A Firefighter's Journal

A Firefighter's Journal

THIRTY-SEVEN YEARS ON THE FIREGROUNDS AND IN THE FIREHOUSES OF PHILADELPHIA

Robert John Marchisello

ISBN-13: 9781976325281
ISBN-10: 1976325285

To firefighters everywhere—we truly share a special bond.

Contents

Prologue
Screams

October 14, 1981—Lieutenant, Engine 24

Confined to the tiny drab-green office, I'm pecking away at the dreaded keyboard once again. Like most young fire lieutenants, I hate this tedious part of my job. I want to be doing something more important, like training my platoon, racing to another fire, or saving lives. Even fire-prevention inspections would be better than this. I'm supposed to be a fire officer, a platoon supervisor, a leader of men. But here I am, doing the boring job of a clerk.

I roll another Form 76-12, "City of Philadelphia—Report of Fire Alarm," more commonly referred to as a fire report, into the typewriter. It's the Philadelphia Fire Department's version of an after-action report and the fifth one I've done so far today. This one is for a simple rubbish fire, way up an alley behind a vacant run-down row home. No damage was done to anything that anyone will ever care about, no harm was done to anybody, and no insurance claims will be filed. But for some ridiculous reason, I have to explain in complete detail how many feet of three-quarter-inch booster line (the fire department's smallest hose) were stretched to the seat of the fire. What time were we dispatched? What time did we arrive? How long were we there? What was the nozzle size? What was the pump pressure? Who attended the alarm? What orders did I give my company?

I never learned how to type, but in the few years since my promotion, I've developed a feel for the keyboard. I still curse when I have to pause and search for one of those less frequently used keys, like the *U* or *X*, and where's that damn hyphen? Almost ominously, Blue Öyster Cult's "(Don't Fear) the Reaper" is playing on the radio. I turn up the volume and tap my left foot to its distinctive cowbell beat so I can hunt and peck with rhythm.

The office of Engine Company 24 is located by the apparatus floor, the garage bay where our shiny red American LaFrance pumper is parked. Over the music, I can hear the guys joking around and laughing as usual as they bask in the cool breeze by the open garage door. Russell is busting Rocky's chops about his height.

"Yo, Rock! I saw you jumping up trying to reach the booster-line tip on that last run. Did you guys see him? He looked like a squirrel monkey trying to snatch a banana off a tree. They should put a step stool on the standard equipment list just for you." Russell, at six foot two, attended Niagara University on a basketball scholarship. Like the actor Joe Pesci, he has a way of making almost anything sound funny.

Mel and Clarkee roar with laughter as Rocky retorts, "Screw you, Russell! You put it way up there, near the top of the reel. The bracket's right here. Even I could reach it if it was in its damned bracket." Everybody cracks up.

I wish I were one of them again—no responsibility, no office, no friggin' fire reports!

Only thirty feet from the office sits the watch desk, the dispatch hub that contains the station's communications equipment. A harsh dispatch tone emits from the speaker of its public-address system, and the laughter out front comes to an abrupt halt. The guys stand motionless as the fire dispatcher announces in a monotone but official-sounding voice, "Tactical phone box two-three-three-six, Twenty-Third and Moore Streets. The fire is reported to be in the eighteen-hundred block of South Twenty-Third Street, a dwelling."

I know it's weird, but I know all of our box numbers. I spring from my paperwork prison and run for our pumper as soon as I hear the numbers 2-3-3-6. "That's us!" I yell. "Second-in!" We scramble for our riding positions, kick off our shoes, jump into our boots, and slide into the sleeves of our running coats in one seamless motion. Rocky grabs the handle and pulls his five-foot-seven frame into the driver's seat. I jump into the officer's seat next to him. The diesel engine roars to life for the sixth time today. We're out the door before the dispatcher finishes repeating the message a second time. In firefighters' jargon, we got out really fast.

Rocky swings our huge pumper onto Twentieth Street, cuts a hard left, and executes a perfect 150-degree turn onto Point Breeze Avenue. There are no illegally parked cars on the corner, so we make the turn without a backup maneuver, a rare event indeed. Point Breeze Avenue, "the Point," as we call it, is an angled street that intersects South Twenty-Third at Moore. Straight up the Point and a quick half left will take us directly to the reported fire. We're responding in a straight line, the shortest distance between two points.

Two engine companies, two ladder companies, and a battalion chief are dispatched to house fires in the city of Philadelphia. The first engine and ladder attack the fire from the front while the second engine and ladder drag their equipment up the back alleys, fighting dilapidated fences, overgrown trees, shrubbery, rubbish, and, of course, angry, barking dogs. First-in is the glory-work position while second-in is the shit-work position. We call it shit work because there's always dog shit in the alleys. We're second-in at Twenty-Third and Moore, but there's an unwritten rule in the department. If you arrive first on scene, you can assume the first-in position. We call it "beating a company in." Most companies in the department have a lot of pride, and Engine 24 is certainly no exception. Stealing another company's first-in fire is one way to demonstrate that pride. The tradition stems back to the days before the paid fire department, when volunteer fire companies would race to beat each other to fires so they could collect extinguishment fees from insurance companies.

For some reason, Engine 60 is listed as first-in for this fire. Maybe it's because, as the crow flies, their firehouse is just a little bit closer than ours. But their route through the tight streets and illegally parked cars of South Philly is more of a zigzag course. Rocky is beginning to taste the glory of beating them in. I can tell because he's pressing a little harder on the accelerator, and I can see that glazed look in his eyes. Russell gets him more fired up by yelling from the crew cab, "We got 'em, Rock!"

I ease up on the siren and glare back at Russell. Then I look at Rocky. "Yo, Rock! Take it easy! There's school kids on the streets!" The diesel's rpms whine down.

"Okay, Loo," he moans, but he still has that intense look on his face. According to the rule book, we were supposed to come to a complete stop at each stop sign and red light. Nobody ever does it. Rocky slows down but rolls through each one as soon as he can see that it's clear. I'm okay with it because I can tell that he has the huge fire apparatus under control. I don't like to violate the rules, but at the same time, I don't want to do anything to diminish my company's aggressiveness.

In less than two minutes, we're making the half left onto Twenty-Third. As we cross Moore, I look east toward Twenty-Second. Engine 60 is nowhere in sight. We beat them in by a mile. My temporary feeling of glee fades when I look down Twenty-Third and see a huge crowd waving at us.

A very large woman is standing in the street, flailing her arms, and wailing at the top of her lungs, "He's in there! I hear him! I know he's in there! I hear him!"

Just behind her I can see dense grayish-black smoke pushing from the crevices of the second-floor front windows of a two-story row home. I figure that the fire probably involves one or more bedrooms. I report over the radio to the Fire Communications Center (FCC), "Engine Twenty-Four. We're on location at Eighteen Twelve South Twenty-Third Street and have a two-story occupied brick row dwelling with medium smoke showing on the second floor and a report of people trapped. Place both engine companies in service with inch-and-three-quarter hose lines (1¾" diameter), and have the ladder companies prepare for rescue." I guess at the address. I just want the responding companies to know that it's on the even side of the block, the west side. The shit-work companies, Engine 60 and Ladder 11, need to know which alley to use.

By some miracle, there's a fire hydrant directly across the street, and surprisingly, no one is parked in front of it, not even the cops. What a treat! Rocky passes the fire, leaving room for the first-in ladder company, Ladder 19.

"I got the hydrant, Loo. Just a length's gonna do it." It's Rocky's way of letting me know that he can handle our crucial water supply on his own. Russell, Mel, Clarkee, and I can focus on the fire.

The fat lady is still wailing as Clarkee and I enter the unlocked front door. It's a bad sign! Maybe the fat lady's right. People don't leave their doors unlocked when nobody's home, especially around here. Russell and Mel stretch two hundred feet of hose line from our pumper and follow behind us. Clarkee is our pack man, the only one in our company assigned to wear a self-contained breathing apparatus. Crouched over and pulling his mask over his face, he knows that his job is going to be search and rescue.

My eyes are filling with tears, and mucous is streaming from my nose because of the acrid smoke, which has filled the first floor. I'm breathing faster, trying to take in more oxygen as I cough out to Russell, "Charge the line!" He relays the message to Mel, who relays it to Rocky. Within seconds our hose swells with water and is ready to confront the red devil himself. A heavy pat jars my back. It's Gerry, the lieutenant from Ladder 19.

"Bob, my pack guy's coming right up." He coughs. "Just gimme a few seconds, and we'll take out the windows." The other members of Ladder 19 are raising their ladders so they can take out, or break, the windows. That will cause the smoke to lift and allow us to advance our hose to the seat of the fire.

The first time I hear the shrill shrieking sound is while Gerry is talking to me. It travels straight up my spine. "What the hell is that?" I holler.

"It sounds like somebody stepped on a fuckin' cat," replies Russell. I laugh. He always finds a way to ease the tension.

The sound cuts through the dense smoke again.

"That ain't no fuckin' cat," cries Gerry. "It's the trapped guy!"

Clarkee, realizing that the sound is a human scream, dashes three-quarters of the way up the steps before I yell, "Clarkee! Wait a friggin' minute, man! Give us a goddamned chance to get the line upstairs." He isn't an experienced search-and-rescue man, so I don't want him to wander too far away from the protection of our nozzle.

As I rush up the steps behind him, I look back at Gerry. "Ger, where's those friggin' windows, man?" I should be more patient. I know from experience that it takes time to get the ladder off the truck, carry it up the street, place it, raise it, climb it, and take out the windows. The man's screams are making me testy. Gerry isn't the least bit offended. He understands all about stressful firegrounds.

As the man screams again, my spine tingles, and the hair on the back of my neck stands straight up. Where the hell is he? "Hang on, man!" I yell into the darkness. "We're coming to get you!"

I reach the top of the stairs with Clarkee. The built-up heat has created an impenetrable barrier three feet above our heads. I look to the right, where a dull orange glow is barely visible through the dense smoke in the middle bedroom. Then I look toward the front bedroom, where I can make out another orange glow. This one's a bit brighter. Two rooms are involved in fire.

I shove Clarkee forward. "Clarkee, he's got to be"—the man screams again—"in the back, man. He's gotta be in the back!" From my position the scream appears to be coming from the rear. Clarkee takes off down the hallway. Only inches away, he's swallowed by the thick black smoke.

Russell is directly behind me with the nozzle. Mel's right next to him. "Where is it, Loo?" yells Russell.

The smoke is beginning to get to me, and I cough my reply. "Front and middle rooms. The guy's in the back. Let's make the turn." We lift our hose line over the banister and turn down the hallway toward the fire. "The middle room—get the middle room first and then the front. I'm going to help Clarkee search for the guy." As I turn, air rushes through the nozzle, followed by a spattering sound as Russell directs 125 gallons of water per minute at the middle room's glow. The water turns to steam that scalds my face, neck, and ears, driving me to the floor. My nose is only inches from the floorboards as I crawl toward the rear. Suddenly, my helmet bumps into something hard. I grope with my gloved hand. It's another helmet.

"Clarkee?"

"No, pack man, Ladder 19!" he replies, his voice muffled by his mask.

I spin him around. "Back! Go to the back! The guy's back there." Mucous is streaming down my face, my ears are burning, and I'm gasping for breath. Everything in my body is telling me to get out of the building. I know Mel and Russell are having the same problem because I can hear them cursing as they struggle for air. We won't bail out. It just won't happen. We're firefighters—and more importantly, there's a life at stake.

Finally, I hear the welcomed sound of crashing glass. I glance back and see that Ladder 19 has taken out the front windows. The smoke, heat, and steam immediately begin to lift. But as the air rushes in, the orange glows erupt into huge walls of flame. I'm fully confident that Russell and Mel can handle the fire. It's only a couple of bedrooms, as we have done so many times before. I resume crawling and bump into another helmet.

"Clarkee?"

"Yeah, Loo!" comes his muffled reply. "The back bedroom's clear!"

That not what I want to hear. "It can't be, Clarkee! Are you sure?"

"Yeah, Loo! I'm positive. Nobody's back there!"

Suddenly it dawns on me. I rapidly crawl down the hallway on burning knees. "The bathroom, Clarkee. Find the bathroom!" It's the only place he could be. Clarkee spins around and follows. The bathroom is about ten feet on the right, and its door is wide open. Shit! Someone could only survive this torrid heat, smoke, and steam, if the door was closed. The screams have stopped, and I'm hoping, wishing, and praying that it's because the poor guy has jumped out a window.

I belly crawl inside a bathroom charged with smoke. As I frantically probe with my arms extended, I hear three rapid taps on the tiny window. It's a warning from Ladder 19. They're about to take out the glass. Instinctively, I curl into a ball and cover my head with my arms. The window explodes, and I'm pelted with hundreds of glass shards. But the shower of slivers brings welcomed relief. I can almost breathe again.

I resume my search, groping around the floor, toilet, and bathtub but still can't find him. I'm beginning to feel confident that he jumped out of the back-bedroom window. But as the smoke continues to lift, I hear the sound of running water. It isn't coming from our nozzle, though. It's a much smaller sound, like a running faucet.

I peer through the shadowy darkness toward the bathtub, and eerily, the ghostly silhouette of a man slowly appears through the rising smoke. He's sitting with his back against the wall, his head slumped down, and his legs dangling over the side of the tub. His limp hand is still clutching the handle of a quart-sized pot resting on his lap. Water from the faucet is steadily running over its top, down his leg, and down the drain. His lifeless head is tilted to the side, and his hair and eyebrows are completely singed away. Folds of burned skin are sagging from his forehead, and a mix of grayish-yellow mucus has run down his chin and pooled on his chest. His eyes are closed, but his swollen purple tongue is hanging from the side of his mouth. The fire never got to the unfortunate seventy-year-old, but the heat, steam, and smoke were just as deadly.

I take my glove off and check for his carotid pulse. There isn't any. I call out to anyone within hearing range, "We need a medic up here to pronounce one." Even though I'm certain that he's dead, I don't have the authority to pronounce him DOA. Fire-department paramedics will need to put on their gear, climb over the debris, and handle the grim task.

Battalion Chief Kenney pops his head into the room. "What do you have, Twenty-Fours?"

"It's a fifty-two ninety-two, Chief," I reply, pointing to the dead man. The Philadelphia police code 5292 means "dead person." It's used so officers can communicate in front of a victim's family or friends without using words like "dead" or "DOA" and upsetting everyone. "We just need to pronounce him, Chief."

Kenney looks in and shakes his head. "Yeah, kid, you sure do. I got the medics on their way up."

Down the hall Russell and Mel have made quick work of the fire, and they look exhausted. I yell in their direction, "Go outside and take a breather. Clarkee will take the tip."

Clarkee hears my command and quickly moves into position. Even though the fire is out, we won't let anyone else touch our nozzle. It's all about company pride. Another unwritten rule: never give up the tip, the nozzle, to another company.

All that needs to be done now is to open the walls and ceilings to check for hidden fire. Chief Kenney has already assigned that to Ladders 19 and 11. The smoke has cleared somewhat, and the heat is beginning to lift as I rest against the wall next to Clarkee. He's crouching with his mask dangling, and he has a firm grip on the nozzle, looking as if he's just waiting for someone to challenge him for the tip. I'm proud of him for it.

Staring at the victim in the tub, I mumble to myself, "You shouldn't have tried to fight it yourself, buddy. Why didn't you just get the hell out?"

Clarkee looks up and shakes his head. "Friggin' shame, Loo. It's a friggin' shame."

Captain Bernard's words of years ago float to the top of my mind: "Bobby, the dead ones are bad enough, but it's the dying ones that will bother you most." Now I know exactly what he meant. I heard this man's last agonizing screams as he was scalded to death. I think back to my lieutenant's indoctrination course when they told us that we'd be making life-and-death decisions. My mind begins to race a mile a minute. Should I have told Clarkee to check the bathroom first? Should I have gone into the bathroom myself? Did the steam from our fire attack kill him? Should I have told Russell and Mel to wait for the windows to be broken? Should I have yelled for the victim to shut the door? When did I hear his last scream? Was there anything else I could have done? For a fleeting second, I wish that I was back in my office typing those friggin' fire reports.

Chief Kenney gently taps me on the shoulder. "You okay, kid?"

I look into his smoke-stained eyes and lie, "Yeah, yeah. I'm all right, Chief."

Sensing that I'm second-guessing myself, he pushes his helmet back. "Listen, kid, you did everything possible here. You guys did both engine and ladder work on this job. There's nothing else you could have done to save him. You did a good job, Twenty-Fours." He gives me a reassuring pat on my back, climbs over our hose, and carefully avoids the fallen debris as he makes his way back down the steps. Chief Kenney is two ranks above me and has about twenty years on the job. His words of encouragement comfort me and temporarily alleviate my self-doubts. I close my swollen eyes to relieve the sting of soot and smoke.

A scream.

I cringe. My neck, back, and arms are all goose bumps.

I hear it again.

My eyes fly open. Was I mistaken? Could it be? Is he still alive? Suddenly it's pitch black again, and I can't see a thing. I sweep my arms through the darkness. Where is he? Suddenly I feel a body beside me. I'm about to check for a pulse when I realize that it isn't the fire victim; it's my wife, Diane. I'm not in a steamy, smoke-filled room; I'm at home and in my own bed. Diane is sleeping as peacefully as a kitten, but my heart is pounding. Tears are streaming down my face, and I've broken out in a cold sweat. I wipe the nightmare from my eyes. Slowly, the greenish blur of our clock radio comes into focus. It's 3:43 a.m. The haunting screams have returned like always. Without warning, every few years, they rise from the recesses of my mind. The nightmare repeats its vivid details each and every time. There's no escape; the screams will haunt me for the rest of my days.

Bright, shiny fire trucks, flashing lights, and firefighters dressed in neatly pressed uniforms posing with a handsome Dalmatian form the public's image of firefighting. Though these portrayals may be accurate in certain situations, the actual business of firefighting is dirty, gritty, physically demanding, and terribly dangerous. The emotional challenges faced by firefighters and the psychological scars they suffer can be just as dangerous and exhausting. Firefighters are human beings with feelings, emotions, and at times self-doubts or even regrets. Because of the things they see, the things they do, and the decisions they make, many firefighters suffer from disturbing dreams and even haunting nightmares. I know firsthand. I was a Philadelphia firefighter for over thirty-seven years.

I don't consider my career to be extraordinary when compared to those of many of my peers. I may have gotten promoted and had some shining moments, but I always considered myself to be simply a firefighter—nothing more. I didn't work in the busiest fire department in the United States. I didn't even work in the busiest fire company in Philadelphia. I certainly wasn't the bravest of the brave, nor was I the most decorated firefighter in the city. I didn't rapidly dart my way up every rung of the promotional ladder, and I surely didn't rise all the way to the top to become fire commissioner.

The one thing that I did do, something that made me different from most firefighters, was to keep a journal. Throughout my career, I recorded dates, times, places, events, and details of my varied experiences. Sometimes I simply jotted notes, and other times I wrote short stories. In my journal, I expressed my feelings, emotions, ambitions, doubts, and fears. I described many of the horrible things that firefighters witness and experience. I wrote about life inside the fire station, firehouse humor, fire-department politics, and the pressures of the job. I even wrote about the gallows humor that firefighters sometimes use to cope with the horrific tragedies they witness. I kept most of my writings to myself. I told my journal more than I ever told anybody, including my closest friends.

So this is my story. It's about a little boy who wanted to grow up to become a firefighter and was fortunate enough to live his childhood dream. It's a firsthand account about the nature of firefighting and the lives of firefighters.

My journal is not just a compilation of blazes and infernos. Firefighters do much more than fight fires. Over the course of my career, I found myself in the middle of situations I never imagined when I raised my right hand and swore the oath. Not in my wildest dreams! Firefighters are summoned to nearly every conceivable type of emergency. It would be much more appropriate to call a fire department an "emergency-services department." Firefighters bear witness to the most horrifying, disgusting, and repulsive situations imaginable. In order for my readers to understand what it's really like to be a firefighter, some of my stories graphically describe many of the gruesome sights, terrifying sounds, and repugnant odors I experienced over the years.

I'm not really sure why I started journaling. In the beginning of my career, my obsessive-compulsive disorder (OCD) forced me to log every detail of my actions, observations, and experiences. I felt compelled to keep a running documentary of my life as a firefighter. As the years passed and I had children of my own, my feelings changed. I reached the point where I wanted to record as much as possible for my family. I wanted future genera-tions of Marchisellos to have something more substantive to remember me by than a simple name on a skimpy family tree. I never intended to write a book, but on several occasions, when I shared my fire stories with friends over cocktails, someone would inevitably say, "You should write a book!"

So I suppose this is simply that book, the journey of my career. It's a chronological compilation of excerpts, accounts, and stories based on the writings in my journal, a journal that spanned over thirty-seven years of service to the citizens of Philadelphia. I was assigned to various fire stations, each with its own distinct neighborhoods, hazards, challenges, and casts of characters—the many firefighters that I lived with, worked with, and grew to love. Most of my assignments were to fairly active firefighting units, and my experiences were as diverse as my assignments. For obvious reasons, I've changed some of the names, dates, places, details, and times. I feel that my career encompasses an excellent cross section of the firefighting profession and what it's really like to live the life of a firefighter.

CHAPTER 1

Childhood Dream

My fascination with firefighting began when I was only two years old. My parents rented a tiny third-floor apartment on Reed Street in South Philly. It had a small kitchen, a tiny bathroom, and one bedroom that also served as our living room and my playroom. My wooden toy box sat under the large window facing Reed. It was the center of my little world.

The closest firehouse was Ladder Company 11, only three blocks away. Whenever I heard their siren approaching, I would drop whatever I was playing with, excitedly climb atop my toy box, and press my face against the window to catch a glimpse of their shiny red hook and ladder as they screamed by. During the warmer months, I would lean against the window screen so hard that a small bulge formed in the shape of my face. My mother would scream hysterically, fearing that I was going to fall through.

I was amazed by all the excitement that the big red truck always created when it flew up the street. People outside stopped, stared, and made the sign of the cross as the men wearing black canvas coats and tin helmets raced by. Even the mysterious gang of men, whose daily hangout was in the variety store across the street, rushed outside when they heard the approaching siren. I later learned that they were number writers, runners, and racketeers, which explained the relief on their faces when they realized that the siren wasn't the cops.

One brisk fall evening, my uncle Alex, who owned our apartment building and lived on the first floor, excitedly shouted up the steps that the factory across the street was on fire. My father quickly scooped me into his arms, and we raced down the stairs with my mother chasing behind. When we got outside, I could see a red glow through the windows of the four-story garment factory where my grandmother worked. Then I heard Ladder 11's wailing siren and saw its red light spinning as it sped directly toward us. Perched on my father's shoulders, I had a great view of all the action.

Spellbound, I watched as Ladder 11 parked at an angle and raised their big silver ladder all the way to the roof. As firefighters were climbing up the ladder, a smaller fire engine arrived from the other direction. Engine 24 screeched to a halt right in front of our apartment and connected their big tan hose to the orange hydrant on our pavement. Wide-eyed, I watched as firefighters bashed down the main door, dragged their hose inside, and disappeared into the thick black smoke. Just then, other firefighters smashed the big windows with their long poles, and within minutes the fire was out. I was absolutely amazed by all the action and excitement, as well as the coordination and the efficiency of the firefighters. After that, I played with the toy fire truck in my toy box until its wheels wore out.

The sound of Ladder 11's approaching siren and its Doppler shift gave me goose bumps as a little boy. And after all these years, whenever I hear the sound of a fire apparatus screaming to an alarm, I still get the same goose bumps, even after responding to thousands upon thousands of fires and other emergencies as a Philadelphia firefighter.

I can't say that the only thing I ever wanted to be was a firefighter. Like most young boys growing up, I went through many different phases. When I didn't hear sirens, I wanted to be a cowboy. More specifically, I wanted to be Roy Rogers. Like so many baby-boomer boys, I had a crush on Dale Evans, Rogers's beautiful wife. But I soon realized that there weren't any cowboys wearing ten-gallon hats and sporting six-shooters while galloping around Reed Street. Besides, Dale Evans already had a husband, the real Roy Rogers! At one point I also wanted to be a soldier. My father was a combat veteran who had served in Italy during World War II. I remember staring at his uniform jacket, which hung in our closet, and rubbing my fingers across his blue Combat Infantryman Badge.

Halloween was one of my favorite holidays. Having previously dressed as a cowboy and a soldier, when I was four years old, I begged my mother to dress me as a firefighter. But no matter how hard she tried, she couldn't find a firefighter's costume. She did the next best thing: dressed me as a police officer. I really liked the gun and handcuffs that came with the outfit, so until the next time Ladder 11 raced up Reed Street, I wanted to become a cop.

When I turned five, my father landed a good job at the General Electric Switchgear Plant in Southwest Philly. My parents finally had the means to buy their own tiny row home on 1800 South Rosewood Street, a predominantly Italian block in South Philly. It was a stretch financially, so my maternal grandparents moved in to help with the bills.

I missed my toy-box observation deck for Ladder 11. But our new home was only a half block from Broad Street, the main two-way drag that bisects South Philly. The sounds of subway trains, buses, trucks, motorcycles, and cars amused my little ears as they traveled along the busy street. There were also plenty of sirens. From my bedroom window, I could look across the lot behind our house and watch all of them pass by. Before long, I learned all the different types of sirens. I knew the difference between police cars, ambulances, and, of course, fire engines. I even knew the distinctive sounds made by our local fire trucks, Engine 10 and Ladder 11. Yes, Ladder 11 came down Broad Street too.

My vocational desires continued to fluctuate throughout my childhood. Whenever I saw a war movie, I wanted to be a soldier. In the spring, I wanted to be a baseball player, and in the fall, I wanted to be a football player. The rest of the time I wanted to be a firefighter, and I wasn't alone. My friend Arthur, who lived around the corner on Moore Street, shared the same cyclic hopes and dreams. We quickly became best friends. Arthur and I began chasing fire engines as soon as we were old enough to leave the neighborhood. We'd often visit firehouses within walking distance. Full of wonder, we would peek inside to catch a glimpse of what life was like for the firefighters who worked there. Did they actually play checkers, chess, and poker to pass the time? Did they really sleep upstairs? If so, who the heck woke them up if there was a fire? And what the heck happened if they were sitting on the toilet when the bells rang? My goodness!

Chasing the lore of firefighting wasn't the only means of fun in our tough little neighborhood. Box-ball, half-ball, wall-ball, dead-box, buck-buck, rough-touch football, and, of course, street fights were common to our urban row-home environment. But in our gang, Arthur and I were the only two whose eyes lit up when we heard sirens wailing in the distance.

One of my favorite fire-chasing memories came on August 27, 1959, during the summer of my eleventh birthday. It was uncomfortably hot and humid in our stifling row home with its black asphalt roof. We didn't have air conditioning, so it was virtually impossible to sleep. I kept flipping my pillow over to its cooler, unperspired-upon side throughout the night, and it was nearly dawn before I finally dozed off. It seemed like only minutes before the sound of distant sirens woke me from my slumber. With half-opened eyes, I listened carefully. They were definitely fire engines, but their sound quickly faded away. Convinced that they weren't coming down Broad Street, I nodded off again. But minutes later I heard more, and these were getting louder. Surely they were coming down Broad this time. I sprang to my feet, ran to the window, and caught the red blur of two pumpers as they zipped past. As their sirens faded, they were replaced by more—lots more. There was a big fire somewhere in South Philly. I jumped into my shorts and sneakers and dashed downstairs. My grandmother, as usual, was already in the kitchen, making homemade pasta. As I reached for the front door, she yelled, "Robbie, *ma cosi stai fa? Dove stai?*" (But what are you doing? Where are you going?)

"Fire engines, Grandma. There's a fire somewhere. Gotta go!" I yelled excitedly as I flew out the door. As I ran down the front steps, I could hear her mumbling, "*Tu sei pazzo!*" (You're crazy).

Arthur came running down the street; he had heard the sirens too. "Hey Bob, there's a big fire somewhere!" His wide, eager eyes filled his black-rimmed glasses. "Did you see where they went?"

"They're going this way, Art!" I exclaimed. "They're going toward Snyder." Lured by more sirens, we sprinted to Broad Street, where two more pumpers zipped past, and we chased after them. It was impossible to keep pace, but we followed them after they turned left onto Snyder Avenue. The chase was on. Two little fire buffs, who wanted to someday be Philly firefighters, were chasing fire engines through the streets of South Philadelphia on a hot summer morning.

More fire engines raced past as we ran ten blocks down Snyder Avenue. We didn't stop running until we reached Fourth Street, where a huge three-story garage had smoke and flames shooting from its roof. Issy's Garage was about seventy-five feet wide by seventy-five feet deep. An attached corner store on one side and an apartment building on the other were also billowing thick black smoke. Totally fascinated, we watched the action unfold. Fire hose was lying everywhere. Some firefighters were climbing ladders to roofs, some were crawling through doors while pulling hoses, and others were lying on the pavement, physically exhausted.

A few things caught my young eyes. A firefighter, with "Captain" written above the number 49 on his helmet, staggered out of the building and collapsed onto the sidewalk. Other firefighters immediately dropped what they were doing and rushed to his aid. It was the first time I realized how physically demanding firefighting really was. It was also the first time I learned that there were other ranks besides fire chief.

Another thing I noticed was a fire engine sitting inside Engine 53's firehouse, only a half block from the fire. I couldn't imagine why they were parked idly in their station with such a huge fire blazing practically next door. At that age I didn't realize that companies from distant stations were moved to cover areas devoid of fire protection.

We hung around until the smoke had been reduced to a few wisps and the firefighters had taken down their ladders and rolled up their hoses. On our way home, we discussed how much better it would be someday to actually *ride* on fire engines instead of chasing after them.

The following October, I was in the sixth grade when a batch of blaring sirens raced past our classroom windows. Even though Francis M. Drexel Elementary School was a public school, I joined the entire class and dropped my pencil to make the sign of the cross. My siren-tuned ears told me that this wasn't a false alarm. There were way too many sirens for that. I craned my neck trying to see if I could spot smoke outside. I didn't see anything, but my teacher, Mrs. Seacrest, saw that I was focused elsewhere. She went into a windup like Phillies's pitcher, Robin Roberts, and hurled the blackboard eraser directly at my head. "Robert! Pay attention!" Rubbing my noggin, I dared not look out the window again. But I didn't pay attention either. I was too focused on the sirens and the hint of smoke in the fall air.

The sirens and smoke were gone by the time I went home for lunch. I disappointedly looked up and down the streets but couldn't find any trace of a recent fire. When I got home, my grandfather was sitting on the front step. As I passed him, I smelled a hint of smoke. When I turned around, I was shocked to see black soot all over his shirt, face, and white hair. "Grandpop!" I cried. "What the heck happened?"

He smiled proudly and replied in broken English, "I'ma sit inna bar. It a catch a fire. I'ma pulla the firebox and a save the whole goddamned place." He was beaming, and I was darned proud of him. I couldn't wait to tell somebody, anybody. So before class resumed, I gleefully told Mrs. Seacrest how my grandfather had been in Smiley's Saloon and saved the day by pulling the firebox.

To my surprise, after lunch Mrs. Seacrest announced to the class, "Robert has a story to share with us."

Honored, I stood at my desk and recounted my grandpa's heroics, even adding the firebox number, which I had memorized: one-eight-eight-three.

Then Mrs. Seacrest threw me a curve. Sneering, she asked, "Now, Robert, why don't you explain to the rest of the class exactly what your grandfather was doing in a taproom at ten o'clock in the morning?"

I looked at her sheepishly, scratching my head, unsure how to answer. "Well, Mrs. Seacrest, my Grandpa really likes beer and whiskey." She smirked as the class erupted with laughter. I had to defend him. "But if he wasn't in there drinking, Mrs. Seacrest, the whole darn bar would have certainly burned to the ground. He's a hero, you know!"

"Sit down, Robert!" she snapped. Maybe Grandpop had been drinking too early in the day, but I was still damned proud of him. He had called my beloved fire department and saved his beloved saloon.

That Christmas, science became my favorite school subject after my parents bought me a chemistry set. I loved it so much that I even did experiments that weren't in the manual. The following year I asked for the largest one they made. I loved learning about chemicals and the equipment that came with the sets. At a young age, I learned to respect chemicals, not fear them. I had a new career quest to fill the icy gap between football and baseball seasons. I wanted to be a chemist. Besides, during the winter it was way too cold for us to chase fire engines anyway.

Before we reached our teens, Arthur and I tracked down several more big fires. One summer, he became enthralled with the Marine Corps and repeatedly dragged me to see *The DI*, starring Jack Webb. I figured it was just a whim, because whenever we heard sirens, it always came back to us joining the fire department together.

As we entered our teens, our gonads kicked in, and we quickly realized that it was much more fun to chase girls than fire trucks. During our adolescent pursuits, we occasionally stopped by the firehouses, but it was for a different reason. We wanted to earn tip money by going to the store for the firefighters. We had learned that a young man needed money to take a girl to the movies. But I still had the bug to be a firefighter. Whenever we hustled tip money, I still longingly peered inside the firehouse, hoping that the bells would ring and the firefighters would spring into action.

No matter what I was in the midst of, the sound of a siren or the sight of a responding fire truck always took priority. One evening, I was playing junior-league baseball at Thirteenth and Reed Streets, a block away from the firehouse. The game with the Tigers was tied two apiece in the seventh inning with two outs and a runner on third. The pitcher wound up and delivered a nice not-so-fast fastball directly down the middle of the plate. I should have crushed it. Unfortunately, at that exact moment, Ladder 11 came screaming out of their firehouse. I instinctively glanced up for a nanosecond. It was too long. Before I could refocus on the ball, it sharply thwacked into the catcher's mitt. "Strike three!" the umpire seemed to yell with joy.

But Coach Mike's earsplitting scream made the ump sound like a church mouse. "Bobby! What the hell are you looking at?" he screamed from the coach's box. "Keep your eyes on the goddamned ball!" We lost three to two.

Arthur was a grade ahead of me, and as we grew older, we became more involved with our own classmates. We still hung together often, but our fire-chasing days were long gone. Without him to share my pursuits, my quest to become a firefighter slowly went dormant.

The classmates I hung around with at South Philadelphia High School were into something completely different: hot rods and drag racing. After getting my driver's license at sixteen, I became infatuated with cars. My uncle gave me a clunker of my own, an old beat-up 1955 Chevy. To support it, I got a part-time job at a service station pumping gas and doing oil changes, lubrications, and tire repairs. My career plans had veered in a new direction. I now wanted to be an automobile mechanic.

After graduating in June of 1966, I had plans to attend an automotive technical school, but I decided to hold off. Instead, a few car-crazed classmates and I piled into one of our old jalopies, drove to Willow Grove, and applied to join the Air National Guard. I hoped that the air force's aptitude test would demonstrate that I was best suited to be an automobile or truck mechanic. Why pay for technical school if I could get a free education and satisfy my military obligation at the same time? In the meantime, I got a full-time job at a car rental as a light mechanic and car jockey.

Luckily, I did well in the electrical/mechanical portion of the test, and after basic training, I was sent to technical school at Sheppard Air Force Base in Texas. But it wasn't for automobile, truck, or even aircraft mechanics. Instead, they sent me to school for refrigeration and air conditioning, a career I had never even thought about.

The eighteen-week air-force technical school was exceptional. We learned about refrigeration, air conditioning, temperature controls, and electrical troubleshooting. They taught us how to diagnose and repair everything from water coolers to one-hundred-ton air-conditioning units. We also learned how to weld, braze, cut, and solder all types of metals. I learned a good trade, and after returning home, I decided to give it a try. I easily found a job making house calls to repair domestic refrigerators, air conditioners, and small appliances.

The technical part of my new job was challenging, and I enjoyed the repair work, but I found dealing with the public distasteful. I looked young for my age, and customers were skeptical about letting someone who looked barely sixteen work on their expensive new appliances. After a year I grew to hate what I was doing and began looking for another career.

Oddly enough, becoming a firefighter didn't enter my mind. This was probably subliminal; during my fire-chasing days with Arthur, my mom often voiced her objection about my joining the fire department. "Robert, being a fireman is so dangerous. Wouldn't you be happier with a nice clean job working in an office when you grow up?" After my experience with house calls, an office job didn't sound too bad.

Mechanical drafting had been my minor in high school, so I landed a job as an entry-level draftsman at a street-lamp manufacturing company in North Philly. I really enjoyed electrical and mechanical design, and within a year I was promoted to design draftsman. This is when my latent OCD surfaced. Technical drawings need to be perfect before production, so I meticulously triple-checked my work. To better myself, I also began studying mechanical engineering at Temple University, and at last, I thought my career was set.

One day in the plant, a forklift operator accidentally knocked a sprinkler head off its pipe, which tripped the fire alarm and summoned the fire department. As we evacuated, Engine 34 came screaming up the block, and my childhood dream began to rekindle. I admired how the firefighters quickly jumped off their pumper and dashed in the building as we ran outside. My old desire started rattling around in my brain again. Then my eyes locked on the newly hired cute little blond secretary, and she smiled back. How could I switch jobs now? Poof! My thoughts of becoming a firefighter vanished instantly.

Her name was Concetta, and she was the niece of Philly's reputed Mafia boss. We hit it off right away and ate lunch together nearly every day. After a few dates, we were going steady. A short time later at a family gathering, I was introduced to the Don himself. If I didn't know he was Philly's Godfather, I'd have never guessed it. He was very friendly, polite, and docile. But he was always surrounded by a group of tough-looking men Concetta also referred to as her uncles. I knew they weren't blood relatives because I recognized many of them from the neighborhood or newspaper photos. They were soldiers in her uncle's "extended" family.

Concetta and I dated for a few years before our romance faded, but we still remained close friends. The company was also faltering, and in October of 1971, my position was eliminated. I had known things were slow, but the layoff was still a shock. As I packed my desk, I wasn't sure what to do with my life. Manufacturing in Philadelphia was dying as many factories moved south to escape Philly's harsh winters and the increasing demands of labor unions. I thought about completing my degree in engineering, but I didn't have the funds to support myself as a full-time student. Totally dejected, I loaded my car and drove home to South Philly to ponder my future.

If anything was a constant in my life, it was the guys from the neighborhood. Like most youths in the city, we had grown up hanging on street corners and continued our trend into young adulthood. The night I was laid off, I decided to seek solace the only way I knew: by hanging on the corner of Fifteenth and Moore Streets with my buds. It was a crisp fall evening as eight of us stood yakking and joking under the streetlight in front of Sisca's Grocery Store.

Lou was a married man in his forties who lived a few doors down the block. He was a Philly firefighter who often stopped to chat with us while walking his russet-colored terrier. That night, as Lou approached, Joe Cal broke his stones as usual. "Yo, Lou! Why the hell do you guys break all the friggin' windows when a house is on fire? You guys destroy more property than you save!"

I was beginning to laugh when suddenly it was as if a mule had kicked me right in the ass. A light in my brain flashed: *Firefighter!* "Why don't I become a firefighter?" I anxiously spent the next hour talking to Lou about his job, and I decided to apply the next day. Just thinking about it kept me up all night.

Enthused about finally pursuing my childhood dream, bright and early the following morning, I rode four stops along the Broad Street subway to city hall. Excitedly, I walked into room 127, Philadelphia's personnel office, and took my place in line. When my turn came, I proudly proclaimed to the chubby redhead behind the desk that I was there to take the firefighter's test. Without looking up, she slid a yellow postcard under my nose. "The title's 'fireman,' not 'firefighter'! And we're not taking applications for that position now. Fill this out, and we'll mail it to you when we announce the test. Next!" I felt as if she had slugged me in the gut with a baseball bat. My aspiration to quickly land a job as a firefighter was dashed.

I soon learned that it was going to be much more difficult to attain my childhood dream job than I had originally thought. To my dismay, I found out that the position of fireman was one of the most sought-after jobs in city government. With such high demand, the examination was also extremely difficult. I knew it was going to be challenging, but I was determined to do everything possible to become a Philadelphia firefighter.

My OCD kicked in, and I began working hard to prepare myself for the rigorous civil-service test. I bought a fire-department test-preparation manual, read every page, made notes, and took all the practice tests. I also bought prep books on grammar, vocabulary, math problems, logic problems, and mechanical aptitude, all of which were possible test categories. Every day, without exception, I studied and took practice tests. Some fire departments required a physical-agility test, so I made it a point to keep myself in good shape with daily sit-ups, push-ups, jumping jacks, and laps at the track.

In addition to general knowledge, some fire-department examinations also evaluated a candidate's knowledge of firefighting practices. In order to prepare myself, I borrowed library books and read everything I could about firefighting. While reading an annual report for the Philadelphia Fire Department, I learned of a volunteer organization called the Philadelphia Reserve Fire Force. Its roots dated back to manpower shortages and preparedness for bombing raids during World War II. They were still around and assisting the paid department at extra-alarm fires. What better way was there to learn about firefighting? And maybe it would somehow help me get hired.

I contacted their chief, Bill Proudman, who said that they were always looking for new volunteers. I joined in January of 1972, and within months I was trained as a reserve firefighter. We responded to plenty of extra-alarm fires, but our activities were limited to stretching hose, restoring equipment, and performing other outside duties. Because of liability, workman's compensation, and fire-department-union rules, we were forbidden to go inside burning buildings. Nonetheless, I still learned a lot about firefighting.

After a short stint on unemployment, I landed another drafting position in North Philly and often hooked up with Concetta for lunch. She saw how determined I was about becoming a firefighter and prayed that I'd soon realize my dream. One afternoon, we were sitting in the park eating our lunch when she gently placed a prayer card in my hand. It was Saint Jude's Prayer. She sweetly said, "Say this daily, and he won't fail you." I prayed to Saint Jude every day. I still do.

On March 27, 1972, the little yellow postcard finally arrived in the mail. Applications were being accepted for the fireman's test, scheduled for a Saturday that coming June. I kicked my prep work into high gear. Using another fireman's entrance-examination book, I took complete practice examinations each Saturday morning until the test. It was one of the tips I had studied—get into a regular test-taking rhythm. The Friday night before the test, I was in bed by eleven, a tough thing to do for a single guy. And on test day, I ate a full breakfast so I wouldn't subconsciously rush through the test because I was hungry. I said one final prayer to Saint Jude as I walked two blocks to my alma mater, South Philly High, for the most important test of my life.

I was feeling fairly confident. But when I turned onto Snyder Avenue, my heart sank. Thousands of young men were milling around the school yard, also waiting to take the test. I knew that the examination was also being given at several other schools around the city. Knowing there were only a few hundred anticipated vacancies, I began to panic. How could I possibly score better than all those guys? I made my way through the crowd and found a few friends. As we chatted, I did my best to calm down. "Most likely," I convinced myself, "I have prepared harder than most. I just have to relax, focus, and try my best."

At nine o'clock sharp, the doors swung open, and we filed inside. We were directed into different classrooms, where we were assigned random seats. A proctor handed us each an answer sheet, two pencils, and an envelope with a six-digit number printed on it. We were fingerprinted and instructed to complete forms with our names, addresses, and social security numbers. We were told to stuff the forms and fingerprint cards inside the envelopes, which were then collected. From that point on, we were identified only by our six-digit numbers. The envelopes would remain sealed until the tests were graded. Only then would names be assigned back to the numbers and the hiring list published. It was a fair system designed to minimize cheating and false identities.

The proctor placed thick examination booklets face down on each desk and then looked at the clock. "It's nine thirty. You have until eleven thirty to complete the test. Ready? Go!"

Nervously, I flipped the booklet over and began. The questions were difficult, but my eight months of study and preparation helped immensely. After a few questions, I felt relaxed and comfortable. I was sure about the answers for about 70 percent of the questions and made educated guesses for most of the others. By ten thirty, I was finished. Unlike the many other test takers who quickly filed out of the classroom at that point, I didn't budge. I reviewed and double-checked every answer. Only a few of us were still in our seats when the proctor told us to stop. I walked out of the classroom knowing that I had done my best, but I still was extremely nervous. My entire future was at stake.

The summer of 1972 dragged on as I waited for my results. It was my first glimpse into how slow things work in city government. A month later, I joined a few corner buddies and took the police department's entrance examination. I knew I would be much happier as a firefighter, but it was a good plan B.

The days trudged by at my drafting desk, and I couldn't wait to get home each night to check the mail. But through June, July, and August, no results arrived. Finally, on Saturday, September 16, I was leaving the house for a rough-touch-football game when I bumped into the mailman coming up the steps. He ruffled through his bag and handed me a wad of mail. Tired of being disappointed, I casually shuffled through the stack of bills and junk mail. But this time I noticed a small yellow postcard tucked in the middle of the pile. My heart nearly stopped! I closed my eyes, took a deep breath, and slowly slipped it out. It was from the City of Philadelphia Personnel Department and bore the title "Final Results of Examination." I said another prayer to Saint Jude before flipping it over. When I saw my results, I nearly did a backflip! My score was 87.5, but more importantly, my rank on the eligibility list was 221. I was ecstatic. I had to pinch myself over and over to make sure I wasn't dreaming. To top things off, we won the football game that day too!

My uncle had a friend who was a battalion chief in the fire department, so I called him to find out exactly where I stood. Chief Freddy Buck told me that the city was already hiring a hundred firemen off the new list for a class scheduled in November. "Some guys won't pass their physicals, background checks, or interviews, so you'll probably be called for the second class. Congratulations!" Wow! I was that close. "Listen, kid, give me a call when you're about to be interviewed. I'll put in a good word for you."

Later that month I also received my results from the police department, and surprisingly, I scored even higher! I finished in the top hundred on their hiring list. Preparing for the fire-department test obviously helped. It was a no-brainer for me, though. Just like my fourth Halloween on Reed Street, if I somehow couldn't wear a firefighter's uniform, I'd settle for that of a police officer.

In February of 1973, I received a letter from the city's personnel department. I tore through the envelope and found a notice to appear for a physical examination. Yes! But as I read further, I realized it wasn't for the fire department; it was for the police. I wasn't exactly sure what to do. I was bored as hell as a draftsman and certainly didn't want to ruin my fallback plan, so I took the physical.

A few weeks later, I got another notice. This was the one I had been waiting for. My physical-examination request for the fire department had arrived. I went through all the medical evaluations again except for the chest x-ray. When the nurse asked if I had recently had any x-rays, I told her that I had just taken one for the police department. "Okay, Robert. You don't need to take another one. We'll use the one we already have."

In the middle of March, I received my interview notice from the fire department. This was the final step! I excitedly called Chief Buck, and he coached me about what to say and, more importantly, what not to say. "Tell them that the main reason that you want to become a firefighter is because you like helping people. Tell them that you want to settle down and are looking for a steady job. Don't tell them that you chased fire engines as a little kid. They'll think you're some kind of screwball or something!"

I swallowed hard. "Okay, Chief. Thanks for the advice." I had had no idea that my childhood dream or endeavors to learn about firefighting might possibly harm my chances.

The interviews were conducted by two pair of fire chiefs who asked all sorts of questions about my background, interests, and work experience.

They also asked me why I wanted to become a firefighter, and I was careful to answer as coached by Chief Buck.

During the second interview, one of the chiefs leaned forward. "Listen, kid. You're going to see a lot of disgusting, nasty, and ugly things on this job. Can you handle it?"

"Yes, Chief," I responded without hesitation.

Then he narrowed his eyes. "Son, are you willing to put your life on the line for the citizens of this city and for your brother firefighters?"

Surprised by his candor, I gulped my reply. "Yes, I am, Chief."

Then the other chief took off his white hat. "Hey, kid, do you know a battalion chief named Freddy Buck?"

Whew! "Yes, Chief, he's a friend of my uncle," I replied with a small smile. He winked, said that I had done well, and told me there was a good chance that I'd be in the class scheduled to begin in April. It felt good to know that someone was watching out for me.

By the end of the first week in April, I still hadn't received my hiring notice. Concerned, I called Chief Buck, who said that the candidate's letters had been mailed the week prior and that I should have already received one. I immediately called the fire department's personnel office and explained to the sweet girl on the other end that I had completed all phases of the hiring process but hadn't received notification that I was hired.

"Something must be wrong, sir. All the letters were mailed March twenty-seventh."

I almost fell through the floor. Could it be that I had somehow failed the interview, the background check, or even the physical? I had gotten this far; what the heck went wrong?

"Sir," she added, "why don't you give me your phone number? I'll look into it and get right back to you." It took fifteen minutes for her to call back, but it seemed like an eternity. My heart was pounding a mile a minute, and I nearly jumped out of my skin when the phone finally rang.

"Mr. Marchisello, we have all your paperwork, but it appears that you didn't take your chest x-ray." I quickly told her about the police physical. "Oh, those morons! Let me look into this, and if everything's okay, you'll get your notice of appointment in the mail within days." I thanked her profusely, but she cautioned, "Now, listen, the class is scheduled to begin Monday, April twenty-third, but don't give notice to your employer until you receive our letter."

I was on pins and needles for two days, but when I got home that Wednesday, my notice of appointment was there. I had done it! At twenty-four years of age, I was about to become a Philadelphia firefighter. A dream since the age of two, my career was finally about to begin.

By now you might be wondering, what ever happened to my friend Arthur? He never got the chance to become a Philly firefighter. My childhood friend's passion to be a marine resurfaced in 1966. He transferred from the United States Naval Reserve to the United States Marine Corps, went through basic training all over again, and was quickly shipped to Vietnam. On February 25, 1967, my dear friend with the black-rimmed glasses was killed by small-arms fire near Duc Pho, Quang Ngai Province, South Vietnam. His name, *Arthur A. Johnson*, is inscribed on panel 15-E, row ninety, of the Vietnam Veterans Memorial in Washington, DC.

CHAPTER 2

Class 141

O n Monday, April 23, 1973, I raised my right hand and swore the following oath:

> I solemnly swear that I will well and truly perform the duties of my
> position, Fireman, to the best of my ability. I will obey and uphold
> the Constitution of the United States, the Constitution and Laws
> of the Commonwealth of Pennsylvania, the Home Rule Charter,
> Ordinances of the City of Philadelphia and all rules of the Fire
> Department. I so solemnly swear.

The Philadelphia Fire Department, like most professional fire departments,
is a paramilitary organization. Newly hired firefighters, called cadets, must
complete an arduous basic-training program before being assigned to companies in the field.

Our first day was the only easy one. After reciting our oaths, we completed forms, signed paperwork, and were measured for uniforms, helmets,
coats, and boots. After a short orientation film about firefighting, Assistant
Chief Bowen asserted, in no uncertain terms, that the following eight weeks
were going to be rigorous. If we didn't pass all the written exams and practical exercises, we'd be fired.

Our training began the following day, and so did my journal.

APRIL 24, 1973—CADET, FIRE TRAINING COLLEGE

At eight o'clock sharp, birds were chirping melodious songs of spring as
seventy-six male cadets of Class 141 stood silently, in military formation,
in the yard of Fire Training College. Dressed in dark-blue uniforms with

laminated name tags neatly pinned on our chests, we all sported well-trimmed, regulation-style haircuts. A stern cadre of instructors, all fire officers wearing starched white shirts, lined up facing us.

One of the instructors, a fortyish man with wavy black combed-back hair and a menacing scowl on his face, slowly paced along our front row. Occasionally he paused in front of a cadet, eyeballed him from top to bottom, and then shook his head in disgust. After he reached the end of the line, he leisurely strolled to the center of our formation and executed a perfect about-face so that he was facing us.

Suddenly, in the booming voice of a drill instructor, he barked, "Class One Forty-One...ten-hut." I instantly snapped to attention in unison with the seventy-five other cadets. "My name is Lieutenant McMillan. You will address me and each one of these instructors behind me as 'sir.' Do you fuckoffs understand?"

"Yes, sir!" Class 141 shouted in unison for the first time.

McMillan slowly paced to the left end of our front row, put his hand on a cadet's shoulders, and yelled, "Beginning with this man, count off!"

"One...two...three...four...five...six...seven...eight...*eight*...nine..."

"Stop! Stop! Stop! You fuckin' assholes have got to be kidding me." McMillan turned and looked at the cadre behind him. "Fifteen thousand fuckin' applicants, and we hired a bunch that can't even count right! This is fuckin' unbelievable!" He turned back to the class. "Now let's try this again, you bunch of assholes! Beginning with this fuckin' cadet, count off!" It appeared that cursing was going to be as much a part of firefighting as hoses, nozzles, ladders, and red fire trucks.

When we finally got the counting part correct, McMillan loudly barked, "Class One Forty-One, parade rest!" Most of the class properly obeyed the command, but a few didn't have a clue what the military drill term "parade rest" meant. After darting through the ranks to check each man's posture, McMillan returned to the front and snarled, "For you fuckin' hippies with no military experience, 'parade rest' means to stand with your feet facing outward, twelve inches apart, and your hands tucked behind your backs, right back hand resting in the left palm. Do you assholes understand?"

"Yes, sir!" we shouted.

McMillan continued, "Now, before we begin our morning workout, I want to explain one thing to you bunch of fuckoffs. The Philadelphia Fire Department does not tolerate lateness. We're open twenty-four hours a day, seven days a week, and three hundred sixty-five days a year. People depend on us, and we depend on each other. If you're late one time while you're here for training, you're going to be standing tall before Chief Bowen, explaining why we shouldn't fire your stupid ass."

That was my introduction to the Philadelphia Fire Department. It may have been profane, but we understood that McMillan was using vulgarities to emphasize the serious nature of our new positions. As in the military, orders are meant to be followed, and similar to battlefield conditions, there's no room for debate on the fireground. I carefully listened to every word and followed every command. After working so darned hard to get hired, I wasn't about to screw up. I wanted to be a Philadelphia firefighter more than anything else in the world.

Located about ten miles from the Liberty Bell, Fire Training College, more commonly referred to as Fire School, sat atop the hills of the city's Roxborough neighborhood. We were the 141st class to be trained as a unit since the Philadelphia Fire Department was organized as a paid entity on March 15, 1871. Before that, new hires were sent directly to their firehouses for mostly on-the-job training. Our class was divided into four platoons, A, B, C, and D. I was the sixteenth member in the D platoon, and "D-16" was written under my name on my name tag.

Fire School's main focus was a looming five-story drill tower with several window openings that had shutters instead of glass panes. A large safety net sat ominously stretched beneath its windows. In the adjoining building were an auditorium, classrooms, and a garage, appropriately called the apparatus floor, housing two fire apparatuses (fire engines). Outside was a large paved drill yard, where we did daily calisthenics and various training evolutions.

The quarters of Engine 39 and Ladder 30 were attached to the auditorium building, but we were forbidden to go near the firehouse or socialize with its firefighters. I correctly presumed that the brass didn't want the veteran firefighters to corrupt the strict sense of military discipline being drilled into our brains every day.

The cadets of Class 141 were between nineteen and thirty-one years old, at least five feet six inches tall and had a minimum vision of twenty-fifty, which had to be corrected with glasses to twenty-twenty. With few exceptions, everyone had been born and raised in Philadelphia. Most of us were from blue-collar, working-class families, had grown up hanging on street corners, and had a sense of street smarts. We were attracted to the job for various reasons. Most wanted a reliable and stable job, some were descendants of fire-fighting families, and a few didn't have a clue what they were getting into. I later learned that there were others like me who were realizing their childhood dream. I kept my mouth shut about that and about my experience as a fire reserve after some classmates found out that a fellow cadet had been a volun-teer firefighter and began calling him "Buff," a derogatory term for a fire buff.

The first thing we'd do each morning would be to stand at attention, salute the American flag, and recite the Pledge of Allegiance. During the first week, we were reciting our pledge when an instructor angrily dashed to the rear of our formation and began scolding a cadet. He was shortly joined by other screaming and yelling instructors. I couldn't hear their exact words, but as usual, an awful lot of expletives were flying around. Obviously, some-one had upset them, but I dared not look back. As we began our jumping jacks, I spotted the cadet in question being escorted through the apparatus floor and upstairs to Chief Bowen's office. Uh-oh.

The next day we learned that the cadet had been fired for some unknown infraction. I guess the most important lesson I learned was that if you don't comply with the rules, you're gone!

Each day our pledge was followed by a demanding round of calisthenics and a run of a mile or so around the drill yard. Afterward, we'd assemble in the auditorium for a written quiz based on our homework reading assign-ment. The class then split into our respective platoons, and we'd rotate through different training evolutions or classrooms throughout the day. At the end of each day, we were familiarized with the concept of housework, a daily chore done in all firehouses. We'd sweep and mop floors, empty trash cans, wipe down desks, and clean fire apparatuses before reassembling for a recap of the day's activities and our homework assignment. Sometimes, if the instructors weren't happy with our performance, we'd receive a scolding laced with four-letter words before dismissal.

I briefly joined a car pool with a few other cadets from South Philly. Things went well until we hit heavy traffic a few times and were nearly late. With McMillan's stern tardiness caveat seared into my mind, I opted to travel solo and left my home at six thirty in the morning for the half-hour drive. Arriving early had its benefits. I had more time to review my notes or practice evolutions that were giving me difficulty. About half the class was there by seven anyway, and we'd gather around the huge coffee pot on the apparatus floor. It was there that we cultivated the first bonds of camaraderie shared by firefighters everywhere.

The deputy director of Fire School, Battalion Chief George Yaeger Sr., had two sons, Eddie and George Jr., in our class. Eddie was quickly nicknamed Chief's Kid 1, and quick-witted George became Chief's Kid 2. More simply, we called them CK-1 and CK-2. Another son, Michael, had been hired about a year before us and was assigned to Engine 11 in South Philly. Even though most of us hadn't met him, we referred to him as CK-3.

South Philly's Jim Alberici was the first of the many hilariously funny firefighters I'd meet during my career. He easily could have been a stand-up comedian. Each morning he'd settle in around the coffee urn with fellow comics CK-2 and Southwest Philly's jocular Billy Hopper, and they'd hilariously mimic and exaggerate the idiosyncrasies of our instructors. The trio of funnymen quickly gave nicknames to many of our fellow cadets. "The General" was the most serious cadet, "Porky" barely eked under the maximum weight requirement, "Big Bird" was the tallest, "Dirt" earned his nickname after someone spotted a smudge on his shirt, "Tour de France" was the oldest, and "Double D" was the wackiest.

The trio also took potshots at each other. Jimmy would often poke fun at CK-2, saying, "If it weren't for your father upstairs, CK, you'd still be hanging on some street corner in Parkwood."

CK-2 would snap back, "Yeah? If it weren't for your paisans in that South Philly car pool, you'd never find this damn place!"

They drew bigger and bigger crowds each day. I loved the morning comedy routine so much that I made it a point to finish reviewing my notes and prep work by seven thirty. I wanted to sip my coffee and enjoy the sideshow to help relax my nerves, especially before major exams. One of the instructors, Lieutenant Terry Kelly, told us that it was a great introduction to firehouse life. He was right. Bantering, joking, and kidding followed me throughout my career and became one of my favorite aspects of the job.

About half of our training involved classroom studies, while the other half consisted of practical drills and evolutions. In class we studied the department's rule book, directives, operational procedures, equipment, hydraulics, pump operations, flammable-liquid fires, hazardous materials, sprinklers, standpipes, first aid, fireground tactics, aircraft fires, ship fires, and the chemistry and physics of combustion. We also learned about emergencies involving subways, elevated trains, elevators, escalators, and bridges.

In the practical sessions, we learned how to use most of the department's equipment. We were instructed on the proper techniques for using hand tools like the fire axe, ceiling hook, Halligan tool, claw tool, and power saw. We practiced stretching and rolling hose line, identifying the different types of hose layouts, whipping a stream around inside a building, and directing a stream from the outside. We had to recognize, identify, and know how to properly use an endless array of nozzles, fittings, and adapters. During search-and-rescue training, we were blindfolded and had to crawl around the fire tower searching for a bulky mannequin, which we had to drag outside.

We were trained to be skillful with rope. It seemed like every piece of equipment, other than the fire truck itself, had a particular array of hitches, half hitches, and safety knots to be tied for raising it aloft. The bowline, sheet-bend, and clove-hitch knots were so important that we had to master tying them blindfolded. The most exciting thing we had to do with rope was rappel down the tower. We tied one end to the chimney, wrapped the other end around a hook on a waist belt (ladder belt), and slid down five stories from the roof.

We also had to become extremely proficient with ladders. To develop our confidence in climbing, we began with scaling ladders. These ancient-style ladders, similar to those once used to attack fortifications, were designed to be climbed at a ninety-degree angle. They had one beam supporting the rungs and a large hook at the top. Beginning at ground level, we'd place the hook of the ladder into the second-floor window, climb straight up, straddle the sill, and climb back down. The next day, instead of climbing down after we straddled the sill, we lifted the ladder and hooked it into the third-floor window. Then we swung out and climbed up again. We added an additional floor each day, and by the end of the week, we were climbing up and down the five-story tower with ease. A final exam, of sorts, was to climb to the fifth floor, clasp the hook of the ladder belt on the beam of the ladder, lean back, and raise our hands in the air, as if to say, "Look, Mom, no hands!" It was an excellent way to overcome a fear of heights; once we were done with the scaling ladders, there wasn't a ladder in the department that I was afraid to climb.

And then there was the life net. Each cadet had to jump from a tower window into a circular life net supported by eight fellow cadets. It was actually more of a task to catch someone than to be the jumper. A 150-pound person lands with a significant impact, and if you're not holding the net properly, you could get seriously injured. Our group had the misfortune of holding the net when the rotund figure of Porky appeared on the window ledge. For levity, we backed away and pretended to refuse to catch his two-hundred-pound frame. The rest of the class got a pretty good chuckle out of it, but the instructors weren't as amused. After they yelled at us and forced us to catch him twice, we had to run up and down the fire tower five times as punishment.

Running up and down the fire tower was penance for any sins committed during training. The more severe the sin, the more trips one had to make up and down the steep stairs. One day, Captain Bense, who didn't teach too often, was giving a lecture at the podium. Sitting directly behind me was a cadet who had a lazy eye condition which caused one eyelid to droop. Not overly familiar with everyone, all Bense could see from his vantage point was the lazy-eyed half of his face. Thinking he was dozing, Bense immediately screamed, "You, five trips up the tower, now!" A few of us realized what had happened and began giggling. Bense got furious and screamed,

"You think that was funny? Five laps, all of you!" I joined seven others as we ran our laps, but we couldn't stop laughing the entire time. That and the Porky incident were my only two penance runs.

As we progressed, all the quizzes, examinations, and practical evolutions were graded. Cadets who didn't finish with an average score of seventy or higher would face termination. At the other end of the scale, the cadets with the three highest averages would be rewarded US Savings Bonds. I was doing extremely well until I completely screwed up one of the evolutions.

My partner, Steve, and I had practiced the two-man twenty-foot ladder raise several times with ease. But our practice ladder was an older model with only one set of heel plates. Heel plates were supposed to be placed against the ground for stability, as opposed to the opposite rounded end of the ladder. During our graded evolution, I was positioned at the end of the ladder farthest from the building, the end that was supposed to be raised to the top. I looked down and saw a set of heel plates. That couldn't be right! Surely our devious instructors were trying to trick us. I boldly rotated my end of the ladder toward the wall, which completely confused Steve, who had no choice but to go along with what I was doing. Cadets performing other evolutions ducked for cover as I swung my end of the ladder over their heads. When we raised the ladder into position, I was beaming. They didn't fool me! But unexpectedly Captain Brown screamed, "What the fuck was that circus act, Marchisello?"

"Sir," I replied confidently, "I had the heel plates at my end, sir."

Captain Brown angrily pointed to the top of the ladder. "And what the hell are those?" The ladder was a newer model that had heel plates at both ends. I got a zero for the exercise.

I felt better a few days later when I heard Captain Brown also scream at a group of cadets across the yard. Unbelievably, a group from the South Philly car pool had raised a thirty-five-foot extension ladder upside down. This was nearly impossible to do! My "circus act" was quickly forgotten the following morning when CK-2 dubbed the quartet "the Flying Tetrazzini Brothers."

During week five, the instructors knew that our training wasn't preparing us for the reality of the severe heat and smoke we'd soon encounter on firegrounds. They found two old couches in a neighbor's trash, dragged them into the basement of the tower, and set them ablaze. It was time for pack-man training. We each donned a self-contained breathing apparatus (SCBA) and climbed the exterior fire escape to the roof, where thick balls of black smoke were belching from the rooftop's fire-tower door. We were then ordered to descend through the darkness of the tightly sealed tower. Once we reached the searing heat of the basement, we were to climb back to the first-floor exit. The trek was hot, blinding, and extremely scary, but since we could breathe, I didn't think it was all that bad.

I wasn't prepared for what our cunning instructors had us do next. We were ordered to climb to the roof again, where we got our first lecture about the use of the breathing apparatus. "Sissies wear packs! Real firemen can take a beating in smoke and heat! Now drop your packs and get your asses down those steps again!"

This time the trip was brutal. We coughed, gagged, and choked our way down through the dense smoke and stifling heat. When we reached the basement, conditions were unbearable. I was clinging to the cadet in front of me as we crawled along the wall, desperately searching for the outside stairs. Unexpectedly, Lieutenant Kelly's voice bullhorned from somewhere in the darkness, "Stand at attention, cadets, and recite your name, payroll number, and platoon, or you're not getting the hell out of here." To say that I was impressed is an understatement. There wasn't a hint of distress in his voice, yet I could barely breathe. How was that humanly possible? I choked my name and staggered outside, barely making it to fresh air before passing out. Our faces were covered with so much grime and mucus that I couldn't recognize my classmates. It was my very first dose of smoke—the first of many.

Even though we were told that SCBAs were only for sissies, the 141st learned their benefits. We'd have nearly twenty years on the job before the "sissy culture" attitude finally gave way to mandatory use of SCBAs for everyone during interior firefighting.

In our seventh week, they bused us to a string of vacant row homes in North Philly that were scheduled to be demolished. We practiced raising ladders, taking out windows, and opening roofs. We also got hands-on experience overhauling, which means ripping apart walls, ceilings, baseboards, and trim to check for fire extension. It was a great practical exercise for those of us who would be assigned to ladder companies. Everything went well until an overzealous Tetrazzini Brother leaned over the roof and took out the windows of an occupied home a few doors down. When we got back, Chief Bowen almost popped his cork while screaming at the instructors. We could hear him yelling from the washroom as we laughed our asses off.

With graduation approaching, we excitedly discussed our upcoming station assignments. The 140th had been assigned to training stations that housed an engine company, ladder company, and rescue (emergency medical) unit. The objective was to give rookies varied experience by rotating them into the diverse units. The program was well intentioned, but there was a problem. There were only a handful of training stations, which meant that senior firefighters from those stations were being unwillingly transferred to make room for the rookies. Complaints flooded politicians and Local 22, the Philadelphia Firefighters' Union. Fire Commissioner Joseph R. Rizzo, Mayor Frank Rizzo's brother, was taking a lot of heat but remaining resolute for the time being. Of all the training stations, I was hoping for the busiest, Engine 68 and Ladder 13 in Southwest Philly.

On Tuesday evening, June 12, during our last week of Fire School, I took a break from my studies to pal around with my buddies at Fifteenth and Moore. Of course, I was the first of the group to detect a slight odor of smoke wafting through the night's warm, sticky air. But it was Bo (everyone in my crowd had a nickname) who first spotted smoke drifting in the sky. "Yo, Mitz"—my nickname was Concetta's pet name for me—"look at all that smoke!" A huge cloud of black smoke completely obscured the nearly full moon. I instantly knew it was an extra-alarm fire.

"Come on, Mitz," Bo yelled excitedly. "Let's go check it out!"

"Nah." I shrugged. "I got my final exam in two days and need to review my notes. Besides, I'm going to be seeing my share of fires beginning next week."

"What? Are you afraid we'll see how easy it is to pour water into a burning building?" Bo taunted. Then he turned to the guys. "Mitz chased fire engines all those years as a kid. Now he don't want us to see what he's going to be doing for a living."

"Okay!" I relented. "But only a few minutes. I've got to study." We piled into Bo's car and followed the smoke seven blocks up Broad Street.

Nothing in either my training or my days chasing fires with Arthur had prepared me for what we saw. There had been an explosion, and the scene was utter chaos. Firefighters were being pulled and dragged from under collapsed walls and debris. Others were being quickly wheeled past us on stretchers as flames shot nearly one hundred feet into the air from the huge burning building at Thirteenth and Washington. Fifty-five-gallon drums soared high into the night sky, trailing flames like rockets. I watched one soar over a hundred feet before it smashed down onto the roof of Ladder 11 with a thunderous crash.

"Screw this," Joe Cal whispered in my ear. "You can keep your new friggin' job, Mitz."

After the police pushed us away, we slowly piled back into Bo's car. Nobody said a word as we rode home. The news was all over the radio. Several firefighters had been injured and possibly killed during the explosion. I sat there silently. I wanted to be a firefighter so badly that I had never stopped to think what the hell I was getting myself into.

The fire we witnessed would be recorded in Philadelphia Fire Department history as the Levey-ink-plant fire. Two huge explosions ripped through the five-story building as firefighters battled the flames. The seven-alarm blaze blew out the building's back wall on Kimball Street and tossed firefighters against the walls across the street like bowling pins. Some of them were buried under tons of bricks and cinder blocks. Killed were Fireman Robert Malley, thirty-seven, from Engine 24, and Fireman John Welsh, thirty-two, of Ladder 5. Forty others were injured, seventeen seriously.

There was no comedy routine by the coffee urn on Wednesday morning. Everybody had heard the news. With somber faces and hushed tones, we could talk about nothing else. The brother of CK-1 and CK-2, Michael from Engine 11, had narrowly missed getting killed. An astute chief, Joseph McCreery, had sensed that something wasn't right and ordered CK-3's company out of the building moments before the blast.

The instructors held a brief moment of silence before our morning pledge and workout. Afterward, we assembled in the auditorium, where teary-eyed Captain Bense officially informed us about the tragic deaths of Malley and Welsh. "Last night we lost two brothers, Bob and Johnny. Their death is a death in our family, our brotherhood of firefighters. It's the price we must accept for the profession we've chosen. We will mourn, of course, but we will also carry on as usual. People need our help regardless. For Class One Forty-One, your challenging final exams will still be held tomorrow. Hopefully you'll pass and graduate on Friday."

A pall hung over the 141st during our final days at Fire School. Our enthusiasm about station assignments and class standing was tempered by the presence of two brightly waxed pumpers parked on the apparatus floor, being prepared as funeral hearses.

As promised, our comprehensive final examination was tough. But despite my twenty-foot-ladder circus act, my OCD helped me finish seventh in the class. It didn't matter much. Effective Monday morning we'd no longer be cadets. We'd be rookies trying our best to be accepted into close-knit fire companies. No matter how good or how bad we did in Fire School, we'd need to prove ourselves as firefighters.

Friday June 15 was graduation day. Early that morning we milled about the auditorium wearing our dress uniforms for the very first time. Seemingly overnight, the instructors' stern faces were replaced with warm, amicable smiles. The instructors moved among us like proud parents, satisfied that they had done their job. The rest was up to us.

Captain Bense called the 141st to attention. "Okay, it's time for your station assignments. There's been a change. Most of you are not—I repeat, *are not*—going to training stations." Politics had prevailed. "When I read your name and assignment, proceed to the front of the class, pick up your transfer, and then return to your seat." Alphabetically, my name was halfway down the list. "Robert Marchisello, Ladder 19, Platoon B."

I was disappointed. Even though it was one of the South Philly firehouses Arthur and I often visited as kids and was close to home, I had been hoping to get my start in a busy engine company. On the other hand, I could have done worse. Ladder 19 was fairly active and responded first-in with Engines 24, 47, 49, and 60.

Unlike those of most cadet classes filled with hope and promise, Class 141's graduation ceremonies had a somber undertone. During our commencement, Fire Commissioner Joseph Rizzo had no choice but to address the line-of-duty deaths (LODDs) of Firemen Malley and Welsh. He wisely got it out of the way quickly so the rest of the ceremony would have some sense of normalcy. As we walked to the front of the class to receive our certificates and handshakes, worried families, including my parents, hoped and prayed that the recent tragedy wasn't an omen for their loved ones' futures.

After the ceremony we were directed to another room, where we were split into two groups for Saturday's funerals. Sadly, Class 141's last official duties together were funeral details. I was assigned to Fireman Malley's services in Southwest Philly. Some of my classmates were assigned as honorary pallbearers. Unfortunately, their first ride on a fire truck wasn't what they had expected. Instead of enthusiastically responding to a fire with flashing lights and blaring sirens, they took a slow, solemn ride in a funeral procession.

Such was the beginning for Class 141. A few classmates left the job for various reasons long before they were eligible to retire. But most of us stayed on the job and made careers in the Philadelphia Fire Department. Graduates from Class 141 would fight some of Philadelphia's biggest and deadliest fires in the ensuing years. Some of my brothers eventually became chief's aides, paramedics, hazardous-material technicians, technical-rescue specialists, fire boat pilots or engineers. Over a third of us would get promoted to lieutenant, many rising to the rank of captain. Seven would become battalion chiefs, and three of those would rise to the rank of deputy chief. Looking back, I guess it wasn't too bad for a group who, on April 24, 1973, were referred to as a bunch of fuckoffs and assholes who couldn't even count right.

CHAPTER 3

Captain Blood the Rookie

A s in most urban areas, there are two basic types of fire companies in
Philadelphia. Engine companies, which are primarily responsible for
attacking and extinguishing fires, and ladder companies, whose main duties
include search, rescue, forcible entry, laddering, ventilating (taking out windows and opening roofs), and overhaul operations.

Ladder Company 19, located at Twenty-Fourth and Ritner Streets, was
quartered with Engine Company 60. A Seagrave tiller-style (steerable rear
wheels) tractor trailer, its key feature was a hundred-foot hydraulically operated main ladder mounted on its trailer section. It carried a full complement
of ground ladders, tools, and equipment, including a scaling ladder and a
life net.

Because of its close proximity to the Atlantic and Gulf oil refineries,
the station also housed two specialized pieces of fire apparatus. Engine
160, a foam pumper used for fighting oil fires, was staffed by Engine 60's
firefighters. Chemical Unit 3 carried extra foam, a high-expansion foam
generator, technical-rescue gear, hazardous-materials equipment, and an air-
supply bank for filling SCBAs. It was one of three such units strategically
located around the city. When Chemical 3 was dispatched, a firefighter
from Ladder 19 would relinquish his laddering duties and serve as its driver
and operator.

The first shift in the firehouse is unforgettable for every firefighter.
For me it was a monumental culmination of endless months of waiting,
preparation, and training. No longer a cadet, I had become a rookie, and
like most rookies, I spent my first day filled with apprehension, nervousness,
and anxiety. I desperately wanted to fit in and be accepted by the veteran
firefighters.

At the time, Philadelphia firefighters worked a rotating three-shift
schedule. The shifts, referred to as Platoons A, B, and C, worked two

ten-hour days (8:00 a.m. to 6:00 p.m.) and two fourteen-hour nights (6:00 p.m. to 8:00 a.m.), followed by two days off. I was assigned to Ladder 19's B Platoon, and I recorded my first day in the firehouse in my journal.

June 19, 1973—Rookie Firefighter, Ladder 19

I turned onto Twenty-Fourth Street filled with anticipation, and there it stood—the big two-story, ornate red brick firehouse with its distinctive black slate roof. Built the same year my father was born, 1921, it's the same place Arthur and I frequented more than ten years ago to hustle tip money. Black bunting, a sad reminder of the recent line-of-duty deaths, was still draped over its big red manually operated doors.

At 7:00 a.m., an hour before my first shift, I stepped out of my car wearing my summer dress uniform: a light-blue shirt with epaulets and dark-blue serge trousers. I smartly placed my uniform cap on my head, popped open my trunk, and idiotically grabbed more belongings than I could handle. With so many things in my arms, I could barely close the trunk with my elbow. With my personnel folder dangling from my mouth, I lugged my helmet, boots, running coat, work uniform, work shoes, and toiletries bag across the street. Miraculously I made it through the open apparatus doors without dropping anything. It was certainly an ungracious entrance on my first day. Luckily, no veterans were around to notice my awkwardness. I'm sure if they had been, they would've wondered, "What kind of simpleton did they send us?"

My helmet clunked as I fumbled it onto the red bench next to Ladder 19's apparatus. Luckily, the firefighter sitting at the watch desk didn't notice. After I folded my coat over the bench and set my boots upright, I stood there holding the rest of my stuff, not knowing what to do next.

"Are you in the engine or ladder?" a friendly-sounding voice said from the top of the stairs. I looked up and saw a firefighter with bright-red hair leaning over the railing.

"Uh, the ladder. I'm in the ladder," I answered nervously.

The A Platoon's Richie Doc waved me up the steps. "Come on up. I'll take you to the meet the captain."

After I introduced myself to Richie, we walked down the hallway to the last room on the right. On its glass windowpane was the department's logo with the words "Office—Ladder 19" stenciled below it. Richie knocked softly and said, "Hey, Cap, your new guy on the B Platoon is here."

Captain Jack Bernard's bright friendly smile seemed to fill the doorway as it swung open. "Welcome to Ladder Nineteen, kid. Here, let me take that," he said, grabbing the personnel folder I had tucked under my chin. "Come on in and sit down." His welcoming demeanor instantly eased my tension. I hadn't even made a run yet, but my affable captain made me feel like I was already part of the company.

After he closed the door, Captain Bernard gave me a short but spirited pep talk. "By no means are we the busiest, kid, but we catch our share of fires. Always take pride in yourself and our company, and learn from the veterans." Bernard explained that he worked on the A Platoon, not mine, which I found disappointing. Even though I'd just met him, I knew it would have been great to work directly under his supervision.

After our chat, the captain handed me a red frontispiece for my helmet and a locker key. "Get changed, kid. Then go down to the kitchen and have a cup of coffee. I'll be down at eight, when they ring the bells for roll call." Richie was waiting outside, and he escorted me to the locker room. I hastily slipped out of my dress uniform, hoping and praying that we wouldn't get a run while I was clad in nothing but my underwear. Thankfully the bells remained silent, and I finished dressing into my work clothes. I tied my shoes loosely so I could easily kick them off in case we got a run.

My 141st classmates Tour de France, Eddie Hill, and Dirt, who was one of the Flying Tetrazzinis, had also been assigned to my firehouse. Tour de France got Engine 60, and it was his first day too. I spotted him wandering the hallway, looking just as confused as I did. "In here, Tour. This is the B Platoon's locker room." I was comforted by the fact that someone else also looked completely out of place. I waited for him to change, and we headed down to the kitchen together.

The drab tan kitchen off the right side of the apparatus floor had four steps leading to its large open doorway. Inside, about a dozen firefighters were sitting on wooden benches that lined a large laminate table, chatting and laughing. The room instantly went quiet, and heads turned toward Tour and me, two fresh-faced rookies, as we warily walked inside. Our light-blue work shirts and dark-blue trousers, a uniform change issued only to the 140th and 141st classes, highlighted our newness. Everybody else was wearing older-issue gray tops and bottoms. Hopefully blue uniforms would shortly be standard issue for the entire department.

Most of the veterans shook our hands and introduced themselves, but a few at the other end of the table merely smiled and nodded in our direction. They all resumed their conversations while Tour and I poured ourselves coffee and sat together at one end of the table. Heeding the advice of our instructors at Fire School, we sat there silently. "A rookie is all ears and no mouth!"

While I was sipping my freshly brewed coffee, the bells suddenly rang. The loud clanging nearly jarred me out of my skin, and I winced as I spilled hot coffee onto my lap. "Will this be my first run?" I wondered. No, it wasn't. A loud voice from the apparatus floor followed the long ring. "Roll call!" Like newborn sheep, we followed the herd down to the apparatus floor.

Two rows of firefighters formed beside Engine 60's pumper, and two rows lined up next to Ladder 19. I joined the oncoming platoon in the front row by the ladder. Captain Bernard stood before us and commanded us to attention. After surveying both rows, he ordered us to stand at ease and pointed at me. "This is Bob Marchisello, our rookie from Fire School." I think he spotted the wet coffee spot on my trousers, because he had a half smile on his face as he spoke. I hoped that he didn't think I had peed myself! Thank God he didn't make any comments. The eight o'clock alert tone buzzed from the watch desk, and Bernard officially proclaimed, "Platoon B is on duty. Platoon A, you're dismissed." Our row remained in formation while firefighters from the off-going platoon scurried out through the open apparatus doors.

Somewhere in his forties, my lieutenant moved from the end of our row and took Bernard's place in front. His name was Lieutenant Mattox. Staring down at his roll-call slip, he doled out our assignments. "Eddie, you're driving. McGinn, you're tillering." (He'd be steering the rear wheels.) "Walt, take the pack. Gerry, you've got the inside hook and Chemical 3." I was assigned a six foot ceiling hook and instructed to follow McGinn around on the fireground.

After roll call, Eddie, Walt, Gerry, and McGinn rapidly gathered around, introduced themselves, and welcomed me to the company. Our thinly built tillerman, red-haired Mike McGinn, led me to my riding position, showed me where and how to lay out my gear, and gave me pointers.

"Listen, we got all the riding positions covered today, so you're an extra guy. I've got the outside hook, so just follow me around." We walked to the rear of the apparatus, where Mike showed me our array of ladders. "The twenty-eight and thirty-five are our workhorses down here. If we're second-in, we'll take either the sixteen or twenty."

"Does our twenty-footer have heel plates at both ends?" I asked curiously.

"Yeah!" he said with a big grin under his bushy red mustache. "Do they still have those old single-plate ones at Fire School?" I smiled and nodded but didn't elaborate about my Fire School circus act.

My six-foot hook was in a tube under the tillerman's seat. "This is your hook," he pointed out. "Before you take out a window, tap on it three times. You don't want to smash glass into the face of any firemen operating inside."

Mike looked at his watch. "Come on, let's get a cup of coffee. Housework begins at eight forty-five. I'll take you through all the compartments after we're done." I could already sense that McGinn had taken a keen interest in my development as a firefighter.

Everyone except the officers and watchman was back in the kitchen kidding around and talking. As soon as we walked in, Engine 60's rather large Tony Mongano shouted, "Yo, Mike! Give the friggin' new kid a break. He's got all day, which is more than enough to learn everything *you* know about firefighting." Everyone laughed.

"Screw you, Tony! I just want to make sure he don't become a fuckin' bum like you," McGinn responded. The laughter got louder.

Smiling, I topped off my coffee and sat on the bench next to McGinn. At exactly 8:39 a.m., the kitchen speaker blasted, "Attention, Engine 60 and Ladder 19, Nineteen Twelve Durfor Street, a defective refrigerator." It was my first run! Dashing through the kitchen door, I jumped down the short set of stairs and landed on the apparatus floor with a loud *whomp*! I sprinted to my riding position as though I was trying to beat out an infield hit. I was running so fast that I had to grab the apparatus's side handle to stop myself from sliding onto Twenty-Fourth Street.

I kicked off my shoes, but my laces were so loose that one of them sailed completely underneath our apparatus. I slid into my left boot without a hitch, but when I tried to put my right foot into the boot, it hit something. "Uh-oh!" I remembered in horror that I had kept my housework rags in my boot at Fire School. Shit, they were still there! It was too late to do anything because Eddie already had the engine running and everybody was climbing aboard. I had no choice but to climb into my rear-facing jump seat with my right foot sitting in my boot at an uncomfortable sixty-degree angle.

Walt climbed aboard and took his place facing me. Two beeps from the floor pedal signaled that McGinn was ready in the tillerman's cage. Eddie dropped the shifter in drive and revved the engine, and we raced out the door, following Engine 60 and Engine 160 down Twenty-Fourth. All those years of listening to sirens as a kid, and on my very first run, I could barely hear ours over the loud roar of our diesel.

Minutes later we arrived on Durfor Street. "Follow me!" McGinn shouted as I clumsily slid my hook from its tube. I tried my best to hide my hobble as I followed him up the street and into a small row home. Engine 60's officer, Captain George, was already inside and standing in front of a white refrigerator that had a hissing sound coming from its freezer. I knew it was a nontoxic Freon leak but stood there silently holding my hook like a shepherd. All ears, no mouth!

Balding and bearing a thick gray mustache, George stuck his nose into the freezer and sniffed once. "It's only Freon and don't need to go outside. Ladder 19, you're recalled."

McGinn tugged on my coat. "Let's go. We're outta here!" As we returned to our apparatus, a concerned look came over my mentor's face when he noticed the wobble in my gait. "Why are you limping?"

"Uh, I twisted my ankle playing softball last night. I'll be fine," I lied.

Luckily, the apparatus hadn't run over my shoe. Before we backed into the station, I pretended that it belonged to someone else and nonchalantly kicked it out of our path. I dallied before removing my boots and, when the coast was clear, quickly pulled the huge wad of rags wedged in the right one and tossed them into the trash can. Then I tightened my shoelaces a little. After these minor adjustments, I was ready for my second run.

It was the first of thousands of runs that would span my career. Even though the call was uneventful, I learned something, even if it was only about shoes and boots. For the rest of my career, I religiously checked my gear and equipment at the beginning of each shift.

My first day was filled with activity. After housework, I helped Eddie finish washing Ladder 19. McGinn kept his promise and methodically walked me through all the compartments. "Bobby, do this every day until you memorize where every single piece of equipment is kept," he said. Eddie, Walt, and Gerry also took turns giving me advice and pointers. Everybody was helping the new guy. It made me feel good.

For lunch, Mongano put together delicious Italian hoagies. He also made a huge mess. After eating, Tour and I cleaned the entire kitchen, the lowly task expected from rookies. We understood that we'd be at the bottom of the hierarchy until a fresh batch of blue shirts took our places. Personally, I didn't mind the rookie chores at all. I was elated to simply be there.

At one o'clock, Mattox yelled from the apparatus floor, "Ladder, block checks!" and we spent the next two hours doing fire inspections. Eddie took the lead this time and explained every step of the block-by-block process. With straight brown hair and a hooked chin, Eddie had more interest in block checks than the rest of the guys did. They rolled their eyes as he meticulously showed me how to conduct a thorough building inspection.

After we came back, McGinn told me to sit at the watch desk to learn the duties of the watchman. That's where I formally met Engine 60's driver and pump operator, Frank Castellucci. The big guy with a linebacker's build had been buzzing around checking equipment, cleaning compartments, and washing the pumper all morning. When we left for block checks, he was still at it, sliding around underneath on a mechanic's creeper, performing maintenance checks. Earlier in the day, Gerry had said, "Bob, that's the hardest-working man in the department. He puts about six hours a day into that pumper."

Frank was pulling his shift on watch duty when I walked into the ten-foot by ten-foot cinder-block watch box. His features were dominated by jet-black wavy hair and black-rimmed glasses. He stood up and offered his massive hand as soon as I walked in. "Hey, kid! Come in and sit down next to your buddy here." Tour had been in the watch box all afternoon. My eyes almost popped out of my head from pain when Frank clamped down with his viselike handshake.

Frank wasted no time. "Listen, Bobby, the first thing I want to tell you is that the reputation you make during your first year or so will follow you throughout your career." He looked toward Ladder 19. "See that friggin' truck? That's your toolbox. Learn your compartments. Know how to use and maintain every piece of equipment it carries. When you get qualified to drive, keep that ladder in tip-top shape, even if it takes all day, understand?"

Frank took off his glasses. "I was just explaining to your classmate that the best tool you have isn't on that truck; it's your friggin' head. Don't let anybody tell you anything different." Frank pointed his hot-dog-sized finger toward the apparatus floor. "More than half these friggin' guys don't think; they just react. When we get a job, take a second to think about what you're doing. It could save your friggin' life someday!"

Frank spent his entire watch shift giving us tips and pointers. I sat there mesmerized by his down-to-earth, common-sense approach to firefighting. Of all the lessons we had learned in Fire School, nothing could compare to his practical advice. McGinn and Eddie were good teachers, but the man I affectionately began to call Uncle Frank was the first of my many great mentors. The work habits and lessons I would learn from him during my rookie days laid the foundation for my career.

After my first lesson with Uncle Frank, we got our second run. We were first-in ladder on box two-four-four-three for a reported church fire at Twenty-Sixth and Tasker Streets. Four engines, two ladders, and two battalion chiefs were dispatched on the full-box alarm. I kicked my shoes toward the wall this time, and my boots felt a lot more comfortable without rags stuffed inside them. Engine 60 was second-in, so we went out the door first. My heart was pounding, but the call turned out to be a minor electrical problem, and we didn't do anything except shut off the power. As we were leaving, I saw my 141st classmates Bobby T. and Porky, both assigned to 24's, the first-in engine. I waved as they were reeling up their booster line under the watchful eye of a husky blond-haired firefighter, apparently *their* mentor.

We didn't catch a fire on my third run that day either, but I was unexpectedly caught in the middle of a controversy.

JUNE 19, 1973—ROOKIE FIREFIGHTER, LADDER 19

Captain George's policy stated that the last firefighter on watch during each shift would clean the kitchen and make two fresh pots of coffee. Walt had the last watch, from four to six, but when there were new guys around the house, the rules were different. Tour and I covered his chores and readied the kitchen for the oncoming platoon.

"There's so many things to remember that I'm bringing in a notebook tomorrow," I told Tour, but before he could answer, we got our third run. "Attention, Engine 49, Ladder 19, Battalion 1, and Rescue 11. Broad and Jackson Streets, an automobile accident."

With two runs' worth of experience under my belt, I jogged to my riding position like a seasoned veteran. I gently kicked off my shoes and donned my gear, and I was about to climb aboard when a heavy hand grabbed my coat and jerked me backward. "What the f—" I yelled.

A dark-haired firefighter from the oncoming platoon slipped past me, indignantly proclaiming, "You're relieved!"

I dejectedly stepped down but shot him an angry glare. Then I heard a thunderous voice behind me boom, "Get the fuck back on that apparatus, fireman!" It was the voice of the C Platoon's Lieutenant Muck. He certainly had an odd way of introducing himself.

I started to climb aboard again, but the firefighter snarled, "You're relieved, new guy. Get off!"

I stepped back down, looked back at Muck, and shrugged my shoulders. "He said I'm relieved, Loo."

With daggers in his eyes, Muck stomped toward us, pointed at the firefighter, and screamed, "You! Get the fuck on the main." (Sit on the main ladder.) "I said he's making this fuckin' run!"

Astonishingly, the firefighter resisted. "Loo, I'm making this darn run. He's been relieved!"

Gee! I'd thought that on this job, orders were orders!

I was climbing up and down like a yo-yo until Muck popped his cork. He began screaming wildly at the firefighter. "I said the new kid's making this fuckin' run. Now, either get on the main or get the fuck off the truck and face charges." The threat finally forced the disgruntled firefighter to relinquish his seat. Cursing under his breath, he climbed over the engine compartment and onto the main. I scrambled aboard before Muck had a chance to yell at me again. I never imagined the simple act of making a run could be so difficult.

We made it all the way to Broad and Jackson before getting recalled by 49's (a radio message that our service wasn't needed). I knew I was the new guy, but I was pissed at the veteran for putting me in such a position. I glared at him during the entire ride, but he refused to make eye contact. After we got back, he and Muck got into it all over again. While they were screaming and yelling at each other, I went upstairs to change into my dress uniform for roll call. My first day was over, and I was batting zero for three. Three runs, no fires.

I never expected my first day to end with a confrontation between a firefighter and his lieutenant, especially one that was about me. Lieutenant Muck's authoritarian ways and disparaging attitude often resulted in confrontations with his firefighters. I was glad that he wasn't my officer. I only saw Muck at change of shifts, but the very next week, I unwittingly became the target of his wrath again.

Tour was on a run with 60's, and I had just finished my afternoon kitchen chores when Muck came marching up the steps. "What the fuck are you doing in here, rookie?" he roared. "You should be at the watch desk learning these friggin' streets!" I tried to explain that I was only doing my rookie chores, but he abruptly cut me off. "How would you make the run to Twenty-Eighth and Ernst Streets?"

Obviously he didn't know that I had grown up in South Philly because it was a no-brainer. "Loo," I replied, "I'd make a left onto Twenty-Fourth Street, a right onto Passyunk, and a right on Twenty-Eighth to Ernst."

He pounded his fist on the kitchen table. "You're fuckin' wrong!" he screamed. "You make a right and then a left on Snyder!" He was dead wrong, but I bit my tongue and kept my mouth shut. Rookies didn't argue, especially with officers.

In the coming shifts, I was making plenty of runs and getting pretty good at cleaning the kitchen, but I was anxiously awaiting my first *official* fire. I *thought* it had come on June 28 when we responded to a fire in the housing projects. Medium smoke was pushing from the second floor as Eddie and I took out the windows. Then we joined the rest of our company inside and wrestled a smoldering mattress down the steps and out the front door. But according to McGinn and another firefighter in my company, Frenchy, it didn't count. Engine 60 and Ladder 19 had handled the fire alone. In order for me to officially lose my firefighter's virginity, all hands had to be placed in service on a tactical box or more. The wait continued.

July 5, 1973—Rookie Firefighter, Ladder 19

I couldn't catch a damned break. Early in the morning of July 5, I actually missed my first all-hands fire. At 4:30 a.m. I was sitting in the watch box with Uncle Frank, listening to a fatal four-alarm blaze at the Chesterfield Hotel in North Philly. Four civilians had been killed, and several firefighters were injured in the fire, but as they say, we didn't turn a wheel. All was quiet on the southern front.

Because of the hotel fire, someone needed to drive the reserve car parked in our lot to pick up a backup fire marshal. No surprise—that task fell to the new guy, me. Frenchy, our acting lieutenant for the shift, had me take my gear off Ladder 19 and drive to Engine 20 to pick up the fire marshal.

I placed my gear on the red bench and drove to Chinatown, where I picked up a lieutenant and took him to investigate an automobile firebombing at Fourth and Wharton Streets. Right after he finished and got back into the car, tactical box one-six-six-one came over the radio for a reported dwelling fire at Twenty-Second and Morris Streets. Naturally, Ladder 19 was first-in.

I was okay with it until Captain George reported heavy fire showing and placed all hands in service. "Damn!" I yelled, slamming my fists against the steering wheel so hard that the lieutenant nearly jumped out of his seat. "I just missed my first friggin' fire!"

I think he felt sorry for me. "Okay, kid," he said. "Respond to the fire, and I'll drop you off."

Heavy gray smoke was still pouring from the windows by the time we pulled up. I hastily thanked the lieutenant and hopped out. But as he drove away, I realized, to my abject horror, that I had left my gear on the red bench. I felt like a turtle without a shell. What was I going to do now?

It didn't take long for Battalion Chief Tynann to spot me standing there cluelessly. After doing a double take, he stormed in my direction. "Where the hell were you, and where the hell is your gear?" he screamed, his eyes darting up and down my body. The chief's verbal onslaught had me paralyzed. My mouth was moving, but nothing was coming out.

Luckily, Uncle Frank was operating 60's pumper between us. He quickly came to my rescue. "Chief! Chief! Frenchy sent him to pick up a backup fire marshal, and he just got back. I brought his gear. It's here in the compartment."

Tynann's scowl turned into an understanding smile. "Okay, kid, get your gear on and join your company." Whew! Thank God for Uncle Frank.

I got a little action pulling ceilings and opening walls, but it certainly didn't count as my first fire. All hands had been placed in service, but I wasn't one of them at the time. I was still a virgin firefighter!

When one fire company is overstaffed and another company is shorthanded, the overstaffed company sends, or details, a firefighter to the understaffed company. In Ladder 19 everybody took turns being detailed to other companies. But if the detail was to a slower company, Mattox usually sent me instead of the veterans.

July 31, 1973—Rookie Firefighter, Ladder 19

As usual, I arrived for work an hour early, placed my gear by my riding position, and began my ritual of checking each compartment. "Marcello! Marcello!" It was Mattox. He still didn't know how to pronounce my name.

"Yo, Loo," I said, peeping over the top of our apparatus. "What's up?"

"You're detailed today."

Since I had just been detailed to 49's on our last day shift, I knew it wasn't my turn. The detail had to be to someplace slow. "Okay, Loo. Where to?"

"Boat Three." He giggled.

My jaw dropped. No place was slower than Fire Boat 3. I shrugged my shoulders and slapped my hands against my thighs. "Okay, Loo, Boat Three."

Tony Mongano belly laughed at my disappointed face as I grabbed my gear and walked dejectedly to my car. "Yo, Bob!" he called. "Try not to fall in the river!" I replied with both of my middle fingers.

Fire Boat 3's station on the Schuylkill River was nestled between the Atlantic Refinery and the Philadelphia Gas Works. The firehouse, a plain one-story tan-and-brown cinder-block building, looked rather odd without an apparatus floor. Resembling a tugboat with water cannons and ladders, the *Benjamin Franklin* was facing upstream, tied to its adjacent dock.

Unsure what to do with my gear, I piled it by the door leading to the boat before I went inside. As in every firehouse during shift change, a gang of firefighters was in the kitchen, sipping coffee and chatting away. At least I was familiar with that aspect of the job. I poured myself a cup and joined the group, whose average age had to be around fifty-five. Glenn Miller's "Moonlight Serenade" was softly playing in the background, and it made me feel more like I was hanging with my father and his friends than sitting in a firehouse.

I was trying to figure out how to join in on a conversation about pensions, Social Security, and Medicare, when the B Platoon's officer sat beside me. Lieutenant Pete Iazzonni, barely forty, brought the crew's average age down to fifty. Cheerful and friendly, Iazzonni took me on a tour of the boat and explained how they operated on the firegrounds—or let's say the *firewaters*.

In addition to Iazzonni, the boat's staff consisted of a fireboat pilot, a fireboat engineer, and three deckhands. Imagine that—I was a deckhand for the day. I felt more like a recruit in the navy. In rookie tradition, or maybe out of respect for their age, I did the lion's share of the housework. The guys, who had done their time in busy companies before their semiretirement, treated me to hamburgers for lunch. I repaid them by cleaning up, doing the dishes, and pulling all the afternoon watches.

Outside the watch-desk window was an array of piping networks and hissing steam lines for the refineries. An occasional tugboat would chug its way along the river pushing a barge, but other than that, nothing was happening on the predominantly industrial stretch of the Schuylkill. Bored as hell, I passed the afternoon studying for my six-month probationary exam.

Fireboats automatically respond to box alarms located within a block or so of the river. Shortly after four o'clock that afternoon, as I was about to do my duty and make coffee for the oncoming platoon, a long buzz came over the public-address system. It was a box alarm for Thirty-Sixth and Wharton Streets. I hastily checked the response file, and to my utter surprise, we were listed to respond. We actually had a run!

I flipped on the fire lights and pressed hard on the bells. "Celotex Corporation! Thirty-Sixth and Wharton! A building fire!" The pilot, the engineer, and Iazzonni slowly made their way toward the boat. Unbelievably, the other two deckhands casually strolled into the storage room to retrieve their gear first. They didn't even have it out!

I threw my gear onto the deck, scampered aboard, and was stepping into my boots when Iazzonni exclaimed, "No! Just put on your helmet and gloves. If you go overboard with your gear on, you'll sink like a rock." I'd never thought of that.

Unlike my shipmates, I was raring to go within seconds, but they didn't show an ounce of urgency as they casually meandered aboard. I wanted to scream, "Come on! We *are* going to a fire, you know!"

It seemed like an hour before we started to chug up the Schuylkill. We were going so slow I wanted to get out and push the darned boat, especially after I looked north and saw clouds of black smoke drifting across the river. Yup! I missed another one. Ladder 19 was first-in.

Iazzonni tapped on the window of the wheelhouse and told us that we were actually going into service. I couldn't believe it! My first working box alarm, and I was aboard a damned fireboat. Because so many fire hydrants had been open with the summer's heat and humidity, pressure in the area's dead-end mains was extremely low. Capable of pumping six thousand gallons per minute, our job on the boat was to supply water to the engine companies.

Heavy smoke was still pouring from the building as we slowly docked. The first person I saw was Uncle Frank. With a few folds of heavy hose draped over his shoulder, he was dragging several hundred feet behind him. That man was as strong as an ox!

"Bobby," he said, laughing while he handed me a heavy brass coupling, "I forgot you were at Boat Three today. Looks like you missed another friggin' job."

"Tell me about it," I said as I connected the coupling to one of the boat's discharge outlets.

We supplied a few more companies, and within fifteen minutes, the black smoke turned gray. Once they had an adequate water supply, the companies quickly knocked the fire down. After that, there was nothing else for me to do but watch. I felt like I was buffing fires with Arthur again.

Suddenly I heard laughter from the roof. "Look! It's Captain Blood the Rookie!" It was Frenchy, McGinn, Eddie, and Gerry. With smoke drifting over their heads, they were standing at the roof's edge, saluting me.

"Argh," shouted McGinn. "It's Captain Blood on his pirate ship in the mighty Schuylkill. Argh. Argh!" I felt bad enough about having missed another job, yet there they stood, breaking my balls. I flipped them the bird, which only made them laugh harder.

I should have had two jobs under my belt by now. Instead, I was Captain Blood the Rookie, a virgin pirate. Sigh!

The name stuck. The next day Frenchy and McGinn said that the nickname was mine until I caught my first all-hands fire. We did respond to more fires, but they were all handled by one engine and ladder, one engine and two ladders, and even two engines and one ladder. It seemed that I was going to be Captain Blood the Rookie forever.

At the time, the task of the pack man in a ladder company was search and rescue. It wasn't the most fitting assignment for a rookie, let alone for one who was still a virgin. Search-and-rescue personnel often operate alone, frequently above the fire, without hose lines for protection. It's one of the job's most dangerous duties and is usually reserved for veterans.

Since I wasn't qualified to drive or tiller the ladder or drive Chemical 3, I was pack man more often than not. Uncle Frank, my worried mentor, constantly gave me advice and safety tips about conducting searches under heavy smoke and heat conditions.

I tried to make the best of the situation and learned to don the pack quickly and efficiently. It kept me in shape too. Every time we responded to the high-rise towers in the nearby housing projects, which was quite often, I'd race up to the fire floor and arrive before everyone else. I even got to stomp out a few rubbish fires before Engine 60 got up there.

Unsurprisingly, I was pack man the evening that I finally lost my firefighter's virginity.

August 26, 1973—Rookie Firefighter, Ladder 19

On the night of August 26, on our very first run, I finally caught a job that met the guys' criteria for my first official fire—an all-hands working box alarm for an apartment fire at Thirtieth and Wharton Streets.

Halfway there McGinn, who was sitting across from my rear-facing jump seat, kicked my boot. "Yo, Blood! This might be it." When I turned around, I saw a column of thick black smoke blowing across Wharton Street. Heavy fire was showing from the second-floor rear windows when we pulled up, so I slipped on my mask, raced inside, and followed 47's hose line upstairs. As they battled the flames in two rear rooms, I methodically searched the front room, middle room, and bathroom. I'd be the first to admit that it was scary as hell crawling around inside the darkness of a burning building. The smoke was so thick that I couldn't see a thing. I circled around each room, hugging the walls and sweeping the floor with my extended Halligan tool. Luckily, nobody was in any of the rooms.

I was doing pretty well until 47's knocked down one of the back rooms and I hastily crawled inside to continue my search. The floor was covered with red-hot smoldering debris. It felt as though I was crawling over a bed of hot coals, and my knees were burning like hell. Thankfully, nobody was in there either. Whew!

After the heat lifted, it was such a relief to get off my scorching knees. After removing my mask, I joined McGinn, Frenchy, Walt, and Eddie in pulling ceilings, opening walls, and ripping apart baseboards, doors, and windows. McGinn stopped for a second, put his arm around my shoulder, and announced loudly, "Yo, guys! The rookie's no longer the virgin Captain Blood! This was his first official job." Smiling, he poked me in the chest. "Listen, even though you're not a virgin anymore, you're still a rookie." The guys gathered around and congratulated me.

When we returned to the firehouse I disappeared into a bathroom stall, rolled up my pants, and checked my knees. They were swollen, red, and covered with blisters. I had second-degree burns. They hurt like hell, but there was no way that I was going to report an injury on my first official job. That's all Frenchy and McGinn would need to hear. I'd probably get another nickname, like "Mr. Wimp the Rookie."

In any case, I was Captain Blood the Rookie no more!

I treated my burned knees with over-the-counter burn ointment and ban-
dages. The blisters hurt for about a week, but the injury was well worth the
cost. My handle, Captain Blood, was gone, and I was finally accepted, to
some extent, by the members of my company. It had taken two months and
seven days to bust my cherry, a little longer than I had originally imagined.
But it was over, and I was glad to have a fire under my belt.

Before long, the cold weather would set upon Philadelphia. The fall and
winter were certain to bring more fires.

CHAPTER 4

Free Fall

Rookie firefighters must be careful not to fall victim to devilish pranks and practical jokes. During my first 4:00 a.m. solo turn on watch duty, a man identifying himself as the chief fire dispatcher called on the intradepartmental phone (fire phone). "Fireman," he commanded, "we need you to test your station's emergency alert system. I want you to flip on the lights and press the bells for thirty seconds." Everyone was asleep, and I wasn't about to fall for his ruse. I covered the speaker with my hand for a minute and then told him that the test was successful. He didn't buy it. "Fireman!" he screamed. "We didn't get your signal. Now hit those damned bells!" When I didn't react, he began to curse at me, so I slammed the phone into its cradle. He didn't call back. Obviously someone in my station had set me up. My main suspects were Mongano, Frenchy, or McGinn.

All summer long, whenever I sat out front, the same trio unsuccessfully tried to dump a bucket of water on my head. But as soon as I heard the second-floor window slide open, I'd dart away, and the water would splash harmlessly on the sidewalk. One night, however, I was sitting on the bench with Mongano (the setup man) and darted away as usual after hearing a noise from above. I looked up, and sure enough, Frenchy (the other setup man) was poised at the window holding a bucket. I pointed at him and was beginning to laugh when suddenly McGinn jumped out from the side of the station and drenched me with the garden hose. They got me!

It was difficult for them to get me with bedtime antics because I would stay up most of the night waiting for a call. But my villainous comrades were patient, and they studied my habits. One night, I went to my bunk at my usual time, 4:00 a.m., and quickly fell asleep. Suddenly my bunk jerked and jolted me awake. Wide eyed, I clung to the mattress as my bed was dragged halfway across the room by a rope tied to the back of 60's pumper. They got me again!

The following week, after checking my bedframe for ropes, I climbed into bed. This time I smelled a vaguely familiar fragrance but couldn't place the scent. The following morning when I looked in the mirror, I was white from head to toe, covered with talcum powder. Yet again!

Whether I was the victim of the pranks or not, I quickly grew fond of the quaint firehouse sense of humor.

Burly Tony Mongano, the funniest guy in the station, loved to make me laugh. With his black slicked-back hair, mustache, and olive complexion, he looked more like one of Concetta's mafioso uncles than a firefighter. One day, while Tour and I were cleaning the dishes after lunch, he brushed us aside and wisecracked, "Do you want to see how I cleaned dishes when I was a rookie?" Tony then grabbed a stack of dirty plates and one by one, tossed them out the open window. Astonished, we watched as they sailed onto the lawn like Frisbees. "Fuck these motherfucking dishes!" he proclaimed. "Everybody should clean their own fuckin' dish. That's my take!" We doubled over with laughter before dashing outside to retrieve them.

Tony could dish it out, but he could also take it. He was the first firehouse prankster that I actually turned the tables on.

September 25, 1973—Rookie Firefighter, Ladder 19

We'd been responding to more fires recently, so I guess a quiet night was in the works. Only two runs—both false boxes. That was it. But at least there was some fun inside the station to help pass the time.

Captain Bernard had borrowed a mannequin from Sears to dress up as a firefighter for Fire Prevention Week. The stark-naked dummy was standing outside Ladder 19's office with a huge cardboard sign hanging around its neck. Boldly printed on it were the words "Don't touch." To the mischievous minds of Frenchy and McGinn, it was like an open invitation.

Around eleven that night, I made my usual trip to the bunkroom to check my bed for ropes, baby powder, or other booby traps. It was all clear. But lying face up and tucked snugly under the blanket of Mongano's bed was the mannequin. Giddy that I wasn't the target this time, I had to restrain myself from laughing too loudly because Tony was in the TV room just a few feet down the hall. He was still there when I went down to the watch box for my midnight to two o'clock shift, so I propped the door open, knowing full well that I'd shortly hear him cursing.

Sure enough, just before one o'clock, his roar broke the station's silence. "Frenchy! You motherfucker!" A loud thump preceded another yell. "Fuck this motherfucking dummy!" I laughed my ass off, hoping that he hadn't tossed it out the window. I should have known better.

When I went up to my bunk at four o'clock, the mannequin was in my bed. That explained the thump. A muffled chuckle, sounding like Mongano's, came from the darkness as I dragged it out into the hallway. Across the hall, Tony's locker was wide open, almost like it was calling to me. I couldn't pass up the opportunity. So instead of returning the dummy to where Bernard had placed it, I dragged it into the locker room and dressed it completely in Tony's uniform, even his shoes and cap. I finished it off with a nice tight Windsor with his tie. Now, Tony had this nasty habit of staying in bed until five minutes before roll call. He'd never be able to dress in time for the eight o'clock bells. Oh sweet revenge!

At seven, the watchman sounded seven short rings. Per regulations, it was time to get up and dress for roll call. As usual, Mongano didn't budge. The trap was set. As we dressed, they all laughed when they saw whose name tag was on the mannequin's uniform. Knowing what was coming, we hid down the hall, and at 7:55 a.m., Frenchy opened the bunkroom door and hollered, "Let's go! It's time for roll call."

Tony groggily rolled out of bed and stumbled into the locker room, where he exploded for the second time of the shift, "Frenchy! You mother-fucker!" He was still blaming Frenchy! He raced to strip his uniform off the mannequin and tossed it headfirst into the hallway, shouting, "Fuck this motherfucking dummy!" It crashed into the wall and unfortunately landed squarely at the feet of a completely unamused Lieutenant Muck. Uh-oh! I thought he was going to have a conniption. But he didn't say a word.

Instead, he grabbed the mannequin, dragged it into the office, and began yelling at Mattox. "Your fuckin' clowns broke the captain's dummy. Look! Its arm is hanging off, and there's a big hole in its fuckin' chest."

A few minutes later at roll call, he growled at us, "You B Platoon jokers haven't heard the last about that mannequin. Dismissed!"

If it had been up to Muck, I'm sure there would have been a complete investigation. Maybe even formal charges would have been filed. But even though Captain Bernard pretended to be mad, I could sense that he understood pranks were simply part of the job. Our punishment was direct: strip and wax all the linoleum floors on the second floor. I admired that he didn't blow the incident out of proportion. I didn't realize it then, but I was learning how to be an officer from Bernard, along with how not to be one, from Muck.

Out of nowhere, I developed a persistent erratic thumping in my chest, which at times made me feel light-headed. Alarmed, I visited my doctor, who sent me for tests and diagnosed my condition as severe premature ventricular contractions (PVCs). PVCs cause the heart to have an extra beat. If they are occasional, they're not much cause for concern. Mine were frequent. Presuming that my condition was caused by excitement and stress, the doctor prescribed a low dose of Valium and Quinaglute, a medicine for heart-rhythm disorders. I didn't mention a word to him about being a firefighter, fearing that he'd say that I was unfit for duty. The medicines reduced the PVCs' intensity, but they were still there, especially when I skipped my Valium, which I wasn't about to take at work.

With the cooler weather, we began responding to more fires. We even responded to my first extra-alarm fire, a three-alarm blaze at the Atlantic Refinery. The increased pace wasn't helping my PVCs. Neither was my irritation from being routinely assigned as pack man. On my own at most fires, I wasn't learning much from the veterans.

November 19, 1973—Rookie Firefighter, Ladder 19

"The night was clear and the moon was yellow. And the leaves came tumbling down." The ominous opening lyrics of "Stagger Lee" by Lloyd Price imply calmness before the storm. Likewise, when I arrived at work one clear evening, leaves were gently floating around a bright crescent moon. I should have heeded it as a warning.

I rolled my eyes when Mattox assigned me as pack man again, but as usual he didn't react to my displeasure. I didn't have a problem with being pack man. With the recent surge in fires, I'd even been learning my limitations. When my ears began to burn with pain, I knew it was time to retreat. But I still would have preferred to learn all the aspects of ladder work, not just the pack man's duties.

Right after roll call, I dutifully checked my pack and laid it at my riding position with the straps fully extended so I could slide into it easily. I might not have known what the heck I was doing on the fireground, but at least I could get that pack on quickly. The bells rang just as I finished. "Engine and Ladder, Twenty-Eighth and Jackson Streets, special assignment (somebody had pulled the firebox)." I put on my gear and slid into my pack, but as suspected, it was a false alarm. Within ten minutes we were back in the firehouse, and I laid my pack out again, ready to go. It was time for my rookie chores.

Uncle Frank came into the kitchen as I was cleaning up. "Yo, Uncle Frank," I said. "Maybe we'll catch a job tonight, huh? It's pretty cool outside."

He looked over his glasses while pouring his coffee. "Are you pack man again?"

"Sure!" I responded. "What else would I be?"

He slammed the pot down on the burner. "You shouldn't—"

The bells interrupted his rage. "Everybody! Three and one! Twenty-Fifth and Wharton! Full box for a building." Within seconds, I was in my pack again, and we were screaming up Twenty-Fourth Street. We were first-in ladder, and 60's was third-in, so they pulled out behind us. Even with a week's worth of Quinaglute in my system, my PVCs were thumping erratically.

McGinn was sitting facing me, and halfway there, he yelled, "We got a job, kid." I looked over my shoulder, and three blocks ahead was a four-story commercial garage with medium black smoke rolling from its large open door. When we pulled up, 24's was hooked up to the hydrant across the street, and that big blond-haired mentor of Bobby T's and Porky's was leading the way as they stretched their hose inside.

McGinn jumped off the apparatus before it came to a stop. I did too, but the extra weight from my pack made me stumble like a drunkard. Luckily, I regained my balance before falling flat on my face. Inside the building, a fully loaded commercial trash truck was fully involved. Engine 24's Captain O'Brien pointed toward the top of the building and yelled in our direction, "Ladder Nineteen, get those windows up there!" I looked up and through the smoke could barely make out a narrow catwalk surrounding several dozen pull-down windows at roof level.

"Drop that friggin' pack and come with me, kid!" McGinn gestured. I slid out of my pack and trotted behind him to a slim set of metal stairs that zigzagged fifty feet up to the narrow catwalk. I felt like a freed man without the thirty extra pounds strapped on my back, and we quickly zipped our way upward. But the closer we got to the top, the thicker the smoke became. When we reached the catwalk, it was unbearable. Tears filled my red, burning eyes, and snotters (a firefighter's term for mucus) were pouring out of my nose. It was impossible to see McGinn through the blackness as we felt our way around the catwalk, unlatching windows and pushing them open. I prayed that the catwalk wouldn't come to an abrupt end and send us plummeting to our deaths.

About three-fourths of the way around, the smoke finally lifted enough that I could make out McGinn's black, soot-covered face. I knew I looked the same.

"Now you look like a real fireman." He coughed. "Nice job hanging in there, kid!" It was a major compliment from a firefighter with a reputation as an excellent smoke eater.

We climbed back down and helped overhaul the trash that had been dumped from the truck while 24's hosed it down. After we finished, I slung my pack over my shoulder and headed back to our apparatus.

As I passed Mattox, he snidely remarked, "You got a pretty dirty face for a pack man, Marcello." I wasn't sure if it was a compliment or an admonishment that I shouldn't have taken my pack off, so I just nodded and climbed back into my seat.

We returned to the station, and I repositioned my air pack again and headed upstairs to wash the soot off my face. When I was halfway up the steps, the alert tone buzzed: "Box two-four-four-nine, Twenty-Fourth and Morris Streets, the fire is reported to be Twenty-Fifth and Morris Streets, a garage." Ladder first-in, engine second-in. I flew back down the stairs and was in my jump seat with my pack on before Eddie started the engine this time.

As we swung the turn off Twenty-Fourth, I could see over McGinn's shoulder that Uncle Frank was right behind us, and Captain George was pressing hard on 60's siren. My heart was thumping hard again, but I believed that it might have been because I was so proud to be heading to fight the red devil with firefighters like McGinn, Frenchy, and Uncle Frank.

We screeched to a halt in front of a two-story garage pushing heavy black smoke from around its doors. We had passed the place only ten minutes earlier. How could we have missed all the smoke?

While 24's flaked their 1½" attack line outside, Ladder 11's pack man, Johnny DeRose, and I forced the side door open. Balls of black smoke rolled over our heads as we crawled inside to unlock the overhead door. Our hand lights were as useless as they'd be to a blind man as we groped our way through the dense smoke and searing heat. It was reassuring to be alongside a veteran like DeRose for a change. Feeling our way along the door, we somehow located the lock mechanism and banged away at it with our Halligan tools until it snapped. The door easily lifted open.

Captain O'Brien, Porky, and that big blond guy quickly advanced their line inside to attack the orange flames lapping at the fresh supply of oxygen. "Hey! Ladder Nineteen!" Battalion 5's chief yelled as soon as he saw me. "Get the back of that roof opened up—now!" I dropped my pack by Uncle Frank at 60's pumper, swapped my Halligan for an axe, and zipped up our thirty-five-foot ladder to the roof.

Through the heavy smoke, I could barely make out the outlines of firefighters toward the back of the roof. "Yo, Ladder Nineteen?" I yelled toward them.

"Marcello? We're back here." Mattox waved me toward their position.

I started straight for him, but after only a few steps, I suddenly found myself plunging into the heat and blackness. Unknowingly, I had stepped right into a ventilation hole my company had cut in the front of the roof. I was in a free fall! It's funny what thoughts go through your mind when you're plunging twenty-five feet through the darkness. For me, it was the vision of Malley's flag-draped casket. Was I about to join him? Even if I was lucky enough to survive the fall, would I survive the flames?

Fortunately for me, 24's had battled the flames away from my landing zone. Unfortunately for them, they were directly in my path. Something soft gave way and broke my fall as I thumped down. It was the big blond guy's head. I bounced off as he was going down. Captain O'Brien began screaming, "Everybody out! The roof's coming down!" But it wasn't the roof; it was me, the rookie skydiver.

Remarkably, I wasn't seriously injured as I landed on my ass a few feet short of the flames. Adding insult to injury, I had come down on a heap of smoldering fire debris, and my ass was burning! Screeching in pain, I quickly sprang to my feet. As firefighters were evacuating and dragging their fallen comrade to safety, Captain O'Brien quickly turned his light toward my agonized scream.

"Where the hell did you come from?" he exclaimed. "Are you hurt?"

"No, Cap, just burned my ass a little," I replied in embarrassment as I picked up my helmet.

"Yo, we got another injured man here," he yelled, and several firemen rushed to my aid. As they were whisking me away, he shined his light toward the ceiling and said, "This damned place ain't collapsing. He fell from the goddamned hole in the roof. Let's get that line going again."

McGinn and Frenchy practically slid down the ladder, grabbed me by the arms, and sat me on 60's rear step. "Ouch!" The blond guy was already in Rescue 14 being treated, so Battalion 5 called another rescue for me. Uh-oh! That meant a trip to the hospital, and my PVCs were pounding away. "I'm fine, Chief," I exclaimed as I jumped to my feet. "Can I go back with my company?"

"No, you cannot!" he said sternly. "You just fell twenty-five feet, and I want you to get checked out."

"But I'm perfectly fine, Chief. I don't need to go to the hospital," I pleaded.

He furrowed his brow. "Sit back down! You're going to PGH," he barked, referring to Philadelphia General Hospital, "and that's final."

Uncle Frank didn't spot me until they placed me onto Rescue 11's hospital cot. Deeply concerned, he raced over and asked, "Bobby? Are you okay?"

"Frank, it was my fault," I explained. "I stepped right into the friggin' hole. I should have known better."

"Yeah, I know, Bobby. But if you weren't the damn pack man, you'd have been up there with your company in the first place." He then winked and smiled reassuringly. "It was a dumb rookie mistake, kid. Learn from it, and make sure it doesn't happen again."

My PVCs were worse than ever during the ride to PGH. The more I worried about them, the worse they got. When we arrived at the ER, they placed me on a gurney and wheeled me next to the big blond guy. He was lying there writhing in pain with a big cervical collar around his neck.

"I'm sorry I fell on your head, man. Are you okay?"

He rolled his eyes, stared at the ceiling, and growled like an angry dog. I wasn't sure if it was because he was in pain, he was angry with me, or both. Before I could find out, they rolled me into a different treatment room.

A team of nurses treated my bruises and the second-degree burns on my butt. When the doctor came in, they told him that it didn't appear that I had any major injuries. As he checked out my limbs for breaks, he noticed the soot on my face. "It looks like you took a lot of smoke. Let's listen to those lungs." Oh no! He was surely going to hear my PVCs.

"My lungs are fine, Doc. You don't need to check them out," I begged, my eyes wide with fear as I tried to get off the gurney. "The soot on my face is from a trash fire, that's all."

"Sit back down! I'm not releasing you until I check your lungs."

I reluctantly eased back onto the gurney, silently praying that he wouldn't pick up the PVCs.

He moved the stethoscope around my back. "Take a deep breath… again…another."

Suddenly he stopped telling me to take deep breaths but kept listening. Uh-oh! Then he moved the stethoscope around to my heart. "Nurse, let's get an EKG on him."

EKG! Oh God! If he detected the PVCs, I could lose my job for medical reasons.

"What's the matter, Doc?" I asked, trying to sound unconcerned. "Are you picking up those little extra heartbeats?"

"I sure am," he replied, looking troubled. "Apparently you can feel them?"

I tried to play it cool. "Oh yeah. My family doctor has me on Quinaglute, but I forgot to take my pill today." I was lying my burning ass off, but he didn't look convinced. So I lied some more.

"I was fine until I fell through the roof, Doc. The excitement must have triggered this little flurry, that's all. I'll take my pill as soon as I get back to the station, and I'll be fine. I promise."

He placed his stethoscope over my heart again and listened attentively. Then he took off his glasses and looked at me seriously. "Okay. Since you're under treatment, I'll let it slide. But I want you to promise me that you'll take your pill every day. I also want you to see your doctor and tell him what happened tonight. I'll write you a return-to-duty note effective in two days. Okay?"

Okay? I was elated! My little fibs had actually worked. I jumped up and vigorously shook his hand, promising that I'd comply.

I hopped into my boots and rushed down the hall before he could change his mind. As I passed the next treatment room, I heard that familiar growl again. The big blond guy, his neck stiffened by the brace, was propped up on a gurney and staring directly at me.

I stepped inside with trepidation and offered my hand in peace. "How are you feeling?"

He sat there for a few seconds before his frown slowly turned to a smile. "You know, that was a hell of a way for you to introduce yourself." He chuckled as he reached for my hand. "I'm a little sore and need to wear this stupid collar for about a month. How about you?"

"I'm just fine." I laughed. "I'm so sorry for falling on your head. Really!" We began laughing uncontrollably.

The doctor heard the commotion and stomped into the room. He put his hands on his hips, looked at me, and barked, "Are you still here? I told you to go home and get some rest!"

I waved good-bye and dashed out of the room, my heart still pounding.

Yes, it started out as a beautiful fall evening. But before it was over, I almost fell to my death and literally came within a heartbeat of losing the job I loved so much. On the bright side, though, I abruptly met a great firefighter who would eventually become one of my best mentors, John Buggy.

CHAPTER 5

Bubba

The fireground can be an extremely dangerous place, even for those who are cautious. But my walking right through a roof's ventilation hole was a stupid rookie mistake. It violated Uncle Frank's most basic rule: think before you act! Thank God my fall didn't snap Buggy's neck or seriously injure either of us. It was a tough practical lesson about fireground safety, but it taught me to be careful in the future.

A few weeks after the fall, the medicine made my PVCs subside, but they were still there. It would take years for my OCD-driven brain to adapt to the disorder and chaos encountered on the firegrounds. Only after I realized that our actions and decisions actually restored order would the PVCs disappear completely.

I spent my first Christmas Eve as a firefighter in the firehouse. Shortly after midnight, a thoughtful group of about two dozen Christmas carolers came inside the station to sing. I sat on the steps with a half-dozen melancholy firefighters enjoying the soft familiar melodies. One of the carolers, a pretty brunette, instantly caught my eye. I stared and smiled at her until she took notice and smiled back.

I was thinking about my next move when suddenly Mongano's loud, discordant voice thundered from the second-floor hallway, "What's that damned racket down there? Some of us are trying to sleep up here!" The startled chorus reacted with horror and went completely off key. My eyes widened in disbelief, and I turned as red as our fire trucks. The shocked brunette quickly broke eye contact as the well-intentioned choir quickly finished the verse and scrambled out the door.

Tony later claimed that he had thought the two dozen carolers were outside the firehouse and wouldn't hear his futile attempt to make us laugh. Such is the dark side of firehouse humor.

Aside from Tony's misguided attempt at comedy, Christmas Eve was rather quiet. We only had three runs.

My first New Year's Eve in the firehouse was quite different. We had seven runs, and two of those were all-hands fires. It set the stage for a very busy January and February. Even though I was still the company's pack man more often than not, I was gaining experience.

One gray winter's day, Mattox summoned me up to his office. To my amazement, the briefing he had in mind was the last thing I had expected.

February 5, 1974—Rookie Firefighter, Ladder 19

After finishing my rookie chores, I headed to our quiet locker room to study for my probationary examinations. While browsing through my notes, I heard Mattox's voice echo in the hallway. "Marcello? Where's Marcello?"

I popped my head out the door. "Right here, Loo."

"Listen, Marcello," he said, nervously twirling a pencil between his fingers. "I'm taking off Friday, so Chief Tynann wants me to qualify you as an acting lieutenant and put you in charge of the company."

"Come again?" I sputtered.

He twisted his lips into a half frown and half smile. "Well, you're not qualified to drive, and Tynann's not wild about some of the other guys, so he told me to give you a crash course. You're going to be in charge."

In charge? I barely knew where the siren pedal was, and I was going to be in charge?

I stood there in shock as Mattox showed me how to prepare the company roll call, make logbook entries, and complete a fire report. One minute I was studying for my probationary exam, and the next I was training to be acting lieutenant. My OCD was in a tizzy trying to keep pace with the rapidly shifting gears.

Just before midnight we caught an all-hands fire on box one-two-seven-nine at Nineteenth and Moore Streets. It was difficult to observe Mattox's fireground decisions while groping around inside as pack man, again. I still couldn't wrap my head around the fact that I was going to be in charge Friday, even though I was completely clueless.

On February 8, 1974, with less than eight months' field experience, I was in charge of a fire company for the very first time. The city even gave me 10 percent more pay for the shift. The guys broke my balls all day, calling me the "acting rookie." But luckily, we didn't have any fires. If we had, though, I knew that McGinn, Frenchy, Eddie, and Gerry had my back.

A few weeks after my acting-lieutenant debut, Mattox got transferred. Our replacement, newly promoted Lieutenant Conaway, was an excellent officer. On his first day, he gave me a pep talk. He must have done his homework, because the first thing he said was that I was no longer steady pack man. "Everybody's going to take turns doing everything around here. I want to get you qualified as a ladder driver, tillerman, and chemical-unit operator as soon as possible." He glanced down at the company's personnel data and paused for a second. "Ha! I see that you're already qualified as an AL," he said, referring to my stint as acting lieutenant. "Oh well, I want you to spend an hour a day with me anyway to learn my version of a lieutenant's duties, okay?"

Okay? I was elated! Conaway truly cared about my growth and development as a firefighter. We went driving and tillering nearly every day shift, and he had Uncle Frank train me on Chemical 3's equipment every night shift. Fueled by his enthusiasm, I scored a 94 on my first probationary exam and immediately began studying for the next. Under his recommendation, I even enrolled in the fire-science program at Community College of Philadelphia.

Conaway did his best to make me feel like part of the company. He even gave me a few gray work uniforms so I wouldn't stand out in a crowd. With my running gear getting nice and dirty from all the fires, I was beginning to blend in. For a little while, anyway.

In early March, the department decided to change helmet styles. Our traditional black helmets were replaced by rather odd-looking yellow helmets with huge one-piece visors. Unfortunately for me, the yellow Philadelphian-style helmets were first issued to firefighters who graduated in the 140th and 141st classes. So much for blending in. I stood out like a sore thumb! Whether riding on the apparatus or operating on the fireground, I got strange looks from the public as well as from other firefighters. But I never imagined that I'd actually get attacked for looking different.

MARCH 6, 1974—ROOKIE FIREFIGHTER, LADDER 19

At 10:37 p.m. we were dispatched to the 2100 block of Tasker Street to assist the police. Lieutenant Conaway had us raise a ladder to the second-floor window of a row home to check on the welfare of an eighty-year-old woman who hadn't been seen or heard from for days. Basically, they wanted to make sure that she wasn't sick, injured, or dead. Naturally, that type of task usually fell to newer guys and rookies like me.

Wearing my gray uniform, boots, gloves, and brand-new yellow helmet, I climbed to the window, pushed it open, and poked my head inside for a sniff. Thankfully, there wasn't a hint of death's putrid odor. I squeezed my way inside and plopped belly first onto the floor, when all of a sudden, a blood-curdling scream pierced the darkness. Then something hard whacked the top of my helmet. *Thwack!* Another scream was followed by a second *thwack*. This one broke my visor completely in half. Dazed and confused, I looked up and saw the very much alive, feisty octogenarian wielding a broom handle.

Cocked and ready to take another swing, she screamed, "Spaceman! I'm being attacked by spacemen! Somebody help!"

I grabbed the broom handle before she could swing again. "Relax, lady. I'm a fireman. We're just here to make sure you're okay."

She tried to wrestle the broom handle out of my hand, but I kept a firm grip on her weapon. "If you're a fireman, why are you wearing a space helmet? Somebody please help me!"

Having heard the commotion, Conaway sent Frenchy to my rescue. Thank God he was wearing his traditional helmet. The lady quickly calmed down, looked at me, and screamed, "You better get a helmet like him, you, you spaceman, you!"

Firefighters remember their firsts. Their first day of training, their first day in the firehouse, their first run, their first fire, and tragically, their first fire fatality. Veteran Philly firefighters irreverently refer to victims burned beyond recognition as "crispy critters." I tried not to think about it much but knew it was only a matter of time before we responded to a fatal fire.

April 4, 1974—Rookie Firefighter, Ladder 19

Over the past month, I'd noticed this gorgeous slender brunette walking past the firehouse around four o'clock every afternoon. I thought surely she was a teacher at my alma mater, Vare Junior High. Hoping for a chance to flirt with her, I took a seat on the front bench with Frenchy and, of all people, Mongano. I should have known it was a recipe for disaster.

Stunning with her long, flowing hair, angelic white blouse, and short black skirt, she appeared on cue. She was walking with an attractive, forty-ish blond woman, certainly another teacher. As they neared, I discreetly distanced myself from Mongano and took a position by the curb.

"Hi, girls," I said softly, hoping that they'd be the only ones within hearing distance. "How beautiful...it is today."

The brunette gave me a pretty smile. Yes! But it was the older one who batted her eyelashes and flirted back. "Yes, it is indeed!" the older one replied, sizing me up and down. "So, are you handsome firemen having a quiet day today?"

Before I could respond with something nice, Mongano loudly blurted, "Hey, Marchisello! It looks like you hooked the wrong fish! Release that one, and cast your line again."

Her eyes flew open with embarrassment, and she stormed away, pulling the petite brunette by the arm. I guess I should have known better than to make a move in front of Tony.

Maybe all wasn't lost. As they turned down Ritner, the brunette looked back, smiled, and gave me a cute little wave. Tomorrow's another day—sans Mongano, of course.

As soon as they were out of view, the bells rang. "Everybody, two and one! Full box for an apartment fire, Sixteen Hundred South Twentieth Street." Within seconds, we were out the door. After three weeks of other assignments, it was my turn to be pack man again. Feeling like a seasoned veteran, I buckled myself into my pack and opened the air bottle. As soon as we turned onto Twentieth, Frenchy kicked my boot. Over my shoulder I could see black smoke blowing across the street ahead of us. We had a job! Wasting no time, I pulled the mask over my face, tightened the straps, and put on my gloves. This search-and-rescue man was ready to go.

Engine 24 was already stretching their hose line upstairs as we lurched to a stop. I jumped off the apparatus in a flash and was attaching my mask to the regulator when an older man grabbed my arm. "Bubba's burning up in there, man! Save Bubba!" he cried.

Captain O'Brien's crew had already made the turn in the hallway and started attacking the flames in the middle bedroom, so I searched the rear first. Luckily, no Bubba. As soon as they knocked the bulk of the fire down, they advanced their line to the front bedroom, which was also fully involved. Visibility was zero as I crawled into the red-hot middle room, groping around for Bubba. During my methodical clockwise sweep, I tried to duck walk, but piles of smoldering debris toppled me over again and again. My knees were scorching once more.

My search was nearly complete when my helmet clunked into something metallic. It was a bedpost. Uh-oh! While rising to my feet, I spread my hand across what I presumed was the foot of the bed, but all I could feel were the scalding springs of the mattress. As I tried to maneuver myself to check further, my air tank bumped into the doorframe, causing me to lose my balance. Trying to brace for a fall, I extended my arm toward the center of the mattress. But instead of springs like I expected, my right hand landed on a round object. Unfortunately, this object had a nose and eye sockets. Yep, I'd found Bubba!

My hand sprang back with instant repugnance. As the smoke lifted, I shined my light on the horrific remains. Bubba was charred black, with white blotches along his legs and torso. A large split in his abdomen revealed his boiled pink intestines. His ears, fingers, and toes were completely burned off, and his arms and legs were contracted pugilistically. Charred, stretched facial skin revealed his teeth, creating a vision of a ghastly smile on his face.

"We have a victim!" I cried, my voice muffled in my mask. Chief Tynann and Captain O'Brien dashed into the room.

The chief had us stand by until the fire marshal investigated and photographed the scene. The fire's cause? Bubba fell asleep while smoking. After they finished, four of us tried to lift him, but he was stuck to the springs. As I tugged on his ankles, I felt his flesh sliding over his shinbones. After several yanks, we finally sprang his torso loose and wrapped him in a yellow blanket.

After he was on his way to the medical examiner, I felt responsible. I was the search-and-rescue man, and Bubba had died on my watch.

McGinn was quick to notice my guilty look. "Bobby, don't ever take these things personal. This guy was dead before we left the station. Understand?"

After work Frenchy, McGinn, Eddie, Mongano, and I went to the bar across the street for a few beers. McGinn put his arm around my shoulder. "Bobby, today you're no longer a rookie; you're a firefighter." We joked about my failed attempt with the brunette and my remorse over Bubba. My knees were killing me once again, but needless to say, I wasn't about to go to PGH. It took two weeks' worth of burn ointment to help them heal this time.

Most likely scared off by Mongano's rather crass attempt at humor, neither the pretty brunette nor her older coworker ever passed by the firehouse again. C'est la vie!

CHAPTER 6

The Disciple

B ecause of Conaway's continuous and thorough training, I passed my exams for ladder driver, tillerman, and chemical driver on April 15, 1974. As promised, Conaway immediately posted a new schedule, in which everyone rotated assignments, even pack man.

Uncle Frank had taught me how to operate the special equipment carried on Chemical 3. Most frequently, chemical units were dispatched to working fires for the simple task of filling air bottles from their air cascade system (a series of larger bottles). Most of the other equipment was fairly easy to operate, although the Jet-Axes gave me pause. Designed to breach walls and metal garage doors, the three differently sized explosive charges had long cords, similar to Claymore mines. Once the unit was primed, the main charge could be detonated from a safe distance by pushing a button. There was no way to practice using the shaped explosives without blowing holes in the firehouse walls.

Chemical 3's most complicated piece of equipment by far was the high-expansion foam generator (Hi-Ex unit). To operate the complex piece of equipment, one had to follow about twenty steps meticulously. One misstep, and there would be no foam. Though it was rarely used, Uncle Frank had me practice putting it in service over and over. During one practice session, he casually mentioned that a firefighter named John Newman was the "Hi-Ex unit expert." Transferred a few years before, Newman had placed the unit in service on several occasions.

May 3, 1974—Firefighter, Ladder 19

Chalk off another first—driver and operator of Chemical 3. What were the odds that my first run would be for the Hi-Ex unit? One out of a hundred, a thousand?

At 8:33 a.m. the bells rang, and Frenchy yelled from the watch desk, "Chemical Three, box six-three-five-five, Philadelphia International Airport." All hands had been placed in service for a basement fire in a building on airport grounds.

"Okay," I thought, "they'll be using air bottles like crazy, fighting a basement fire. This call should be a piece of cake." So as soon as Frenchy and Eddie pulled the ladder out, I depressed the clutch, shifted into first gear, and made my first run driving a fire apparatus.

Lieutenant Conaway blocked traffic and threw me a reassuring salute as I pulled onto Twenty-Fourth. But before I even turned onto Passyunk Avenue, the radio squawked: "Battalion Seven's aide to Chemical Three. Proceed to Gate Fifty-Five and meet airport police. They'll escort you to the fire building. The chief wants you to place the High-Ex unit in service."

Say what? I couldn't believe it. Uncle Frank had told me that it hadn't been used at an actual fire for nearly a year. Just my luck! I mentally walked through the twenty steps during the rest of the run.

A group of firefighters helped me remove the cumbersome generator from its compartment and place it near the fire building. I must have looked like an idiot talking to myself, as I systematically walked through each step. Surely that's what 69's pump operator was thinking as he stood there watching my every move, with his arms folded. I figured that he was waiting for this fresh-faced, yellow-helmeted rookie to screw up. But thanks to Uncle Frank's repeated training, foam was flowing into the basement within minutes. Yes!

I was standing there proud as a peacock, admiring my handiwork, when someone patted me on the back. It was 69's pump operator. "You did everything right, kid. Nice job!" As he turned and walked back to his pumper, I noticed the name on the back of his coat: Newman. The Hi-Ex-unit expert had been watching my back the entire time. Thanks, John!

In addition to part of the Schuylkill (a.k.a. Sure-Kill) Expressway, Engine 60 and Ladder 19 were first-in at three of the city's deadliest intersections:

Sixty-First and Passyunk Avenue, Twenty-Sixth and Penrose Avenue, and Twenty-Sixth and Hartranft Streets. Needless to say, we responded to more than our share of accidents. Extricating victims from the crushed remains of automobiles was a challenge until the Jaws of Life were issued to all PFD ladder companies several years later.

MAY 11, 1974—FIREFIGHTER, LADDER 19

Late in the afternoon we responded to Sixty-First and Passyunk for a car that was wrapped around a telephone pole. Somewhere in the mangled wreck were the remains of the driver, though it was difficult to figure out where his head and torso were. One arm was hanging out of the passenger's window, and one leg somehow was curled underneath the driver's side. The rest of him was somewhere in between. Blood was dripping from the twisted metal and pooling in the street as we pried the car apart using manually operated hydraulic jacks and hand tools. It took nearly an hour to retrieve his body. We were soaked in blood. I even had brain tissue on my running coat and fecal matter on my boots. Uncle Frank washed us off with 60's booster line before Lieutenant Conaway made us available.

Before May was over, Lieutenant Conaway was transferred, but it wasn't because he had done anything wrong. As a matter of fact, he was rewarded with a busier company. The administration wanted to make room for a punitive transfer. The administration wanted fire officers to withdraw from the Philadelphia Firefighters' Union, Local 22. Not only did Lieutenant Jack Plumley refuse, he was running for a position on the union's executive board. His punishment, Ladder 19, was a good distance from his home.

I was very upset about losing the officer who had brought me so far in such little time. But then I met Jack. A veteran of Ladder 12, one of the city's busiest, Lieutenant Plumley was a terrific firefighter. Totally gung ho, he picked up right where Conaway left off and continued training me. He even kept our assignment list. After four shifts as tillerman, it was my turn to drive.

May 30, 1974—Firefighter, Ladder 19

It was another first—my first night driving Ladder 19. Though I was fairly confident about my abilities, I'll admit I had a case of the jitters. Especially concerning were some of South Philly's tight turns where people carelessly park so that their cars are sticking out on corners.

Our first run, which came at 9:20 p.m., was like a practice run. It was a special assignment with 24's for a falsely pulled firebox at Twenty-First and Moore. The turns were fairly easy, and it made me feel more relaxed.

Just before midnight Lieutenant Plumley and his banjo joined me on the front bench. While strumming chords, he shared valuable firefighting lessons, practical dos and don'ts that I'd never have learned from textbooks.

The bells abruptly interrupted his melodic tutelage. "Chemical Three, Sixth and Washington, all hands working on the box." I was about to go stop traffic as usual when I realized that I was driving Ladder 19. Oops! I dashed back inside and pulled out so the chemical could respond.

Grinding gears, Mongano pulled Chemical 3 beside me. "Fuck this motherfucking stick shift!" he cursed. He made me laugh so hard that while backing in, I nearly hit the station's tight doors.

As Chemical 3's siren faded, the bells rang again. "Engine! Second alarm, Sixth and Washington. A lumber yard." The fire was spreading quickly. Before I could climb down from the cab, Ladder 19 was dispatched on the third.

I restarted the engine, and Eddie signaled with two beeps from the tillerman's cage. Within seconds, I was flying down Passyunk. Fueled by adrenaline, I was driving way too fast! It was obvious by the way Plumley was hanging on for dear life. Recalling Uncle Frank's words—"What the hell good are you if have an accident and don't get there?"—I reduced my speed drastically.

Flames were leaping a hundred feet into the sky, and five alarms had been sounded by the time we arrived. The deputy chief was barking orders at Plumley before we came to a full stop. "Lieutenant, place your main to the roof of that exposure so we can get some lines up there!"

Instead of simply reacting, Plumley paused a few seconds, rubbed his chin, and pondered a plan. "Think for a few seconds, and you'll gain minutes." It was something he had just talked about between verses on the bench.

"Okay, Bob," he said decisively, "pull forward and jackknife so the turntable is at the corner of the building closest to the lumber yard." The jackknife maneuver was something Conaway had made me practice repeatedly. One backup later, I was in position to raise our ladder.

After the companies climbed to the roof and began shooting their streams at the fire, the chief gave Plumley new orders. "Prepare for ladder-pipe service." (Attach a hose nozzle to the end of the ladder and help extinguish the fire.) Remarkably, that's exactly what Plumley had anticipated. We were perfectly positioned for both duties. His plan was brilliant, and our stream was soon darkening the flames.

That's when a chief from headquarters, who was part of the administration, spotted Plumley. With arms flailing, the chief rushed toward him in a rage. I couldn't hear his rant over the sound from the pumpers, but he was furious.

"Was something wrong with my driving or my ladder operation?" I wondered nervously. "Did I get my lieutenant in trouble?" The barrage lasted five full minutes. After that Plumley casually strolled back. He was giggling as though they had just exchanged jokes.

"What the heck did we do wrong, Loo?" I asked.

"We didn't do anything wrong, Bobby. He hates me because I still won't quit the union. I'm sorry, guys, but he's keeping us here all night."

Plumley's fortitude was impressive. Veteran chiefs quaked with fear when chiefs screamed at them, but not my new Loo! He smiled the entire time.

A cover-up ladder caught an all-hands fire on Twenty-Sixth Street around five in the morning. We would have been first-in. Oh well.

During the ensuing months, things began to change in the firehouse. Captain George was promoted to battalion chief, and newly promoted Captain Jones replaced him. Jones had a case of OCD that put mine to shame. Intense, serious, neat, and orderly, he was a direct contrast to Plumley's laid-back, jovial, and nonchalant style. It was fun to watch their interactions in the firehouse. Jones worried about everything, while absolutely nothing bothered Plumley. In the long run, though, they were equally effective officers.

McGinn, who was on the lieutenant's list when I arrived, got promoted and was transferred. Walt and a few guys from 60's also got transferred. Three blue-shirted, yellow-helmeted rookies from Fire School, Joe Krieble, Barry-Barry, and Ralphy-Boy, replaced them. Tour and I happily taught them everything we knew about cleaning the kitchen and making coffee. Though we were still new guys ourselves, we were officially off rookie status.

From day one, Uncle Frank had preached that until I worked in an engine company, I'd only be half a fireman. It was a good time for me to try to make the switch. Effective January 1, 1975, in order to reduce our working hours, the department was adding an additional shift. Bargaining agreements between Local 22 and the city paved the way for the D Platoon. Massive transfers were anticipated, so I submitted a transfer request for Engine 45 in North Philly, Engine 68 in West Philly, and Engine 24 in South Philly. Getting it approved would be another matter—unless I had a connection.

Plenty of promotions were also coming with the D Platoon expansion. In addition to training me each day, Uncle Frank had studied hard for the lieutenant's test. Though I wasn't eligible for the test myself, I frequently studied with him. Because of Uncle Frank, I began studying for lieutenant before I even finished my probationary exams.

October 6, 1974—Firefighter, Ladder 19

Ever since I submitted my transfer for an engine company, Uncle Frank had been preparing me for the move. At 60's pump panel, he peered over his glasses. "Bobby, I'm going to train you to be the second-best pump operator in the city."

Puzzled by his odd opening statement, I asked, "Why shoot for second best, Uncle Frank? Teach me to be the best."

With a broad smile on his face, Uncle Frank replied, "I'm the best, kid, and you'll never be as good as me!"

My side was splitting as Chief Tynann's car pulled onto the apron during his rounds (when he visited the firehouses under his command). While he was upstairs with the officers, his backup aide, Engine 49's Joe Tiesi, joined us at the pumper.

My dad's age and balding, Joe had a friendly demeanor that made me feel as if I'd known him my entire life.

Out of nowhere, Uncle Frank said to him, "You're a backup aide for the commissioner, aren't you, Joe? Why don't you help this poor kid get transferred to an engine company?"

At first, his answer didn't appear to have anything to do with my transfer. "Bob, why don't you join the Sons of Italy Lodge and come to our weekend Catholic retreat in Malvern next month?"

"Why would I do that?" I replied naïvely. "Do I need to pray for a transfer?"

"Praying won't hurt." He chuckled. "But the fire commissioner will be there praying too."

Then I understood.

The next day I joined the lodge and signed up for the retreat.

A few days later, on October 9, 1974, Battalion Chief Walter Long, of the Sixth Battalion, collapsed and died from an apparent heart attack while operating on box five-two-two-one, Sixteenth and Indiana. It was the department's third line-of-duty death (LODD) of my short career.

A month after his funeral, it was time for our spiritual sojourn to Malvern. I didn't expect it to be much fun. Calling ourselves Rizzo's disciples, fellow firefighters Angelo, Johnny, and I behaved like altar boys during the day. But as soon as the sun went down, we sneaked off campus and partied the nights away at a bar near Villanova University. Girls actually flocked around us after Angelo told them that we were studying for the priesthood. Blitzed on ethanol and reeking of perfume, we didn't get back to our rooms until the wee hours of the morning.

On Sunday, our last day, Joe took me to meet Commissioner Rizzo. My head was still pounding from the night before as Joe asked about my transfer. Rizzo thanked me for going to the retreat with him and gave me an assuring nod. It was like a scene from *The Godfather*. I felt as if I should have knelt down and kissed his ring.

A few weeks after the retreat, Chief Tynann's regularly assigned aide, Joe Monte, retired, and his party drew a huge crowd. Since Uncle Frank, Tour, and Mongano brought their wives, I brought my date, a petite nurse named Donna. It was her first, and last, firefighters' party.

Mongano was his usual self, even though his wife tried to keep him in check. Throughout the night his crass jokes and wisecracks frequently made Donna's cheeks match her red zinfandel. She didn't fully comprehend Tony's twisted sense of humor, and she looked horrified, especially since I was laughing my ass off.

Trying to explain his behavior, I said, "He just does that for laughs. Look around; most of us are quiet and refined." As she panned the catering hall, the door to the men's room suddenly flew open and slammed into the wall. Several firefighters came rolling out, cursing and slugging away at each other.

Donna gently tapped me on the shoulder. "Yes, quiet, refined, *and* gentlemen too."

Near the end of the year, the promotional lists were published. Uncle Frank scored well in the lieutenant's test, and he got promoted and transferred. The administration didn't feel that Plumley was far enough from home, so they transferred him even farther. He had taught me so much in such little time, and I was going to miss him terribly.

Luckily, my decision to become one of the commissioner's disciples paid off. On January 4, 1975, I was transferred to Engine 24 on the newly formed D Platoon. Amen.

CHAPTER 7

Never Give Up the Tip

Wedged between Twentieth Street and angled Point Breeze Avenue, Engine 24's firehouse was the smallest in the city. Built in the 1950s, the tan brick triangular building's obsolete hose tower beaconed sixty feet above its flat roof.

Inside, behind the apparatus floor, a small multipurpose room served as the kitchen, locker, and television room. Literally feet away from the kitchen table was a miniscule bathroom with a single urinal, stall, and sink. A person standing in just the right spot, at just the right time, could smell the aroma of someone frying bacon mixed with the stench of someone taking a dump. Oh my! In the center of the room, a solid green door led to a tiny cramped bunkroom. The station's tight quarters, with firefighters always close to their pumper, enabled 24's to get out fast.

Engine 24 was busy and had a reputation as an aggressive firefighting company. Its district was made up mostly of economically deprived neighborhoods. Their thousand-gallon-per-minute 1972 Ward LaFrance pumper shared the apparatus floor with a Dodge van, designated Rescue 14. An emergency-medical-services (EMS) basic-life-support (BLS) ambulance, Rescue 14 was staffed by firefighters assigned to the company. Most detested their turn on rescue duty, but a few actually embraced it. Each shift had one such firefighter who was trained as an emergency medical technician (EMT) and who worked the BLS unit on a steady basis.

Walking into 24's for the first time, I was apprehensive but not as nervous as on my first day at Ladder 19. I had to prove myself all over again. Thankfully, my wait for a fire wasn't as long as it had been for Captain Blood the Rookie.

January 4, 1975—Firefighter, Engine 24

It was the first shift for the newly formed D Platoon and also my first day at 24's. The kitchen was cramped with firefighters waiting for shift change as I discreetly tried to make my way to the coffee brewer. A boisterous voice rose above the kitchen chatter and stopped me dead in my tracks.

"Well, if it isn't the airborne firefighter who nearly broke my friggin' neck!" Big John Buggy stood out like a mountain as he arose from the bench. "Don't tell me you're on the D Platoon? With me? Seriously?" What a reception!

Sensing my embarrassment, Buggy winked in a fatherly way. "Come here," he said, patting his hand on the bench next to him. "I'm glad you made the move to Twenty-Four's. It will be safer for you *and* everyone on the floors below you." As I sat next to him fixing my coffee, he placed his huge arm around my shoulders and said in a much lower voice, "I'm glad you're here, Bob. We have a great crew on the D."

My platoon was a mix of firefighters from 24's other shifts. I was the only outsider. Thin, with dirty-blond hair, Lieutenant "Sharpie" Sharpe was a well-respected firefighter and officer. The rest of the guys, with the exception of Two-Streeter Al "John" Fry, had more time on the job than I did. John had been assigned to 24's from Fire School about a year ago. After roll call, Buggy quickly branded us his two new "mopes" and proclaimed himself to be our mentor. From what I'd seen, he was going to be a great one.

Sharpie was a terrific officer. After Buggy finished taking me on a familiarization tour of the compartments, he called me into the office for a half-hour chat. He said that I was going to be tip man (nozzle man) for the entire month of January. It was the best job in the company! I'd be crawling the hallways right alongside him. What a great way to learn!

Afterward, as we mopped the floors, Buggy pulled me aside. "Listen," he said sternly. *"Never give up the tip!* I'm pack man and will be right behind you and Sharpie. If things get really bad, I'm the only one you'll relinquish that tip to. Nobody else! But it better be friggin' unbearable for you to bail out." With a reassuring slap on the back, he added, "You know, I'm excited to have you and Johnny on the D Platoon with me. You guys are going to learn a lot together."

Unlike in my days at Ladder 19, I didn't have to wait long for my first job with 24's. Around noon, Johnny had just whipped up a delicious-smelling batch of creamed chipped beef and home fries. I was setting the table when we got our first run. We were first-in on tactical box seven-five-six, Twentieth and Morris Streets. I stopped traffic while our driver, Joe, pulled off the apron, and then I jumped on while the apparatus was still rolling. Buggy grabbed my arm and pulled me into the forward-facing jump seat across from him. Joe swung the turn, and within seconds we were racing down the Point with our siren screaming. It was amazing how fast we got out of the station.

Adjusting the straps on his pack, Buggy gave me a reassuring wink, and as soon as we turned from Twenty-First onto Morris, the smell of burning wood filled the air. Ahead, black balls of smoke were billowing from the second floor of a row home. Joe stopped for a moment. Johnny jumped off and wrapped a few folds of our 2½" hose around the hydrant (took a wrap) and then gave Joe a thumbs-up. As we zipped down the block, our heavy brass couplings plopped onto the asphalt. Joe slammed to a stop just short of the fire, leaving room for Ladder 19. We got there so fast that we could barely hear the other companies responding in the distance.

As Buggy and I flaked our 1½" attack line along the sidewalk, Sharpie briefly scanned the smoke conditions. "Okay, piece of cake," he said confidently. "It's the front bedroom."

How could he tell exactly where the fire was located? It was like he had a sixth sense. I was awestruck.

Leading the charge, Sharpie had us poised at the top of the stairs within seconds. "Okay, let's get the line over the railing and make the turn," he said. Buggy was right on my heels, skillfully taking up the slack, making it easy for me to advance. "Stay low. Don't open the tip until you get to the door and see the glow."

Stay low? I was gasping for breath with my nose hugging the floor. I couldn't possibly get any lower.

"Keep moving. You've got it," Sharpie said reassuringly as we crawled forward. When we reached the bedroom door, a loud crash illuminated the room in bright crimson. Ladder 19 had taken out the windows. "Okay! Open it up, and whip it around."

With our nozzle opened fully, I spun the stream in circles around the ceiling. Trying to breathe, I kept my nose close to the stream, a trick we had been taught in Fire School. Guess what? It didn't work.

After the flames darkened, Sharpie choked out, "Okay, let's get to the window and blow it out." (A wide pattern sprayed from a window draws smoke and heat with it.)

Buggy, coughing behind us, added, "Sweep the floor with the stream first so you don't burn your knees." Oh! That was the trick.

Within minutes the smoke lifted, and we could breathe again. Ladder 19's Ralph Campana and fellow Malvern-retreat-mate Angelo joined us and began pulling ceilings. "Hey! Look who's tip man," kidded the fun-loving Campana.

As he tugged on an unyielding piece of lath, Angelo added, "Yeah! But he had to become a disciple first."

Buggy didn't have a clue what Angelo meant, but he patted me on the back anyway. "Good job, kid!" It meant the world to me. My first job as a tip man was under my belt!

The next day we got to do it all over again. It was another dwelling fire, this time only three blocks from our firehouse. We were there so fast that Joe and Johnny had to raise our twenty-four-foot ladder and take out the windows before the ladder companies arrived. This time the fire involved two bedrooms, and as we advanced, our stream struck a portable heater. My entire body was tingling, but with Sharp and Buggy's encouragement, I pushed on until the tingles went away.

I was loving it at Engine 24. Not only had my transfer come through, but Buggy was a terrific mentor, and the platoon oozed with esprit de corps. And the fires kept coming. By the end of my first two weeks, we had responded to several more dwelling fires and a four-alarm fire in a huge apartment building in West Philly.

I was getting the experience I wanted.

JANUARY 22, 1975—FIREFIGHTER, ENGINE 24

A bitterly cold wind wreaked havoc with our stream as it poured water into the five-story abandoned factory. Second-in on the first of three alarms several hours earlier, I felt like a Popsicle by the time Chief Bankhead told us to take up (gather our equipment and return to our station). It took another half hour to chop our hose from the ice and pick it up before heading back to our cozy little firehouse.

Dinner was five-alarm chili, of all things. Its delectable aroma wafted across the apparatus floor while we thawed out and restored our hose. We didn't finish until nearly eleven o'clock, just in time for a long buzz over the speaker. "Tactical box seven-three-four, Eighteenth and Wharton Streets. The fire's reported in the eighteen-hundred block of Latona Street, a dwelling." Joe bucked Federal, and two blocks later we made the turn onto Latona. Another job!

Heavy smoke was pushing from the second-floor windows of a house in the middle of the block. Johnny took a wrap, and we plopped our hose down to the block again. It was getting to be routine. But this time, a woman clad in a nightgown was screaming hysterically in the street. Only moments ago, she had seen a woman's agonized face press against the second-floor front window and disappear back into the smoke. Someone was trapped!

The door was locked, but one good whack of Buggy's Halligan got us inside quickly. Lugging our attack line, Buggy and I followed Sharpie as he dashed up the stairs, where orange flames were lapping across the hallway ceiling. The middle room was fully involved, and the fire extended into the hallway. "Knock it down, and push it back into the middle room!" Sharpie yelled.

The flames overhead quickly darkened as we advanced. As soon as we reached the middle room's door, Sharpie veered off to search the front bedroom.

Buggy was right behind him. "Don't let it get the hell out of that room, or Sharpie and I will be trapped!" he cried through his mask.

I swept the floor and crawled halfway inside while whipping the stream over my head. Joe and Johnny had taken out the front windows, but the middle room's glass was still intact. The steam was unbearable, and I could barely breathe as I inched forward. "If you ever have trouble breathing," they had said in Fire School, "tuck your nose under the collar of your running coat for some fresh air." Guess what? That didn't work either.

I heard a commotion in the hallway. "Grab the legs. I got the arms!" It was Sharpie. They had found a victim. As they passed the door, Ladder 11 took out the middle window with a loud crash. Still blinded by the smoke, I aimed the stream toward the sound. It worked. The smoke and heat began to lift.

As they struggled to get the victim down the steps, I heard Sharpie yell to Ladder 11's captain, "There's another one by the front window on the right side!" Footsteps raced down the hall as I switched the nozzle to a fog stream. Seconds later I heard them dragging a second victim down the stairway.

Fresh air flowing from the doorway replaced the smoke and heat. Gasping for breath, I turned my head to the side to catch a lungful. Shockingly, somebody on the floor was staring back at me. I rubbed the smoke from my eyes and blinked hard until the face came into focus. Unfortunately, it was a third victim, a ghastly resemblance of Bubba. The victim's sickeningly sweet odor of burned flesh flooded my nostrils. I slithered closer to the window. "We have a fifty-two ninety-two!"

A woman and two men died in the fire. After the fire marshals reconstructed the scene, they determined that the man in the middle room had died quickly from smoking in bed. The couple, asleep in the front room, was awakened by the smoke. Attempting to flee down the steps in a panic, they swung the front-room door open and were quickly enveloped by the flames. The second man fell right there. The woman made it to the front window before collapsing in a heap.

The three deaths marked the beginning of a tragic year for 24's. Though we weren't the busiest company in the city, we had the most first-in fire deaths during 1975.

We returned from the Latona Street fire shortly after four o'clock in the morning, just in time for my turn on watch duty. As the last man on watch, I thoroughly cleaned the kitchen and brewed two pots of coffee. By seven thirty the kitchen was crammed with two platoons of firefighters noisily chatting away. One of the oncoming platoon's firefighters—I'll call him Jerry—poured himself a cup and sat down across from me. The only thing I knew about him was that his sarcastic laugh had been the loudest when Buggy jokingly called me an airborne firefighter on my first day.

Dipping his spoon into a nearly empty sugar bowl, Jerry screeched, "Who the fuck had last watch?" The kitchen instantly hushed.

"I did. Why?" I fessed, aware that he suspected me.

"The sugar bowl's empty, rookie. Fill it!" he demanded as he smugly slid the bowl across the table.

Bleary eyed from lack of sleep, I was already twisted before his vicious attack. I glared at him with daggers in my eyes. "How long have you been here?" I asked arrogantly.

He puffed up his chest. "I've been here for over three years!"

"Three years? Then you should know where the fuckin' sugar is! Go fuckin' fill it yourself!" I flung the sugar bowl back across the table. The kitchen simultaneously let out a load "Whoa!" I rose to my feet, but Joe quickly jerked me back down. Sitting at the other end of the table, Buggy winked with approval. It was the last time anyone called me a rookie.

On January 28, I *officially* came off rookie status after scoring ninety-eight in my final probationary examination. I wasn't done with my studies, though. Johnny and I were preparing for our first promotional examination.

Buggy had never had aspirations to become an officer, and he jokingly scoffed at our new ambition. Whenever he saw us studying, he laughingly called us lieutenant-wannabe mopes. But deep down inside, we knew he was rooting for us. After all, we were his understudies.

CHAPTER 8

The Medicine Wagon

In 1975 Philadelphia's EMS system comprised twenty rescue units. Only two of those, Center City's Rescue 1M and 7M, were staffed by fire-paramedics as advanced-life-support units (ALS). All the others, including Rescue 14, were BLS units staffed by firefighters trained in first aid and, in some cases, a state-certified EMT.

We at 24's were lucky to have one EMT assigned to each platoon. Some BLS stations didn't have any. Gino was the D Platoon's EMT, and he handled 50 percent of our rescue burden by working Rescue 14 steadily. After soliciting our input, Sharpie posted an assignment-rotation list that scheduled the remaining six of us to rotate into the rescue on a monthly basis.

Gino loved rescue duty, and he was good at it. A veteran firefighter of 24's for several years, he had rotated between the engine and rescue just like everyone else before volunteering for EMT school. Though he hadn't yet applied, he was considering volunteering for the department's Fire Paramedic Program, which was still in its infancy at the time.

The rest of us were non-EMT rescue drivers (NERDs). Gino served as the attendant (doctor) and was primarily responsible for patient management.

My first stretch of rescue duty came in February. Buggy may have been my mentor on the fireground, but Gino was our company's rescue guru. Throughout January he taught me emergency medical techniques, and we practiced CPR. He also had me read his EMT textbook. Enthused by the TV series *Emergency*, I was actually eager for my new experience. But it didn't take long to find out that EMS wasn't exactly like Johnny Gage and Roy Desoto made it appear on television.

Our first run was to an apartment house for an unresponsive person. After following a trail of fecal matter up a set of stairs, we found an older man lying prone in the hallway. His pants were stained brown from the fecal matter, which had run down his leg and over his shoes. The stench was awful!

Gino checked the poor guy's carotid pulse and shook his head. "He's ice cold, man." Then he placed his stethoscope over the man's chest and listened intently. "Uh-uh!" Finally, he lifted the man's eyelids and shined his penlight into his eyes. "Fixed and dilated, Bob. This guy's a fifty-two ninety-two." As I turned back toward the steps, Gino said, "No! Not yet, Bob. Here." He handed me his stethoscope and penlight. "Check him out for yourself. You need the experience." My on-the-job training officially had begun. We had eight more calls that day.

It was a frigid February, and I knew the inevitable was about to happen. On my second day in Rescue 14, I missed an all-hands first-in working fire with 24's. It was a good job too! (It sounds odd, but firefighters often refer to a working fire as a "good job.") People were jumping from the windows just as 24's turned onto Catherine Street. We responded to treat the injured and transport them to the hospital.

It seemed as though every shift in Rescue 14 was an endless series of runs. The night shifts were the worse.

FEBRUARY 8, 1975—FIREFIGHTER, ENGINE 24, DETAILED TO RESCUE 14

Anticipating a long night in Rescue 14, I slept until eleven o'clock in the morning. It was a good thing too. We were up all night.

As usual, Rescue 14 wasn't in the station when I walked into the firehouse at 5:00 p.m. Seizing the moment, I jogged downstairs, got changed, jogged back up to the kitchen, and poured myself a cup of coffee. I couldn't wait until I was senior enough to get a locker in the kitchen like practically everyone else.

Everybody was laughing about the C Platoon's fire the previous night. One of their new guys had been on watch around three o'clock in the morning. Suddenly, he heard a man frantically banging outside on the overhead door. He looked up and saw fire blowing from every window of the store across the street. Instead of ringing the bells, he tiptoed into the officer's bunkroom and gently tapped his lieutenant on the shoulder. "Hey, Loo," he whispered, "I think there's a fire across the street."

The lieutenant jumped to his feet and sprinted to the apparatus floor. It looked like daylight outside. The flames were shooting halfway across Twentieth Street. He calmly turned to the new guy. "You *think* there's a fire across the street! You *think*? Did you ever *think* about hitting the lights and bells? Now hike the company out, you moron!"

I was still giggling when Rescue 14 backed into the station. Seconds later, Gino and I jumped in for our first run of the night, a seizure victim in West Philly. The cops must have gotten tired of waiting for us to make the four-mile trek; by the time we arrived, they had already taken the patient to the hospital. We returned to the firehouse just in time for dinner. The mouthwatering aroma of roast beef filled the kitchen. I'd yet to see the rescue guys finish a meal uninterrupted, so I knew I had to eat fast. Anticipating a call any second, I quickly gorged myself on two helpings of roast beef, mashed potatoes, and creamed corn. My belly was trying its best to keep pace with the rapid food intake, but there's always room for ice cream, right? I rapidly shoveled a heaping plate of butter pecan into my mouth and finished just in time for our second run. I was so stuffed that I felt like a balloon about to burst as we dashed to the apparatus floor.

Minutes later we arrived at a wedding reception on Broad Street. We pushed our way through the crowd to a seventy-eight-year-old man who was slouched in his chair, clutching his chest. Gino took one look at his ashen face. "Bob, get a nasal cannula on him and start him on O-two." As I looped the cannula around his head, he suddenly vomited. A brownish mix of partially digested steak, potatoes, and who knows what else spewed onto his light-blue three-piece suit.

Now, I can take the blood, the guts, and the gore, but the smell of vomit always makes me want to puke myself. As Gino wiped away the brown slurry to clear the man's airway, the smell worsened. A sickening mix of roast beef and butter pecan was inching its way up my esophagus like magma through a volcano. I was about to erupt. Thankfully, Gino exclaimed, "Bob! We got to roll fast. Go outside and get the hospital cot."

Outside? Thank god! I flew through the crowd so fast that a woman shrieked, "Oh my God! The man must be in bad shape! Look how fast that fireman's running." If she only knew! After a breath of fresh air and a few deep gulps, I was fine. When I returned with our stretcher, Gino had thoughtfully wrapped the man with a tablecloth to suppress the smell.

That run opened the floodgates. Over the next ten hours, we had ten more runs. The worst was for a man who had been hit by a car. His left leg was fractured so bad that it was perpendicular to his thigh. He also had a compound fracture of his right arm and a severely bleeding wound on the back of his head. We bandaged and splinted him as best we could before transporting him to Graduate Hospital.

The other calls—an unconscious man, a diabetic coma, two stroke victims, a lady with difficulty breathing, a man who had fallen, a child with a 103-degree fever, and another cardiac case, sans the vomit—kept us on the street until sunrise. I guess we weren't busy enough; some joker called in a false alarm at 7:12 a.m.

On February 13 we were transporting a seizure patient to Saint Agnes Hospital, and Gino was in the back treating the patient. While sitting at a red light, I heard a loud bang as a car whizzed through the intersection. About a second later, a man thumped down on the ground right in front of us. He'd been struck and hurled into the air by a hit-and-run driver. We placed a cervical collar around his neck, strapped him on a backboard, and slid him on the floor next to our seizure patient. When we arrived at the ER, Gino told the nurse, "We've got two for the price of one this time!"

We averaged about ten runs each shift for the rest of the month. The calls included diabetics, drug overdoses, seizures, strokes, stabbings, shootings, accidents, and cardiac-arrest cases. Four of our patients needed CPR. Even though I was learning a lot, I never expected to wind up in the limelight while working rescue.

February 21, 1975—Firefighter, Engine 24, Detailed to Rescue 14

Just before noon we were dispatched to an expensive Center City restaurant for an unresponsive person. A fiftyish heavyset man lying face up was in cardiac arrest. "Bob!" Gino exclaimed, "Go outside and call a code blue" (have an ALS rescue unit dispatched to our scene). I trotted to Rescue 14, called the code blue over the radio, and returned to Gino, who was doing chest compressions. I opened the man's airway and filled his lungs with oxygen after every fifth compression. Sensing that someone was watching, I glanced up and saw a local television news camera filming our every move.

Minutes later, Rescue 7M's fire paramedic, John Bankhead (a relative of our chief), placed his defibrillator paddles over the man's chest and looked intently at the monitor. "We got V-fib! Clear!" We halted CPR, and John zapped an electric charge through the man's chest, causing his body to jerk violently. John placed the paddles back on his chest and studied the monitor again. "We've got sinus rhythm." The news crew stood there with their mouths open while the paramedics started an IV and pumped drugs into his body. The four of us placed the man on Rescue 7M's hospital cot and wheeled him into their vehicle before they dashed off to Jefferson Hospital.

As we were restoring our equipment, the news crew interviewed us. We told them that we merely had kept the guy alive with CPR until Rescue 7M arrived and that Rescue 7M had been the ones who actually saved him with their defibrillator and drug therapy. Even though they took everyone's names, they only mentioned Gino and me on the six o'clock news, calling us heroes. So much for the media getting their story straight.

As expected, I missed several fires with 24's during my month of rescue duty. We responded to most of them with Rescue 14, and we placed our equipment on the hospital cot and set up a first-aid station. Like a fire buff, I'd simply watch the firefighting effort as we stood by. If we got dispatched on the initial assignment with 24's, we'd often help them connect to the hydrant or raise a ladder to take out the windows. It freed my coworkers to attack the fire and conduct search and rescue. I felt more like a part of the team on those calls.

For many people in our district, Rescue 14 served as their primary-care physician. As a consequence, many of our calls weren't for medical emergencies. We were dispatched for coughs, colds, fevers, nausea, flu-like symptoms, and even doctor's appointments. They seemed to know that the magic words to say to FCC call takers were "difficulty breathing" or "chest pains." Duping the system assured them a free and speedy ride to the ER.

By my last night shift of the month, the novelty of rescue duty had completely faded. I was pining to get back to firefighting. That morning, Gino and I joined Buggy for a cup of coffee in the kitchen after returning from our thirteenth run of the shift. Engine 24's oncoming driver/pump operator had pulled onto the apron to complete his preshift checks.

All of a sudden, a twelve-year-old boy ran through the open doors and burst into the kitchen. Panting for breath, he exclaimed, "My mama told me to come get the medicine wagon!"

"Okay, son, calm down," Buggy reassured him. "What's wrong with your mama?"

"She has a…um…um…chest paints. Eh, that's what she told me to say." Chest *paints*?

Buggy got the boy's address and told him to tell his mother that we were on the way. I disgustedly splashed my steaming coffee into the sink and yelled toward the bathroom, "Yo, Gino! The wagon train is under attack on Twentieth Street. They need the medicine wagon." Buggy was running around the kitchen whooping and hollering as we pulled out of the firehouse. After transporting her to the hospital, I overheard her tell the ER nurse that she had the flu. Duped again!

Years later the department officially renamed the rescues as medic units. By the time I retired, their number had swelled to over fifty in order to keep pace with the city's primary-care demand.

CHAPTER 9

Avenue Y

On February 28, 1975, Firefighter Michael Iaquinta from Engine 55 collapsed while operating at a nine-alarm blaze on box one-six-seven-nine at Ninth Street and Glenwood Avenue. He died shortly thereafter from an apparent heart attack. His LODD marked the beginning of a tragic year for Philadelphia firefighters.

During the month of March, it was my turn to be pack man and to back up Buggy, of all people. It was another busy month, and unsurprisingly, he didn't relinquish the tip to me once. If anything, he showed that he was one hell of a tip man and could hang in there with the best of them.

As the company's backup man during April, it was my job to ensure that our pumper was supplied with water before I joined the attack team. An essential but less celebrated assignment, backup also meant taking a beating while humping hose line in the heat and smoke.

APRIL 2, 1975—FIREFIGHTER, ENGINE 24

The soft cool breeze blowing across Seventeenth Street didn't make me feel any better. Back propped against a wall, I sat on the sidewalk with a dozen other exhausted firefighters trying our best to recover from the nasty beating we had just taken. There must have been something extra dreadful in the smoke that morning. That familiar horrible feeling suddenly overwhelmed my stomach, and I vomited not only my breakfast but what seemed to be the previous day's lunch and dinner. The odor of my own gastrointestinal slurry made me puke even more.

At 8:14 a.m., we had responded with Ladder 5 to Seventeenth and Washington for a pulled firebox. Though it would have been unusual for that early in the morning, we thought it was most likely a false alarm. But to our surprise, the assignment was upgraded to a box as we pulled onto Twentieth. We looked up and saw a huge column of black smoke marring the beautiful azure sky. Box three-four-two wasn't false; we had a job.

We followed the smoke to a well-involved three-story apartment building near Seventeenth and Ellsworth. Joe pulled right next to a hydrant, so he didn't need help connecting to it. I was free to hump our hose line behind Sharpie, the tip man, and the pack man. After knocking down the fire on the first and second floors, we began to advance up to the third. The smoke was more acrid and bitter than usual, but our main concern was the intense rush of heat rising from below. The first floor had reignited. Choking and gasping for breath, we were suddenly crawling inside what felt like a searing, soot-filled chimney. There was nowhere to go but up. Luckily, the chief saw what was happening and placed 10's beneath us. By the time we hit the third floor, the welcoming sound of splashing water was coming from below. God bless the shit-work companies.

After the fire was knocked down, the chief ordered us outside for a breather. I just about made it out before collapsing and puking on the pavement. My head was pounding, and I felt queasy as Buggy made his way along the beaten and bushed row of firefighters. Working Rescue 14, my mentor was dishing out bursts of oxygen from his resuscitator and cups of water he had gotten from the concerned lady whose home we were resting against. He knelt beside me with concern, filled my lungs with oxygen, and handed me a cup of water.

As soon as he saw that I was okay, he shook his head. "Look what you did, you friggin' mope. You threw up all over the nice lady's sidewalk!" As sick as I felt, I had to laugh.

Back then, it was commonplace to see exhausted firefighters sprawled on the pavement, gasping for breath and spilling their guts after an interior attack. To many of us, it was like a badge of honor, proof that we could hack it without wearing an SCBA to protect our lungs. We weren't sissies! We were, however, extremely naïve; we routinely filled our lungs with carcinogens and other toxic products of combustion. We'd hack up black sputum for days afterward. The carbon monoxide from that fire gave me a smoke headache that took over twenty-four hours to shake. It wasn't my first, nor was it my last.

Although our assignments were scheduled on a monthly basis, Sharpie made adjustments whenever somebody was off. The following night shift, I got my first chance to drive 24's. As with my first night driving Ladder 19, the wait for a fire wasn't long. At 11:58 p.m. we caught an all-hands job, second-in, at Thirty-Third and Reed. Thanks to Uncle Frank's intense training, my first pump service seemed like it was routine.

On May 20, I was filling in as Rescue 14's driver when mechanical problems forced a traffic helicopter to slam down on the Atlantic Refinery's grounds. Thanks to his skill, the pilot narrowly averted a disaster when he autorotated to a hard landing between two oil storage tanks. Thankfully the aircraft didn't burst into flames, but the pilot was screaming in agony. No matter how gently we touched him, he screeched with pain. Rescue 7M had to pump morphine into his veins before we could get a collar around his neck. Gino presumed correctly that he had broken his back.

On July 3, Firefighter John Fagan, Battalion 3's aide, died from an apparent heart attack while on duty. Sadly it marked the department's second LODD of the year.

The fires slowed down drastically with the summer's heat, but the warm weather also brought more false alarms at street-corner fireboxes. With some problem boxes being pulled several times a day, the department tried several approaches to quell the nuisance.

Dispatches to cold fireboxes (those without an accompanying phone call) were reduced to an engine and ladder, and in some cases only a single engine. Termed "special assignments," those companies would turn off their warning lights and sirens within three blocks of the pulled box, hoping to diminish the offender's cheap thrill. It didn't work. The false alarms increased.

Then, in an attempt to alert neighbors and discourage offenders, they installed fireboxes that sounded a deafening whistle whenever the lever was pulled. The effect was negligible, but replacing the air canisters that powered the whistles proved to be extremely costly. The false alarms continued to rise.

A less costly option was to have firefighters apply a stubborn purple dye to the firebox lever each time the box was pulled. The theory was that it would act as a deterrent or that we'd catch the culprit purple handed. Unfortunately, it seemed as though the only ones who ever got dye on their hands were the firefighters. It was virtually impossible to wash off.

One night I was in a nightclub talking to a shapely blonde, and as usual, my Italian hands were flying all over the place. In the midst of our conversation, she gently grabbed my arm and flipped my wrist over. "Why do you have ink all over your fingers?" she asked curiously.

I didn't want to get into the whole firebox dye theory, so I ad-libbed. "I got fingerprinted today."

Her reaction was surprising. She slid her chair closer, crossed her legs alluringly, and whispered in my ear, "Ooh, I find that so exciting! Are you connected to the mob or something?"

It was time for a little fun. "Well, I was in a relationship with the Don's family a few years ago," I answered truthfully, referring to Concetta. The woman was totally captivated.

Another thing they tried in an attempt to stop false alarms was called the "Box Watch Program." A firefighter and a police officer used an unmarked car to stake out problem fireboxes during the hours they were most frequently pulled. When it was my turn, I picked up the little black Rambler, call sign Robert 4, at Engine 31, along with a plainclothes officer, and parked halfway down the block from box one-six-three-nine at Twenty-First and Fitzwater Streets.

Predictably, the neighbors quickly made us out. A white guy dressed in a ridiculous-looking Hawaiian shirt sitting with a black guy in a small black sedan with cheap hub caps and a VHF antenna didn't blend very well with the neighborhood. Things were quiet until 10:45 p.m., when a tall youth suspiciously began lurking around the firebox. After checking to make sure the coast was clear, he leaned against the pole and inched his fingers upward toward the handle. We were poised, ready to jump out and chase him down, when he suddenly spun around, pointed at us with one hand, and grabbed his crotch with the other.

"Hey, you jerk-offs," he shouted, "I almost got ya! Ha!" He was gone before we could open the doors.

The fireboxes kept getting pulled until the department wisely decided to remove them during the eighties.

In addition to rewinding fireboxes, softball was a good way to stay active during the summer, so many stations played each other after their day shifts. Between innings, we would take in more calories than we'd burn, by replenishing ourselves from silver cans. To make the games more challenging, the losing team paid for the beer. Since we didn't have enough players to field a team of our own, we hooked up with Engine 60 and Ladder 19 for our nonleague beer-game fun. Between May and July, we played after nearly every second day shift.

During pregame warm-ups, I usually paired up with Ralph Campana. For fun, Ralph loved to break my stones by tossing wicked curve balls across the diamond. Just before they reached my glove, the balls would break nearly a foot down and away. He'd laugh hysterically as I chased after them while cursing under my breath.

Since unused ball fields were hard to find around the city, the Gulf refinery let us use the well-maintained employee field on their grounds. It was ironic, considering what was to come.

August 17, 1975—Firefighter, Engine 24

I wrote this entry filled with sadness and pain. An endless stream of tears rolled down my cheeks and smeared the pages of my journal.

The morning began with screaming sirens penetrating the drone of my window air conditioner. "Most likely there's a box alarm somewhere," I thought as I crawled out of bed. I usually prefer more than three hours of sleep before work, but the weekend was a special occasion—my twenty-seventh birthday. The sexy red head I'd been dating, Peggy and I celebrated, in our own special way, until nearly three in the morning.

A five-minute cold shower chased some of the sleep from my eyes, but I was still dragging. Then I heard more sirens. There was a fire somewhere downtown. I turned on my fire radio while dressing, and for a minute, nothing but squelch hissed over its speaker. Then four long beeps abruptly pierced the silence. "Fourth alarm on box five-nine-eight-eight, Penrose and Lanier Avenues, Gulf refinery. The following companies will respond: Engine Twenty, Engine Sixty-Five, Engine Sixteen, Engine Forty-One, and Ladder Four." Even though 24's was on the first alarm and most likely there already, I dashed out the door and jumped into my car.

I wasn't surprised to find the apparatus floor empty when I arrived at the firehouse. Johnny was already there and brewing a fresh pot of coffee in the kitchen. Sharpie, Joe, and Buggy came in by seven thirty, and we were ready to go. But when Sharpie called the FCC, they said that the D Platoon was to stand by at their stations until further notice.

We waited until nearly nine before the C Platoon's driver, Eddie Soloman, pulled our pumper onto the apron. The rest of his platoon, all of our 3½" hose, and our Stang gun (portable water cannon) were still at the refinery. Eddie had been told to return to the station, pick us up, and return to the fireground. We piled on and headed up the Point, toward the column of dense black smoke.

Flaming Tank 231 was located at Fourth Street and Avenue Y, inside the 723-acre refinery complex. Even though the six alarmer had been placed under control, black smoke was still billowing from its roof as we entered the main gate. Eddie pulled next to a yard hydrant supplying our hose. We followed our line a thousand feet to our C Platoon firefighters, who were cooling the tank just north of 231 with a stream from our Stang gun. A few feet away, Engines 160 and 133 were pouring foam on the stubborn flames coming from 231's roof.

We helped by rolling a few fifty-five-gallon foam cans to the foam pumpers before a battalion chief ordered us to return to our station. Third-in on the first alarm, we were shocked to be leaving so soon. But since the yard hydrant's pressure was extremely good, our pumper wasn't needed. The chiefs figured that we'd do better by covering sparsely protected South Philly. If it weren't for that twist of fate, I might not have been writing in my journal.

As we returned to our pumper, I spotted Ralph Campana maneuvering Chemical 3 around hose lines on Avenue Y. "Yo, Ralphy-Boy!" I yelled. "No curve balls today."

Instead of throwing a witty reply like I had expected, he just stared at me with an eerie glaze in his eyes. The usually jovial thirteen-year veteran didn't say a word. His mind seemed to be somewhere far, far away.

I waved and tried again. "See you later, Ralph. We're taking up! Somebody's got to protect South Philly today." He turned again and silently looked right through me. Then he shifted his eyes back to the road. I shrugged it off and climbed back onto our pumper, figuring that he was simply focused on what he was doing.

After we were back at the station, Johnny and I were making the beds when Buggy stuck his head in the bunkroom door. "Did either of you mopes stop to think about what we're going to do without our three-and-a-half-inch hose line or Stang gun if we respond to a big fire today? Come on, let's put a plan together," he said, while motioning us to follow him to the apparatus floor.

Collectively, we decided that the best we could muster for a big fire was an old nozzle we called the "New York hosepipe." It wasn't nearly as good as our Stang gun, but attached to a 2½" hose, it could flow around three hundred gallons per minute.

"Always have a plan," our mentor preached as we checked the nozzle. "And now that we do have one, you two mopes can finish making the damned beds."

As we turned toward the bunkroom, I slapped Buggy on the back. "You're going to make officers out of us yet, Hoss." (We had begun calling our muscular, large-framed mentor Hoss, after *Bonanza*'s Hoss Cartwright.)

"You two as officers!" he scoffed. "God forbid!"

As usual on Sundays, Johnny made his signature creamed chipped beef and home fries for breakfast. Because of our late start and a box run to Twelfth and Christian, we didn't sit down for "breakfast" until nearly two o'clock. While eating and watching the Phillies in the comfort of our tiny air-conditioned kitchen, I couldn't help but think about our brother firefighters still toiling in the heat and humidity back at the refinery. Surely they'd be mopping up soon, and we'd be called back to retrieve our equipment. That call never came.

At 4:24 p.m. we got dispatched, first-in, to 2200 Alter Street for a dwelling fire. "I bet it's that same vacant we've had three times!" I yelled to Buggy. Over the past few months, vagrants had repeatedly lit up the same run-down vacant on Alter Street. Buggy nodded nonchalantly. It would take more than a vacant to get him excited. As a matter of fact, up to that point, I had never seen him get excited.

Sure enough, as we turned up Alter, medium gray smoke was rolling from the basement of the same old place. Sharpie peered into the basement window. "It's only a large pile of rubbish," he said before placing the fire under control. Johnny and I crawled through the basement window and quickly extinguished the fire.

After Johnny crawled back out, as I was about to follow, Buggy pointed to the end of the nozzle, which was missing its fog tip. "Look! You mopes lost the fog tip. Go find it." I quickly spotted the perforated brass nozzle cap among the debris by the window. But as soon as I picked it up, Buggy forcefully grabbed the back of my collar and yanked me out of the basement like I was a rag doll.

My first thought was that the building was about to collapse, but when I looked up, everything seemed fine. "What the frig, Hoss?" I yelled.

"Come on, we got to go!" he screamed. "There was a flash at the refinery, and firefighters are trapped in the flames." It was the first time I ever saw him run.

As soon as I had one foot in the crew cab, Joe took off. With Sharpie pressing on the siren harder than usual, we flew down Twenty-Third and onto the Point. Ahead of us, a cloud of black smoke filled the southwestern sky. It was ten times larger than it had been in the morning. As we zipped past Engine 60 and Ladder 19's empty firehouse, I made the sign of the cross, praying that my brother firefighters were safe.

By the time we pulled into the main gate, a huge wall of crimson flames was dwarfing the Penrose Avenue Bridge. It looked as though the entire refinery was in flames. A chief screamed our orders over the radio.

"Twenty-Four's, protect the tank north of Two Thirty-One." It was the same tank we had been cooling in the morning. We jumped off and tried to track down our Stang gun, but the hose feeding it was now under a lake of burning oil. It was time for our New York hosepipe. As we were stretching our 2½" hose toward the tank, Buggy shot me a little "I told you so" wink.

Out of the corner of my eye, I spotted a large-framed firefighter with foam covering his running coat walking past in a zombie-like trance. "Hey, buddy. Are you okay?" I called out, but he didn't flinch. His eyes fixed in the distance, he walked right past us, looking as though he had just seen the devil himself.

"Let him go!" Buggy yelled. "He's in shock. We've got to get water on that tank."

Flames were roaring like a blowtorch as we took a position on the containment dike and aimed our hosepipe at the tank. But the yard-hydrant system had been damaged by the fire, and even with our pumper augmenting the pressure, our stream splashed well short. We had no choice but to scoot down into the containment area and advance nearly fifty feet through the waist-deep sea of foam so our paltry stream could reach.

The radiant heat on the tank was so intense that our stream quickly turned to steam. With such low pressure, we were lucky if one hundred gallons per minute were reaching the scalding tank, which contained naphtha solvents. The amount of water required to protect an exposed petroleum storage tank is huge. We weren't even close. I looked at Buggy, but his normally reassuring smile wasn't there. Neither was Sharpie's. That's when I became worried that the tank could possibly explode. Shit!

After fifteen nervous minutes, a battalion chief suddenly emerged on the dike behind us. "Get the hell out of that foam!" he screamed.

Sharpie sloshed a few steps toward him and cupped his hands around his mouth. "Our stream won't reach the tank from back there, chief."

"There's oil under that foam! We just lost several guys back on Avenue Y the same way. Now get the hell out of there!"

He didn't have to tell us a third time. We quickly dragged our hose out of the foam and retreated to the other side of the dike. By then the fire had risen to eleven alarms, one of the largest in the department's history. With our line basically useless, we assisted incoming companies stretching their hoses from city hydrants outside the gates. Several explosions and large fireballs ripped throughout the plant. About a hundred feet away, flames under a network of pipes made a loud hissing sound before the pipes exploded thunderously. Flames spewed sideways, as though they were being shot from a flamethrower. It was the second time I saw Buggy run.

Just after eight o'clock, the chief who had ordered us out of the dike told us to take a break by our pumper. "Before you sit down," he said, flinching from another explosion, "take your axes out of the compartment. There's a chance that we might lose this whole fuckin' place. If we do, cut your lines and head straight down this road. Smash through the fence if you have to."

Reeking of foam and oil, we quickly downed lime drink provided by the Second Alarmers Association (a volunteer mobile canteen service), with our worried eyes focused on the looming firestorm. Luckily, incoming companies got the upper hand, and it never reached that point.

In true brotherhood, Tony Watson, an off-duty firefighter from 10's, made his way around the refinery taking phone numbers so he could call our loved ones and tell them we were okay. Some families weren't as fortunate. Several firefighters, many in critical condition, had been transported to hospitals and burn centers. Six of our brothers were still missing as I wrote my journal entry.

After our break, we helped more companies stretch hose lines. The fire roared brightly in the night sky, but the rumbles, hisses, pops, and explosions gradually subsided. Rumors of the missing firefighters circulated around the fireground, and the first name I heard hit me like a ton of bricks. It was Ralph. Someone had seen him get swallowed by a sea of flames as he loaded foam into Engine 160. How I hoped they were mistaken. Six hours after our shift ended, we piled into the back of a police wagon for an unusually quiet ride back to our firehouse. Our shift was over.

Physically and emotionally drained, I went down to the dim basement to retrieve my car keys. I was at my locker when, all of a sudden, a ghostly wail reverberated from the running gear room. I'd never heard anything like it before. Spooked out of my skin, I quickly snatched my keys and flew back upstairs.

I ran into the kitchen panting, and Buggy did a double take. "You look like you just saw a friggin' ghost."

"I didn't see one," I thought, sloughing off his observation, "but I may have just heard one."

I prayed, "Please, Lord, make the events of this day be nothing more than a nightmare."

Unfortunately, it wasn't a nightmare. Eight Philadelphia firefighters lost their lives at the Gulf-refinery disaster. Killed that day were Ralph Campana, forty-one, from Ladder 19; John Andrews, forty-nine, from Engine 49; Joseph Wiley, thirty-three, from Ladder 27; Roger Parker, twenty-eight, from Ladder 27; Robert Fisher, forty-three, from Engine 33; and Hugh McIntyre, fifty-three, from Engine 56. A few days later, Lieutenant James Pouliot, thirty-three, from Engine 20, and Carroll Brenek, thirty-three, from Engine 57, died at the burn center.

During the investigation into the catastrophe, it was learned that hours before the fire, a seagoing oil tanker named the *Afran Neptune* had been pumping Venezuelan crude oil into seventy-five-thousand-gallon Tank 231. Two employees tasked with monitoring the process fell asleep, and as the oil level rose, it forced highly flammable vapors out of its roof vents. At 6:04 a.m. the vapors found an ignition source, and flames flashed back to the tank, causing a mighty explosion and fire.

Unknown to fireground commanders, Tank 231 had leaked oil throughout the day. It insidiously floated on the water and under the foam that accumulated around Engines 133 and 160. As firefighters working in the area disrupted the foam blanket, the oil's vapors were ignited by Engine 133's red-hot exhaust pipe. The resulting flash fire quickly enveloped Campana, Andrews, and Fisher. The others were killed or severely burned as they rushed to the aid of their brother firefighters.

The eight firefighters who died left eight widows and twenty-one children. Fourteen more firefighters were injured, some of them so seriously that they never returned to the job. The fire department lost four pumpers.

In addition to Engines 133 and 160, Engines 16 and 40 were also lost to the flames.

Personally, I found it sobering to think how small changes in a sequence of events could have produced such drastically different outcomes. If our hose line that morning had been supplied by our pumper instead of by a yard hydrant, we still would have been at the refinery when it flashed. If I had stayed at Ladder 19 instead of being transferred to 24's, would I have been helping Ralph near Engine 160? If that battalion chief hadn't come by and chased us out of the oil-filled dike, would we have also been casualties? On that tragic day, it was simply fate that dictated who died and who got to go home.

I often wondered if that glazed look I saw in Ralph's eyes that morning had been an eerie and awful premonition. A few months later, I read in *Philadelphia Magazine* that his wife said that he had sensed something was wrong before he left for work. She said he was uncharacteristically reluctant to leave the house. The father of four even backed his car halfway down his block to have one last look at her before driving away. I can still see him on the Gulf-refinery ball field with oil-storage tanks and flare towers in the background, laughing as I chased after his nasty curve balls.

As for that ghostly wail, maybe it came from the ventilation system, or maybe it was the spirit of Bob Malley crying as eight more Philadelphia Firefighters rose to the pearly gates of heaven. I never heard that spooky spectral sound in 24's basement again.

CHAPTER 10

Mumbles

To firefighters, a LODD is a death in the family. Because of the Gulf-refinery tragedy, we had eight of them in our PFD family. In brotherhood, firefighters from around the country and Canada joined us at each viewing, church service, and burial.

Fires and other emergencies don't stop for firefighter funerals. Despite our broken hearts, we honored our fallen brothers mostly by getting back to what we did best—helping people and saving lives. As a show of appreciation, many residents tipped their caps, waved, or even saluted us during the ensuing weeks as we responded around our district. A few weeks later, someone paid us a different type of tribute.

September 10, 1975—Firefighter, Engine 24

John and I were sitting across from each other after returning from a roofer's tar-pot fire. Suddenly a very loud *ping* rang out from behind us. We looked at each other curiously, thinking that something might have snapped in our rear axle, but the apparatus was rolling along just fine. After we returned to the firehouse, I was about to walk to the kitchen when I heard John yell, "Whoa! Look at this!" There was a bullet hole in the side of our pumper, for God's sake! It had struck only feet behind our seats, just above the discharge outlets. Whether it was intentional or simply misdirected, we'll never know. But fate was on our side. If Joe had been driving just a tad bit slower, one of us could have gotten shot. Wow!

A few days later, we were dispatched to a reported dwelling fire. As our overhead door rose, we saw an old beat-up Oldsmobile Toronado blocking our path on the apron. Its engine was running, and the driver's side door was wide open, but the driver was nowhere in sight. Hoss quickly jumped in, backed it onto Twentieth, and left it there. When he climbed aboard our pumper, he showed me his hands. They were smeared with blood.

When we returned, the Oldsmobile was surrounded by police officers. It turned out that moments before we got the run, the driver had come to our station for help. He had been shot. But instead of entering our side door, he mistakenly ran into the Seventeenth Police District, where the cops rushed him to the hospital. I doubt if the two incidents were related. Maybe September was just gunshot month in our district.

Gunshots or not, Sharpie was a great officer. During nonemergencies, he'd often explain the rationale behind his orders. Many fire officers of the era didn't feel the need to justify their commands to their subordinates. Orders were orders, and they were to be followed without question in military fashion.

September 26, 1975—Firefighter, Engine 24

After assigning our work chores on that gray September morning, Sharpie added, "Oh, and we need to check our roof drain today." It wasn't something we routinely did, so he gave us the reason behind his order. "Last week, the roof of a firehouse in the second division collapsed because debris was clogging their drain spout," he said. "The administration has issued a general memorandum stating that each station's roof drains must be checked and cleaned monthly. Then by the first of the month, the company officer, *moi*, needs to type yet another memo stating that the task was completed." We giggled as he walked away in disgust over the extra paperwork.

"Okay!" Hoss declared as soon as Sharpie was out of sight. "You two mopes get the twenty-four-footer and place it to the roof. And don't forget to raise it three rungs above the eave!"

Our unofficial noncom veteran of Ladder 10 observed carefully as we carried the ladder and raised it as though we were still in Fire School. "Good," he said with a wink. "I'll heel (steady the bottom) while you mopes go up and check the drain."

"Yes, Hoss. Anything you want, Hoss." John sniggered as he climbed upward.

When he reached the top, John yelled in awe, "Holy cow! There's about two feet of water up here! Bob, bring up a hook."

I grabbed our six-foot ceiling hook and was about to climb up when I spotted Mumbles staggering across the Point. Mumbles, a homeless alcoholic who frequented our firehouse, got his nickname because he did just that—he mumbled. He mumbled when he walked, he mumbled when he talked, he mumbled when he drank from his bagged bottle, and we could even hear him mumble through the bathroom door when he did his business. As he approached Hoss, he mumbled something and nodded toward the restroom. Even Mumbles knew Hoss was in charge of the operation.

"Yeah. Go ahead, Mumbles, you mope," Hoss replied sternly, waving his beefy finger at him. "But don't make a friggin' mess this time. We're tired of cleaning up your shit!"

Once I made it up the ladder, I saw that John hadn't been exaggerating. There was at least two feet of stagnant water pooled on the roof. Leaves and other debris were floating on its surface. Perched atop the ladder, I handed John the hook, and he probed below the murky water until he snagged a large plastic bag from the drain opening. Suddenly a swirling vortex formed as hundreds of gallons of filthy water gushed down the drain. But 24's roof drain doesn't empty into a traditional downspout; it empties into a closed sanitary system tied in with all the firehouse drains. The sudden torrent overwhelmed the drainage pipes and caused blackish water to spout like a geyser from every sink and toilet. Unfortunately for Mumbles, he was perched upon the toilet seat closest to the roof drain.

"Yow! That toilet just exploded right in my ass!" he screeched as he darted from the bathroom, dripping wet. It was the first time we ever heard him speak clearly. Clutching his bottle in one hand and holding his pants up with the other, he dashed across Point Breeze screaming, "Yow! They tried to drown me! Yow!"

Hoss was rolling with laughter, and I was doubled over so badly that I could barely climb down the ladder. After we cleaned up, we posted a sign on the bathroom door: "Old faithful."

That cool crisp October brought many fires, but unfortunately I missed them all. It was my month to drive the medicine wagon again. After another endless array of calls and abuse of the EMS system, every trace of enthusiasm I'd had back in February was gone. Like most of my peers, I learned to tolerate rescue duty as a necessary evil that went along with being assigned to 24's.

Even though 24's was busy, it had a high personnel turnover rate. The reason was simple: Rescue 14. Firefighters often transferred to companies that didn't staff rescue units, even if they were slower. Three of our platoon mates transferred out by the beginning of the bicentennial year. Among the replacements was mustachioed Bob "Lumpy" Lombardo. Hired the year before me, the former West Philly firefighter was fun to be around, and we soon became close friends. Lumpy had narrowly cheated death at the Gulf fire. As Engine 16's acting lieutenant that day, he literally ran out of his boots to escape the flames as they consumed his pumper.

Totally into the job, Lumpy's enthusiasm was contagious. John and I were already studying for lieutenant, but Lumpy's zeal made us kick it into high gear. To Hoss, though, who didn't aspire to a higher rank, Lumpy was simply his third mope to train. Whenever we put our noses in the books or discussed firefighting strategy, Hoss would mock, "What are you studying? This job's simple. All you need to know is put the wet stuff on the red stuff!"

Hoss teased us just to be funny. We cared for our mentor and knew that, deep down inside, he'd be proud as a peacock if we ever got promoted.

One day we rolled up to a fully involved dwelling fire that was extending in both directions. As we clambered around, frantically stretching hose lines, Hoss casually strolled to our side of the pumper. "Now, you three mopes can either throw your books at this fire, or you can hang on to my coattails and learn what's really important?" We were laughing so hard while fighting the fire that the other companies thought we were nuts.

Hoss instilled a great deal of company pride in us. These were his two cardinal rules: never give up the tip, and never let another company beat us in. We went above and beyond to please our mentor by memorizing all the fire box numbers in our district. Since box numbers were the first thing announced during dispatches, we figured that if we knew them, we'd get out even faster.

One day, we were huddled around the watch desk quizzing each other. "Where's box four-six-one?" John asked.

"Eighteenth and South Streets," I quickly replied.

Astonishingly, as soon as the words left my mouth, the alert tone buzzed, and the dispatcher announced, "Box four-six-one, Eighteenth and South Streets." We looked at each other with utter amazement. By the time Hoss came trotting from the kitchen, we were already on the pumper, ready to go.

"Are you mopes memorizing box numbers again?" he asked, smiling with approval. "You might get a jump on the other companies, but you still can't leave without me, mopes!" We laughed our asses off while fighting *that* fire too. A different batch of companies thought we were nuts.

As we rolled into our nation's bicentennial year, the winter was bitterly cold, and we were busy. Sharpie adjusted the schedule so that we'd drive the pumper the month after our turn driving Rescue 14. I found out that for some families, lightning could strike twice.

MARCH 6, 1976—FIREFIGHTER, ENGINE 24

I recognized the address as soon as we got dispatched. It was the same house Gino and I had responded to the previous month for a fatal cardiac arrest. How could I forget it? Our Laerdal suction unit had been full of the woman's vomit, and I had gagged continuously while cleaning it out.

That March day, though, it was my turn to drive the pumper, and when we turned the corner, heavy black smoke was pouring from the same exact address. Lumpy jumped off and wrapped our hose around the hydrant. I was looking in the rearview mirror, waiting for his sign, when suddenly, out of the corner of my eye, I saw the woman's husband dive through the smoke from the second-floor window. We heard his body smack onto the sidewalk from a half block away. Having suffered severe head trauma, he was dead on arrival at Graduate Hospital. He died exactly one month after his wife.

May 16, 1976, was a beautiful spring Sunday. But instead of clowning around as usual during evening roll call, we were standing at attention, listening to three rounds of seven bells clanging over the station's joker system (a system of bells controlled by the FCC). Sadly, four more Philadelphia firefighters had lost their lives in the line of duty. That day, around noon, firefighters had battled a basement blaze in Barson's Overbrook Delicatessen in Northeast Philly. As they were operating, the terrazzo floor they were standing on suddenly collapsed and toppled them into the flames. Killed were firefighters David Stewart, fifty-two, Ladder 28; Aloysius Welsh, forty-nine, Ladder 20; Bernard McSloy, thirty-two, Ladder 28; and Richie Iannacone, twenty-nine, Ladder 34. My knees buckled when I heard the last name. Outgoing and friendly, Richie had been at 49's when I was at Ladder 19, and I knew him well. Coming only nine months after the Gulf fire, their deaths were a horrific blow. For the first time, I wondered if I'd actually survive my career.

On June 8, we were returning from an apartment fire when we got dispatched to the elevated railroad at Twenty-Fifth and Reed Streets. A worker painting the overhead wire supports accidentally brushed a thirty-thousand-volt transmission line. Workers in the nearby garment factory saw an intense blue flash before the painter fell twenty-five feet onto the tracks below. Unbelievably, the poor guy was sitting there very much alive, even though his body was still smoldering. We actually joked around with him while carrying him down. We were sure that he'd make it. But a day later, Gino found out that the electrocution victim had died. In our business, sometimes when you think people will live, they die, and sometimes when you think they're dead, they're actually alive.

While filling in as Rescue 14's driver on June 23, we responded to Twentieth and Tasker for an unresponsive male on the sidewalk. He was easy to spot because a swarm of flies was swirling over his body. We thought he must be dead. But when we gently rolled him over, we heard a familiar mumbling. Holy cow! It was good ole Mumbles. Covered in vomit, feces, and urine, he was still clutching his bottle in a bag. Gino figured that he may have drunk a lethal amount, so we wrapped him in sheets, loaded him in the back, and took him to Saint Agnes Hospital. Yes, I gagged in the process, but it was nothing compared to the ER nurse who barfed her guts up when she unwrapped him. It was just another disgusting and boring day in Rescue 14.

JUNE 23, 1976—FIREFIGHTER, ENGINE 24, DETAILED TO RESCUE 14

Hoss was shaking his head, listening to our Mumbles story, when box six-three-five-five, Philadelphia International Airport, sounded over the kitchen speaker. We never paid much attention to the airport box, not only because we didn't respond to it, but also because it came in often for minor aircraft emergencies. Off-airport companies typically responded to Gate 55 and stood by until either Engine 77 or 78 (the two PIA fire stations) reported that the aircraft had landed safely.

As we chatted away, 78's report crackled over the watch-desk radio, but this time the officer's voice was more excited than usual. My ears perked up when I heard, "Confirmed multiengine aircraft crash, and strike out the second alarm!" Seconds later we were flying down the Point with 24's right on our tail, responding to the PIA.

Allegheny Airlines flight 121, a Douglas DC 9 with 106 people aboard, encountered severe wind shear while trying to land. The tail section struck the ground and split the aircraft into two pieces. By some miracle it didn't burst into flames, but there were numerous injuries.

Fire radio directed us to proceed to Gate 55 and wait for airport police. According to procedure, we weren't supposed to cross the runways unescorted. But when we arrived, there weren't any police at the gate. Unsurprisingly, they had all responded to the crash site. We radioed that we needed an escort, but after several minutes, the only vehicles that arrived on scene were the second-alarm companies. Forming a long line behind us, they impatiently sounded their sirens and blasted their horns. Out on the taxiways, we could see dozens of emergency vehicles darting in all directions, like roaches scattering after a light is suddenly turned on in a dark filthy basement. I looked to Gino and shrugged my shoulders, and away we went. Truthfully, I was more worried about getting hit by one of the numerous ground vehicles than an aircraft. I proceeded slowly and carefully, and we safely made it to the crash site.

The scene was surreal. The aircraft was sitting flat on its belly, covered with foam, its tail section lying several yards away. Firefighters had corralled most of the injured into a triage area, but some were still aboard the aircraft. The copilot was trapped in the cockpit, and we were directed inside the plane to help remove him.

We rolled our hospital cot (wheeled stretcher) next to the crippled airliner and climbed in through an emergency exit. First-alarm firefighters already had a cervical collar around the copilot's neck, and they were lashing him to a backboard as we made our way over the strewn baggage in the aisles. As soon as they finished, we helped them maneuver him back out the exit and onto the wing. I looked down to where we had left our hospital cot, but it was gone. Uh-oh! Evidently, it had been used for another patient.

We lugged the backboard to the back of Rescue 14 and slid it flat on the floor. To help keep it stable, a firefighter from 40's climbed in with Gino for the ride to Methodist Hospital's ER.

When we returned to the crash site, our hospital cot was sitting about a hundred feet from the plane, which was a good thing. We had to make two more trips to the ER with injured victims.

Shortly after the airliner crash, Gino was accepted into the paramedic program. We were glad for him, but it was bad for us. Instead of coming back to 24's after completing his training, he'd be assigned to an ALS rescue in another station. Suddenly, in addition to taking our turns as rescue drivers, we had to take our turns as doctors too. Having two NERDs in the rescue was not a good idea.

One hot August day, Hoss and I were paired together in Rescue 14. I won the coin toss, so I opted to drive. Our fourth run of the shift was for a man who had passed out while washing his car. As Hoss was reporting that we were on scene, I jumped out and got to the man first. He wasn't breathing and had no heartbeat, and his eyes were fixed and dilated. There were no signs of rigor, so I yelled for Hoss to call a code blue.

As I was doing chest compressions, Hoss trotted over with the resuscitator. But as soon as he looked at the guy, he growled, "He's friggin' dead! I'm canceling the code."

A small crowd had gathered, and I didn't want to make a scene, so I spoke through my clenched teeth, "Hoss, there's no rigor, man!"

He knelt down next to me and whispered, "Listen, I've been to a thousand of these. He's dead. Now I'm the doctor, and I'm canceling the code." I was sure that the man was dead too, but I was only following Gino's rule: unless you're absolutely certain, resuscitate. Mad as hell, I argued with my mentor during the entire ride back to the station. It was the first and only time we had words.

Just as we were backing into the firehouse, we got dispatched to the same address. I slammed the shifter into drive and screamed at Hoss, "I told you! How are we going to explain this one?" Hoss sat there silently, looking concerned, as we raced back to the scene.

I slammed to a stop in front of the man's house, but his body was still on the sidewalk, covered with a sheet. The call was for his daughter, who had passed out from grief. After we revived her, she refused to go to the hospital.

During the ride back, Hoss stared directly ahead. "You were right," he apologized softly. "From now on, we'll follow Gino's rules, okay?"

"Sure, Hoss," I replied. "I guess we just need to adjust to life without Gino."

A few seconds later, he slowly turned and smiled wryly. "You're still a friggin' mope, though!" We laughed for the rest of the ride back to the firehouse.

That fall we were practicing a dry run for our river-emergency (water rescue) boxes when Hoss lost his footing and blew out his knee. He was in terrible pain as we loaded him into the back of Rescue 14. Complications from severe ligament damage forced our beloved mentor to leave the job with a service-connected disability. We were heartbroken.

Without Gino and Hoss, it seemed as if the rest of us were always either driving the pumper or working in Rescue 14. To top things off, Lumpy got drafted to attend EMT school, and the rest of us were scheduled to follow shortly thereafter. The only way out seemed to be a promotion.

But that fall's retreat at Malvern was more than a spiritual sojourn; it was my saving grace. Commissioner Rizzo asked me how I was doing at 24's. His disciple had to be honest, and six weeks later I was miraculously transferred to Engine 10. I absolutely loved the firefighting aspect of 24's but had had enough of rescue duty.

New Year's Day 1977 was my last day at 24's. As I was loading my things into my car, Mumbles staggered out of the corner bar. "Yo, Mumbles!" I yelled. "Do you want to use our bathroom, you mope?"

He stuck both of his middle fingers in the air and mumbled something unintelligible. I'm pretty sure it was "Screw you and your exploding toilet!"

CHAPTER 11

Brownie's Barometer

In 1953 Engine 10 moved from their firehouse at Eighth and Morris to the quarters of my childhood favorite, Ladder 11. Ten years later, both companies moved a half block south to their new station on the corner of Twelfth and Reed. The modern one-story tan brick building sported a flashy glass atrium that allowed sunshine to brighten its otherwise dull interior. Out front, a small well-maintained lawn seemed to diverge from South Philly's concrete sidewalks. In 1975, to keep up with the increasing pace of fires, Battalion Chief 1 was strategically relocated there from 49's.

Though only ten blocks from 24's, 10's was different in many ways. It wasn't sitting in the middle of a poverty-stricken neighborhood, so there were far fewer first-ins. Most of 10's fires were shit work. And when they did catch a first-in, they arrived with Ladder 11 and Battalion 1, a small army compared to what we had at 24's. Most importantly for me was that 10's didn't house a rescue unit.

Unlike 24's, 10's was a two-piece engine company. In addition to their regular 1,000-gallon-per-minute pumper, they also ran with a smaller, more maneuverable 250-gallon-per-minute pumper called Tac 10. For tactical box and box alarms, both vehicles responded together with the radio designation "Unit 10." Slightly larger than a pickup truck, Tac 10 was great for the narrow, congested streets of South Philly.

Commissioner Rizzo's tac-pumper concept was designed to keep pace with the high fire demand of the 1970s. Staffed by an officer and five firefighters, six tac-pumpers were strategically located around the city. The company's officer and two firefighters rode on the tac, and three firefighters rode on the pumper. The tac was dispatched solo for rubbish, automobiles, wires, and other minor fires. The pumper, though shorthanded, would remain in service to protect the district. If the company was dispatched on a second or greater alarm, the tac and its driver would remain behind to provide a small but valuable water supply for the ladder. The tac-ladder combination would respond together as a unit. I was excited by the transfer because the tac-pumper combination gave me the opportunity to learn something new and different.

Everyone at 10's had more time on the job than I did, so once again I was the new guy. But that was fine because I inherited two new mentors. Buddy Yeager, who transferred into 10's after spending years in North Philly's busy Engine 27, became my new "Hoss." Thinly built, unlike Buggy, yet just as gritty, Buddy had plenty of knowledge and experience to share. I also had Mike Casella. Assigned to 10's since Fire School, "Mikey" had the same sort of down-to-earth, common-sense approach to firefighting as Uncle Frank.

In addition to my mentors, our company captain, "Brownie," was a great fire officer to work for and learn from. Our white-haired leader was experienced, open, and friendly. But on my first day, Buddy cautioned, "Listen, if the captain's face turns red, don't mess with him. That means he's getting pissed. We call it 'Brownie's barometer.'"

It wasn't long before I got a taste of 10's shit work and witnessed Brownie's barometer firsthand.

January 14, 1977—Firefighter, Engine 10

It was a bone-chilling twenty-two degrees, and heavy wet snow was falling as I followed the same path that Arthur and I had traveled so many years ago. I figured that it was better to walk the seven blocks for my shift rather than drive. It was the right decision. Cars were spinning, sliding, and skidding all along the slippery streets of South Philly. By the time I stepped through 10's kitchen door, an inch of snow had accumulated on my uniform cap.

The second I entered, Buddy spotted me. "Christ!" he shouted over the din of the kitchen. "Look at all the snow on your head. How freaking far away did you park?" Everybody roared. Neither Buddy nor DeRose ever missed much. They were quick to mock anything or anybody for a laugh, and I loved it.

By eight o'clock that night, nearly three inches of snow covered Twelfth Street. Brownie was concerned about the small margin of error for a fire vehicle to slide sideways on South Philly's narrow streets. After two slippery box runs, he decided that we needed to put on our snow chains, but we didn't get a chance to start.

About a mile away, an emotionally distraught woman ran outside her house, smashed her large front window, dashed back inside, and set the house on fire. By the time we unraveled our chains, flames were shooting from her windows.

"Box one-four-three-nine, Broad and Wolf!" came the yell. "Engine fourth-in, chief first."

Frankie Rags (Battalion 1's aide) pulled out and fishtailed across Twelfth. He corrected quickly and made a right onto Reed Street. We followed behind them with Tac 10, but with 250 gallons of water over our rear wheels, we hardly skidded. Recently plowed Broad Street was a breeze, and with our electronic siren wailing, we were only two blocks away from the fire when 49's gave their report. "Heavy fire showing with report of people trapped. All companies in service with inch-and-three-quarter hose lines." (The department had switched from 1½" to 1¾" hose for interior attacks.)

Tac 10 makes stretching hose quick and easy. We stopped next to a hydrant on Broad Street, and I jumped out and wrapped a few lengths of 2½" hose around its base. Mikey and Brownie took off, plopping our hose behind them. By the time Buddy pulled our pumper next to the hydrant, Tac 10 was positioned by the alley. Fourth-in, our tactical position was the rear of the dwelling.

While Buddy hooked our pumper to the hydrant, I connected Tac 10's hose to its discharge outlet. Once our water supply was established, I took off to help Brownie and Mikey, who were already stretching another 2½" hose up the alley. I began sprinting, eager to help them, which was a bad move. I quickly slipped, belly flopped, and skidded headfirst completely across Broad Street. The only thing that stopped my slide was a sewer inlet, which I grabbed onto like it was third base. Coach Mike would have been so proud of me!

Covered in snow, I jumped up and began pulling our 1¾" attack line from Tac 10.

Obviously, Mikey had witnessed my imitation of Pete Rose. "Slow down before you kill yourself, Bobby!" he chided as he casually dragged a hose up the alley behind me.

We connected everything together, and Mikey charged the line. Heavy smoke was pushing from the back of the house as we crawled inside through the back door. I was the tip man, but there wasn't much fire to extinguish. Our job was to protect 49's rear. After knocking down the fire on the first floor, they had advanced their line upstairs. The kitchen flared up a little, but it was easy to knock down. Other than that, we only hit hot spots and smoldering debris. Welcome to the world of shit work! We hadn't done much of it at 24's.

With visibility near zero, Brownie shouted, "Let's get some of this smoke out of here." As I edged toward the front window, I crawled over a large spongy mass. I immediately knew that it wasn't debris. It was a charred body. I bolted upright like a frightened cat. Brownie shined his light on the remains. "That must be the mother. There's supposed to be a toddler in here too."

I scooted around the body and aimed a wide fog pattern at the window as Brownie and other firefighters looked for the child. I joined the search as soon as the smoke lifted enough to see. A large fallen piece of drywall was lying against the stairs, so I tossed it aside. Something looked out of place underneath. I shined my light closer and, to my dismay, saw that it was the back of a small charred skull. We had found the toddler.

We covered both remains with yellow disposable blankets and hosed down a few more hot spots. Chief Cowden cut the assignment down to two and two (two engines and two ladders). I guess one benefit of being a shit-work company was that we didn't have to carry the bodies outside. Tradition called for the first-in companies, 49's and Ladder 19 in this case, to share that unpleasant task. "Take up, Ten's," Cowden said. "Nice job." We were done.

As we were dragging our nearly frozen hose back to Tac 10, I slipped on a patch of ice and fell flat on my ass. A tall man wearing a black coat and hat helped me to my feet. It was Commissioner Rizzo.

"Are you okay, Robert?" he asked, remembering me as one of his disciples. The commissioner and his brother, Mayor Frank Rizzo, had grown up in the neighborhood, so he had responded to the scene. Over his shoulder, I spotted Brownie nervously wondering why I was having a conversation with the commissioner. Most likely he thought I was in some kind of trouble. A relieved look came across his face when Rizzo tipped his hat at him and climbed into his black sedan.

I had slipped and fallen twice. Now it was Brownie's turn. After we finished restoring our hose, I climbed into Tac 10. As our captain approached, he hit a patch of ice. For seconds, it seemed, his arms were flailing as he desperately tried to regain his balance. But instead, his short dance culminated with his feet flying out from underneath him. His helmet flew off and landed with a loud crash just as he slammed down on his ass. It looked like a scene right out of a Warner brothers' cartoon. Across the street, DeRose was slapping his thighs laughing. Mikey and I began laughing hysterically. After he pulled himself up, Brownie didn't say a word; he just glared at us. His face was as red as our fire truck. It was Brownie's barometer! I immediately wiped the smile off my face and looked straight ahead.

He climbed in and snatched the microphone from its cradle. "Unit Ten available!" I don't know how I made it back to the station without busting a gut while sitting next to him.

Rumors were swirling that the lieutenant's examination was going to be held that summer. I began hitting the books even harder, studying several hours a day. I missed studying with Johnny and Lumpy, but Buddy wanted to give this test a try, so we sometimes studied together.

Less than thirty years old, Battalion Chief Bruce Cowden was one of the youngest chiefs in the department's history. When he saw how hard I was studying, he often took the time to chat with me about fireground strategy and tactics. Many times, after he returned from a fire, he'd explain the decisions he made and, more importantly, the reasons he made them. If the time came, he wanted me to be as prepared as possible to advance in rank.

Many of 10's jobs were shit work with 24's. On January 29 we responded to box three-four-two at Seventeenth and Washington. The three-story apartment fire was nearly identical to the one where I had thrown up on the lady's pavement. Just like then, 24's knocked down three floors of fire, and 10's advanced behind them, protecting their rear. The main difference this time was that we found a four-year-old deaf girl burned to death on the second floor. Oh, and I didn't vomit either.

Until February I hadn't experienced the main disadvantage of working a tac-pumper company—responding to a fire shorthanded.

February 23, 1977—Firefighter, Engine 10

My job was pack man on the pumper. At 11:20 p.m. we were in the kitchen playing crazy eights. I wasn't into playing cards, but the crew was too much fun to resist. I was sitting next to Brownie when he made an awful move and threw down the wrong hand.

DeRose was so focused on the cards that he thought I had made the move. "Now that's a stupid move, you dope!" he guffawed. Brownie's barometer turned bright red faster than I could throw a single PVC. We sat there in awkward silence while the captain stared down DeRose.

Thankfully, the bells rang a second later. "Tac only, automobile fire!"

As soon as Brownie hit the apparatus floor, DeRose cried, "Now that's what I call getting saved by the bell!" We were rolling on the floor.

A minute later the bells rang again. This time Buddy, Mikey, and I responded with Pumper 10, fourth-in, on a box alarm at Thirteenth and South Streets. The three-story vacant was well involved when we arrived, and the only hydrant available was more than a block away. While Mikey hooked up, Buddy and I stretched our entire 2½" hose bed to the rear. Then we ran back to our pumper, picked up our attack line, jogged back to the rear again, and connected everything together. We'd yet to get a drop of water on the fire but were already out of breath. Naturally, the chief then ordered us to attack the fire on the third floor, but instead of entering from the rear, he wanted us to enter from the front. Where else? The two of us dragged our line around front, flaked it out, and hauled it up two flights of stairs for only ten cents' worth of fire. It took less than a minute to put it out.

"Take up, Ten's."

As they were extinguishing the car fire, Brownie and Tac 10's crew didn't hear the dispatch. They showed up after we had restored our last length of hose.

Brownie rotated our assignments weekly. Since Buddy and I were the only ones studying for lieutenant, he made us take turns filling in for him whenever he was off or serving as acting battalion chief. The experience helped with our studies.

In early March Ladder 11 was shorthanded, so I got a chance to tiller my childhood favorite. As we were responding to a fire in 24's district, we passed by my old third-floor flat on Reed Street. Maybe it was my imagination, but when I glanced up, I thought I saw a little boy with his face pressed against the window. Chills ran up my spine.

Engine 10 and Ladder 11 were first-in at two subway stops along the Broad Street Line. As kids, my friends and I would beat the fare by twisting our small bodies through the exit turnstile at one of those stops, Tasker-Morris. For hours, we'd escape the summer's heat by riding the subway back and forth along its cool subterranean tracks. I wasn't afraid of getting caught by the cops, but what did scare me was horsing around on the platform. The thought of falling on the tracks and being run over by a subway train was horrifying. It was one of my biggest childhood fears.

MARCH 9, 1977—FIREFIGHTER, ENGINE 10

The familiar odor hit my nostrils as soon as we got halfway down the stairwell—that special blend of electric machinery, dirt, and body odor, with a hint of urine that marks the smell of Philly's subways. The dreaded call, "man under a train," had come in right after lunch, of all times.

The northbound train was stopped at the platform, with its sliding doors fully open. At the base of the steps, an attractive middle-aged woman was wailing: "Oh my God! He jumped right in front of the damn train. I'm think I'm going to throw up." I quickly darted past her, more willing to deal with whatever was under the train than with her vomit.

From the platform I saw blood and gore smeared on the front of the first car. There was no sign of the man on the tracks ahead. Obviously, he was under the train. Great!

Subways are powered by six hundred volts from a third rail, which runs parallel to the tracks. SEPTA (the Southeastern Pennsylvania Transportation Authority) had shut the power down, which we confirmed with a third-rail tester before crossing onto the tracks.

Brownie knelt and aimed his light along the length of the train. About three cars down, we saw a large lifeless mass. Shuffling sideways, between the train and the wall, we made our way to the victim. Blood and guts were everywhere. The man's head was nearly ripped from his body, literally hanging by a thread. One leg was severed above the knee, and the other was grotesquely twisted underneath his back. His torso had bloody gashes everywhere, and his left hand was missing.

Virtually all of his bones were crushed. As we lifted him onto the stretcher, his body felt like a massive lump of jelly. Fortunately, I was at the foot end and didn't have to contend with the dangling head. One of the guys gagged, but thankfully for me, he didn't throw up. We covered the gruesome remains with a yellow disposable blanket, passed them up to the platform, and continued searching for his hand and leg.

The leg was easy to find. The wheel of the train had crimped it so tightly that nary a drop of blood had oozed from it. The hand was more elusive. Crawling under any train would be scary for most people, but there I was, living one of my worst childhood fears. After twenty minutes of crawling underneath a subway train in a dimly lit tunnel while searching for a man's hand, I felt like I was about to scream. Suddenly somebody yelled, "Found it!" I scampered back to the security of the platform like a scared rabbit.

Hose testing was a spring ritual in the fire department. Each spring we'd charge our hose lines to 250 pounds per square inch and hold the pressure for ten minutes to see if they had survived the busy winter months.

APRIL 9, 1977—FIREFIGHTER, ENGINE 10

We were testing our bulky 3½" hose line in the parking lot next door. Half the line was done and ready to be restored as soon as we stripped the other half to make room. Just as we pulled the last length of the remaining line off, a police officer pulled up, rolled down his window, and said, "Why aren't you guys at the big fire?"

"What fire?" Brownie asked curiously.

The cop grinned and pointed to a massive cloud of black smoke obscuring the western sky. "Get the line back on, quick!"

"Box five-nine-eight-eight, Penrose and Lanier, Gulf refinery" blasted over the apparatus radio as we frantically hauled our hose back onto the bed.

"Chief only, first-in!" DeRose yelled from the station. With that amount of smoke, we knew that this was going to be an extra alarm, so we quickly piled the hose on without rhyme or reason. We were two-thirds complete when Chief Cowden simultaneously pulled the second and third alarms.

We screamed up Reed, looking like a ragtag outfit with our hose all disheveled, as we responded to the same box that had claimed eight of our brother firefighters less than two years earlier. This time the fire didn't involve a storage tank. Instead, a huge oil barge that had been docked by the refinery to off-load crude oil had exploded. The barge's captain had been aboard the vessel and was killed instantly.

Once on scene, we had to untangle, stretch, and connect our jumbled-up line to our Stang gun and protect nearby piping networks. It took us twice as long to get in service. Thankfully, no firefighters were injured in the six alarmer, but the odor of oil and protein foam brought back horrible memories.

Sadly, the barge fire wasn't the top story that day for Philadelphia firefighters. Firefighter Edward Smedley, from Ladder 28, suffered a massive heart attack while returning from a fire in Northeast Philadelphia. Overshadowed by the barge explosion, his LODD didn't even make the newspapers.

In mid-May we were dispatched, fourth-in, to a box alarm in a traffic-congested neighborhood. While other companies were hung up making turns, we quickly zipped by with Tac 10 and stole the fire. Yes! After we returned to the station, I found out that the lieutenant's examination would be held on June 25. It was crunch time. I followed the same rules I had for the entrance exam: study hard, take practice exams, get a good night's sleep, and eat a nice breakfast on test day.

There were five parts to the examination. Three of them were held that Saturday. The first was a tactical problem-solving exercise that had us write narrative responses to two challenging fire scenarios. The second was an administrative-skills exercise that focused on proper grammar and technical report writing. The main portion that day was a 125-question multiple-choice test.

I felt good about the examination, but so did everyone else I spoke with. The other two parts were out of our hands. Supervisors were required to complete a competitive performance evaluation for each candidate, and 10 percent of our final grade was allotted for seniority. With only four years on the job, I knew seniority wasn't my forte. I had my doubts that I'd succeed.

Chief Cowden thought otherwise. The following shift he called me into his office and told me that I was going to be Frankie Rag's backup aide. I was astonished because that position was usually reserved for senior firefighters.

"Listen, Bob," he said, "chances are you'll make lieutenant, and this will be great experience for you. You'll witness the dynamic conditions on the fireground firsthand. There's only so much you could learn from books." The experience proved worthwhile.

August 31, 1977—Firefighter, Engine 10, Detailed as Battalion 1's Aide

I caught my first working box as a chief's aide. At 7:29 a.m. we were dispatched to box four-one-two, Sixth and Mifflin Streets, for a dwelling fire. When we arrived, heavy fire was showing from the rear, and yellow-gray smoke was rolling over the heads of three people perched at the second-floor front windows.

It was really tough to resist the urge to jump out of the car to help pluck people from the windows or stretch hose lines, but chief's aides must remain in the car to communicate and keep track of things. Besides, there was plenty to do. The chief requested rescue units, utilities, and other resources. He also tactically placed companies and gave progress reports as fast as I could write them down. It was more hectic than I had imagined.

Cowden's orders were direct, concise, and methodical. There wasn't a hint of excitement in his tone, even though four people were injured and a ten-year-old girl died at the blaze. His calmness was contagious. The company officers didn't get nervous or agitated; neither did their firefighters. I thought that if I ever got promoted, I'd strive to be cool, calm, and collected on the fireground, like Chief Cowden.

Between observing Chief Cowden and listening to Mikey constantly remind me to "slow down before you kill yourself," I began to develop my composure on the fireground. "You can't think straight if you get excited," Cowden once told me. I always considered those lessons to be among the most important of my career.

On October 4, I was filling in for Frankie Rags again, and we responded to another fire fatality at Ninth and Spruce Streets. After the fire was under control, Cowden returned to the car, opened the back door, and began rummaging around as if he was looking for something. I asked if I could help, and he replied, "Yes. Help me find that black cat that gets in here every time you drive me. I've had two fire deaths the past couple of months, and you were my aide for both of them."

That fall, each lieutenant candidate's officer was called to the Municipal Services Building (MSB) to complete the performance-evaluation portion of the exam. It required them to place each member of their platoon in slots above or below five hypothetical firefighters, ranging from inferior to superior. To make it competitive, only one member was permitted in each slot. Categories ranged from firefighting to station duty. Since the evaluations were based on each test taker's assignments over the past twelve months, I was evaluated by both Sharpie and Brownie. With several lieutenants' vacancies anticipated, I was getting anxious for the results of the examination. But the cool, crisp fall meant more fires, which kept my mind occupied.

NOVEMBER 30, 1977—FIREFIGHTER, ENGINE 10

We responded first-in to a firebombing in my old Reed Street neighborhood. Vinny, my kindergarten playmate, once had lived in the house that we found fully involved. I had played in there as a young boy. As 10's tip man, I found it helpful to be familiar with its layout.

But the most interesting thing about this fire was the dim-witted arsonist who set the house ablaze. He had the correct house number but was on the wrong street—Mole instead of Hicks—where his intended target lived. Instead of tossing his Molotov cocktail through the window of someone he suspected of killing his friend, the moron set fire to the home of an innocent family watching television in their living room. Seven adults and one child suffered injuries.

I didn't know it at the time, but that was my last first-in fire as tip man. On Friday night, December 16, I was off duty getting dressed for a night of clubbing. The phone rang, and the voice on the other end said, "Hello, Robert? This is Commissioner Rizzo."

Certain that it was one of my buddies horsing around, I cockily replied, "Yeah, sure! And I'm General George Patton. Which idiot is this?"

After a brief pause, he insisted, "Robert, this *is* Commissioner Rizzo!"

Suddenly, I recognized his voice. "Holy shit! I just sassed the fire commissioner," I thought before apologizing.

"I'm sorry, Commissioner. I thought it was one of my friends clowning around."

"Ah, that's all right. I understand." He laughed. Whew!

"Robert, I'm calling to congratulate you. You finished number ten on the lieutenants' list and will be promoted on January ninth." I almost fell through the floor. I had never expected to place so high. Rizzo then gave me a short pep talk about being an effective leader and team player. Naturally I yes-sirred him to death.

Lumpy and Johnny, my study pals from 24's, also did well enough to get promoted with me. Buddy finished further back on the list but would be promoted before it expired two years later.

Until I was promoted, I was used around the battalion as an acting lieutenant. My first stop was Ladder 19, where I got to spend another Christmas Eve. For some odd reason, no Christmas carolers came around that night. The guys told me that they hadn't seen them since Christmas 1973.

Before my promotional physical exam, I gorked myself up with Valium so my PVCs wouldn't screw up my EKG. It worked. I spent my last night at the rank of firefighter back at 10's, where the guys threw me a nice farewell dinner. The next day I was promoted and reassigned.

CHAPTER 12

Loo

On January 9, 1978, a huge promotion ceremony was held in the Mayor's Reception Room at city hall. I raised my right hand and swore my oath alongside fifty-four other newly promoted lieutenants, twenty-six captains, seven battalion chiefs, one deputy chief, and one assistant chief. The place was jammed with family, friends, elected officials, dignitaries, and the media. Mayor Frank Rizzo, who began his career as a police officer, presided. Afterward he took time from his busy schedule to pose for photos with individual promotees and their families. It was a nice touch.

After the festivities we received our new ID cards, badges, and insignia. Then we were ushered into another room for our assignments. I was hoping to fill one of the vacancies in either West or Southwest Philly. It was wishful thinking. Joe Tiesi, who by then had become Rizzo's driver, spotted me in the crowd. "How would you feel about working in Center City?" he asked.

I wrinkled my nose. "I'd prefer to go west, Joe. Why?"

"Well," he said, smiling, "he"—meaning Rizzo—"wants you at Forty-Three's. He said that if you can handle it there, you can handle it anywhere."

"Is this a done deal, Joe?" I asked disappointedly. Joe nodded and pulled a copy of the transfers from his jacket pocket. There it was in black and white, "Firefighter Robert Marchisello, Engine 10/B transferred to Lieutenant, Engine 43/A." The commissioner wanted his disciple to work in one of Center City's spit-and-polish firehouses.

Blocks away from the Schuylkill River, Engine 43, Ladder 9, Battalion 5, and Rescue 7M's firehouse sat among rows of office buildings on Market Street. Surrounded by daunting high-rises, subways, underground trollies, expressways, tunnels, railroads, and commercial properties, 43's didn't respond first-in to many dwelling fires. Hence my disappointment. The companies I preferred to work were in low-income residential areas. That's where the fires were.

Engine 43 was busy, but it was a different kind of busy. High-rise and alarm-system investigations were common. Center City's large population, swelled by commuters, shoppers, and workers, added to 43's call volume, but most of those turned out to be minor incidents, recalls, and false alarms. Many of their actual fires were shit-work jobs on their periphery in South, West, and North Philly.

The limelight of Center City also meant cleaner apparatuses, pressed uniforms, shiny shoes, and a spotless firehouse. With the mayor, fire commissioner, and other high-ranking city officials frequenting the area, 43's officers had to ensure that things were always prim and proper. A firefighter standing outside with his shirt untucked might result in a scathing reprimand for his officer, along with a long memorandum of explanation.

Rescue 7M and its two paramedics per shift were assigned to 43's. Any EMS-related personnel issues, equipment malfunctions, civilian complaints, and controlled-drug issues were the responsibility of 43's officers. A bad day for the rescue often meant a bad day for 43's officer. Engine 43 was the paperwork capital, and I had virtually no typing experience.

But 43's also had its plus sides. The first-in fires to which they did respond were uniquely challenging. Fires in high-rises, sub-sub-subbasements, subways, large apartments, and commercial buildings are more difficult to fight than dwelling fires. Incidents involving underground transformers, steam lines, escalators, elevators, trapped window washers, and the like were much more probable in Center City. Additionally, 43's was one of three Squrt pumpers strategically located throughout the city. Our Squrt's fifty-four-foot articulating boom, with its attached master stream nozzle, was tactically advantageous at large fires. There were 136 extra-alarm fires in 1978, and 43's responded to most of them.

As the A Platoon's lieutenant, I was one of four shift supervisors. The captain and other two lieutenants worked the other shifts. In short order, I found out that Rizzo was right. If I could handle 43's, I'd be able to work anywhere.

January 10, 1978—Lieutenant, Engine 43

My first night as an officer wasn't exactly what I had expected. My first challenge was simply finding a parking spot. The handful of spaces in the lot behind the station were all occupied, so I had no alternative but to hop the high curb on tiny Ranstead Street and park illegally. That sucked!

Then, as I was carrying my gear to the pumper, a couple of firefighters sitting at the watch desk looked my way and said, "Hi, Loo." I did what I'd done a hundred times before. I turned and looked to find the lieutenant they were greeting. Nobody was there. *I* was "Loo." Red faced and embarrassed, I shrugged my shoulders and tried to make light of my faux pas. They giggled. Their first impression of me certainly wasn't very impressive. As I made my way to the office, I didn't recognize a soul on either the A or C Platoons chatting in the kitchen.

Connected by a common bathroom, the offices of Engine 43 and Ladder 9 had large windows with panoramic views of the apparatus floor. Years ago, during one of my details there, a firefighter jokingly had referred to the offices as guard towers. The officers, or guards, could easily watch their inmates while they worked. I'd never expected that one day I'd be one of the guards.

Lieutenant Esterwall of the C Platoon was banging away on the typewriter inside the small fifteen-foot by twenty-foot office crammed with desks, file cabinets, wall lockers, and a small bed. I cleared my throat, and he jumped up and shook my hand vigorously.

"You must be Bob. I'm not even going to try to pronounce your last name. I'm Fran." As fast as he popped up, he spun around and plopped back down into the typing chair. "I'll be done with this report in a second. It's my seventh of the day."

"Seven?" I thought. "The last fire report I did took me a half hour!" Amazed by how fast he was pecking away, I asked if he had taken typing lessons.

"Nah!" He laughed. "After a few months in this place, you'll be a master typist too."

With my OCD? I didn't think so.

A few seconds later, Fran zipped the report from the typewriter, signed it, and tossed it into the outgoing mail bin. "Welcome to Forty-Three's," he said as he spun around in the chair. "First of all, let me tell you that this place is a nuthouse. With that said, there's a few things pending tonight. This morning we found a dent in the side of Rescue Seven-M. Nobody's sure what platoon did it, so the chief wants each officer to interview their paramedics. I'm sure they won't admit to anything, but he wants detailed memos prepared for each interview. You'll also need to type the roster for your platoon, showing your transfer. It's nine parts precarboned, so be careful not to make mistakes. And one of your guys screwed up a fire report as acting lieutenant yesterday. The chief sent it back. It's so bad that it needs to be completely redone."

Great! I hadn't even started my shift, and I was already backed up with hours of paperwork.

"Is there anything else, Fran?" I asked cautiously.

He laughed again. "Nah, but something else will probably pop up. It always does in this damned place. I'm going to get a cup of coffee and head home."

I barely had time to change into my work uniform before the bells rang for roll call. It was time to meet my firefighters. They appeared to be a tight-knit and well-motivated mix. Riley was my senior man. Quick-witted and experienced, he was a backup aide to the assistant chief. I could tell at roll call that Russell, who had been hired the year before me, was the platoon's comedian. The others had less time. "Zee-Spud" got his nickname because his bushy black mustache, eyebrows, and black-rimmed glasses resembled Hasbro's Mr. Potato Head. "Hoagie Man" got his nickname after making too many trips to the deli up the block. Smitty was our newest firefighter, with less than a year out of Fire School, and they were still working on a nickname for him. Motorcycle-riding Bob Snead and his partner Richie B. were my fire paramedics in Rescue 7M.

After introducing myself, explaining my expectations, and laying down a few ground rules, I told them that my office door was always open. Then, since I had never been assigned to a Squrt, we immediately headed to the apparatus floor so they could give me a quick tutorial. The optimal Squrt position was called the cobra. The Squrt backed into position and raised the lower and upper booms so that the V pointed away from the fire. With the master stream nozzle perched on top, the setup resembled a cobra ready to strike.

The bells cut short my first lesson. "Engine, Ladder, and Chief, Twenty-Two Hundred Delancey Place, a fireplace!"

An accumulation of creosote had ignited in the chimney and was easily extinguished, but the call added another fire report to my list. As soon as we returned, I interviewed the paramedics about Rescue 7M's dent. Just as Esterwall had predicted, they imitated *Hogan's Heroes'* Sergeant Schultz: "I know nothing!"

I was wondering how to prepare *detailed* memos stating nothing, when the bells rang again. This time it was for a falsely pulled box at Nineteenth and Chestnut. "Good," I thought. "No fire report required."

My joy lasted for only a second. "Attention Engine Forty-Three, Twentieth and Market, a fuel spill." Yep! That run required another fire report.

The mounting paperwork was beginning to wreak havoc with my OCD. I was champing at the bit to get started, but when we returned to the station, dinner was ready. I felt it was important to bond with my guys, and firehouse dinner was a great way to do that. The reports, memos, and roster had to wait.

We chatted and joked around for an hour after dinner. Just as I was about to excuse myself, the bells rang again. This call, on which we were third-in, was for an odor investigation. It took nearly an hour to resolve. Engine 4 eventually found a burned-out fan motor on the twenty-fifth floor. Since we had been placed in service, another fire report was added to the pile.

It was after midnight when I typed my first keystroke. I pecked throughout the night. Interrupted by two more box alarms, I finally signed my last report five hours later. The trash can was filled with crumpled rosters, fire reports, and memos when I finished. Too wired to sleep, I browsed the Squrt operations manual while lying in my bunk. That did the trick. As I began to doze, I felt something under the pillow. It was a tampon. I'm not sure, but I think it had something to do with breaking my cherry as an officer. Funny, guys!

Satchmo, Ladder 9's lieutenant, had gotten promoted at the same time as I did. He also found a tampon under his pillow. The guys were trying for a laugh, so I figured I'd give them one. At roll call that morning, I stood before them and asked, "Did anybody lose their personal protective equipment last night?" As they were looking at each other quizzically, I slid the tampon out of my pocket and dangled it over my head. "Anyone?" They doubled up laughing.

On the ride home, I tried to convince myself that the mountain of paperwork was an anomaly. My return to the firehouse in less than ten hours would surely be less hectic. It had to be! I wanted to spend more time getting to know my guys and training with the Squrt. Naturally, it didn't turn out that way.

January 11, 1978—Lieutenant, Engine 43

My second shift at 43's began with another illegal hop-the-curb park job on Ranstead Street. Of course! Up in the office, Esterwall was pounding away at the keyboard again. Of course! I spread my thermal underwear on the bed, took off my shirt, and had just pulled my dress pants down to my knees when the bells rang. Of course! It was a gusty twenty-two degrees outside. Could anything else go wrong? Of course!

I quickly pulled up my pants. Then, in my rush to zip up, I yanked the pull right off my zipper. I made my way to the apparatus clad in a T-shirt and with my fly wide open, hoping not to freeze my balls off, literally.

Luckily, Engine 20 placed the fire under control, and we were quickly recalled. I cranked up the heat as we meandered through rush-hour traffic, returning to our firehouse. We were only a block away from my thermal underwear when, you guessed it, another box alarm. We turned around and went flying back down Market, third-in to a building fire.

It was no recall this time. Engine 4 had heavy smoke showing from a four-story commercial building and ordered all companies to go in service with 1¾" lines. We pulled next to a hydrant about a block away from the fire, stretched a few hundred feet of 2½" hose, and reduced it to 1¾". Fire was blowing out of the third-floor windows, but at street level, without my thermals, I was freezing. The frigid winds were going right through me.

The chief ordered us to make an interior attack on the third floor. Great! I actually couldn't wait to get inside the burning building to warm up. But halfway up the stairs, the chief ordered us back outside. The fire had gone through the roof, and he was shifting us to a defensive attack (fighting the fire from the outside, as opposed to an offensive attack, where the fire is fought from the inside). Crap!

The chief requested the second alarm, and this became the perfect fire to use the Squrt. But when I looked down the street, two unattended ladder trucks and two pumpers had us completely boxed in. To make things worse, we didn't carry a Stang gun for defensive firefighting. Our only master stream nozzle was mounted on our boom. It was time to improvise. I called for the biggest nozzle we had for our 2½" hose. It wasn't the best, but it sufficed. With a little extra pressure from Russell, our stream reached the fourth-floor windows. Zee-Spud, Smitty, and I were wrestling with our stream's heavy nozzle reaction, and we were getting soaked. That's when our deputy chief spotted us.

"What's this circus act, Lieutenant?" he growled. "Where's your Stang gun?"

I explained that we were a Squrt pumper and didn't carry one.

"Then why isn't your Squrt positioned here?"

"Chief," I stammered, "we arrived on the first alarm and were directed inside with our attack line. By the time we were ordered out, our pumper was boxed in."

He looked at our pumper, then back at me, then back at our pumper, and then back at me again. "Oh, okay. But don't let it happen again."

An hour later, Zee-Spud couldn't feel his feet. Fearing frostbite, we sent him to Hahnemann Hospital with Rescue 7M. The rest of us were encrusted in ice by the time we were released from the fireground. I was frozen to the bone, but luckily I hadn't gotten water in my boots like Zee-Spud did. By the time we returned to our station, it was after midnight. The clasps on my running coat were so frozen that I had to run hot water over them to unclasp them.

Once again, I typed through the wee hours of the morning. Zee-Spud's injury reports added to my fire report, a fire report graciously left behind by Esterwall, and two more fire reports we picked up after midnight. Finally, at 6:00 a.m., I checked under my pillow for tampons. It was clear. I climbed into bed and quickly dozed off. It seemed like a nanosecond later that I was startled by the fire phone. It was 7:10 a.m.

"Engine Forty-Three, Lieutenant Marchisello," I answered groggily.

A friendly voice on the other end cheerfully replied, "You sound like you just crawled from between the sheets, Lieutenant."

Thinking it was Lumpy breaking my stones, I cockily replied, "Well, I just did, and you woke me up, pal!"

Instead of chuckling as I had expected, the voice began screaming. "What the fuck are you doing in bed, Lieutenant? Don't you know the rules? You're supposed to be out of the rack by seven. Where the hell's Captain Ruff?" Suddenly, I was awake!

"Sorry, Chief, he's not in yet," I replied apologetically to one of the oncoming chiefs. It didn't soothe the beast.

"Have him call me the minute he gets the hell in!" *Click!*

Completely dejected, I sat there holding my head in my hands, wondering why I had tried so hard to get promoted.

Such was my introduction to the rank of lieutenant. Bob Ruff, 43's captain, walked in a few minutes afterward. When I told him that one of his chiefs had just blasted me and ordered me to have the captain call him immediately, he sloughed it off.

"Oh, don't worry about him. He's never happy unless he's yelling at somebody. Let's go have a cup of coffee. I'll call him later."

My new captain chuckled when I told him about my first two paper-work-laden shifts. "Bobby," he said reassuringly, "I promise, it's not always that bad. Don't worry about it." Ruff had an easygoing way that made me feel relaxed. I knew right away I had found a new mentor.

The following week all the newly promoted lieutenants were sent to Fire School for the department's officer's indoctrination program. Topics included supervision, administrative duties, fire investigation, form preparation, special operations, firefighting strategy, and company tactics. The instructors, most of them chiefs, delivered lectures enhanced by their real-life experiences.

During one presentation, Assistant Chief Miller, director of staff services, explained the different support units under his command. Then he told us that at some point during our careers, we'd all be required to fulfill staff positions. Everybody shuddered at the thought. Staff positions were nine-to-five jobs that didn't directly involve firefighting.

For me, the best thing about the course was that I got a chance to commiserate with my fellow promotees. I wasn't the only one whose first few shifts as an officer had been hectic. One lieutenant's firefighters had put diesel fuel into the tank of their gasoline-driven reserve pumper. When they started it, black smoke belched from its exhaust and stained the ceiling with soot. The pumper had to be towed to the shop. A good friend of mine had had to complete a ton of paperwork after his company, Engine 9, slid on an icy street and rear-ended Ladder 21. Another newbie had been yelled at because his station's apparatus doors were left open too long after their rescue unit got dispatched on a run, a violation of the department's energy-conservation directive. Misery loves company. I returned to 43's feeling somewhat better.

The hustle and bustle of Center City was still there. At 8:35 a.m. on my first day back, we were dispatched to a crash involving two underground trolleys. Sixty-six commuters suffered various injuries after one trolley smashed into the rear end of the other. A few injuries were serious, but many victims went to the hospital mainly because of the potential for huge settlements from SEPTA. The operation was labor intensive. Each patient had to be triaged, collared, placed on a backboard, and carried out of the lengthy dark tunnel.

For my dress uniform, I was using a tight-fitting borrowed blouse coat. My new one arrived just in time for another LODD funeral. On February 7, 1978, Ladder 3's firefighter John Brightcliffe (brother of Class 141's Bill Brightcliffe) was electrocuted as the thirty-five-foot ladder they were lowering came too close to a 13,200-volt transmission line. Even though I was off duty the night of his death, I wrote the following entry in my journal.

FEBRUARY 7, 1978—LIEUTENANT, ENGINE 43

Billy Brightcliffe's brother, John, died in the line of duty tonight. This job scares the shit out of me sometimes. And now I'm responsible for the lives of other firefighters! Please, God, help me make the right decisions on the fireground.

High-rise fires weren't as common as dwelling fires, but 43's responded to as many of them as any company in the city. My first as an officer came that February. It involved one apartment on the twenty-first floor. Had it been a dwelling fire, it would have been a piece of cake, but with no easy way to ventilate a high-rise, it was an ass-kicker. We connected to the standpipe (a vertical water pipe with outlets on each floor) and crawled nearly a hundred feet through the heat and blinding smoke just to find the burning apartment. When Ladder 9 forced the door, the heat that rushed into the hallway made it feel as if we were in hell. The water from our attack line quickly turned to steam, which had nowhere to go. My ears got scalded, and they were red for weeks afterward.

Runs to high-rise buildings weren't always for fires. Operations involved many things: alarm systems, odors, power outages, and suicidal jumpers. Strange things often happened in the high-rises of Center City.

MARCH 7, 1978—LIEUTENANT, ENGINE 43

At 3:54 a.m. we responded to Nineteenth and Spruce for a reported high-rise fire with people jumping out the windows. The fire alarm was blaring, and the crowd gathered in the street was pointing at a light haze showing from the sixth-floor window. A young woman was screaming that she had seen a man jump out and land on the roof of the building next door. We grabbed our high-rise equipment and made our way up the fire tower as Ladder 9 raised their main ladder to the roof next door. We connected to the sixth-floor standpipe, stretched down the hall, and felt the door. Amazingly, it was cool.

We slowly pushed the door open to reveal nothing more than a light haze inside. The haze smelled familiar; it was the smell of dry powder from a fire extinguisher. It turned out that as a college prank, an art student had discharged an extinguisher under the door of his classmate's room, pulled the fire alarm, and yelled, "Fire!" The joke backfired. His classmate, fearing that he was trapped, panicked and jumped out the window. He landed three floors below, suffering numerous injuries. Ladder 9 lowered the victim in a wire basket while the hapless prankster watched from the back seat of a police car.

It didn't take long to get a few extra-alarm fires under my belt as a Squrt company officer. To deploy our boom properly, we needed to get close to the fire. Captain Ruff had advised me to ask for a position for the Squrt as soon as we were dispatched. It usually worked well. Most chiefs would clear a path and have a water supply waiting for us when we arrived. But some chiefs disagreed about the best way to use their relatively new toy. Sometimes higher-ranking chiefs trumped the orders of lower chiefs and moved us to different locations. That meant disconnecting everything, repositioning our Squrt, and connecting everything together again. Not only was it a pain in the ass, but it never seemed to make any difference with the fire. At one fire we were relocated twice. The deputy chief didn't like where the battalion chief had placed us, so he moved us to the other side of the building. Then his boss, the assistant chief, didn't like where the deputy chief had us positioned, and he moved us again. It was getting old! I devised a plan for our next extra-alarm fire.

MARCH 24, 1978—LIEUTENANT, ENGINE 43

The delectable aroma of roast beef filled the kitchen. Dinner was ready. But just as I grabbed a plate from the stack on the table, 16's requested a second alarm in West Philly. Ugh! There was no doubt that we were going, so we zipped to the apparatus floor way before the dispatch was announced.

As soon as our front wheels hit Market Street, I requested a position for the Squrt. Battalion 11's aide relayed orders from the chief. "Set up on the south side of the fire and protect a row of exposed dwellings." The south side was a wall of flames when we arrived. We backed in, connected to a hydrant, and raised our boom into the classic cobra position. By the time we were set up, the fire was at four alarms, and Commissioner Rizzo was on scene giving orders over the radio.

In short order, our wide fog pattern was cooling the exposures. After they were well soaked, we began alternating our stream from cooling the exposures to knocking down the flames. The tactic worked nicely. The fire on the south side quickly subsided. All of a sudden, a deputy chief came strolling around to our side. He looked from our stream to me. "Who the fuck told you to put the Squrt here, Lieutenant?" he yelled. I was ready for him.

"Commissioner Rizzo, chief."

He looked back at our stream. "Oh! Nice stream. Which way did he go?"

I pointed west. The deputy chief turned and briskly walked eastward. It had worked. Yeah!

Lying was risky. But Rizzo was autocratic on the firegrounds. I figured that the other chiefs would never challenge me if I said we were following the commissioner's orders. I was right, and I employed the same ruse a few times afterward. It always worked.

That spring I received my associate's degree in fire science. But instead of pursuing a four-year degree in the same field, I went back to Temple University to resume my studies for a bachelor's degree in mechanical engineering. Still worried about my PVCs, I wanted a good plan B. The fireground is a dangerous place. I'd seen far too many firefighters suffer career-ending injuries. A few close calls convinced me that I had made the right decision.

April 18, 1978—Lieutenant, Engine 43

I thought we were goners. We had just stretched our line through the rear door when a thunderous crash rained heavy debris on our heads. It seemed like the entire place was coming down. Luckily, it was only waterlogged drywall from 24's fire attack. My visor split in half again, and my neck was stiff. Thankfully, none of my men were injured.

June 4, 1978—Lieutenant, Engine 43

Another close call. At 4:01 a.m. we responded fourth-in, to Thirty-Eighth and Girard. We were advancing our attack line toward the rear second floor when a horrendous collapse occurred directly ahead of us. Another minute and we'd have been crushed under the third floor. Fortunately, no firefighters were seriously injured by the partial collapse. Five people perished in the two-alarm blaze—three adults and two children.

Firefighters understand and accept the dangers of firefighting. It's our job. When I swore my oath, I never imagined that those dangers might include what occurred on a warm humid morning later that summer.

CHAPTER 13

Shootout

I first heard about the radical group MOVE in late 1977. Engine 10's kitchen was packed with firefighters waiting for Brownie to ring the six o'clock bells for shift change, and as usual, bantering filled the small, overcrowded room. Ladder 11's comedian, Phil, was reading the *Philadelphia Daily News* and firing off jabs between each article. Anybody could be the target of Phil's humor, so I made sure to sit behind him. Out of sight, out of mind. It worked.

The kitchen roared after each of Phil's hilarious slap shots. Even the people he made fun of couldn't help but laugh at themselves. Phil turned the page, glanced at another article, then scanned for his next victim. His eyes locked on Bob, the only black guy in the kitchen.

"Yo, Bob!" he shouted. Bob's eyes got wide as saucers when he realized he was in Phil's crosshairs. Pounding his finger on the paper, Phil yelled, "Your brother John is saying that you should join his movement! He says all blacks are his brothers, and they should join as soon as possible."

Good-natured Bob smiled. "Okay, I'll bite. John who? And what movement should I join?"

Phil retorted, "Well, Bob, his name is John Africa, and the movement is called MOVE. All you need to do is change your last name to Africa. Bob giggled.

Phil scanned the article again. "Oh, oh, wait a minute, Bob. I don't think you'll qualify after all," Phil said as he lifted up the paper and pointed to a MOVE member's photo. "You have to let your hair grow into natural dreadlocks, and I don't think Brownie will be too wild about that!" Everybody knew about Brownie's strict enforcement of Rizzo's military hairstyle regulations. The kitchen exploded again.

Brownie was by the watch desk when he heard his name followed by all the laughter. His barometer turned bright crimson, and he rang the bells a few minutes early.

DeRose looked at Phil. "I guess you got us an early out again." We were giggling as we lined up for roll call.

MOVE was a radical countercultural group. Their communal head-quarters was in a pair of old run-down Victorian brick twin homes at 307–9 North Thirty-Third Street, in the Powelton Village section of West Philadelphia. Vincent Leaphart, alias John Africa, founded MOVE in 1971, and all the members adopted the same surname, Africa. They sported long dreadlocks, and their back-to-nature way of life opposed science, medicine, technology, and most of all government. In their backyards, they processed human waste and garbage into compost, creating foul odors that attracted rats, mice, and roaches. Because of their support for animal rights, they claimed that it was morally wrong to exterminate the vermin attracted to their filth. Frustrated neighbors were subjected to profanity-laced rhetoric loudly voiced over bullhorns all hours of the day and night. Those who complained were threatened with physical violence.

Despite the threats, neighbors constantly complained to city hall about the vermin, rotting garbage, fecal odors, and the loud, incessant, inconsiderate messages. They also reported that on several occasions, they were physically threatened and that MOVE members had brandished weapons. These unlawful actions and a refusal to comply with Health Department and Department of Licenses and Inspection's regulations brought close scrutiny from the Philadelphia Police Department. MOVE refused to either conform or leave the premises.

In March of 1978, Mayor Frank Rizzo ordered a starvation blockade that included metal barricades, police security, and a shut-off water supply. In the event of a fire or other emergency, the plan called for the fire department to provide a fully staffed engine company twenty-four hours a day. Twice I was detailed as the officer in charge of that engine. Both times, MOVE greeted us with barrages of profanity and insults.

The first time, a MOVE member quickly recognized me as the officer. "Hey, motherfucker in the white shirt," he yelled through his bullhorn. "You must be the lieutenant, huh? You too young to be a chief, man. Listen, you shouldn't be helpin' these damned cops, man. You firemen's supposed to be good guys, not evil fuckers like them pigs." I ignored him, but the insults were unsettling. They lasted until he found his next victim, a young police officer he began calling a teenage pig.

The second time I was there, one of the men assigned with us was a friendly, soft-spoken black firefighter with a tremendous firefighting reputation. As soon as a MOVE member spotted him, he began an obscenity-laden verbal assault. He was relentless, calling him every slanderous name you could imagine. He even cranked up the volume on his amplifier and told the firefighter that he was a traitor and a disgrace to the black community. It was a warm spring evening, and everyone, including many curious black neighbors, looked to see who the object of MOVE's rage was.

The courageous firefighter just sat on the back of the pumper, pretending not to hear the rant. Twice I told him that he could go around the corner, but he refused. "No, Loo, screw him. He's not going to get my goat." Finally, *I* had had enough. I ordered the entire company to take a break and get something to drink at a nearby grocery store. I didn't allow anyone to return to the pumper until the cover of darkness was on our side.

Later that night, it was time for a little revenge. MOVE harbored a large number of stray dogs in their compound. Around three o'clock in the morning, things became still, and MOVE was sound asleep. I began barking like a dog, which woke up the real dogs, who began barking back. When the dogs got quiet, a cop on the other side barked a few times, and the dogs went crazy again. Between the cops and firefighters on the detail, we kept the dogs and the MOVE members up all night. Revenge is sweet!

When we weren't in MOVE's crosshairs, the details could be very amusing. We would sit on our pumper and enjoy the show as MOVE sympathizers probed the police line for weak spots so they could attempt to sneak food, water, or other supplies into the perimeter. Sometimes police officers would spot them and give chase. We saw one guy, dressed in a business suit, walk nonchalantly toward the barricade. Before police could react, he quickly pulled a small care package from under his jacket and lobbed it inside the compound. The startled police gave chase, and he ran. As the MOVE members scrambled to retrieve the goodies, the guy abruptly changed direction and headed directly toward us. When he got close, we jumped off to block his path. He went into a wide-eyed, wing-tip-induced skid while trying to make an abrupt ninety-degree turn. His cartoonlike movements were hilarious. Police apprehended him a block away. Before the night was done, there were two more tosses. We called them Berlin airlift missions.

Occasionally, rats would dart from the barricades or from underneath police vehicles, and we'd laugh our asses off as startled firefighters and heavily armed officers scampered away like frightened little girls.

The unsuccessful two-month starvation blockade lasted from March 16 to May 8. In a ten-point court order, the Philadelphia District Attorney agreed to drop all charges against MOVE. The city would provide food and water for the children if the group would agree to evacuate the compound within ninety days. By August 3, MOVE hadn't budged. A Philadelphia Common Pleas Court judge ruled that MOVE had violated the deadline and issued warrants for twenty-one adults. He then set a ten-day arrest deadline, which was set to expire on August 12.

August 8, 1978—Lieutenant, Engine 43

It was warm and muggy when I reported for my shift. Nothing was hanging or pending in the office. Believe it or not, Esterwall wasn't sitting at the typewriter. Wow!

At nine o'clock we were dispatched with Ladder 9, Battalion 5, and Rescue 7M to Van Pelt and Pine for an automobile accident. As we were cleaning up the spilled antifreeze and gasoline, Snead told me that the driver had refused to go to the hospital and that they were returning to service. Then he added, "Oh, by the way, Loo, a cop told me that they're going to evict MOVE around six o'clock this morning."

"Again?" I guffawed. "It's probably just another dry run."

Bob smiled. "Yeah, you're probably right. But he seemed to think it was real this time."

A week earlier, at five o'clock in the morning, police requested us to proceed to the compound to stand by as they evicted MOVE. We waited until almost eight o'clock before learning it was a dry run.

When we returned from the accident, I went upstairs to see if Chief Hoeffel (Battalion 5 on our platoon) had heard anything regarding MOVE. His door was closed, so I decided not to bother him. We got two more box runs shortly after midnight, but each time Hoeffel beat us back to the station. Surely if he knew anything, he'd have told us.

At 4:30 a.m. the entire station responded to another box alarm, at Twenty-First and Walnut. After we reset the falsely pulled box and returned to the station, Chief Hoeffel was sitting in my office. "Bobby, I just got a call from Deputy One. The entire first alarm is to meet at MOVE again, five o'clock, no lights or sirens. Rescue Seven-M goes too. You're fourth-in, right?"

"Yep. We're fourth-in, chief. Just like last week." I giggled. "I guess we'll see you back here for coffee at eight."

At 4:45 a.m. Russell steered our Squrt west onto Market Street. "Attack at dawn, just like Pearl Harbor!" he joked. I was convinced this was just another dry run as we followed Rescue 7M through the deserted streets of West Philadelphia. But when we hit Powelton, we realized that this was the real deal. It was a beehive of activity. Already on the scene were hundreds of police officers, city officials, emergency communications vans, the police stakeout team (SWAT), a police armored vehicle, a bulldozer, a demolition crane, and SPCA trucks.

I looked at Russell and remarked, "Banzai! Today is the day that will live in infamy!"

The assistant chief was at the corner, directing fire-department apparatuses into preplanned positions. He had his game face on. "What do you need from Forty-Three's, Chief?" I asked as we pulled up.

He briefly looked up from his clipboard. "Listen, Lieutenant. Take the green top hydrant on Thirty-Fourth and stretch a three-and-a-half down Pearl to the Giant Deluge Gun. Don't hook up, but bring your three-way" (a connection used to supply three two-and-a-half-inch hoses from a three-and-a-half-inch hose). "Be on the F-four band. Got it?"

"No problem, Chief." I nodded before signaling Russell to proceed.

The Giant Deluge Gun is an old fire truck that's been around since the fifties. It has a huge water cannon mounted behind its cab. Arthur and

I once saw it used at a six-alarm warehouse fire. Capable of discharging twenty-five hundred gallons per minute, it was positioned on Pearl Street, west of Thirty-Third, with its massive gun aimed directly at MOVE's basement windows. If needed, we were one of three engines ready to supply the thirsty beast with water. We had our line stretched within minutes.

The MOVE members, fully aware of the impending attack, shattered the quiet with their bullhorn. "You're a bunch of murderers and baby killers! Fuck you all!" Barking dogs accompanied Delbert's opening rant like a group of tuneless background singers.

When they learned of the judge's order, MOVE had fortified the front of their structure with a decrepit wooden fence. Unlike the times I had been there before, the compound looked like a medieval fort, completely out of place in the neighborhood. As we stood by the Giant Deluge, the first purplish shades of dawn rose behind the compound. The outline of the twin MOVE houses looked eerie, as if it was a forewarning of bad things to come. It was a premonition I'll never forget.

At 5:45 a.m. the air grew tense as a sandbagged garbage truck rolled in front of the compound. A plainclothes officer, using it as a shield, read MOVE its official notice through a bullhorn: "We have in our possession writs of attachments and bench warrants for occupants of Three Oh Seven to Oh Nine North Thirty-Third Street, issued on August second, nineteen seventy-eight, which has ordered the police to take you into custody. Each of you is ordered to surrender immediately. Leave your weapons, and come out with your hands over your head. You have three minutes to walk to the street."

A male MOVE member bullhorned his response: "Long live John Africa."

Several minutes went by. The plainclothes officer spoke again. "You have not surrendered. We are proceeding to tear down the fence." A bulldozer, driven by a uniformed policeman behind a protective shield, rumbled up Thirty-Third and crumbled the fence to the ground. Startled rats, some as big as cats, scampered everywhere. We laughed as reporters, cops, and city officials scurried away in a panic.

After the rats came the dogs. Lots of dogs. The scene went from tense to hysterical as animal-control officers armed with nets chased after them.

The elusive canines kept the dogcatchers busy and provided entertainment for the police and firefighters. One black-and-white spotted mongrel in particular was stealing the show. After a lengthy chase, three dogcatchers finally cornered him. The dog darted around in circles as each of them futilely swung his net and missed. The mongrel broke free and scampered up Thirty-Third as the exhausted dogcatchers bent over trying to catch their breath. In the background another SPCA worker darted past, chasing a mangy cat with a big net. It was like a scene from *The Three Stooges*, and we couldn't help but laugh.

After the animal situation was under control, Monsignor Devlin from the Philadelphia Roman Catholic Archdiocese's Commission on Human Relations pleaded with MOVE to comply with the judge's order and exit peacefully. The bullhorn blared in return, "You bastard! You ain't no fuckin' priest. We'll never give up." The priest pleaded for them to send the children out. It prompted more curses from the bullhorns.

Next, a large crane, with "Little Giant" written across its boom, maneuvered into position. Police extended the crane and broke all the windows within range. The MOVE members called the cops names and made feeble attempts to throw pieces of window casing at them. Then the plainclothes officer told MOVE that uniformed police were going to enter the house to arrest them and would use force if necessary. Through the shattered windows, we saw several MOVE members scamper down the basement steps. Two dozen police officers from stakeout cautiously entered the house. It was nearly seven o'clock. We'd been there two hours.

Like most police and firefighters, I believed that MOVE would surrender without incident. It was only a matter of time. As police officers searched the floors above the basement, a casual air developed outside. Many officers had been on the MOVE case for years and put little credence into the group's threats of violence. The attitude spread quickly as police, firefighters, and other officials casually strolled in front of the compound without fear. If MOVE had planned to do anything drastic, everyone thought, it would have already happened. Even our assistant chief moved his command post forward, directly across the street from the compound.

Riley, who was a backup aide for the assistant chief, asked if he could go shoot the breeze with the chief. Curious to find out how the plan was proceeding, I tagged along. The chief was standing among a throng of police officers.

As we neared, a big smile wiped away his game face. "Riley, I didn't realize you were here." He gave me a quick once-over. "Lieutenant." Well, at least he acknowledged me.

As the chief moved away to talk on his radio, I noticed two police officers standing a few feet away. One of them was teasing the other about his baseball cap. "Yo, Ramp, that cap's not part of our uniform." I smiled and tipped my helmet at them. Ramp tipped his cap back, and they laughed.

Behind us, I overheard the chief talking. Police had decided to try to flood MOVE out. Instead of the Giant Deluge, they wanted an engine company inside to pour water into a hole, while others aimed their streams into the basement from outside. After the chief ordered a ladder company to cut a hole in the floor over the basement, I jumped at the opportunity.

"Chief, Forty-Three's will gladly take the inside," I offered, wanting a more meaningful role.

He smiled in approval. "Okay, Lieutenant. Stretch from your three-way. Make sure you take at least twenty-five feet of line inside and keep the pressure low. We don't want to hurt any kids. Don't forget—be on the F-four band."

As we walked back to our crew, Riley chuckled. "See, Loo. Just a little chitchat, and we got a decent assignment."

"You're right," I replied. "It certainly pays to know people who know people."

This was a nationally publicized event, and I was glad we had a major role. Everybody was enthusiastic as I reviewed our plan. Russell would stay with the pumper and supply us water. Hoagie Man was to stand by at the three-way and charge the line when we were ready. Riley, Smitty, and I would go inside with the hose. I clapped my hands like a quarterback breaking out of a huddle. "Let's get it done!"

As Ladder 6's K-12 saw buzzed in the background, we flaked our hose outside. Riley threw the nozzle and a few folds of hose over his shoulder.

"I'm ready to go, Loo." I nodded, and we headed toward the front door. All of a sudden, things got very tense and quiet. Approximately fifty police and firefighters, with rifles, pistols, and nozzles aimed at the basement, took cover in front of the building. As we stepped inside, it felt as if we were advancing into an enemy bunker.

The first thing to hit me was the putrid stench. The odor of roaches, feces, and urine overpowered the exhaust fumes lingering from the K-12. The place was a filthy mess. An old dilapidated sofa blended well with the tattered trash bags strewn about the living room. The only thing that looked neat and orderly was the perfectly square hole cut by Ladder 6. About a half dozen police officers with weapons drawn lined the back wall. I felt both reassured and unnerved at the same time.

"Battalion Eleven to Engine Forty-Three, charge your line." I nodded to Smitty, who gave Hoagie Man the thumbs-up. Within seconds, our hose swelled with water. Our line was charged, or more appropriately, we were locked and loaded.

Outside, a police officer gave MOVE their final warning. "We are going to pump water into the premises that you now occupy." A few seconds later, we got the order. I peered into the hole to make sure no one was directly below; then we opened our nozzle. Over the splashing we heard male voices cursing us from the basement. My engineering-oriented mind was calculating how long it should take to fill the basement when we were abruptly ordered to shut down. Only three minutes had elapsed. I was hoping that MOVE had opted to surrender, but I was wrong. Monsignor Devlin's voice came over the bullhorn once again, imploring MOVE to send out the children before the hoses were turned back on.

"Fuck you! Leave us alone!" came the reply.

Several minutes passed as we knelt by the hole. Things got eerily quiet again as we waited for the order to resume. A few feet from the hole, I spotted a partially rolled-up scroll. Written in large print on the top line was, "This is the house that John Africa built."

As I reached for it, one of the officers lining the wall screamed, "Hey! Drop that!" Startled and offended, I glared back at him, but his eyes weren't focused on me; he was staring straight down the hole.

"Hey!" he said insistently. "Drop that carbine! Drop that carbine!"

Pop! Pop! Pop! Three rapid shots came from the basement. *Pop! Pop! Pop!* Three more. Then all hell broke loose. Ferocious gunfire erupted between MOVE and the officers outside returning fire. I felt like we were in the middle of the OK Corral. The smell of gunpowder quickly overpowered the putrid stench. We rapidly retreated from the hole and flattened ourselves against a nearby wall. It was just in time. Bullets tore through the floorboards where we had been kneeling. Plaster fell from the ceiling as the shots continued skyward. MOVE was trying to kill us! Over the din of gunfire, an electronic siren added to the chaos outside.

Suddenly, the officers on the other wall began screaming, "Hands up! Put your fucking hands up, now!" A few dripping-wet MOVE women and children froze in fear at the top of the basement stairs. One of the officers used his body as a shield and miraculously escorted them safely outside while the gunfire still raged. It was one of many heroic acts that morning.

I feared that we might get hit by errant police bullets as well as those from MOVE. But for the moment, we seemed to be safe where we were. My decision was simple: stay put until the gunfire was over. At least that was the plan. Then the police decided to lob several canisters of tear gas into the building. I don't know if it reached the basement, but it certainly filled the first floor. I regretted that we weren't wearing air packs, but who could have predicted this? Our eyes quickly swelled, and mucus poured down our faces. When you're exposed to tear gas, only one thing goes through your mind. Get the hell out! It was time for another decision.

Through the haze of tear gas, I saw a glimmer of light shining from a window on Pearl Street. The gunfire was subsiding somewhat, so it was time to enact plan B. I gave the order to bail out. Should the officer lead his men into unknown danger, or should he be the last to leave the danger inside? In this case, I decided to lead the way and jumped first. The four-foot drop was more than I had predicted. I landed with a thud but was uninjured. A police officer quickly swung his revolver in my direction. I curled up, waiting to be shot.

"Hold your fire! It's a fireman!" another officer screamed.

Whew! I quickly rolled away to give Smitty and Riley safe landing spots. Smitty hit the ground and rolled toward me. A second later there was another thump as Riley crashed to the ground.

Everybody was out. "Let's go!" I yelled. As gunshots echoed in the air, we sprinted east on Pearl Street and ducked for cover behind a set of steps several doors down. "Is everybody okay?" I asked.

"Where's Riley?" cried Smitty.

Oh no! We were missing Riley! I peered over the top of the steps, and there he was, lying on the ground right where he had landed. He tried to get up but fell back down.

"Oh God, he's shot?" I exclaimed. "Let's go!" We ran back, grabbed him under his arms, and dragged him down Pearl Street. It seemed like an eternity as more shots rang out, but we finally reached the safety of the steps again. Worried sick, we propped him against the wall and began checking for wounds.

"Riley, where are you shot?" I cried.

Riley looked at me pathetically and winced. "No, Loo, it's my damned ankle. I think I broke it when I landed."

I was totally relieved. "Your ankle? It's only your ankle?"

He replied with a wry smile, "Yeah, my ankle, Loo. That was a heck of a drop. How friggin' high did you make us jump from?" Suddenly we began laughing hysterically. I don't know if it was Riley's dry humor, the relief of having survived the awful shootout, or a combination of both, but we couldn't stop.

A police officer braved his way to our position. "Are you guys okay?" We were laughing so hard that we couldn't answer. Aiming his revolver at the compound, he shook his head and said, "What the hell did they use in there? Laughing gas?" We laughed even harder.

After the gunfire ended, paramedics placed an air splint on Riley's ankle, and we wheeled him to the rescue. He was still giggling and gave us a thumbs-up as we lifted him into the back for a trip to Presbyterian Hospital.

As we made our way back to our pumper, police were arresting several suspects. They were dragging one of them out of the compound by his dreadlocks. Smitty shouted, "Good! That son of a bitch tried to kill us." I felt the same rage but managed to remain silent.

Hoagie Man and Russell were unharmed, thank God! Several others weren't so lucky. One police officer, James J. Ramp, the officer who had been teased about his baseball cap, had been shot and killed. Seven other police officers, five firefighters, three MOVE members, and three bystanders were injured during the melee. The siren we'd heard was from a police armored vehicle brought forward for cover as the wounded were being rescued.

I feel that we cheated death twice. If we hadn't gone inside, we might have still been standing near where Ramp was killed. If we hadn't retreated from the hole so quickly, they certainly would have shot us through the floorboards. Amen.

In addition to Riley, firefighters Bob Lentine, John Welsh, and Dennis O'Neill were injured while operating exterior hose lines. Fire paramedic Bob Snead of Rescue 7M was blasted in the face with buckshot as he pulled wounded Police Officer Charles Stewart to safety. Stewart, shot in the leg and shoulder, had fallen next to Officer Ramp. In a true act of courage under fire, Snead shook off the blast and continued dragging Stewart away from the gunfire. Snead didn't seek treatment for his own injury until all the injured had been tended to. It was only then that he agreed to go to the hospital himself.

A few weeks later, I was summoned to the Philadelphia Police Administration Building to be interviewed by detectives. They took statements regarding 43's actions that morning and asked for my perspective of events as they had occurred. Then they showed several different videos of the firefight. Snead's heroic actions were clearly visible. The blast violently rocked his head, but he didn't pause in his rescue attempt. It was a truly amazing act of heroism.

Upon my return to the firehouse, I prepared a memorandum detailing Snead's actions and put him in for the department's highest award, Heroism. It was approved by Chief Hoeffel and forwarded through channels.

But nobody ever received any awards from the city. When I later inquired about the status of Snead's award, I was told that Mayor Rizzo didn't want the media to pounce on any accolades associated with the tragic events of that day. Rizzo had been severely criticized by the press for quickly razing the compound with a wrecking ball and bulldozers before evidence could be collected. In return, Rizzo slammed the press for glorifying MOVE and said that the incident was partially their fault.

I was pissed that Snead's actions were getting brushed aside because of politics. I tried to push the issue a few times but was rebutted by several chief officers. In a nutshell, I found out how true the saying is that "you can't fight city hall." Months later, the Fraternal Order of Police (FOP), Lodge 5, held a ceremony recognizing the five firefighters injured during the skirmish and awarded them plaques. Many police officers gathered around Snead and thanked him personally. It's a shame that Snead received more attention from the FOP than from the Philadelphia Fire Department. Nobody ranking higher than Hoeffel ever officially recognized his heroics.

Before the compound was destroyed, police removed fifteen weapons, including two sawed-off twelve-gauge shotguns, three .30-caliber carbines, and several handguns. Nine MOVE members, known as the MOVE nine, were charged with Ramp's killing, and in 1980 they were found guilty of third-degree murder during a rancorous, circus-like trial. One MOVE member, tried separately from the others, was acquitted of murder charges.

CHAPTER 14

Whoosh! Whomp! Whomp! Off to Staff

Things quickly returned to normal after the MOVE shootout. In September we responded second-in to a fire at the Fifteenth Street stop of the Market-Frankford Line subway. Heavy black smoke was pouring from every stairwell and ventilator upon our arrival. Visibility was zero as we crawled down two levels to combat a huge newspaper-stand fire. Somewhere in the darkness, we heard a loud crash. It was Satchmo slamming onto the tracks. While trying to find the paper stand, he had fallen from the platform. Satchmo's injuries were only minor. Thank goodness he didn't hit the third rail. After the fire was out, Hoeffel asked SEPTA to run a few trains through the tunnel at high speeds. They cleared the smoke instantly. It was a nice tactic to remember.

During our lieutenant's indoctrination course, the chief fire marshal had told us that they were looking for a few company officers to be trained as backup fire investigators. Each platoon had six backups that could be activated whenever the full-time investigators were committed to other investigations. The training sounded interesting, so I applied. That October I was accepted and detailed to the fire marshal's office (FMO) for a month. Some of the training was formal, but most of it was practical and involved riding with different investigators each day. It was a great learning experience. After my training I was placed on the FMO's backup list.

Back at 43's, it seemed as though there was always something new going on. That fall the department hosted two Venezuelan firefighters who wanted to learn Squrt operations. For two weeks they responded with us to extra alarms. Of course, they didn't speak a word of English. A few guys understood a little Spanish and tried to converse with them, but mostly they just stood there and nodded. That was good because I didn't want my "Rizzo placed us here" ploy to spread internationally.

Speaking of Rizzo, he was always in the neighborhood. One chilly day, luckily on another platoon, Rescue 7M made a run, but nobody bothered to close the overhead doors. Uh-oh, that was a violation! A veteran firefighter was on watch when the commissioner pulled onto the apron. The veteran hurried the new guy out to shut the doors, but Rizzo stopped him in his tracks. "Where the hell do you think this heat comes from?" he growled to the rookie.

The new guy naïvely pointed at the ceiling heaters. "From up there, Commissioner." Rizzo went ballistic. He lined everybody up, and lectured about energy conservation for fifteen minutes. After hearing the story, I became a door Nazi.

On January 26, 1979, I was clubbing at Franny O'Brien's. I was fairly well buzzed when a raven-haired beauty passed by our table. I tapped her on her shoulder and told her that she was the prettiest girl who had ever come in the place. She glanced back with a beautiful smile but kept walking. After a few more glasses of scotch and water, I couldn't remember my own name, but when she passed a second time, I definitely remembered her. I tapped her shoulder again. "I meant what I said, and I've been coming here over four years." Luckily for me, her girlfriend struck up a conversation with my pal, and we began talking. She was as charming as she was pretty. I was trying my best not to slur my words. We chatted until closing time. I asked for her phone number, wrote it on a napkin, and placed four stars next to her name, Diane.

At seven o'clock the following morning, I pulled up Ranstead Street and parked on the pavement once again. From my car, I saw a pair of legs dangling from the Salvation Army's clothing drop bin near Twenty-Second Street. I curiously walked up to the motionless legs, hoping that it wasn't the aftermath of a mob hit. I rapped on the bin, and a blood-curdling scream came from inside.

"Help! I've been stuck in here all night. Get me out!" It was a homeless man who had gotten stuck while rummaging for clothing. I tried to pull him out but couldn't get enough leverage. I told him to stay put while I got help. He cried back, "Where the hell do you think I'm going to go?" It was a cheap run for Ladder 9, who got him out within minutes.

The next week I called Diane and asked her for a date. I couldn't remember what she looked like, but I knew that four stars meant that she must be hot. I'd been fooled by alcohol before, so I was unsure what to expect when I knocked on her door. She was even prettier than I remembered. I wiped my brow. "Whew!" After our first date, I knew that she was the one.

As usual, the winter months brought plenty of extra-alarm fires. On February 21, 1979, we responded on the second alarm to a gas explosion with a resulting building fire at Thirty-First and Jefferson. As we turned onto Thirty-First, a brilliant flash and a huge *whoosh* violently rattled the cab of our pumper. It scared the crap out of me! I looked up and saw bricks flying through the air. A second explosion had blown the building apart, injuring three firefighters from the first alarm. We had to back the Squrt over tons of bricks and other debris to get into the cobra position. I spotted a deputy chief heading directly toward us, but he made an abrupt turn when he saw Commissioner Rizzo standing a few feet away. I didn't need to use my ruse that time. Ha!

At 12:30 a.m. on March 27, we responded, fourth-in, to a hotel fire at Fifteenth and Catherine. As we were stretching our attack line to the door, I heard a sickening *whomp!* One of the hotel's tenants had jumped from the third floor, barely missing us. Paramedics quickly rushed to his aid as we advanced our attack line inside.

With a year's experience as an officer under my belt, I was getting more comfortable in my new position—that is, until I was abruptly ordered to report to headquarters. Gulp! Had Rizzo learned of my ruse?

April 2, 1979—Lieutenant, Engine 43

The plush chair outside Assistant Chief Miller's office was very comfortable, but it was the last place I wanted to be sitting. "Why have I been summoned to the basement of the Fire Administration Building (FAB) in my Class A uniform?" I wondered nervously as I squiggled in the chair. "Why to see Chief Miller?" They never called people downtown to tell them they were doing a good job. Did someone complain that we had driven too fast down Market? Did we not have a flagman posted on every run? Or God forbid, did I get caught lying about the commissioner positioning us on the fireground?

Maybe it was because of the chief on another shift who had summoned Satchmo and me up to Battalion 5's office for a face-to-face dressing down. When we got upstairs, he was pointing at his bed, yelling, "What the hell is this shit?"

I stared at the bed, trying to figure out what was wrong. It looked fine with neatly made tight corners. I gave the chief a puzzled look.

"Your idiot paramedics made the fuckin' bed wrong!" he screamed. "The sheet goes on first, then the blanket, and lastly the spread! Those idiots put the blanket on top of the spread!"

I was awestruck that a battalion chief was in such a tirade over something so trivial. All of a sudden, it dawned on me that Snead had most likely done it just to mess with him. The thought made me snicker, and that sent him into a rage. No matter how much he yelled, I hadn't been able to wipe the smile off my face.

Could it be that he had gotten so annoyed that he sent a memorandum downtown over a mismade bed? No, it couldn't be, I thought. That was way too petty an issue to forward up the chain of command. The brass at headquarters would have thought that he was out of his mind.

"The chief will see you now, Lieutenant," Miller's secretary said with a flirtatious smile. I was way too nervous to smile back. I tucked my uniform cap smartly under my left arm, walked in, and stood at attention before the chief's desk.

Like most chiefs of the era, Miller appeared to be my father's age. An imposing man with graying hair accented with a small pompadour, he sat there motionless, staring at a piece of paper.

"Mark-is-ello, am I pronouncing that correctly?" he said without looking up.

"Yes, Chief."

"Marchisello, do you have any idea why you're here?"

"No, Chief," I replied while trying to think of what to say if it was about my ruses.

Miller pulled the paper closer to his eyes. "I'm holding a few lists here, Lieutenant. Guess who is number one on the list to work in the Fire Prevention Division?" He didn't give me a chance to respond. "Marchisello's number one for Fire Prevention!

"Guess who is number one to work as an FCC shift supervisor? Marchisello is number one on the list for the FCC!"

Oh shit! That was the worst job in the department.

"Guess who they've been asking for upstairs in the fire marshal's office? Yep! Marchisello. You're a qualified backup fire marshal, correct?"

"Yes, Chief. I was trained last fall."

"It says here that you're studying engineering at Temple. What kind of engineering is that?"

"Mechanical engineering, Chief." How the hell did he know that?

Miller finally looked up. "Well, it seems that you're in pretty high demand, Lieutenant. Obviously you're going to be transferred into one of these staff units shortly. You'll be there for three years. This is why I called you here today. I want to know if you'd rather work in our Research and Planning Unit. It's more tailored to your engineering background. You're going to need to do a stint in staff, son, so why not do something you like? If you accept the deal, I'll let you off with two years, not three."

To me, it sounded more like a commuted prison sentence than a deal. Completely blindsided, I asked for time to think it over. He gave me four days before he'd offer the "deal" to other lieutenants.

Decisions, decisions.

When I returned to 43's, I asked Hoeffel for his advice. He said that Miller was most likely bluffing, but if I refused, he might order me into one of the other jobs for spite. Then he added, "If you take the position, you'll be out of there in only two years, and they'll never bother you again. You'll learn your way around headquarters and find out what's important and what's not. You'll learn the players and who to call if you need something done. Over the years, I've found that those with staff experience make better field officers."

It was a Catch-22. I felt like I had little choice but to make the move. I called Chief Miller and accepted the job. I was going to staff.

My transfer wasn't effective until a week later. My last night in the firehouse, we responded to an apartment fire at Fifteenth and Mount Vernon. The place was going pretty good, and just as we pulled up, a man jumped from the second-story window. *Whomp*! That night I wrote in my journal, "As heartbreaking as it was to see another person jump from a burning building, I'm going to miss fighting fires for the next two years."

CHAPTER 15

Research and Planning

The following Monday I started my new job at research and planning. Located two levels below ground, in the bowels of the FAB, R&P's offices sat between the FCC and the city's Office of Emergency Management (OEM). Even though my main goal was getting my sentence over with and returning to the field, I figured that I'd make the best of it and learn as much as possible.

My new boss, Deputy Chief William Richmond, was a perfect gentleman and an excellent leader. A firefighter's fireman, Richmond had worked in some of the city's busiest firehouses before being assigned to staff. He brought a firehouse feel to our fluorescent-tubed office. The other officers assigned to the unit, six captains and two lieutenants, had more time on the job than I did. So once again, even as a lieutenant, I was the new guy, a white-shirted rookie, so to speak.

As junior project officer, my tasks were varied. My biggest project was to write an operational procedure (OP) for the I-95 tunnel that was being constructed through Center City. A few years prior, the department had had an extremely difficult time extinguishing a gasoline-tanker fire on the Schuylkill Expressway underpass near Thirtieth Street. Because we didn't have a practical way to apply foam to the raging inferno, several structural supports were damaged, and the congested expressway had to be closed for months.

Fearing a similar type of incident, the PFD required the Pennsylvania Department of Transportation (PennDOT) to install a foam-sprinkler system in the I-95 tunnel. In theory it was a great idea. But in practice the system's design was ultracomplicated. It was broken into numerous control zones, each with corresponding valves located at different street locations. To apply foam, firefighters needed to identify the exact zone of the fire and then find its proper valve and water-supply connection. The complicated design could have qualified as a Rube Goldberg device. It was my job to take all the technical gibberish and incorporate it into a user-friendly procedure. It consumed much of my time during the first four months there.

As in most office environments, we often juggled several projects simultaneously. It seemed that there was always something more pressing than whatever we were working on. A priority was to issue new Scott 2,200 psi (as opposed to 1,980 psi) air packs to each company. The major change for the department was that they were finally issuing enough packs for all firefighters riding on the apparatus. Delivering the equipment and training several companies each day got me out of the office, however briefly.

Most other projects kept me at my desk. It seemed that each chief's staff meeting resulted in changes to the department's OPs or directives, and we had to quickly revise and distribute them. Sometimes the changes were drastic enough to necessitate complete rewrites.

Personally I found the research projects most interesting. Whenever a new piece of firefighting equipment came on the market, we'd gather information about it, determine its applicability, and evaluate its practicality. The same thing was true about innovative firefighting techniques. When assigned these projects, we'd do the research, draw our own conclusions, and call New York (FDNY), Baltimore City (BCFD), Chicago (CFD), or other large departments to see if they had experience or opinions before performing our own field evaluations.

Even though we were in staff, we maintained our firehouse sense of humor. One time we suspected that an FCC supervisor was snooping around our office late at night and leaking information about our projects to the field. We set him up by leaving phony pictures and memos on our desks hinting that the department was in the process of purchasing small-ladder trucks, similar to those used by utility companies. We even listed the companies that'd be getting the so-called tactical ladders. The next week we fielded dozens of inquisitive calls from officers and firefighters in the field. Got him!

Commissioner Rizzo rarely came down to our office, but occasionally he'd pass by our hall window en route to the FCC. A few times every week, I'd try to fool someone by looking at the window, waving, and saying, "Hi,

Commissioner." Naturally everyone would swing around to look, but he wasn't there. Eventually, they got used to the prank and ignored it. But when a fun-loving battalion chief was detailed to our unit for a week-long project, I got him with the same trick nearly every day. That Friday, the chief's last day, I looked up at the window, waved, and said "Hi, Commissioner!" The battalion chief, thinking that it was yet another joke, rose to his feet, swung around, snapped his heels together, and saluted. But this time, Rizzo *was*, in fact, standing there. He eyeballed the battalion chief, shook his head, and continued down the hall as the embarrassed chief chased after him apologizing. Got him!

There were some perks to working staff. One was having every weekend off. I spent nearly every one of them with Diane and her adorable son, Alex. I had finally met that special someone. Our love grew and blossomed while I was at R&P.

Another perk was that staff personnel were generally given better performance ratings than in the field. In the field, "outstanding" and "superior" grades were strictly controlled. It wasn't uncommon for battalion, deputy, or assistant chiefs to unfairly lower grades given by company officers, even if they didn't know the firefighter being rated. Chief Richmond's rating for me was far superior to what I'd have gotten in the field. It didn't matter much to me at the time. I'd rather have had a lower rating and still have been in the field. Little did I know that that rating would soon prove to be invaluable.

When summer vacations kicked in, I filled in for the EMS, communications, water liaison, safety, and apparatus officers. It was a good change of pace, and I even responded to a few extra-alarm fires as the department's safety officer.

The biggest planning project for the fall was the department's preparation for the visit of Pope John Paul II. Our detailed plans included over-the-top fire protection and EMS coverage for every inch of ground he was scheduled to visit within the city limits. The culminating event was the celebration of a huge outdoor Roman Catholic Mass on Benjamin Franklin Parkway. Most of us were assigned to command first-aid stations. Mine was Aid Station 6 at Twenty-Second and the Parkway. On October 3, I was assigned a doctor, four nurses, and three EMTs, and we handled thirty-eight medical cases at our station alone. Most of them were minor issues like bee stings, syncope, cuts, and bruises, but there were also a few trauma cases, a stroke, and a heart attack. When the papal motorcade passed, we got a close-up view of the pope.

Rizzo surrounded himself with the best and brightest chiefs in the department. Miller and Richmond were perfect examples. Consummate professionals with the perfect blend of field and staff experience, they were sharp, proactive, and quick thinking. Yet, in their hearts, they were basically down-to-earth firefighters. For me, they were paragons of leadership. I learned a ton just by watching them.

When William J. Green III won the mayoral election in November of 1979, Miller and Richmond rightly anticipated that changes were coming. With the city suffering financial woes, cuts to the fire department were likely. Before the new mayor was even inaugurated, Miller had us discreetly develop several cost-saving measures. We also completed impact studies for closing up to four engines and two ladders, along with long-term plans to combine several pairs of fire stations.

In December, there was an opening in the office for the assistant apparatus officer's position. I jumped on it. Though I was still assigned to R&P, I would no longer be chained to my desk. My new job got me out of the office much more. But the more I interacted with the field, the more I missed it. I was yearning to get back to the business of firefighting.

When Miller was interviewing my potential replacements, I learned that Hoeffel's suspicions were right. Once Miller set his sights on somebody, he'd learn as much as possible about the person and then have his secretary type phony staff lists with the unsuspecting officer's name atop each one. That's when he'd call the officer in and make *an offer the person couldn't refuse*. It didn't upset me. As a matter of fact, I took it as a compliment. I didn't know it, but things were about to change anyway.

Sure enough, as soon as Green took office, talks about fire-department cutbacks began. As predicted, Rizzo gave Miller two weeks to develop budget-saving measures, but we were already 90 percent done. The top recommendations we submitted upstairs were based on attrition. Firefighters hired shortly after World War II were retiring in droves. Based on our statistical analysis, refraining from replacing them would meet the desired budget reductions within two years and would cause the least amount of hardship to our fellow firefighters. We recommended that station closings be employed only as an ugly last resort.

The new administration didn't want the political blowback from closing firehouses, but they weren't willing to wait two years either. Less than a month later, they responded with their own plan: layoffs and demotions. Included were staffing reductions for both engine and ladder companies, disbanding tac-pumpers, and eliminating certain staff positions. Most shocking was the abolishment of the department's highest civil-service rank, assistant chief. Miller and six others would need to either resign or face demotion back to deputy chief. The demotions would bump down the chain of command and result in approximately two hundred firefighter layoffs. Miller was rightly furious. Not only was his attrition proposal flatly denied, but his job as staff services chief was being eliminated.

The firefighters' union, Local 22, didn't take the cuts lying down. They staged massive protest marches around city hall nearly every day. They also held a humongous march around the FAB. The morning of the march, Miller called us into his office. "I just got a phone call from upstairs. Now, I've had to give some shitty orders during my career, but this one tops the list! They want you guys to guard the doors and deny them entry. Now here's what *I* want you to do: go up there and stand near the doors, but stay out of sight. If they attempt to come inside, hold the doors open for them!"

The protest was a sight to behold. Nearly a thousand fire officers and firefighters marched up Spring Garden Street. Many of them feared retribution, so they wore Groucho Marx or monster masks. Nobody tried to get inside the FAB.

Among the cuts was the elimination of my position, assistant apparatus officer. I was finally going back to the field! But I was also in jeopardy of being demoted, along with approximately fifty other lieutenants. The department's personnel office prepared demotion and layoff lists in top-secret sessions that rivaled the Manhattan Project. According to civil-service regulations, demotions and layoffs were determined by two factors: total time in the department (which wasn't good for me—most lieutenants had more than my paltry seven years on the job) and the employee's latest performance rating. That was my saving grace! My little detour through staff, with its higher performance ratings, kept me from getting demoted.

Miller, along with five of the assistant chiefs, opted to retire. Only one accepted his demotion back to deputy chief. For me, it was an introduction to the crazy upside-down world of politics. Prior to the cuts, Miller had been as loyal to the administration as he was talented. Yet he was gone in a flash. The department let go of one of its most outstanding managers. Unsurprisingly, he was quickly scooped up by one of the city's largest hospitals to run their safety department.

My last project at R&P was to help balance the department's field staffing levels. Several companies had been decimated by the layoffs, while others remained overstaffed. We had to process massive transfers to ensure that each company received a proper balance of drivers, tillermen, EMTs, and experienced firefighters. When the time came to replace the demoted lieutenants, Richmond smiled and said, "Here's the vacancies, Bob. Pick wherever you want to go." I selected the second company on the list, Engine 24, on my old D Platoon. I had been in staff for eleven months, but it felt like I was going home after a long voyage at sea.

CHAPTER 16

Back to 24's

E ngine 24's D Platoon had been hit hard by the layoffs. Sharpie had gotten promoted to captain a few years back, but his replacement had been demoted, and four of the platoon's firefighters were laid off. The survivors, Mel, Clarkee, and Eric, had less than eight years' combined service. When I helped Richmond with the transfers, it had only taken a couple of calls to add some much-needed experience. Joey, an aggressive firefighter demoted from lieutenant, jumped at the chance to work 24's, and I was able to coax Russell to transfer from 43's. Rounding out my platoon were big strong Stevie D. from Ladder 11 and tough little Rocky from Ladder 32. On my first day back in the field, our first as a team, we were put to the test.

March 7, 1980—Lieutenant, Engine 24

It was 7:00 a.m. as I slowly pushed open the door to 24's tiny office. Half expecting to see Sharpie sitting at the desk, I found it hard to comprehend that I was now in charge of my former platoon—a platoon that once included Hoss, Lumpy, Fry, and Sharpie. Not wanting to disturb the off-going officer, I quietly retrieved my roll-call list off the desk and turned back toward the door.

"Hey! You must be Bobby." Captain Charlie O'Mahoney hopped out of bed and entered the dimly lit office. We had only met once, but I instantly remembered his friendly smile. "Welcome to Twenty-Four's. Have a seat," he said, gesturing to the desk chair. Square jawed, with salt-and-pepper hair and a well-trimmed mustache, Charlie O', as he was affectionately called, lit a cigarette and plopped next to me on the typing stool.

"Now, I remember who you are," he said, staring at my face. "You were at Forty-Three's on the A before they drafted you into R and P, right?"

Charlie O' took a long drag on his unfiltered cigarette. "I'm glad you chose Twenty-Four's. Look, you can run your platoon as you see fit. Just make sure you pass on anything that affects the other platoons, the apparatus, or the station, and we'll get along just fine." He took another drag. "If anything is pressing or if you need my advice, you can call me at home any time, day or night."

Born and raised in a rough neighborhood of Southwest Philly, Charlie O' had a reputation not only as a tough-as-nails firefighter but also as an outstanding officer. He had developed his firefighting skills at 57's and 68's, the busiest companies in Southwest Philly. I understandably felt comfortable around him and considered myself lucky to have him as my captain.

As we headed to the kitchen for coffee, I heard a familiar voice followed by bursts of laughter. It was Russell, who else? He'd already zeroed in on Joey and was humorously welcoming him back to the rank of firefighter.

"Yo, Joe, do you remember this tool? It's called a mop. You dunk it in this bucket, wring it out, and push it across the floor." Everyone in the kitchen, including Joey, was laughing. Even though the faces were different, it seemed as though I had never left. I was ecstatic to be back in the field— back at 24's again.

Roll call was interrupted by box seven-seven-four for a reported fire at the Tasker-Morris Subway. It felt so damned good to be back on a fire truck as we zipped out of the station. Moments later 10's placed the small rubbish fire under control, and we were recalled. As we were backing into our firehouse, Battalion 5 pulled onto the apron. My chief was well-respected Tom Kinney, from South Philly's Two-Street neighborhood. (Chief Kinney was in the Fifth Battalion at the same time Chief Kenney was in the First. We responded to fires with both of them, which made for some confusing fire reports.)

Kinney greeted me with a firm handshake. "Since we were down here for that run, I figured I'd make Twenty-Four's the first stop on my rounds." After we reviewed our staffing quotas, my new chief laid out his expectations. Nothing was earth shattering. He seemed friendly and knowledgeable, and I instantly knew I was going to enjoy working for him. As he was about to leave, he stopped at the door. "Oh! One more thing. I don't want my companies leading off with their booster line. If you have anything more than light smoke showing from any structure, use your inch-and-three-quarter."

I knew what he was getting at. Some officers liked the challenge of fighting one-room fires with their booster line. But there were times when the fire got away from them and they lost the place, suffered injuries, or both. It's something we had never done when I was at 24's or anywhere else.

"No problem with that, Chief," I replied.

It was an unusually slow morning, so I had a chance to get familiar with the guys. For lunch, Clarkee grilled scrumptious cheesesteaks and served them with homemade french fries. After only one bite, I realized how sorely I had missed the firehouse meals. It's another reason I was so glad to be back!

After lunch I cracked my knuckles and slid a working schedule into the typewriter carriage. For the past eleven months, Janice, our secretary at R&P, had done all our typing. I couldn't say that I had missed the keyboard at all. My pecking wasn't much better than the turtle speed I'd had when I left 43's.

"Attention Engine Twenty-Four, Eighteenth and Wharton, rubbish." It was a welcome reprieve, even though it was only for a reported trash fire. But as soon as Eric pulled onto Twentieth, a long beep came over the radio. "Tactical box seven-three-four, Eighteenth and Wharton, the fire is reported to be a dwelling at Bouvier and Wharton, Engine Twenty-Four's local." The assignment had been upgraded. Eric pressed hard on the accelerator as the guys clambered around behind me with anticipation. Just as we approached Wharton, a longer beep sounded over the radio. "Box seven-three-four, Eighteenth and Wharton, the fire is located at Bouvier and Wharton, a dwelling with a report of people trapped."

A tall column of dense black smoke greeted us as we swung the turn. I got a good look at the rear as we passed, and medium smoke was coming from the second-floor rear windows. Heavy fire was showing from the front. If people were trapped, their only refuge was the back bedroom. Hopefully they'd closed the door behind them. Luckily, we had a hydrant only fifty feet from the house, but since we were only three blocks from our station, we were going to be on our own for a while.

My heart sank as a soot-covered woman came rushing toward us, screaming at the top of her lungs. Her grandchildren were in the rear bedroom. Mel, Joey, and Russell had our attack line stretched to the front before I finished giving my radio report. The first floor was fully involved, so I told the guys to stretch another attack line and split into two teams. Joey and Mel would hold the first floor at bay while Russell and I advanced the second line upstairs.

The smoke was choking us. By the time we made the top of the stairs, we were gasping for breath. Flames were extending well into the hallway from the front room. As we opened our nozzle and began pushing the fire toward the front, I heard firefighters thumping up the steps. It was the welcome sound of Ladder 11's firefighters.

"Check the back bedroom!" I screamed through the smoke. It was imperative that we keep the flames away while they crawled down the hall to search for the children.

As we made the front room, I heard a ruckus behind us. I glanced back and caught a glimpse of Billy Joyce rushing a lifeless little body down the steps. Globs of mucus were oozing from the child's mouth and over Billy's sleeves. Another firefighter quickly followed with a second child and then a third. The horrific sight didn't help my digestive system, which was already in turmoil from the smoke. I gagged twice before reverse flushing my cheesesteak and fries. How could it be that something so good only a few hours ago could taste so awful now? I wiped my mouth on my sleeve, and we continued our attack until we beat the red devil into submission.

While our attack lines had been advancing on the fire, the foyer had lit up behind us. Luckily, Eric had spotted it and knocked down the flames with our booster line. It was still lying on the front step as we came outside. I opened the nozzle and lapped at its stream like a dog drinking from a hose. After I swished away the taste of vomit and spit it out, I spotted Chief Kinney glaring at me with his arms on his hips.

"What did I tell you about that booster line?" he said angrily.

I looked at the booster and then back at the chief. "You told me not to lead off with it."

"Then why is it on the front steps?"

"We didn't lead off with it, Chief. We had two inch-and-three-quarter lines in service when the fire lit up behind us. Eric saved our asses with the booster."

Kinney looked at our pumper. "They're both *your* inch-and-three-quarter lines?"

"Yep."

"Oh! Sorry. Good job!"

The fire claimed the lives of a three-year-old boy and his two sisters, aged four and seven. The grandmother was severely burned trying to rescue them. The fire was a downright tragedy, but while fighting it, I learned that I had a heck of a good crew. Even though it was their first fire as a team, they worked like they had fought hundreds of fires together.

The three other engines on the box were shorthanded because of the layoffs. Local 22 screamed foul, but the press largely ignored the issue. To them, the layoffs were old news. The Phillies' spring training camp in Clearwater got more coverage.

Exactly a week later, March 14, 1980, Firefighter Bill Donovan collapsed and died at a working fire in Southwest Philly. It didn't get much press either. Donovan's LODD was the first since Diane and I had begun dating. During my stint at R&P, we had fallen deeply in love, and we were planning to get engaged. Donovan's LODD was an eye-opener for her, but she understood that firefighting was a major part of my life. She accepted the fact that worries are a constant companion to every firefighter's loved ones. That made me love her even more.

Firefighting is both a science and an art. One can learn the science aspect of firefighting from training, education, and studies. But some things can't be learned from books or at training sessions. Cultivating the artistic side of firefighting takes longer and is directly related to the number of fires to which a firefighter responds. Certain subtle indicators often predict the behavior of structural fires. By fighting fires repetitively, diligent firefighters often develop a sort of a sixth sense that detects these minor hints and clues. They learn to *read* the fire. It's like learning to play a musical instrument. With repetitive practice, one eventually learns to make music instead of just playing notes.

I didn't know it when I wrote the following journal entry, but I was beginning to develop my artistic side of firefighting while at 24's.

April 24, 1980—Lieutenant, Engine 24

Every window of the run-down three-story vacant row home was boarded up. Flames weren't showing, but fire was ravaging the once-proud home to a hardworking blue-collar family. Dense gray smoke was swirling from between the decaying window boards. The fire was in there somewhere. It was our job to go inside, find it, and put it out.

From outside, the smoke looked densest on the third floor. It was also a darker shade of gray up there. More importantly, it was pushing from the eaves, under intense pressure. I hadn't seen fires on lower floors push that hard from the eaves before, so I knew the fire was on the third floor. But my senses were giving me more information. For some intangible reason, maybe because of the way the smoke was swirling, I knew that the fire was in the front room. There wasn't any science behind my conclusion; it was just a feeling based on my observations.

While giving my report, I waved four fingers out the officer's side window, signaling for the four-length preconnected 1¾" line (as opposed to our three length). "Place both engines and ladders in service." I wanted the second engine to enter from the rear and cover our behinds, just in case my observations were wrong.

With one mighty swing of Stevie D.'s Halligan, the door flew wide open. Smoke poured over our heads, but there was no heat. We opened the basement door—no heat again, little smoke. The second floor had a lot more smoke but little heat. As we advanced to the third floor, my ears felt a slight rush of air coming from below. It was cool, a good sign that nothing was burning below us.

When we got to the top of the stairs, it was completely black and hot as hell! I signaled Clarkee to stop and stay quiet. Listening intently between

Ladder 32's whacks on the window boards, we could hear the fire crackling in the front room. As soon as Ladder 32 pried off enough boards, the front room burst into flames. We made the turn, and within a minute the red devil was dead.

Many chiefs vented their anger by screaming and yelling at their captains and lieutenants. As in the military, wrath always flows down the chain of command. Young lieutenants are at the very bottom of the pecking order.

May 1, 1980—Lieutenant, Engine 24

Around noon on that breezy spring day, the mechanic placed our American LaFrance pumper out of service for scheduled maintenance. In its place we used Engine 101, the Fifth Battalion's decrepitly old reserve pumper. The mechanic said that the maintenance would take less than an hour. Now what harm could possibly come from running with Junk-Wagon 101 for a mere hour? I should have known better. As soon as the mechanic began working on our LaFrance, we were dispatched third-in on the box, to a grain elevator fire along the Schuylkill River.

Sure enough, smoke was in the sky as we puttered our way up the Point. This fire was going to be a worker. Russell tried to accelerate, but when he pressed on the pedal, Junk-Wagon 101 sputtered, bucked, and even hissed. It refused to go any faster than a snail's pace.

By the time we pulled up, the three other engines were connected to the only hydrants in the area. The next closest hydrant was three thousand feet back, where we had entered off Twenty-Sixth Street. Junk-Wagon 101 only had a thousand feet of hose.

"Hey, you!" screamed the deputy chief, a.k.a. *Les Misérables*. "Get the hell to the end of the pier and draft." (Use our pump to draw water from the Schuylkill.)

"Draft? With this piece of junk?" I thought.

"Move!" he screamed again, the veins bulging out of his forehead.

Obviously he wasn't in the mood to negotiate, so I motioned Russell toward the end of the pier. The river's surface was twelve feet below grade. In order to draft, a pumper needs to have a good tight pump. I gulped, knowing full well that our fifteen-year-old rusty bucket of bolts didn't stand a chance.

Regardless, we connected everything together, tightened our fittings, and lowered our hard black suction hose below the surface. The engine coughed, hacked, and gasped for air when Russell revved it up. When he pulled the primer handle, it moaned and groaned and then began to squeal like a stuck pig. We tried every trick in the book but couldn't lift a drop of water from the river.

The racket caught Les Misérables' attention, and he came storming over. "Well, where's the fuckin' water, Lieutenant?"

"Chief, this piece of junk can't draft," I replied apologetically.

You would think that I had just cursed his children by the way he went up one side of me and down the other. "You're shit in my book, Lieutenant! I think that you and your gang of assholes don't know what the hell you're doing! If there's one thing I hate, it's a company that don't know how to draft! Don't you ever train your men? What the hell's wrong with you?"

When I finally managed to get a word in, I told him that we were doing everything correctly, but it was the pumper that was at fault, not me or my men. He angrily pointed his fat finger in my face. "When you finally get off this fireground, and *you will* be the last to leave, you better prove that this pumper failed its last pump test. I want a verbal report and a long memorandum stating all the facts. Now stretch a three-and-a-half-inch line back to Forty-Nine's for your fuckin' water supply."

Just as he promised, we were the last ones to leave the fireground, and as an extra bonus, I inherited the first-in fire report (more typing). When we returned Junk-Wagon 101 to Engine 1, its rightful owner, I looked through their files. It hadn't passed a pump test since the midseventies. No big surprise there.

I immediately called. "Chief, Engine One Oh One hasn't passed a pump test in years."

There was a short pause. Then he brusquely replied, "Okay." *Click.* That was it. No apology in any way, shape, or form. He didn't even tell me not to bother with the long memorandum. "Okay." *Click.* That's all I got.

If I ever got promoted to chief (ha-ha), I promised that I'd never be like Les Misérables.

CHAPTER 17

Charlie O's Principle

Charlie O' became my new mentor. Each shift change with him was a learning experience filled with advice about firefighting and supervising firefighters. One of the very first things he told me was "The rules of the fire department are just guidelines. Common sense should always prevail." Afterward, I always referred to his advice as "Charlie O's principle." A rumor floating around the firehouse illustrated it perfectly.

One beautiful day in June, Engine 24 had just passed Deputy 1's station inspection. Charlie O' was in the office typing the pile of inspection reports the chief had delegated to him. Chiefs loathed typing too, so they often rudely dumped the distasteful chore on to their subordinates. But Charlie O' never complained. He always made things work to his advantage. If the chief was vague about a certain rating, Charlie O' would seize the opportunity and type a higher score. Why not?

A softball game was scheduled after their shift, so that morning a couple of Charlie O's firefighters decided to warm up on the apron. Preston slapped his fist in his glove in front of the open apparatus doors. Norm took a position on the Point, near Federal Street, and bounced his first toss in front of Preston. His next toss was low again. This one hit a pebble and rolled under Rescue 14. Preston crawled under the apparatus while mumbling under his breath, retrieved the ball, and snapped a quick throw to Norm's glove. "Come on! Pick it up a little, will ya." Norm did. He reared back and threw a high fastball that sailed four feet over Preston's head. The ball continued inside the apparatus doors and smashed a perfectly round hole through the center of Rescue 14's windshield. Preston and Norm stood there with their mouths open while the rest of the platoon ran around laughing hysterically.

Preston said that he would go tell Charlie O', but Norm quickly cut him off and headed for the office. "I threw it. I'll go tell him."

Charlie O' was still at the typewriter when Norm knocked on the door. "Hey, Norm, what's up?" he said.

"Uh, Cap. We've got a little problem," Norm replied.

Charlie O' smiled. "Norm, we never have problems; we only have situations. Now what's the situation?"

Norm nodded toward the apparatus floor. "Uh, the windshield of Rescue 14 has, uh, a hole in it, Cap."

Charlie O' put his cigarette between his lips. "Okay, Norm. Let's go take a look. A little hole certainly isn't a problem. It's a little situation, right?"

The rest of the platoon members were sitting on the concrete island by the overhead door with conspicuous guilty smirks on their faces when Charlie O' reached the front of the rescue. His head snapped back in amazement when he saw the windshield.

"I thought you said a hole, Norm. The entire friggin' window's smashed!"

The guys exploded with laughter. Charlie O' snapped his head toward them, took a long drag on his cigarette, and squinted his eyes. "You know, this hole appears to be the same size as a damned softball. Now tell me exactly what happened."

Norm confessed.

Charlie O' inched closer to the guys. "I've always told you guys that every situation has a solution. Now there are two solutions to this particular situation: I can call the chief, which means Norm, Preston, and I will be in trouble and I'll have a shitload of paperwork to do. Or on Rescue 14's next run, somebody will get on the damned radio and report that someone threw a rock through the windshield. Now what do you guys think we should do?" The guys knew that Charlie O' would never hang them out to dry. It was just as important for him to take care of his men as it was to satisfy his superiors. They agreed on the rock story.

Charlie O' asked for a pair of pliers. When the guys gave him puzzled looks, he said, "Did you ever see a rock make a perfectly round hole in a windshield?" He took the pliers and, almost as if he was skilled at it, chipped away a few pieces of glass to make the hole look like an act of vandalism.

"Now park this thing so that it's facing south on the Point and put an A-frame ladder on the apparatus floor." He got more puzzled looks. "Did you guys forget about the chief? He hasn't been around yet, has he? Make it look like we're changing a light bulb."

As Charlie O's luck of the Irish would have it, as soon as they moved the rescue, Battalion 5 turned from Federal Street and pulled onto the apron. Everybody, including Charlie O', quickly gathered on the apparatus floor and began staring at the ceiling, trying not to look guilty.

The chief got out of his car and also looked up. "What's the problem, Chal?"

"I think we have a bad ballast in that light fixture, Chief."

Unexpectedly, the chief began sniffing the air. "Yeah, I think I can smell it." The guys tried their best to restrain themselves, but a few of them let out muffled giggles. The chief sensed something was amiss but just shook his head and went into the office to do his routine business with Charlie O'. He was gone within fifteen minutes.

At the time Rescue 14 was averaging over six thousand runs a year. But as fate would have it, by four o'clock that afternoon, it hadn't received a single call. This was Charlie O's situation, and he wasn't about to pass it on to the next shift. He walked into the kitchen, poured himself a cup of coffee, and said, "You know, when I was a fireman at Sixty-Eight's and our officer stuck his neck out for us, we always bailed him out." He turned around, took his coffee back to his office, and shut the door. Quite coincidentally, a minute later, Rescue 14 got dispatched to Twenty-Fifth and Wharton for an unconscious man under the railroad overpass. A few minutes afterward, the rescue driver reported that a gang of teenagers threw a rock from the overpass and broke their windshield. The call turned out to be a false alarm. Charlie O' typed a small memo explaining the circumstances, and within hours the windshield was replaced by city mechanics.

A few weeks later when I heard the story, I asked Charlie O' why he had handled the situation the way he had. He took a long drag on his cigarette and smiled. "Bobby, that story is just a silly rumor. But let me tell you something. If I was working when something like that happened, I probably would have done the same thing. There's no way I'd let it go downtown. Besides, whether the windshield was broken by a couple of guys playing catch or by rogue juveniles with a rock, the cost of replacing it was the same. Why would I complicate the matter?" He took another long drag. "Furthermore, I wouldn't want to spend a few hours typing memorandums explaining why the guys were playing softball, why the doors were open, why I wasn't supervising them, and most importantly, how I think they should be punished." He took another drag and then winked at me. "Bobby, always use common sense. But most of all, always take care of your men."

That was Charlie O's principle—common-sense decision making. I put it into practice almost immediately.

June 12, 1980—Lieutenant, Engine 24

Sweaty, filthy, and tired, we pulled onto our apron at 11:00 p.m. Our fifth run was another fire death. It was only a one roomer near Sixteenth and Ellsworth, but we found a man's charred body lying on a mattress in the center of the room.

Russell flipped on our flashing lights, and as the apparatus bay's door rose, I saw Clarkee and Stevie D. prying on Rescue 14's front bumper with a Halligan tool. Uh-oh, they'd hit something.

Clarkee nervously ran his fingers through his hair. "Loo, I'm not sure what happened. The patient was in bad shape, and I was rushing. When I slammed to a stop at the ER, I thought I felt a little bump but didn't think much of it. We didn't notice that the bumper was pushed in until *after* we got back to the station. We must have hit a bollard. I guess we have to call the chief, huh, Loo?"

I knelt down to survey the damage. The bumper was pushed in about two inches and had a tiny dent smeared with yellow paint. I did a 360 around the rescue. There were at least a dozen other dents and dings that the city had never repaired.

"Remove the yellow paint with rubbing compound and then forget about it. It never happened."

Clarkee looked at Stevie D. and then back at me. "Thanks, Loo. I really appreciate it."

I had applied Charlie O's principle. If I had called the chief, the rescue would have been placed out of service for the investigation, I would have had a mountain of paperwork to complete, and Clarkee would have gotten a preventable accident on his record. All for a bumper that wouldn't be repaired. Refraining from reporting it was common sense!

I didn't want Charlie O' to get blindsided in case anyone noticed the damage, so the following morning I pointed it out and explained my rationale for not reporting it. He took a long drag and patted me on the back. "Bobby, you're my kind of officer."

That summer, during one of our shift-change tutorials, Charlie O' and I talked about the importance of the portable ladders carried by single-engine companies. "Bobby, make sure you practice with them. You never know when you might need them." Luckily, I followed his advice.

August 14, 1980—Lieutenant, Engine 24

We started the morning off with a bang. I was in the kitchen sipping coffee while Johnny B., the C Platoon's burly ex-marine, was ranting about the Iranian hostage crisis. "I know how to get our damned hostages back. Tell those sons of bitches that we'll drop a nuke on them every day until our people are released! But no, balls-less Carter won't make any threats like that!" We were still giggling when ringing bells ended his tirade. Seconds later, we were out the door, racing to an apartment fire with a report of people trapped.

As soon as we turned onto Eighteenth, we saw dark-gray smoke coming from every window of the three-story end of the row. A man and woman in their thirties, with globs of mucus oozing from their mouths and noses, were perched at the second-floor window, screaming, crying, and gasping for air. Ladders 11 and 19 were nowhere in sight. We didn't even hear their sirens.

Russell and Clarkee stretched our attack line to the front door while Stevie D. and I wrestled our extension ladder off the pumper. Stevie was so strong that he practically dragged me as we dashed toward the fire. We set the heel plates on the ground, extended the ladder, and were lowering it to the sill when the man suddenly reached out and snatched it from our grip. As soon as it stopped bouncing against the window sill, the man swung onto it and scampered down. The woman was still teetering as she struggled to place her bare feet on the rungs. Stevie D. darted up and quickly helped her down as the man sat on our back step watching. So much for chivalry!

Taking advantage of my shift schedule, I made the switch from night to day classes at Temple. At the time, the university required all graduates, no matter their major, to complete four semester hours of physical-education courses. I choose karate.

One of the things we often practiced in class was called the side kick. Standing firmly, we'd raise one leg and kick sideways. By the end of October, I felt as though I had a pretty effective side kick. At least that's what I thought.

OCTOBER 27, 1980—LIEUTENANT, ENGINE 24

Smoke was pouring from the second floor of the vacant dwelling on Clymer Street. Just as Stevie D. was about to whack the door open with his Halligan, I yelled, "Hold up on the door!"

Looking perplexed, Stevie D. rested the tool on his shoulder and backed down the steps. "What's wrong, Loo?"

I climbed to the top step, turned sideways, planted my feet firmly, and looked down at him. "Watch this, pal!"

Incoming sirens from the rest of tactical box were wailing in the background as I precisely raised my right leg, just as I had done a hundred times in karate class, and delivered a firm blow just below the lock. The door didn't budge. In my engineering classes, we studied Newton's laws of motion. Newton's third law states, "For every action, there's an equal but opposite reaction." Since the door didn't budge a single nanometer, my body bore the entire opposite reaction. I was propelled off the top step with my arms flailing. Luckily, big Stevie D. was there to catch me.

"Very entertaining, Loo!" he said, shaking his head. "Can I pop the door with the Halligan now?"

Another effect of the layoffs brought cuts in staffing to the department's marine units (fireboats had been renamed marine units). The officer and the three firefighter positions had been eliminated. Only the pilot and engineer remained to drive and operate each vessel. For staffing, select engine companies were trained as land-based companies (LBCs). Their job was to respond to the marine unit before it got under way. The logic behind the cuts was that there rarely was any urgency for the boat to respond. Waiting for an LBC to arrive wouldn't matter much. Of course, the logic was flawed.

Nine months later, the Passyunk Avenue drawbridge got stuck open after a tugboat passing underneath inadvertently cut its cables. For some unknown reason, a motorist removed the barricades that had been placed in the roadway and drove under the gap between the road and the bridge. He, along with his wife and small child, plunged into the frigid waters some twenty feet below. They landed only a couple of hundred yards from the wharf of scantily staffed Marine Unit 32 (formerly Fire Boat 3). An eyewitness said that the car bobbed in the Schuylkill for several minutes before sinking.

December 4, 1980—Lieutenant, Engine 24 (LBC, Marine 32)

A cold wind was howling as we joined two police boats circling around in the murky Schuylkill River. At 7:10 p.m., Engines 40 and 60, Ladders 4 and 19, Battalion 7, and Rescue 19M were dispatched to the Passyunk Avenue Bridge for an automobile in the river. We were dispatched to staff Marine 32 as the LBC. A critical fifteen minutes had passed by the time we arrived, got into the boat, and cast off.

We could see splashed water marks on the west wall beneath the bridge. They were still there a half hour after the family of three plunged into the chilly waters. I shined my hand light into the dark-green water, searching for an oil sheen, air bubbles, or any sign of life. Clarkee and Stevie D. were on the sides, probing the depths with twenty-foot ceiling hooks, and the engineer was astern, dragging the river with grappling hooks.

Suddenly, Stevie D. yelled that he felt something with his hook. I ran to the back of the boat as the pilot cut a tight clockwise circle. Stevie's eyes were transfixed on the spot where he had felt something metallic. I aimed my light at the spot, which was only twenty-five feet astern. The pilot turned the boat 360 degrees, but it was way too wide. The spot was now fifty feet away. I jogged up to the wheelhouse and yelled at the pilot, "We gotta get to the spot he's pointing to!"

The pilot, a thirty-year veteran, calmly replied, "I can't turn this thing on a dime. I'm doing the best I can."

I felt bad for yelling and apologized. "I know you are, sorry. But my guy felt something over there. Get as close as you can."

The pilot was still maneuvering when a police boat with two officers in dive suits approached. I frantically waved and caught their attention. "There!" I yelled, shining my light on the spot.

The divers quickly disappeared under the surface. The pilot stopped the engines, and we drifted quietly. A few minutes later, one of the police officers surfaced and gave a thumbs-down signal. He had found the car, but the family had drowned.

I stood there wondering whether a fully staffed marine unit would have made a difference.

In the wee hours of the morning on that same shift, we responded on the second alarm to a huge apartment-building fire at Forty-Fifth and Walnut. Working under the guidance of Battalion 7 again, we stretched our line past a burned corpse in one of the apartments. "One DOA by land and three DOAs by sea tonight, Chief. It seems like we're not a good mix," I quipped.

The very next night, we responded to Forty-Ninth and Baltimore on the second alarm. It was in the Seventh Battalion again. The chief cringed when he saw us. "Oh no! Not you again. Take the exposure on the right. I'm pretty sure you won't find any DOAs in there."

In the beginning of 1981, Joey was rightfully repromoted and transferred out of 24's. Many of the EMTs who had been laid off were being rehired and assigned to engine companies with BLS rescues. Two of them—quick-witted "Capo," a former fire dispatcher, and Joe Urick, who, like myself, wanted to transfer from Ladder 19 to a busy engine—joined our platoon.

One of our first runs together was for a pulled firebox. False fireboxes were more infrequent during the colder months. But occasionally someone would pull the handle to remind us that the boxes were still hanging on the poles.

FEBRUARY 7, 1981—LIEUTENANT, ENGINE 24

Suspecting a false alarm on box seven-three-four, we made the three-block trek without our warning lights or siren. As expected, nobody was waiting on the corner, and there were no signs of fire or smoke.

After rewinding the box and applying a fresh coat of purple dye to its handle, we were about to pull away when I spotted the shadow of someone lurking in the alley. Hugging the wall, I sneaked up slowly, jumped out, and landed in my most threatening karate stance. "Aha! Did you pull that firebox?"

Well, my karate pose finally scared the crap out of somebody. Unfortunately, it was a jacketless little boy. The startled ten-year-old tripped over his own feet as he tried to scramble away, but I grabbed him by his sweatshirt before he hit the ground. I could feel him trembling as I pulled him up. His eyes widened with fear when I flipped his right wrist over and saw purple dye smeared on his fingertips.

"Why did you pull that firebox, kid? Is there a fire?" I asked sternly.

He began crying uncontrollably and shrugged his shoulders. My anger turned to pity, and I knelt beside him. "What's your name, sonny?"

His reply was Malcom. I could tell right away that he wasn't a juvenile delinquent. He was too scared. Procedurally, I was supposed to notify the police and fire marshal that a suspect had been apprehended. But I let my emotions outweigh my dutiful obligation.

"Tell me your address, and I'll take you home."

His arm was shaking so much that he could barely point down Wharton. I took his hand and walked him to a nicely maintained row house. It was only a short distance from where we had lost the three children a year ago. I knocked on the door, and a thin young woman, nicely dressed in business attire, answered. She smacked her hands on her cheeks and screamed, "Malcom! How did you get outside? I thought you were in your room. Why are you with a fireman?"

When I explained that he had pulled the firebox, she began crying hysterically, "He must have snuck out. I never let him go outside alone!" She knelt down and wrapped her arms around him. "Malcom, why did you pull the firebox? You know that's not right."

With tears streaming down his cheeks, frightened little Malcom looked up at his mother. "I wanna see the fire engines, Mommy."

She nuzzled him. "He loves fire engines. Every time he hears your siren, he runs to the window to watch you go by. I'm so sorry! I guess he just wanted to see your fire truck up close."

She looked up with sad eyes. "Do the cops need to take him to the stationhouse?"

"No, lady, we won't tell the cops," I said softly. "But do both Malcom and me a favor. Take him to the firehouse, and we'll show him around. He can even sit in the driver's seat. If he knows that he can see us whenever he wants, he won't pull the firebox again."

"Oh, thank you so much." She sobbed before planting a soft kiss on Malcom's cheek. "Tell the fireman you're sorry, Malcom." The teary-eyed boy apologized.

I know that it was the right move. It wasn't what the department's directives spelled out, but it was the right thing to do. Charlie O's principle: The rule book is just a guideline. A good officer makes common-sense decisions based on *all* the facts.

Though Diane was adjusting to dating a firefighter, she really didn't have much of an idea what my job entailed. As they say, a picture—or more appropriately, a video—is worth a thousand words.

July 1, 1981—Lieutenant, Engine 24

Around 7:15 p.m., I was on the apparatus floor, speaking on the pay phone with Diane, who was excitedly chatting away about our plans for Saturday's July 4 barbeque. I was gazing out the open apparatus doors as she talked about hamburgers, hot dogs, and potato salad. Right before my eyes, a huge column of black smoke rose into the pretty summer sky. I cut her off before she got to the baked beans. "Di! I see smoke! Got to go!"

"Oh," she replied in a worried voice. "Call me when you get back, no matter what time!"

I ran over to the watch desk and rang the bells. When the guys asked where we were going, I pointed to the widening column of smoke.

Clarkee's eyes almost popped out of his head. "Holy shit!"

Unsure what was burning, I cradled the microphone as we raced two short blocks to the southwest corner of Twentieth and Washington. Gigantic fireballs were coming through the roof of a two-story commercial building, approximately 150 feet square. The building was a goner, but the exposed houses were the main problem. I requested the box and the second alarm simultaneously, with orders for most of the companies to cover the right side and rear with master streams. When Kinney arrived, he pulled the third.

We returned to the station well after midnight, and I called Diane to let her know that I was okay. There was a huge sigh of relief in her voice when she said, "I saw your fire on the news. It was absolutely horrifying. I was worried sick." I reassured her that I was fine. I knew she believed me because her next words were "I found this new recipe for baked beans…"

I hadn't been chastised by a chief officer since the bashing by Les Misérables over Junk-Wagon 101's drafting debacle. But all good things must come to an end. It was time to get screamed at just for being at the wrong place at the wrong time.

July 9, 1981—Lieutenant, Engine 24

We arrived on the second alarm and were ordered to set up our Stang gun at the rear of the property. The fire was up to four alarms, and flames were leaping through the roof of the five-story office building at Ninth and Walnut.

Chief Kinney, who was assigned to the rear, was keeping a watchful eye on the rapidly changing conditions. From behind us I heard his radio crackle. The incident commander wanted all available manpower at the front of the building. It only took one firefighter to man our master stream, so Kinney directed me to leave Clarkee with our gun and go around front with my other two firefighters.

The three of us hustled down Ninth Street, but as soon as we turned onto Walnut, the entire front of the building collapsed. We dove behind a parked car, and I waited for the bricks to stop bouncing before I poked my head up. The first person I saw as the dust settled was the chief who summoned us. His tirade began from twenty-five feet away.

"What the fuck did I just tell you, Lieutenant? I said get the fuck away from the front of this goddamned building, didn't I? What the fuck's the matter with you? Are you hard of hearing?" His face was red with rage, and more fire was darting from his eyes than from the building. I could swear I actually saw steam coming off his forehead.

I'd been screamed at before, but that was by far the most intimidating. I knew he had me confused with someone else, but he didn't appear to be in the mood to debate the issue.

Unsure what to do, I stood there for a second waiting for orders. Hadn't he just told Kinney to send us around front? But instead of orders, he rushed toward me, screaming louder than I had ever heard anyone scream before. "Get the fuck out of here! Move!"

In less than a minute, we were back at our gun again. Kinney did a double take. "Why are you guys back so soon? What did he want you to do?"

"I'm not sure why he wanted us, Chief." I laughed. "But as soon as we turned the corner, the building collapsed, and he blasted me with both barrels just for being there. Then he chased us away."

Kinney nodded understandingly. "Oh, I see. Wrong place at the wrong time? Don't worry about it. He does that to us chiefs all the time."

The chief's rage toward me that day was simply misdirected. Obviously, he had ordered someone else out of the area before the collapse. But some officers were in his crosshairs for reasons totally unrelated to the fire they were battling.

September 9, 1981—Lieutenant, Engine 24

Alarm-system calls are rarely anything more than accidental alarms or system malfunctions. That's exactly what I was thinking when we were dispatched with Ladder 32 and Battalion 1 to a paper distribution ware-house. But as we turned onto Reed Street, the powder-blue sky ahead was blemished with heavy black smoke.

Constructed of heavy timber, the warehouse was 500 feet by 125 feet and varied from two to four stories in height. Heavy fire was showing from the roof of its center three-story section, and by the time I requested a full box assignment, the fire had spread to the adjacent fourth floor. Recalling the structure's heavy fire load from last spring's inspections, I had no doubt that it was a goner. Luckily, all the employees had evacuated and were accounted for.

Acting Battalion Chief Spitz had no doubts either; as soon as he pulled up, he requested the second alarm and ordered an exterior (defensive) attack on the fire. We quickly set up our Stang gun on Twenty-Fifth and began pouring nearly eight hundred gallons per minute into the center section. It hardly had any effect; the fire kept extending. Les Misérables requested two more alarms as soon as he arrived.

A half hour later, the six-alarm fire still wasn't under control. We were crouching by our gun, trying to shield ourselves from the intense radiant heat, when I spotted Les Misérables and a gaggle of other chiefs dash past us and dart east on Reed Street. A few seconds later, I saw the reason. The incident commander was storming down Twenty-Fifth. He had the same look of rage that he'd had back on Walnut Street. "Uh-oh," I thought, "someone is in trouble." Pretending not to notice him, I circled around a railroad support, making sure to stay out of his view until he had safely passed. Whew! Fortunately, I wasn't the one in his crosshairs.

Lieutenant Earl of 49's wasn't as lucky. As the building burned in the background, the chief began screaming in his face. With arms flailing, he stomped up and down and lambasted the lieutenant for a full ten minutes. This was surely more than misplaced aggression. I couldn't imagine what Earl had done wrong, but I wanted to know so I could ensure that I'd never make the same mistake.

Much later, after the fire was under control and the coast was clear, I made my way over to Earl. "Why the heck was he screaming at you?"

"Bob, it had nothing to do with the fire," he said, shaking his head disgustedly. "Somebody told him that one of my guys is taking street numbers over the pay phone in the firehouse. He threatened to fire both of us if it's true. What am I supposed to do? Bug the pay phone?"

I was bothered by how things that weren't completely within our control could get an officer into deep trouble.

While I was walking back, my sobering thoughts were interrupted when a young employee of the paper company called me over and stated that he was a firefighter elsewhere. "Hey, why didn't you guys make an interior attack on this fire?" he said arrogantly, grandstanding in front of a large group of fellow employees. I was annoyed that he was trying to impress his coworkers at my expense. I also didn't appreciate being second-guessed.

I tilted my head cockily. "Do you really think two hundred fifty gpm from a two-and-a-half-inch mobile line would have put a dent in this fire? The third floor was well involved and extending rapidly!"

He had begun stammering about flow rates and hydraulics when I cut him off.

"How many fires have you fought in buildings this size?"

That caught him completely off guard. "Well, a few years ago, we had this barn fire—" he said before I cut him off again.

"A barn fire? Listen, I'm kind of busy right now, but any time you'd like to discuss fire strategy and tactics or share experiences, stop by our firehouse. We're at Twentieth and Federal Streets. I'd be happy to discuss firefighting with you."

Later, I felt bad for snapping at the guy. His workplace was a total loss, and I'm sure he was worried about his job. Needless to say, he never showed up at our firehouse.

Each January, officers assigned to companies for three years were rotated (transferred). I was safe for another year at 24's, but Charlie O' was rotated to Southwest Philly. I was crestfallen. In addition to Charlie O's principle, I had learned so much from him.

CHAPTER 18

From Paris Green to Machetes

JANUARY 1, 1982—LIEUTENANT, ENGINE 24

Our first run of the year was with Ladder 19, Battalion 1, and Rescue 14. A homeowner on Mifflin Street was cleaning his basement when he knocked over a tin can and spilled a greenish powder. There wasn't a label on the can, but someone had scribbled on its lid, "Paris Green." When Chief Cusick arrived (Cusick had replaced Kenney), I was questioning the owner, who had no idea what had spilled. But I knew exactly what Paris green was: *rat poison.*

As a young boy, I had been tinkering with my chemistry set when I found an old can of the emerald-green powder in our basement. It was in a rectangular tin with "Poison" written next to a skull and crossbones on its label. That didn't deter me from scooping out a little to test it for copper by burning it on a Nichrome wire. When my parents smelled something burning, they rushed down the stairs. My mother nearly stroked out when she spotted the poison label, and the Paris green quickly disappeared from our house.

Cusick had been my instructor for the two hazardous-materials courses I'd had when I was in the fire-science program. When I told him that it was a small spill of Paris green, he replied, "What the hell is Paris green?"

"Chief, it's copper acetoarsenite, a compound that contains arsenic. It's used as rat poison."

Cusick looked at me sideways. "How the hell do you know that?"

"I had this thing for chemistry as a kid, Chief. Long story." I laughed.

"Bob," he said in a serious tone, "you should definitely transfer into Hazmat."

I waved my hands emphatically. "No thanks, Chief. I like it right where I am!"

In 1980 Engine 60 and Ladder 19 had become one of the department's three Hazardous Materials Task Force stations. Each one comprised an engine, ladder, foam pumper, and chemical unit. Firefighters assigned to those companies were specially trained to respond to hazardous-material incidents. I watched curiously as they cleaned up the spill that night. I loved chemistry, but I loved being at 24's much more. I didn't know it at the time, but the incident was a brief glimpse into my future.

That winter, the city announced the captain's examination. The format was 45 percent written, 45 percent oral, and 10 percent based on seniority. I knew how to study for the written portion but didn't have a clue what to do for the oral. Charlie O' was studying for battalion chief, which also had an oral portion, so I gave my old mentor a call. He gave me a few pointers but told me that the most important thing was to practice with other people. Taking his advice, I joined a study group.

I felt pretty good after the written, but it was difficult to gauge the subjectivity of the oral portion. When the results were published, I had finished number 32. At best, it was a gray area. I wasn't terribly disheartened, especially when they promoted twenty-six captains in the first batch. (There were only seventeen vacancies, but in a political move, the fire commissioner overpromoted to reach someone he wanted.) Nonetheless, I was number six on the list with nearly two years before it was set to expire.

Personally, 1982 was a busy year for me. Diane and I had gotten engaged on Christmas Day, 1981, and planned to wed that fall. We were also looking for a house in the city's Overbrook Park neighborhood. In the meantime, I was carrying a heavy course load at Temple. Satchmo, my partner from 43's, had since transferred to one of the busiest stations in the city, Engine 2 and Ladder 3. Their firehouse was close to Temple, so I frequently swapped (MXT'd) with him. Not only was it convenient for classes, but I loved the action. Besides, I always learned something new when I worked there.

June 25, 1982—Lieutenant, Engine 2 (MXT)

It was my last MXT payback for the spring's grueling semester. We began the shift by squeezing our cars into the tiny rear parking lot surrounded by high walls topped with concertina wire. It was safer than the street, but cars still got vandalized back there. I guess that's why some guys called the place Fort Apache. Regardless, 2's was one of my top choices for the next January, when I was due to rotate.

A half hour after shift change, we caught a first-in working fire on Lawrence Street. It was good to be battling blazes again with Frenchy, who was now in Ladder 3, and Chief Hoeffel, who was now assigned to Battalion 6.

After a rubbish fire, a false box, and an automobile fire, we caught another first-in dwelling fire on East York Street. Journey's "Who's Crying Now" was blaring on a radio somewhere in the dense smoke as we advanced our line down the second-floor hall. Suddenly a blur crashed into my hand light, jumped over my head, and scampered down the length of my body. A second later, another blur did the same thing. Were they rats? Fortunately they weren't. I heard a frightened little meow as the occupant's second cat jumped off my leg.

I was just finishing my reports when the bells rang again at five thirty. We were fourth-in at a working apartment fire at B and Westmoreland. Hoeffel directed us to cover the left exposure, where fire had extended into the second floor. The front room of the exposure was going pretty well when Hoeffel called me on the radio. "Battalion Six to Engine Two, give me a progress report."

"Engine Two, we're knocking the fire down, Chief. I *think* we got it."

Hoeffel snapped back, "Bobby, you *think*? You either got it or you don't. Get back to me when you know!"

After I was sure, absolutely sure, I got back to him. "Chief, we got it."

It was a little embarrassing, but it was a good lesson. Hoeffel needed facts, not suppositions. I never used the phrase "I think I got it" on the fireground again.

A few weeks later, back at 24's, I learned another lesson: the word "routine" shouldn't apply to any call, no matter how trivial—even calls as humdrum as rubbish fires.

July 10, 1982—Lieutenant, Engine 24

Philadelphia's three Hs of summer—hazy, hot, and humid—seemed to give the stench of dog shit an extra punch as we stretched our booster line up the alley. Ahead of us a gigantic pile of trash and garbage was burning freely. I recalled how those little old Italian ladies on Rosewood Street often had used brooms and garden hoses to wash the alleys clean on a regular basis. They'd had pride in their neighborhood. For some reason, in more recent days, nobody seemed to care. Well, almost nobody.

After the fire was extinguished, I noticed an angry-looking man standing behind us with his hands on his hips. The disheveled-looking man with charcoal stubble and a dirty white straw hat blended in perfectly with the filthy alley. As soon as we made eye contact, he began barking at me: "When the hell are you going to haul this trash away? You gotta get this damned garbage out of my alley!"

I looked behind myself and then back at him. "Are you talking to me? We're firemen, not trash men!"

I guess that pissed him off, because he pulled a huge machete from his pants. "I know who the hell you are, and you're going to take this damned trash out of the alley."

Behind him, I saw Capo slowly sneak out of the alley for help. Clarkee and I stood there staring the man down. Our only means of defense was our booster line. A direct blast between his eyes would buy us a little time if he charged us.

Capo quickly returned with big Stevie D. They were a sight for sore eyes. Stevie had our Halligan resting on his shoulder like a baseball bat, and Capo was sporting our heavy iron-claw tool. They positioned themselves within striking distance of the man, and Stevie loudly asked, "Hey, Loo, is there a problem here?" The guy swung his head around and quickly recalculated his odds. Seconds after he placed the machete back in his pants, two police officers charged up the alley, tackled him to the ground, and hauled him away.

As we were rolling up our hose, the handcuffed man was sitting in the back of a patrol car. Every time I passed by him, he cursed me. I was already annoyed because the man's arrest meant extra paperwork. The fifth time he cursed me, I saw red. I don't know if it was the heat, the extra typing, or his threats, but I flew into a rage. I charged the car, screaming, "Hey, asshole, I hope that some night your stupid ass is hanging out the window of a burning building. Guess what?" I grabbed my crotch. "Screw you!" The guy went completely bonkers and began kicking at the rear-passenger window. Police officers ran over to quiet him down as their sergeant chased me back to our pumper.

I later found out from the police that the guy had been high on something. I don't know if charges were ever filed, but I was never summoned to testify. But from then on, I carried the Halligan tool whenever we responded to *routine* rubbish fires.

I was due to rotate at the end of the year, and I had begun thinking about my choices. In addition to 2's, Engines 68, 57, and 5 were high on my list. The thought of going back to a ladder company never entered my mind.

July 26, 1982—Lieutenant, Engine 24

The buzzer in the office sounded once. "Engine Twenty-Four, Lieutenant Marchisello."

It was the familiar and friendly voice of Charlie O'. It was great to hear his voice again. "Where are you sitting on the captain's list now?"

"I'm still number six, Cap. Why?"

Charlie O' chuckled. "Yeah. They overpromoted a little, didn't they? You should get promoted before the list expires, but it's going to take a while. That's why I called. You're going to be rotated at the end of the year, so I was wondering if you'd be interested in working here with me. There's going to be an opening in Ladder 13 next week on my platoon."

I had always wanted to work at 68's but had never thought about making the move to a ladder company, so I hesitated. "The ladder?"

"Bobby," Charlie said in a fatherly tone, "you can only learn so much crawling on your belly with a hose. In a ladder company, you'll gain a better understanding of how fire travels and spreads. You're going to be a captain someday, and then they'll qualify you as an acting battalion chief. This will be great experience for you. We're working our balls off out here. It's a no-brainer, pal!"

"Charlie O's never steered me wrong before," I thought. "If I make the move, I'll be working right alongside my mentor. Why hold out for a slim shot at Two's or another busy engine company? I might wind up someplace dreadfully slow."

Charlie O' told me to forward a transfer request and said that he'd take care of the rest. My transfer was in the department mail before I left work.

CHAPTER 19

The Cuckoo's Nest

Charlie O' pulled some strings, and eleven days later, I was transferred to Ladder 13.

Housed in their original 1904 brick firehouse with its modified mansard roof, Ladder 13 shared their quarters with Engine 68, Battalion 7, and Rescue 3. Located on the cusp that divides West and Southwest Philly, it was one of the city's busiest fire stations at the time. Firefighters had nicknamed the three-story firehouse at Fiftieth Street and Baltimore Avenue the "Cuckoo's Nest" after the 1975 Academy Award–winning movie *One Flew Over the Cuckoo's Nest*. On my first day there, I found out why.

AUGUST 6, 1982—LIEUTENANT, LADDER 13

I parked on Fiftieth Street, grabbed my running gear, and walked toward the open apparatus doors where Big Franny was standing outside. Franny had a great sense of humor and a colossal pair of balls. The first time I met him, I had been a lieutenant at 24's. Big Franny had been punitively transferred to 24's on one of the other platoons. On his first day, I was standing outside waiting for shift change when he got out of his car. He walked directly up to me, smiled, and handed me a transfer request to return to 68's. It had to be the quickest transfer request in the department's history. He hadn't even walked in the door yet. Maybe a fix was in; before long he was transferred back to the Nest.

Franny began laughing when he saw me. "You're too sane to be here, Loo. You should hand me *your* transfer request."

"Nah, Fran," I replied. "I actually asked to come here."

The bells rang in the background. "Chief only!" Within seconds, Battalion 7's car was racing east down Baltimore Avenue with its siren blaring. As I was placing my gear by Ladder 13, the bells rang again, this time four short rings. "Squad!" Two firefighters scrambled into Rescue 3, darted out the side garage door, and screamed south on Fiftieth. I was about to go upstairs when the bells rang again. "Engine only, Fifty-Second and Whitby, rubbish!" Charlie O' rubbed my head as he trotted past. In less than a minute, we were the only company left in the firehouse.

Bells ringing, firefighters running around, and companies responding in different directions were the perfect backdrop for a firehouse called the Cuckoo's Nest. I instantly fell in love with the place.

I was drinking coffee in the kitchen when 68's came back from their run. Charlie O' grabbed a cup, and we were chatting when I felt someone breathing down the back of my neck. I spun around, and the first thing I saw was a white battalion chief's cap. Showing respect for the rank, I sprang to my feet. The entire kitchen erupted with laughter. It wasn't the chief; it was Buddy, a mentally challenged adult who frequented the firehouse. He loved wearing his donated cap and serving as the Nest's official greeter.

Buddy sat next to me and said, "Hi, buddy."

I shook his hand and replied, "Hi, Buddy. It's nice to meet you."

As I chatted with Charlie O', Buddy kept tapping me on the shoulder and repeating, "Hi, buddy."

I kept answering him until Charlie O' nudged me. "Bobby, buy him a candy bar, and he'll leave you alone. That's all he wants." Buddy followed me to the canteen like a little puppy dog and eagerly chose a Snickers bar. I tossed a quarter into the coin box, and he disappeared.

Out on the apparatus floor, Ladder 13's driver, nicknamed "the Third," gave me a quick tour of our 1978 Seagrave hundred-foot tiller ladder. After we finished, I was heading upstairs when I heard someone loudly yell, "Yahoo!" Unable to determine where it had come from, I just shook my head. A while later, while I was in the office, another *yahoo* resounded throughout the second floor. I popped my head out the door, but nobody was around. More *yahoo*s occasionally reverberated throughout the morning. Now, Charlie O' was a master prankster, and I wasn't sure if he was trying to set me up, so I wasn't about to ask him if he also heard the *yahoo*s.

Throughout the morning the bells sounded several times for 68's and Rescue 3. In between, several *yahoos* sporadically echoed throughout the station. Ladder 13 didn't turn a wheel (didn't get any runs), so I had time to set up my locker.

Around noon the bells rang five short bursts. I had no idea what that meant, so I began running for the stairs. Charlie O' came strolling out of his office, his cigarette dangling from his mouth. "Yo, pal, it's only lunchtime." As I was following him down the stairs, another *yahoo* bounced off the walls. Charlie O' didn't flinch, so I pretended not to hear it. At that point, I was sure he was in on it.

After lunch, and a few more *yahoos*, the entire office suddenly began rumbling. I looked up, and the fluorescent bulbs were shaking violently. Thinking it was an earthquake or some explosions at the refineries, I rushed into Charlie O's office. "Cap, what the hell's rumbling?"

He was sitting calmly at his desk. "Oh, that?" He giggled. "It's just the guys playing basketball upstairs. It makes a hell of a racket, but it keeps them happy."

I stood there amazed. "There's a basketball court on the wooden floor above?"

Ringing bells snapped me out of my astonishment. "Everybody! Engine third-in, ladder second-in, and chief first-in, Sixty-Third and Walnut Streets, for an apartment fire." As I darted out of the office, I collided with two firefighters rushing down from the basketball game. We bounced around the hallway like pinballs before eventually making it to the stairs. The call turned out to be minor, and we quickly returned to the station. At least the run temporarily ended the hoops fest. The office was quiet again—quiet enough to hear occasional *yahoos* pierce the air.

A little while later, I heard a different noise. This time it was the distinctive clicking sound made by the pawls of a portable ladder being raised. Figuring that it was probably roofers nearby, I didn't pay it much mind. But seconds later, 68's engine started, and I heard the pump engage. I peeked into Charlie O's office, but he wasn't there. Just then, I heard the engine rev up. Something was definitely amiss.

Suddenly a racket came from the small room next to my office. A hose stream was splashing around, and somebody was bouncing off the walls. I darted out into the hallway just as a soaking-wet firefighter came flying out the door. He had been taking a nap so the other firefighters, and Charlie O', decided to drench him.

Another *yahoo* sounded in the background as the firefighter dripped his way to the locker room. At least I knew that the calls weren't coming from him.

As he disappeared from view, the bells rang again. "Everybody, first-in! Forty-Ninth and Spruce, an apartment." Snickers and giggles came from several firefighters as they followed wet footprints down the stairs. The call turned out to be a small rubbish fire, which 68's handled alone. Back in the office, I logged in the run and was done! No fire report. It felt great to be in a ladder for a change.

Around five o'clock that evening, another extra-loud *yahoo* echoed off the walls. I couldn't take it any longer, so I marched through the bathroom that connected our offices. "Okay, Cap, I give up. Who the hell keeps yelling 'Yahoo'?"

Charlie O' began laughing hysterically. "I was wondering when you were going to ask. It's the 'Reverend.' He's working an MXT in Sixty-Eight's today. He constantly reads the Bible and yells 'Yahoo!' whenever he gets high on Jesus."

Charlie O' regained his composure, took a long drag, and leaned back in his chair. "I know we didn't get any work, but how was your first day?"

I tilted my head. "This place is like a friggin' insane asylum, Cap, but I'm going to love it here."

Charlie O' almost fell off his chair. "I knew you would. Welcome to the Cuckoo's Nest, pal."

The following week, on August 13, I responded to my first working fire with Ladder 13. Only moments after I paid my dues, another candy bar for

Buddy, we were dispatched to a raging dwelling fire on Fifty-First Street. For the rest of my time at the Nest, Buddy would be in the kitchen eagerly awaiting his treat as soon as I walked into the firehouse. It was a small price to pay for being stationed there. Besides, I grew fond of Buddy.

Firefighting is hazardous, and everyone who swears the oath knows the risks. Philadelphia firefighters have lost their lives in various ways. Some died from unusual mishaps, like ladderman George Dungan, who died in 1880 after being crushed between the apparatus and the station doors. Hoseman John Hicks died in 1900 after being kicked in the stomach by a horse. And Lieutenant Robert Moorehead perished after he fell into a boiling vat of lampblack in 1919. Like my brother firefighters, I was aware that accidental LODDs were possible. But I never imagined that a LODD could result from an *intentional* act by another firefighter.

When I walked into the firehouse kitchen on the morning of August 14, 1982, I was shocked and saddened by the news. The unthinkable had happened in the Ninth Battalion only hours before.

For some unfathomable reason, off-duty firefighter James Nero snapped. Just before six o'clock that morning, during a fight with his girlfriend, he stabbed her in the abdomen. In a rage, he then drove to the home of off-duty firefighter Robert Upshaw and shot him as he answered the door. Upshaw was struck in the wrist and elbow. Next on the list was Firefighter Stanley Brown. Brown was preparing for his B Platoon shift when Nero knocked on his door. As soon as he answered, he was shot in the head. Nero wasn't finished yet. He got back into his car and drove to his Germantown firehouse, Engine 9 and Ladder 21, where he was scheduled to begin his 8:00 a.m. shift. Kenneth Gallagher had the misfortune of being on watch. Nero walked into the station and shot him in the head too.

After fleeing the scene, Nero barricaded himself in his sister's apartment. He surrendered to police a few hours later. His girlfriend and Upshaw survived the attempts on their lives, but Gallagher lost his life hours after the shooting, and Brown died two days later. Shock reverberated throughout the department. Workplace violence wasn't supposed to happen in firehouses! Our job was dangerous enough.

Nero was convicted of the homicides and was sentenced to two life terms plus fifteen years. It has never been determined why he shot the firefighters. There were rumors that when he was apprehended, he had a list in his possession with more of his coworkers' home addresses.

That fall, just as Charlie O' had promised, we began getting a ton of work. He was also right about getting a totally different perspective of firefighting as a ladder officer. Charlie O' and I would often discuss fireground strategy and tactics for hours. I found his approach as pragmatic and down to earth as those of Uncle Frank, Plumley, and Hoss. It was great working on the same platoon with him.

Charlie O' knew the attributes of each firefighter in the station very well. The Third had the best gift of gab. It seemed that he could talk to anybody about anything.

December 11, 1982—Lieutenant, Ladder 13

When we arrived behind 68's and Battalion 7, the distraught man was perched on the beams of a railroad trestle, nearly a fifty-foot drop to the tracks below. Police officers were trying to coax him down, but every time they approached, he released his grip and threatened to jump.

The chief shut the rail traffic down and positioned Rescue 19M along with a few firefighters at track level. A few years ago, the department removed the antiquated life nets from ladder companies, so there wasn't much for us to do except hope for the best. But Charlie O' had another idea.

He rubbed his jaw while studying the situation intently. "Bobby, get the Third up here. If he can't talk this guy down, then nobody can." The police were apprehensive about letting a firefighter negotiate with the man, but Charlie O' convinced them to let him try.

The Third took his helmet and coat off and slowly approached the trestle. The guy quickly spotted him, but before he could do anything drastic, the Third had him deeply engaged in conversation. Usually boisterous in the firehouse, the Third was speaking so softly that I could barely hear what he was saying. With each sentence he inched closer and closer. Fifty words later he was on the trestle. The guy was so engrossed in the discussion that he didn't even notice.

We stood there silently watching the Third work his magic. Another fifty words, and they were perched side by side chatting away like they were sharing beers in a bar. I watched in amazement as the Third gently took the man's hand and slowly led him back to safety. I have to admit that during the last few seconds, I was scared shitless, worrying that the man would suddenly jump and pull my firefighter with him. But he didn't. The police backed off as the Third helped the man into the back seat of a police car for a trip to the hospital to be evaluated and 302'd (committed involuntarily for mental health).

While congratulating the Third, I asked, "What did you talk to him about?"

He laughed. "You know, Loo, the moon, the stars, usual stuff."

As soon as we returned to the station, I prepared a memorandum requesting that the Third be given an official commendation from the department.

In addition to the fires and other action, I did more laughing at the Nest than anywhere I had been assigned previously. Each platoon had a unique cast of characters, and shift change was like a TV sitcom.

Diane and I had gotten married, and by January she was a few months pregnant. One day she told me that she was concerned that I seemed to get depressed during my four days off. I had to reassure her that it had nothing to do with my adjustment to married life. I gently rubbed her baby bump. "Di, it's just that we have so much darn fun at work. But I love being home with you just as much."

She gently kissed me and then looked into my eyes. "Yeah, right!"

At the Nest, we had a vacancy on our platoon, and it was rightly filled by a firefighter nicknamed "Charlie Tuna." Outrageously funny, he was perfect for the Nest. One day when I was working another swap at Fort Apache, Frenchy told me that Tuna was a *monkey* on the fireground. I wasn't exactly sure what he meant until I actually saw it for myself.

January 28, 1983—Lieutenant, Ladder 13

Fire was blowing out of the first-floor windows of a porch-front dwelling on Kingsessing Avenue. The guys quickly threw a ladder against the porch roof. As soon as I heard the crashing of glass, I turned to tell our pack man, Tuna, to climb into the second-floor window to conduct search, but he wasn't there. Where was he? He had been standing next to me only a second ago.

Suddenly Tuna popped his head out of a second-floor front window. Smoke was swirling around his head. "It's all clear up here, Loo!" How the hell did he get up there? He didn't climb up our ladder. The first floor was well involved, so he couldn't have gotten in that way. When the fire was under control, I asked him.

"Well, when I saw that the fire was on the first floor, Loo," he replied, "I ran up the alley, shinnied up the drain pipe, and climbed in through the back window."

I nodded. "Like a monkey, right?"

"Yeah, Loo." He giggled.

"Well, let me know before you disappear next time, *cheetah*."

In 1983 the Philadelphia 76ers won the 1982–83 NBA championship. We were on night shift during the final buzzer.

May 31, 1983—Lieutenant, Ladder 13

At one o'clock in the morning, thousands of jubilant fans were dancing, cheering, and celebrating along South Fifty-Second Street. The Philadelphia 76ers had just beaten the Los Angeles Lakers by a score of 115 to 108 to win the 1982–83 NBA World Championship.

As we crawled underneath a SEPTA bus, we could hear repetitive chanting. "Moses! Moses! Moses! Doctor J! Doctor J! Doctor J!" they shouted, for

Moses Malone and Julius Erving, adding, "Sixers are world champs! Sixers are world champs! Sixers are world champs!" But one strapping tall youth wasn't celebrating anymore. Somehow he had been dragged under a huge Route 52 bus as it tried to negotiate its way through the euphoric crowd.

There was no way to get to him without crawling through his blood and gore. Sticky red fluid saturated our running coats as we inched closer to his motionless body. I had my doubts that he was alive until one of 68's EMTs placed two fingers over his carotid artery and said, "We got a pulse!"

The victim was lying face up with his partially open eyes rolled upward. Blood was oozing from the back of his head and flowing freely from his leg. A foot-long section of his thigh was peeled back, revealing muscle and bone. The EMT slid his avulsed skin, which was caught atop the axle, back over the wound. Globs of yellow adipose tissue clung to the axle. Another firefighter pressed a white towel over the huge gash. It quickly turned bright red, but it slowed the bleeding to a few drips. Paramedics placed a cervical collar around his neck and slid him onto a backboard, and within minutes, we loaded him into the back of the rescue.

Engine 68's pump operator washed the gore from our running coats, and we climbed back onto our apparatus. As we slowly made our way along Fifty-Second Street, I heard a section of the crowd change their chant to, "Firemen are world champs! Firemen are world champs! Firemen are world champs!" It felt great to be cheered for a change.

CHAPTER 20

Good-Bye, Charlie O'. Hello, Joe the Boss

The dust hadn't settled from the 1980 layoffs before the city was claiming financial woes again. Like always, they turned to the fire department for cuts. On June 27, 1983, the department closed Division 3 and Battalion 6 and consolidated three double fire stations into task forces (an engine and ladder combined as a single unit, which required less staffing). The resulting elimination of four deputy chiefs, four battalion chiefs, and three captains killed my chances of getting promoted. I wasn't terribly disappointed, though; I was happy at the Nest.

In July of 1983, Diane gave birth to a beautiful baby girl. We named her Maria. The very next night, I proudly handed out "It's a girl!" cigars to my brothers at the Nest. That's when I learned that Charlie O' was leaving.

Rather than take his chances with the coming officer rotation, Charlie O' jumped on an opening at Engine 52, which was closer to his northeast home. The guys threw him a great farewell dinner on his last night shift. The following morning, I gave him a big hug and thanked him for all that he'd done for me.

"Bobby, don't forget all the things you learned," he said as he loaded his car. He gave me a reassuring wink and took one last long drag. "We'll cross paths again, pal." I was going to miss him terribly, but luckily his replacement was another legend.

Captain Joe Loughrin earned his reputation as a leather-lunged firefighter at Engine 2. Dedicated, witty, and one of the greatest firefighters I ever worked with, Joe "the Boss" took over at 68's. The department couldn't have picked a better fit for the Nest. Like his predecessor, Loughrin was down to earth, funny, and friendly, yet he also displayed excellent leadership skills.

AUGUST 11, 1983—LIEUTENANT, LADDER 13

At dinnertime Commissioner Rizzo called Joe the Boss and told him that they were about to break ground on our new firehouse at Fifty-Second and Willows.

The sky had turned black, and thunder was ominously looming in the background as Joe the Boss shared the good news with us at the kitchen table. "Yep, it's going to be a one-story building facing Fifty-Second—" Suddenly there was a loud *boom!* We ducked for cover as a brilliant white flash of lightning accompanied the thunderous clap that rocked our firehouse.

"Wow! That was close!" I cried. "I hope it didn't strike anything." I was wrong!

Three minutes later we were racing to an old four-story apartment building at Fifty-Fifth and Chester. Medium smoke was coming from the roof of the recently converted church, which neighbors saw get struck by a lightning bolt. Engine 68 quickly knocked down the fire in the cockloft, but it took us over an hour to rip open the walls and ceilings to check for further extension.

Once we were back in the kitchen, we talked about how lighting strikes can energize electric circuits for blocks in every direction. Sometimes the wiring in nearby buildings gets overheated and ignites wooden construction materials. Those materials can smolder for hours before erupting into flames. A few hours later, our discussion was confirmed.

Three o'clock that morning, the man on watch flipped the master light switch and pressed hard on the bells. "Full box, everybody first-in, Fifty-Fourth and Chester, a building!" Thick black smoke was pushing from every crack and crevice of a large furniture warehouse. It was only a block away from the earlier fire.

The Third raised our main ladder to the roof, and as we climbed upward, Joe the Boss yelled, "Bobby, be careful. This baby's a goner." It was good advice. As soon as we opened the skylights, flames leaped upward. Joe the Boss was right; the building was doomed. I ordered a hasty retreat, and just as we were climbing down, the center section of the roof collapsed. The fire quickly grew to four alarms.

We began getting a ton of fires again in October. That's when I saw for myself what a leather-lung Joe the Boss really was.

OCTOBER 22, 1983—LIEUTENANT, LADDER 13

The smoke couldn't possibly be any thicker as 68's stretched their line inside. Crawling behind them, I was only five feet inside the doorway when the dense, choking smoke drove me to my belly. Gasping for air, I could hardly move. Suddenly I heard Joe the Boss calling from up ahead, "Over here, guys. It's a kitchen fire." He was talking as though he were still sitting in the firehouse kitchen. There wasn't a hint of coughing, puffing, panting, or gasping in his voice. When the smoke began to lift, I was even more amazed. He had been standing upright where the smoke was thickest the entire time! How could anyone possibly take that much smoke?

Wilson Goode was elected mayor in November, and Joe Rizzo's days as fire commissioner were numbered. During the interviews to replace Rizzo, Goode asked each candidate whom they would choose, other than themselves, to be fire commissioner. Almost every one of them had the same answer—Deputy Chief Bill Richmond, my former boss at R&P. I couldn't have agreed more. A brilliant, progressive, and proven leader, Richmond was appointed fire commissioner in early 1984.

The staffing of BLS rescue units was a burden on the EMTs assigned to companies like 68's, so Richmond enacted a new policy. EMTs were to be transferred into ladders housed with rescues and rotated into them. A few of my firefighters, including Tuna, weren't EMTs, so they had to leave. I was initially annoyed when I found out that they were being replaced by rookies from Fire School. But as soon as I met rookies Greg Jenkins and Chris Stewart, I knew that they were exceptional. They were the first rookies assigned to me as an officer, and I wanted to train them properly. The Nest would provide the experience they needed to complement their training. That experience came quickly.

Our deputy chief was a no-nonsense guy and a stickler about opening the roof over the fire. It was one of the first things he'd look for when he arrived on firegrounds, so I always made sure we got it done quickly. But every once in a while, Murphy's Law intervenes and ruins the best of intentions. Luckily for me, appearances can sometimes be deceiving.

May 14, 1984—Lieutenant, Ladder 13

Heavy fire was showing from the top-floor windows of the four-story apartment building. It was critically important to open the roof for this fire, so I paused at the base of the ladder until I heard the welcoming sound of our power saw buzzing away. I was turning to go inside when suddenly an awful clunking noise came from the roof, and the buzzing came to an abrupt halt. The doggone saw had died!

I grabbed an axe and climbed to the roof to help. We had to cut a big hole over the fire. The power saw was sitting on the roof smoking as Chris, Greg, and the Third whacked away with their axes. I yanked on the saw's pull cord, but it wouldn't budge. The engine had seized.

The guys weren't making very much progress, and after only one swing of my axe, I found out why. There were at least five layers of tar and paper over the wood. Our axes were binding and sticking with every swing. The guys had scribed a textbook four-foot by four-foot outline in the tar, but after several minutes we'd only managed to cut one-foot lines on two adjoining sides. Figuring a small hole was better than nothing, we began pounding away at the intersecting lines and finally pushed roughly a one-square-foot section into the fire below. It was only a sixteenth of the size I wanted, but flames immediately began shooting from the opening. The fire was so intense that within minutes the fire burned the roof away, and the hole expanded to more than twenty square feet.

When I reached the ground to go inside, our deputy chief was looking upward. "Hey, Lieutenant, get over here!" I was sure that he was angry about our small initial hole, so I trotted over expecting to catch hell. To my amazement, he patted me on the back. "Nice job, Lieutenant. That's exactly what I like, a nice big hole directly over the fire." If he'd only known.

At 2:30 p.m. on June 8, 1984, it was ninety degrees and humid when an Amtrak train packed with passengers departed Thirtieth Street Station. Five minutes later it derailed near Forty-Ninth and Paschall, about a dozen blocks from the Nest. We were working day shift.

June 8, 1984—Lieutenant, Ladder 13

I peered over the side of the overpass at the unbelievable sight below. Several silver passenger cars of an Amtrak train looked like toppled toys lying on their sides. Cries, moans, and screams were coming from every car. For a few seconds, I was transfixed by the surreal scene, but I quickly snapped back to reality. We had a ton of work to do.

Our first concern was the thirteen-thousand-volt catenary system that powered the huge trains. Luckily, all the wires were still in place on the poles. The chief placed the entire box in service and requested several additional rescue units. He assigned each engine and ladder a different car. We headed down the steep grass slopes carrying tools, ladders, and first-aid supplies. I double-checked the catenary again before we placed our metal ladder against our assigned car. We then climbed up and dropped another ladder into the side door.

Once inside, we triaged the passengers and prioritized their removal. Overall, things weren't too bad in our car. Several passengers were complaining of neck and back injuries. One man had a compound fracture of his lower leg, and there were lots of cuts, bumps, and bruises. The operation was labor intensive. We removed the ambulatory people first and then the fracture case. About a dozen people had to be collared, backboarded, lifted out of the car, lowered to the ground, and carried up the steep embankment. By the time we finished, we were exhausted.

I was sitting on the back step of 68's when a grateful gray-haired woman passenger walked up to me. She placed both of her hands on my cheeks and kissed me on the lips. "Thank you! You guys were our angels today." She made me love my job even more, if that's possible.

Diane had returned to work, so I became Mr. Mom during my days off. At noon on June 13, 1984, I was feeding Maria a jar of Gerber's beets. I dreaded beets day! By the time Maria was done eating, everything within five feet of her high chair was stained with red mung. The *Action News* theme was playing as I dipped a spoonful from the jar. My hand froze when I heard the top story. A Philadelphia firefighter had been killed and several others injured when a burning house collapsed on them. Joseph Konrad, thirty-seven, of Engine 25, had been killed while fighting a vacant-dwelling fire on Tulip Street in the Kensington section of the city. He was the father of five children. My one-year-old daughter looked at her daddy curiously as tears flowed down his cheeks.

Later that summer we moved into our new fire station at Fifty-Second and Willows. Its modern split-level layout was great for getting out fast, but the place lacked the charm of the big old house.

As we were making the move, the department announced the next captain's examination. The current list hadn't expired, but my chances of promotion were nil. Between studying for classes at Temple and babysitting Maria, I devoted every minute I could to preparing for the test. At least if I didn't do well, I thought, I had another year at the Nest, but I was wrong.

A few weeks later, my name unexpectedly showed up on the 1985 lieutenant's rotation list. Because I had just missed the cutoff date, it came as a complete surprise. My days fighting fires at the Nest were numbered.

December 8, 1984—Lieutenant, Ladder 13

Heavy fire was showing from two windows on the third floor of a large apartment building on Osage Avenue. A few windows away, a panic-stricken young woman was perched on the sill screaming for help. There were also two people waving for help at a second-floor window. As my firefighters raised portable ladders to rescue those on the second floor, I hopped on our turntable and scurried up the main ladder as the Third was raising it.

When I got to the top, the woman was frightened out of her mind. "I'm scared of ladders. Please don't let me fall."

"You'll be fine, honey. We do this every day," I lied convincingly. "I'm going to place your feet on the rungs, and then you can come down on your butt, okay?"

She was doing fine until she looked down. Suddenly she panicked and kicked my hand light from its shoulder strap. I watched helplessly as it sailed down and crashed through the back window of a parked automobile. It took a lot of coaxing to unfreeze her, but she eventually followed me down.

I added a memo explaining the automobile's damage to my fire report. Ugh!

I felt pretty good after taking the captain's exam and was hopeful. In the meantime, I submitted five prioritized choices for companies where I preferred to be rotated.

My first choice was a no-brainer—Engine 41. It was first-in at my Overbrook home, had a great reputation, was busy, and most importantly had a lieutenant's opening on the rotation list. After my night shifts at the Nest, Diane usually drove to the firehouse with Maria in the car seat, and we'd swap cars. She'd go to work, and I'd take Maria back home. Engine 41 was close enough that Diane wouldn't need to drag Maria out of bed on cold winter mornings.

But when the tentative rotation assignments were published, they penciled me in for Engine 40. It wasn't even one of my choices! Though officers were permitted to swap, Coxie, the lieutenant who was going to 41's, lived in Overbrook. I didn't even bother calling him. Surely, I thought, 41's had to be his top choice.

It wasn't. A week before the swap deadline, I unexpectedly received a call from Coxie. "Yo, Bob, I heard that you're interested in Forty-One's?"

"Yeah, I sure am," I replied excitedly.

"Well, I want Sixteen's, so I've managed to work out a swap," he said. "Huh?"

"It's a four-way swap, man." He giggled. "Just forward a memo, and Forty-One's is yours."

"Coxie, you're a wheeler-dealer. I love you, man!" I exclaimed. It was the fastest memo I ever typed. I was transferred to 41's effective January 18, 1985.

Two days before my transfer was to take place, I was home doing my Mr. Mom routine when I received a call from a 141st classmate, Big Bird, who was Ladder 13's C Platoon lieutenant. I figured I had forgotten something in my locker, but he was way too excited for that.

"Bob, the captain's list just came out, and we both did well, classmate! You're number six on the list, and I'm number ten!"

The glut of captains was dwindling, so my chances for promotion were excellent this time. I called Diane at work to share the news and then popped the lid on a can of beer to celebrate as I ate my lunch. Maria, who was making a mess of her lunch again, gave me a puzzled look. She knew that it was unusual for Daddy to drink from a silver can at lunchtime. I figured that she should celebrate too, so I popped open a can of cola, poured some in her bottle, and let her taste soda for the very first time in her life. She made a sour face at first and then quickly downed the rest and held out the bottle for more. I poured a little more and said, "This is soda, Maria."

She gulped it down and held the bottle out once again. "Doo-da!" For the rest of the afternoon, she crawled around belching and saying, "Doo-da!"

"Now don't tell Mommy about the doo-da, Maria," I pleaded as I chased after her.

My mother couldn't find a firefighter's costume so she dressed me as a policeman. Behind me is the window where I watched Ladder 11 pass (Halloween, 1952).

Philadelphia firefighters demonstrate the use of scaling ladders (1960s).

My first firehouse, the quarters of Engine 60 and Ladder 19 as it was in 1973.

Captain Blood the Rookie (1973).

Chemical 3, the first fire apparatus I drove (1974).

View from the tillerman's seat of Ladder 19 (1974). The watch box is on the left.

Firefighters removing "Bubba" (April 4, 1974). Note old verses new helmet styles. Firefighter on the extreme left is wearing a driver's helmet used at the time.

Engine 24 and Rescue 14 (1975)

Dinner in Engine 24's tiny kitchen. From left to right: Joe Podgorski (detailed), John Hade, Sharpie, Gino, and Hoss (1975).

The tragic Gulf Refinery Fire, which claimed the lives of eight brother firefighters. (August 17, 1975).

Engine 24's Stang Gun after the Gulf Fire.

Allegheny Airlines crash (June 23, 1976).

Rear view of Allegheny Airlines crash where the tail section sheared off.

Tac-10 (1977).

Fire Commissioner Joseph Rizzo offering congratulations
at my promotion to lieutenant (January 9, 1978).

My first assignment as lieutenant, Engine 43, Platoon
A (1978). I'm second from the left.

"Commissioner Rizzo placed us here!" One of the fires where the ploy worked (1978). I'm behind Riley with my hand on the compartment door.

At my desk at research and planning (1979).

Aide Station #6 during the visit of Pope John Paul II
(October, 1979). Firefighter Dennis O'Neill to my left was
shot in the hand during the 1978 MOVE shootout.

Back to 24's (1980).

With Ladder 13 at the Cuckoo's Nest's new firehouse in 1984. I'm in the center.

Promoted to captain on August 12, 1985. From left to right:
Fire Commissioner William Richmond, Diane, Maria,
Captain Marchisello, Alex, and Mayor Goode.

Back to South Philly as the captain of Engine 49 in 1985. (I'm holding Maria, and Alex is sitting in the driver's seat).

The fire on Passyunk Avenue that was fueled by polyurethane vapors. This was the real test (1991).

There wasn't much left after the building collapsed. The "Shaftway" placards on the left indicated that this was a commercial property that had been converted into apartments.

Celebrating twenty years in the department on April 23, 1993. Battalion Chief Fran Hanson (left) presenting gifts to 141st Classmate Bill Hopper (center) and myself (right).

The firefighters from Engine 60, Ladder 19, and Deputy 1 presented me with my very own chief's car during my last night as captain (we had just returned from a fire, hence the dirty face). Lumpy's sitting behind me (Christmas Eve, 1996).

Posing with Mom and Dad at my promotion to Battalion Chief in 1996.

In my office at the Philadelphia Fire Academy as Chief of the HMAU (1997).

You've got to have a sense of humor to be a firefighter (HMAU, 1998).

Back in the field as Battalion 1 in 2000.

Overturned Xylene tank truck on I-95. I never feared
chemicals because I understood their hazards (2006).

My first major fire as deputy chief (2008).

With my retired aide Bill Gaffney at Engine 53 and
Ladder 27's alumni luncheon in 2009.

My aide Ed Hutt (to my left) and me surrounded by Squad 47's B Platoon (2010).

My last fire, 11th and Callowhill Streets, came in June of 2010.

The three members of Class 141 to reach the rank of deputy chief. Left to right, John Devlin, me, and George Yaeger (2010). Devlin was also appointed as a deputy fire commissioner.

Me and my first and favorite mentor, "Uncle Frank"
Castellucci, during my last night at the firehouse.

My family, Alex, Diane, and Maria, during my last night at the firehouse.

CHAPTER 21

Closer to Home

E ngine 41 was quartered with Ladder 24 at Sixty-First and Thompson Streets in West Philly. Their one-story tan brick firehouse, built in 1957, resembled Engine 24's. It even had the same drab green interior masonry walls. The only difference was that it was a little bit bigger.

At the time the department was desperately trying to find ways to keep pace with the ever-increasing EMS calls. Other cities had implemented a concept called the "First Responder Program," where engine companies staffed with an EMT were equipped with backboards, trauma kits, and resuscitators so they could respond to EMS calls. Commissioner Richmond decided to pilot the same type of program in the Eleventh Battalion. Since Engine 41 was in the Eleventh, whether I liked it or not, I quickly found myself back in the medical business.

JANUARY 18, 1985—LIEUTENANT, ENGINE 41

The ride to 41's on that frigid Friday morning was so short that my car didn't even warm up enough to blow hot air from the heater.

When I was at the Nest, we had caught a lot of fires with Engine 41, so I was familiar with most of my firefighters. Dad, our gray-haired senior man, was the oldest member in the battalion. Bright-eyed rookies Mikey and Foxy had about five years' combined experience between them. Denny, a neighborhood resident and solid firefighter, was our driver for that day's shift. As Denny was showing me around our Seagrave pumper, the bells rang for my first run with 41's. It was a medical call, only a block from our firehouse.

I tossed my coat and boots into the cab, slipped into my work jacket, and climbed aboard. As we were making the sharp 180-degree right turn onto

Thompson, I keyed the microphone and told the dispatcher we were responding. Before I could finish my message, we were on scene. Denny jerked the apparatus to a halt, jumped out, and raced into the two-story row home ahead of everybody. "That's good," I was thinking. "He's really motivated."

At that very second, the dispatcher replied, "Okay, Engine Forty-One, use caution. That's reported to be a shooting. Police are not on location, and the shooter may still be in the house."

"Jesus Christ! Denny! Denny! Hold up. It's a shooting!" It was too late; he'd already disappeared inside. Was one of my guys going to get shot on my first run with 41's? I had no choice but to run into the house after him.

Denny was in a dimly lit living room, kneeling next to the lifeless body of a middle-aged woman slumped on her sofa. Blood was oozing from a small hole in her chest.

"Denny," I whispered as I glanced around the room, "is there any sign of the shooter?"

He looked back with tears in his eyes. "Loo, she's my neighbor. Somebody shot my neighbor!"

Mikey and Foxy trotted inside toting our resuscitator and trauma kit. Police sirens were screaming in the background as we pulled the woman onto the floor and began chest compressions. Sadly, blood spurted high from the hole. She'd been shot in the heart. We applied several four-by-four-inch gauze pads over the wound and resumed compressions while forcing air into her lungs with our resuscitator. We all knew that she was a goner.

Heavy footsteps from behind startled us. Thankfully it was the police. They quickly spread throughout the house with their guns drawn, but the shooter was long gone. Even though we knew it was hopeless, we continued CPR until Rescue 7M arrived. Out of respect for Denny, I greeted the paramedics at the door and told them not to pronounce her dead on scene. They rushed her to the Lankenau Hospital.

Denny was shaken up, but he insisted on finishing his shift. What an ace! We made ourselves available just in time to be dispatched to another medical call. This one was for a man convulsing in the kitchen of his Lancaster Avenue home. As I'd seen so many times while riding with the medicine wagon, an empty prescription bottle of the antiseizure drug Dilantin was sitting on the counter. At least the call wasn't dangerous for us.

Our hoagies arrived for lunch, but before I could unwrap mine, we were dispatched to Fifty-Seventh and Vine for an unconscious man lying in the street. We covered him with a blanket until the rescue took him to the hospital. As soon as they left, we were dispatched to Fifty-Ninth Street for a man who had slipped on the ice and fractured his lower leg. We applied an air splint and waited nearly twenty minutes for Rescue 16M to arrive from their firehouse in East Falls.

When we got back to the station, detectives were waiting to interview us about the shooting, but they only had time to take my name and rank before the bells rang again. Within minutes we arrived at Fifty-Fifth and Lancaster for a woman suffering a CVA (cerebrovascular accident, or stroke). I was getting a quick EMS refresher course on my first day.

The detectives didn't finish interviewing us until 1530 hours (the department had switched to military time). Ladder 24's lieutenant, Bob, smiled as he poked his head through the office door. "So, how do you like the First Responder Program?"

"Well, it's going to keep us pretty busy." I chuckled. "But a problem will arise someday when we're out there tending to a nosebleed and somebody dies in a fire. Years ago, our main problem was false fireboxes. If they decide to implement this program citywide, it will become just as big of an issue."

Our conversation was interrupted when the bells rang. "Engine only, Sixty-First and Vine Streets, special assignment on box seven-six-five-one." Somebody had maliciously pulled the firebox at Sixty-First and Vine. I guess they wanted to let us know that they were still out there.

It didn't take very long to respond to my first fire with 41's. At 0209 hours on January 19, my first night there, we caught a first-in all-hands fire in the 400 block of Simpson Street. Two houses were well involved. My buddy Johnny Fry from 24's, who had since been promoted to captain, was acting battalion chief, and he ran the fire like a veteran chief. I'm sure Hoss would have been as proud of him as I was.

Engine 41's fire calls were a mixed bag of first-ins and shit work, but the medical calls were relentless. They weren't as bad as when I worked the rescue because we didn't transport patients, but more importantly, we still did firefighting. Also, as the officer, I usually wasn't directly involved with patient care and could maintain a safe distance in case they spewed their gastric contents. The pilot program ended on March 1, 1985. There wasn't a teary eye in the battalion.

Our main focus became fires again, and as an added bonus, we were able to get through most meals without making a run for a change. Technically, we weren't supposed to send firefighters to the store to pick up our meals, but just about everybody did it.

March 7, 1985—Lieutenant, Engine 41

Lunch was delayed because we caught a dwelling fire on Fifty-Sixth Street. By the time we returned to our firehouse, it was too late to cook, so we called Vincent's Pizza and placed a huge sandwich order. The plan was simple. While the rest of us restored our equipment, Mikey would drive to Fiftieth and Thompson and pick up our lunch. It nearly backfired.

The moment Mikey returned from the store carrying two huge bags of sandwiches, a long beep sounded a box alarm for a reported apartment fire at Fiftieth and Thompson. It was directly across the street from Vincent's!

"What did you do? Start a fire while you were there?" I asked jokingly.

"It can't be much of a fire, Loo." He laughed. "I was parked right in front of the place only minutes ago."

Incredibly, as we swung our 180-degree turn, we saw a column of black smoke rising in the distance. Seconds later, 65's reported heavy fire conditions with people hanging from the windows. Ladders 24 and 6 made several heroic rescues.

It would have been interesting if Mikey had made those rescues while he was at the store. We'd surely have put him in for a medal, but how would we have explained that he had been picking up our sandwiches? Next time we'd just take the apparatus.

The guys in Ladder 24 were a hilarious bunch of practical jokers who rarely missed an opportunity to pull a prank. Dad would dial his wife on the pay phone, let it ring once, hang up, and retrieve his quarter. Alert to his signal, she would promptly call back, and they'd chat away. But every now and then, the mischief-makers would sneak up to the phone, dial his number, let it ring once, and dash away. Sure enough, she'd call back and ask for Dad. We'd laugh our asses off as he vehemently denied calling home. Sometimes he talked to her for fifteen minutes anyway, and we'd laugh even harder.

Anybody was fair game for the pranksters, even the officers. If we were out on a call, Ladder 24's mischief-makers would often set the clock radio in my office to go off full blast at 0400 hours. They got me several times before I routinely began checking the darn thing before going to bed at night. It was a nuisance, but I loved the humor.

On April 5, the joking around temporarily stopped. Firefighter David Cronin of Ladder 16 died from heart-related issues after battling a fire. It was upsetting to think that an LODD could rear its ugly head even after the last ember had been extinguished.

In 1985 spring arrived with warm weather, lush green grass, beautiful flowers, and unfortunately a hideous fortified blockhouse on top of MOVE's new headquarters. The radical group had relocated to the 6200 block of Osage Avenue. It was just my luck! MOVE was now in 41's first-alarm area. We drove past the unsightly structure a few times while making runs. It was an ugly stark contrast to the well-maintained homes in the neighborhood.

Astonishingly, the city did nothing while MOVE reinforced the blockhouse that sat on the roof of their dilapidated row home. They even constructed gun ports! City hall procrastinated as they worried about political correctness. Before long, it was too late. MOVE was up to its old tricks again. Booming bullhorns, filth, compost piles, trash, and terroristic threats finally drove neighbors to complain to politicians and, more importantly, to the media. Under intense pressure, the city was forced to take action. Just as in 1978, the city first tried to bring the situation to a peaceful conclusion. It came as no surprise that all diplomatic attempts failed miserably.

May 12, 1985—Lieutenant, Engine 41

When I walked into 41's kitchen for night shift on Mother's Day, I immediately sensed something was amiss. Nobody was joking or kidding around. Instead they were all glued to the breaking news on the television. The police were planning to forcefully evict MOVE from their compound at dawn. The first thing that entered my mind was the scene from the movie *Jaws 2* when Sheriff Martin Brody exclaimed, "I don't intend to go through that hell again!" My sentiments exactly, Sheriff!

According to plans, the eviction and arrests of MOVE members for contempt of court, terroristic threats, firearms, and parole violations were to commence at 0600 hours. If they didn't peacefully comply, Squrt pumpers (including 43's, my 1978 MOVE alma mater) would attempt to neutralize the blockhouse using elevated master streams. Other companies were to be strategically placed to support the police department as needed. Luckily, 41's strategic placement was perfect! We were to remain in our firehouse unless needed. Maybe it was because of my experience with the 1978 incident, but I had an ominous feeling that things wouldn't go as planned this time either.

I was in the office reviewing the department's plan when I heard a dispatch come over the speaker. "Attention, Engine Forty-One, Seventy-Four Sixty-Six Rhoads, a dryer." It was my house! My mind raced as I sprinted for our pumper. "Diane? The kids? My house? A dryer?" Then I thought about it. If it had been anything serious, Diane wouldn't have been calm enough to tell the dispatcher that it was only a dryer. She would have been screaming, "My house is on fire!"

My logic was right. Nothing was showing as we passed my rear driveway. I turned off the lights and siren as we turned onto Rhoads. Diane, the well-trained firefighter's wife she was, had evacuated the kids across the street and was standing with several neighbors when we rolled to a stop.

"I was trying to get a jump on the laundry," she explained, "but when I went downstairs, the basement was full of smoke, so I called nine one one. I got the kids out of the house, like you always said I should."

When I gently kissed her cheek, I immediately knew that it wasn't anything serious. I smelled a hint of perfume in her hair, but there wasn't a trace of smoke. It turned out that the dryer vent had vibrated loose, allowing steam and lint to spew into the basement.

I made a few temporary repairs and reassured Diane that it was safe to bring the kids back inside. The guys were giggling as I climbed back into the cab. Denny shifted into drive. "I guess you like working close to home, huh, Loo?" We laughed all the way back to the firehouse.

Of course, my clock radio was set to go off at 0400 when we got back, so I adjusted the time to 0530. I wanted to be awake before the MOVE eviction began. So did everyone else. When I entered the kitchen at dawn, it was already packed with firefighters. Cradling our coffee cups, we watched the live broadcast intensely. It didn't take long for the gunfire to begin. It was uncanny to hear the live pops outside echo in the distance a split second before we heard them on television. We even heard a heavy caliber *rat-tat-tat* that made the other shots sound like cap guns. We had no idea who was shooting at whom, and neither did the media.

At 0800 hours we were saved by the bell. We were relieved. As we were leaving, Ladder 24 got dispatched to the MOVE compound to assist with ground ladders. As they pulled out, I waved to them and made my way to my somewhat less dangerous job, taking care of Maria.

The gunfire had subsided by the time I got home. Later that morning, the Squrts trained their powerful streams on the blockhouse, but they had little effect. The tense standoff lasted all day before police figured out another way to neutralize the threat from the rooftop.

That night, Diane, Maria, and I went to watch Alex's Little League baseball game, only a block from our house. A short while later, we heard a muffled boom in the distance. I didn't think much of it until Diane pointed to smoke coming from the direction of the MOVE compound. It was the beginning of a tragic end to the daylong standoff.

The muffled boom was the sound of an explosive charge being dropped from a Pennsylvania State Police helicopter in an attempt to destroy the blockhouse. Unknown to police, a small gasoline can had been sitting near the blockhouse, and it was ignited by the explosion. Flames engulfed the MOVE compound and quickly spread to neighboring dwellings. Fearing for the safety of his firefighters, Commissioner Richmond delayed fighting the fire because the police refused to declare the scene safe from active shooters. The fire continued to spread throughout the block and eventually jumped to neighboring blocks. By the time Richmond got clearance to attack the fire, it had developed into a major conflagration. Sixty-one homes were destroyed, and eleven MOVE members, including five children, lost their lives in the fire.

Surviving MOVE members and the media vilified the fire department for their delay in fighting the fire. I was outraged at those unwarranted and vicious attacks on my brothers. In my opinion, it was virtually impossible to understand the decisions made at the 1985 MOVE incident without taking into consideration the 1978 MOVE shootout. Commissioner Richmond was thoroughly committed to protecting his unarmed firefighters and wasn't about to expose them to gunfire as had happened in 1978. When Richmond finally got the green light from police, the department did an outstanding job and contained the inferno without further losses.

Other than being in the firehouse that morning, I wasn't involved in the 1985 MOVE incident, and that was just fine with me. I had had my share of MOVE.

Working with such a terrific group of firefighters at 41's and Ladder 24, I had all but forgotten about the captain's list. I figured that there wouldn't be any promotions until sometime in 1986.

JUNE 5, 1985—LIEUTENANT, ENGINE 41

A two-alarm blaze in the 6200 block of Market Street kept us up all night. We were first-in and attacking the fire offensively before the chief yanked us out. I wasn't sure why he pulled us out until we got outside and saw that the flames were through the roof, reaching toward the moonlit sky. We set up an exterior defensive attack and didn't get off the fireground until nearly 0600 hours.

Back at our firehouse, I joined eight other exhausted firefighters sipping coffee in the kitchen. With smoke-stained faces and sleepy eyes, we gazed at the morning news. As expected, there wasn't a word about our two alarmer. Nobody died or was injured, no bombs were dropped, and the Market-Frankford Elevated Line had long since been reopened. It was just another West Philly fire to the media.

"Hey, Loo, fire phone."

I was so tired that I hadn't heard it ring. I wiped the soot from my eyes and picked up the kitchen extension.

"How are you doing, pal?" A smile came over my face. It was Charlie O'. "I heard a good rumor, pal. They're promoting nine captains in August." I stood there silently trying to process the information. The promotion was coming sooner than I had expected. Sure, it meant more pay and an advancement in rank, but I'd be leaving 41's. I was happy, but how would it affect our childcare arrangements?

As usual, Charlie O' was right. At the next chiefs' staff meeting, they announced that a large promotion ceremony was going to be held in August. I waited until it was official before telling Diane. She was elated. It was my first promotion since we had gotten married. When I reminded her that I was surely going to be transferred farther from home, she just shrugged it off. "Don't worry about it. We'll work it out. We always do." As always, she was completely supportive of my career.

My days at 41's were numbered, and I wanted to relish the rest of my time working close to home with such an outstanding group of firefighters. But the fire marshal's office was overwhelmed by the aftermath of the MOVE incident, and they activated me as a backup fire marshal for the rest of June. Diane and I had to scramble to make childcare arrangements while I investigated fires in the Seventh and Eleventh Battalions on steady day shifts.

I had been back at 41's for only a few shifts when I was detailed out again. While assigned to Ladder 13, I had been qualified as aircraft-crash-rescue officer. FAA rules didn't allow acting lieutenants to work at the PIA's firehouses, so I was detailed there occasionally. Once the novelty wore off, though, I found the details there boring...usually.

July 6, 1985—Lieutenant, Engine 41, Detailed to Engine 78

I thought that I was done with airport details when I left Ladder 13, but the Seventh Battalion was shorthanded, and they tracked me down. I was irritated at first, but since we had a family barbeque the following day, I figured that I'd at least get a good night's sleep. Surprisingly I was wrong; we were up nearly all night.

The shift started off with box six-three-five-five to stand by for an approaching aircraft with an unsafe-landing-gear light. An hour later we responded to a first-aid call for a few injuries suffered by passengers when their aircraft hit turbulence. Later yet, we responded to another box six-three-five-five for a bomb threat. We stood by for nearly two hours as the bomb squad searched the passenger aircraft. It was unfounded. At 0300 hours, the fire lights and bells went off again. A large JP-4 fuel spill took us a few hours to clean up.

Actually, I loved the action. But the next morning when I arrived home bleary eyed, Diane looked at me and exclaimed, "You look dreadfully tired. I thought you worked at the airport last night."

"I did." I laughed. "I probably would have gotten a better night's sleep at Forty-One's."

In July, I took my promotional physical. Maybe married life was agreeing with me; my PVCs were practically gone. I didn't even need to pop any Valium to get through the EKG that time.

My last fire with 41's was in my Overbrook Park neighborhood. Diane heard our approaching siren and waved to us as we zipped up Seventy-Fifth Street. After we returned to our station, I cleaned out my locker. It had been nice working close to home.

CHAPTER 22

Back to South Philly

In the Philadelphia Fire Department, one captain and three lieutenants are assigned to each fire company. The captain supervises a platoon, just as the lieutenants do, but also serves as the company's commanding officer.

On August 12, 1985, Diane, Alex, Maria, my parents, and my in-laws all beamed with pride as I pledged to faithfully fulfill the duties of my new position. The promotion ceremony, held in the auditorium of the FAB, included five battalion chiefs, nine captains, seventeen lieutenants, and five paramedic lieutenants.

After the formalities, Diane pinned my shiny new captain's badge on my uniform and planted a soft kiss on my lips. Despite the recent MOVE conflagration, the atmosphere was cheerful. Life goes on in the fire department. Mayor Goode and Commissioner Richmond posed for pictures with individual promotees and their families.

After an hour of celebrating, we lined up for our new assignments. I was apprehensive, afraid that I'd wind up somewhere far, somewhere slow, or worse, somewhere far *and* slow. But instead of being assigned directly to a company, which I would have preferred, I was placed in the captains' pool to fill in as needed. Fortunately, I was assigned to the First Division, which included West Philly.

My first few weeks as captain were great. They used me in busy West Philly companies where I was familiar with most of the firefighters. Even our childcare arrangements were working out. But the joyride didn't last.

When I called the deputy chief's aide to ask where I was needed the coming week, there was a long pause on the other end. "Uh, Cap, it says here that you've been transferred to Forty-Nine's, effective September fourth." Engine 49 was in South Philly and was slower than any company I'd ever worked. It was my turn for a long pause.

Commissioner Richmond's policy was to assign newly promoted officers wherever the vacancies occurred, in promotion-list order. I had hoped that I'd somehow wind up in West Philly. South Philly had never entered my mind, but I could have done worse. There were plenty of companies that were less active and much farther away. On the plus side, my parents, who often babysat during my day shifts anyway, still lived in South Philly. I'd be able to drop Maria off at their house and pick her up easily.

Engine 49, located at Thirteenth and Shunk, was responsible for the southernmost tip of South Philly. Their district included Veterans Stadium, home of the Phillies and Eagles; the Spectrum, home of the Flyers and 76ers; and the Philadelphia Naval Shipyard. Its first-alarm area was a diverse mix of residential and commercial neighborhoods, along with portions of I-95, I-76, and three stops along the Broad Street Subway.

Built in 1956, its one-story, flat slag-roofed firehouse had one large red apparatus-bay door. The building's tan exterior bricks were similar to those used at 24's and 41's. The city architects must have loved tan bricks in the fifties. The firehouse was also home to Rescue 11M, the First Battalion's fire-prevention parade float, and a reserve tiller-style ladder that was out of the station more than it was in. I was responsible for the station, everything in it, and everybody who worked there.

Engine 49 was assigned to the First Battalion, and my chief was George DelRossi. An avid basketballer, George was a decisive, quick-thinking, and excellent fireground commander. My three lieutenants were Uncle Pete, Gerry, and Pete-Pete (not to be confused with Uncle Pete). All of them had more time on the job than I did. As a matter of fact, Uncle Pete had been fighting fires when I was in elementary school. Gerry had been working Ladder 19 the day we heard the man scream to death on Twenty-Third Street, and Pete-Pete had worked on another shift at the Nest when I was there.

On my C Platoon, Danny Phillips was our senior firefighter. Pleasant, with a round face, Danny had been an outstanding tip man for many years at 24's before transferring. Gruber and Riles were veterans of the Nest. Gruber (aptly named after the *McHale's Navy* character Lester Gruber) was an avid gambler. His favorite pastime was organizing battalion-wide sports pools. Big Frank (not to be confused with Uncle Frank) lived close by and was as strong as an ox. He'd been at 49's since Fire School. Big Frank was eager and hardworking. He quickly became my go-to guy in the firehouse. Our platoon's rookie, Flash, had gotten his nickname after outrunning everybody during a building collapse at an extra-alarm fire.

Engine 49 had been a revolving door for captains. Many of those before me had pulled strings to cut their stays short. Richmond, fair minded as always, put an end to that. As a rule, he was going to keep his officers at their assignments until they were due to be rotated. It was a good move for the department. Unfortunately, I just happened to land at 49's when it was implemented.

September 5, 1985—Captain, Engine 49

I guess the previous few captains of 49's had anticipated short stays. Instead of preparing new station policies, they had covered their predecessors' names with correction fluid and typed their own names over them. I decided to take a fresh look at each policy and, if necessary, make changes for the better. It was my first shot at station manager, and I wanted to do it right. Besides, I didn't expect a whole lot of fires to interrupt my work.

I didn't decide to call it quits until 0300 hours on my first night at 49's. I knew it was time to knock off when my policies began swirling around my brain. The military-style bunk squeaked horribly and sagged about a foot when I climbed aboard. The tattered feather pillow collapsed as flat as a pancake under my head. Before dozing into a deep REM sleep, I made a mental note to add obtaining new station bedding to my growing list of things to do.

Within seconds I was jolted out of my skin by the harsh ringing of bells and the bright fire light on the ceiling over my head. I jumped out of bed in a stupor and had no idea where I was. But years of Pavlovian conditioning guided me out of the office, onto the apparatus floor, and into my gear. I was sitting in the cab of our pumper before I was fully awake. Big Frank was already in the driver's seat and revving the diesel. "Second-in, Cap," Big

Frank said calmly. "Tactical box, Ten Hundred Emily for a dwelling." In a flash, we were racing up Thirteenth.

It's a good thing that Big Frank was an excellent driver because 49's had some of the tightest turns in the city, especially late at night when illegally parked cars extended well into intersections. But with only two effortless turns on our route, we arrived on scene within three minutes. As we pulled next to a hydrant on Eleventh, I glanced down Emily. Fire was blowing out of the front windows of a row home in the middle of the block. Engine 53 was already on scene, and they reported that someone was trapped inside.

We stretched our hose line up the alley and quickly attached our attack line. The mighty deadbolt on the rear door was no match for Ladder 11's Halligan, and within seconds we were crawling inside the kitchen. Engine 53 quickly knocked the fire down in the living and dining rooms before advancing upstairs. As a shit-work company, we moved forward to cover their rear.

As we maneuvered our line to get a better shot at a stubborn hot spot, I noticed that the front door was only partially open. Gasping for air, I crawled over and tried to open it fully, but it didn't budge. Something was blocking it. I shined my light down the length of the door until I spotted the obstruction. It was a charred body wedged between the door and wall. The unfortunate woman was still clutching a fistful of keys. Sadly, the home-owner lost her life in the blinding smoke while trying to find the right key to unlock her door's double-keyed deadbolt.

As we were restoring our equipment, we heard a horrifying scream pierce the night. The woman's daughter had arrived on scene and had been informed of the tragedy. I'll never forget the sound of her horrendous shriek. I hoped it wouldn't give me more nightmares.

At the Emily Street fire, I quickly learned that I had a good crew on my platoon. Flash needed more experience, as I expected, but Gruber, Danny, Riles, and Big Frank were a nice blend of veterans.

The Philadelphia Naval Shipyard (PNSY) had its own fire department, but people inside the naval base often called 911 during emergencies, which connected them directly to the Philadelphia Fire Department. We'd often get dispatched to incidents inside the shipyard without their fire department's knowledge.

SEPTEMBER 18, 1985—CAPTAIN, ENGINE 49

I couldn't help but stare at the victim's wedding ring. When he left for work that morning, his wife had had no idea that he'd never be coming home. An alleged drunk truck driver had barreled into the fence installer as he was working and killed him instantly. When we arrived inside the PNSY, the man's mangled body was tangled inside several yards of cyclone fencing. When the shipyard's firefighters arrived on scene, they had no idea that we were already there. Nobody had called them. Working together, it took us over a half hour to cut his body from the twisted mess.

Time passed quickly, and before I knew it, fall became winter. February was particularly bone chilling. After spending so many cold winters on the job, I was usually well prepared for subfreezing temperatures. *Usually*, that is!

FEBRUARY 12, 1986—CAPTAIN, ENGINE 49

It was a bone-chilling eighteen degrees as Gruber steered our pumper southbound onto I-95. About a half mile ahead, gray smoke was blowing across all lanes of the expressway. As I pressed on the siren, I felt like Moses parting the Red Sea of taillights. It seemed as if the panicked drivers were trying to climb over each other to get out of our way.

As we neared the source of smoke, a coatless man in a shirt and tie was waving frantically. Behind him, flames were swirling underneath the front wheel wells of his late-model Cadillac. Its engine compartment was well involved.

Gruber stopped short of the fire and parked at an angle to protect us from errant drivers. As Flash and Danny dragged our booster line to the fire, I helped the man into our crew cab to shelter him from the bitter cold. Then I went to his car, reached inside, and pulled the hood release. It came as no surprise that it didn't make a popping sound. The thin metal cord that releases the hood mechanism easily burns away during engine-compartment fires. In order to get to the seat of the fire, we now had to forcibly pry the hood open.

As Danny and I banged away at the mechanism, Flash was extinguishing the fire by aiming the stream underneath the wheel wells. Unfortunately for me, he missed. My inexperienced rookie unintentionally misdirected the stream and blasted me square in the neck. Ice-cold water splashed on my face, went into the opening at my collar, and ran down my chest. It continued down my legs and collected in my boots. I was thoroughly soaked. With seventeen-mile-per-hour winds, I quickly turned into a human icicle. By the time we were done with the fire, my ice-crusted mustache felt as stiff as a whisk broom. I could barely speak into the microphone to tell the FCC we were available.

When we returned to our comfortably warm firehouse, it took several minutes to undo the frozen clasps on my running coat. My boots had nearly an inch of water in them. I flipped them upside down and leaned them against the front wheel to drain. Everything I was wearing, including my thermal socks and underwear, was dripping wet.

I sloshed into the office and thrashed through my locker, looking for my spare thermals, and suddenly it dawned on me. They were still sitting on the dining-room table at home. Diane had washed them, but I had forgotten to bring them to work. I had absentmindedly picked up my keys, which she had placed on top of them as a reminder, and left my thermals behind. What a goof I was!

I tried to reassure myself, "Well, this *is* Forty-Nine's. What's the chance that we'll catch a fire in the next couple of hours?" I changed into a dry uniform and hung my thermals over the piping-hot office radiator to dry.

An hour later they were still slightly damp, so I decided to join Gruber, who was watching a movie in the kitchen, in order to give them more time to dry. It was a bad decision. The bells rang as soon as I sat down. As the overhead door rose, a blast of frigid fifteen-degree air rushed into the apparatus floor. I stepped into my wet boots, and cold water instantly soaked through my thin uniform-issue socks. Shuddering, I slid my arms into my still-dripping running coat and jumped into the cab. We swung a 180 and raced west to a reported hotel fire.

The recently vacated big old hotel and bar had been a haven for drugs and prostitution for years. I had previously fought fires there with 24's, 10's, and Ladder 19. Luckily, those fires had been contained to one room, and two engines and ladders had handled them. We were third-in, so I was certain that we wouldn't go in service. Of course I was wrong!

"We have a three-story vacant hotel, seventy-five feet by a hundred and fifty feet, with heavy fire showing on the second floor," 60's officer reported. "Have all companies go into service with inch-and-three-quarter hose lines."

Passyunk Avenue was full of smoke as we made the turn. Engines 60 and 24 had taken the two hydrants on the fire's side of the street, closest to the hotel. Our choice was either a hydrant on the same side but roughly a thousand feet away or one directly across the street from the hotel. I glanced up and saw that fire was leaping from four windows. Screw the traffic! We took the hydrant across the four-lane street.

Our orders were to stretch an attack line to the third floor. Anticipating that the fire could change into a defensive operation, we stretched our larger 3½" hose before attaching our attack line. The bitterly cold wind piercing through my wet gear made me feel as if I were in Antarctica. I couldn't wait to get inside the warmth of the burning building! We followed 60's line up the stairs until it veered off into the smoke-charged second floor. Then we climbed up another flight, dropped to our bellies, and began crawling forward in the dense smoke. The orange glow we saw in the darkness ahead wasn't a good sign. The fire had jumped to the third floor, *our* floor!

Flash was our pack man, but Danny and I were gasping for air. Only seconds ago, I had been freezing, but now, the heat was unbearable. I couldn't wait to get back outside again! Suddenly, the orange glow turned into a huge fireball. The red devil had found a fresh supply of air. I banged on Flash's helmet. "Open it up, now!" Our stream disappeared into the flames without any effect. Suddenly I heard screaming and yelling coming over my portable radio. That could mean only one thing: Deputy Chief Fanning had arrived.

He might have been a screamer on the fireground, but few chiefs could read a burning building as well as Fanning. But his rant seemed more intense than usual this time. I raised the radio to my ear. "Deputy One to Battalion One, get everybody the hell out of that building now. I repeat. I want everybody out of that damned building!"

If Fanning was ordering us out, things had to be really bad. We quickly retreated down the hall and backed our line down the stairs. A frigid blast of air quickly reminded me how cold it was outside. Suddenly, I was freezing again. I momentarily locked eyes with Fanning. He looked relieved that we had made it out. I think I even saw a trace of a smile on his face. Then, as if he had caught himself being soft, he screamed, "Get your gun in service on the west side, Captain!" The flames were now through the roof.

Since we had already stretched our large hose, we were able to quickly attach our Stang gun and start pouring water into the building within minutes. In the meantime, Fanning had pulled the second and third alarms. It was the aged hotel's swan song. We wouldn't be making any more fires there. Good riddance!

Fanning's positioning of companies was impressive. He quickly had every square inch of the building covered with overlapping streams, and the fire soon began to die down. But as the heat faded, ice began to form inside my boots. I didn't want to turn into an ice sculpture, so I began hopping around.

A firefighter from 69's was sitting motionless by his company's gun, which was next to us, so I hopped closer to make sure he was okay. I'd seen the firefighter, who was in his sixties, around before. His name was Louie. The intense cold had virtually no effect on him. He looked like he was simply enjoying a day at the beach. My face was so frozen that I was barely able to ask if he was okay.

"I'm just fine, sonny—eh, I mean Cap," he replied nonchalantly.

I was jumping around and rubbing my arms, and there was Louie, nearly twice my age, enjoying a day at the park. I couldn't help but ask, "Aren't you cold, Louie?"

He laughed. "This ain't nothing, kid. We'll be home in a few hours."

A crackle on my radio interrupted our chilly chat. It was Fanning. The police wanted to open the eastbound lanes of Passyunk Avenue, so he decided to release 49's. My strategic positioning had paid off! Not only did we get in service quickly by stretching across the heavily traveled street, but our apparatus placement was getting us off a bitterly cold fireground.

As we were taking up our equipment, Louie still looked like he was sunning himself. Absolutely astonished by his endurance, I exclaimed, "Louie! It's friggin' fifteen degrees out here! How the heck is it that you're not freezing?"

He stared straight ahead and chuckled. "Cap, I spent weeks in a freezing foxhole in Bastogne. Believe me, kid, this ain't nothing!" Suddenly, I was too embarrassed to be cold.

That morning, I brought my gear home and placed it next to our heater. My numb toes didn't thaw out until later that evening. The brutally cold month of February wasn't over. We responded to a five alarmer at Thirteenth and Callowhill on the twenty-seventh and then a six alarmer at Fourth and Brown on the following night, the twenty-eighth. Both were in subfreezing temperatures. I surely didn't forget my spare thermals for either of them. I never forgot Louie either; he's a true American hero.

CHAPTER 23

Learning My ABCs

Captains in the Philadelphia Fire Department are trained to be acting battalion chiefs (ABCs). My turn came in March of 1986. In order to be qualified, I had to run the battalion for several shifts under Chief DelRossi's watchful eye. My last shift with him was like a final examination. We had two working fires that night, and George felt that I was ready. But first I had to kiss the ring. We drove to Deputy Chief Fanning's office for his official endorsement.

"Be prepared," George cautioned, as I nervously followed him into Fanning's office. "He's probably going to grill you."

Stout with a round face, an olive complexion, and brown hair, Chief Fanning rose from his chair as we entered. He looked me up and down and then said, "I remember you from the hotel fire on Passyunk Avenue. You guys just made it out in the nick of time."

Fanning's demeanor was much different from what I'd seen on the firegrounds. He was relaxed, cordial, and even giddy. "So, George, you think this kid's ready, huh?"

"I have full confidence in him, Chief," DelRossi affirmed.

Fanning turned to me and looked over the top of his glasses. "I have one question for you, Captain."

What was he going to ask? High-rise operations? Shipboard firefighting? Refinery fires? I gulped.

Fanning smirked. "Okay, kid. What's Battalion One's northernmost boundary?"

It was a no-brainer for me. If I knew anything, it was the district! "Broad and Lombard, Chief!"

Fanning laughed. "This kid knows his shit, George! They're usually so worried about fireground issues that I always get them with the boundary question." Then he looked back at me. "Okay, kid. If DelRossi says you're qualified, that's good enough for me. I'll approve the paperwork." I felt as though I'd been anointed as an acting cardinal by the pope.

ABCs cover for chiefs when they're on vacation, sick, or off duty for other reasons. In addition, if a chief responds to a second or greater alarm, the FCC often sends his aide to pick up a captain to serve as an ABC and restore the battalion to service while his company runs shorthanded with an acting lieutenant.

I got my first chance to fly solo when Chief DelRossi attended a staff meeting nearly a month later. It was only for a few hours, and we only had one run, a recall. I was eager for another chance.

May 3, 1986—Captain, Engine 49

Huddled around the watch desk, we listened to the companies dispatched on the second alarm at Fifty-Sixth Street and Paschall Avenue. When our numbers weren't called, I slammed my fist on the desk. "Shit!" Flash was so startled that he nearly jumped out of his chair. I repeated my tirade after they also bypassed us on the third and fourth alarms. "Why the heck aren't they sending us?" I yelled. "We're closer than half those companies!" Then it dawned on me. They must have been saving us so I could restore the battalion. It made sense; DelRossi had responded on the second.

A minute later, the fire phone rang. I was expecting to be told that DelRossi's aide was en route to pick me up. Over the chatter from the fire in the background, the supervisor said, "Cap, we need you because of the extra-alarm fire."

"Okay!" I replied eagerly.

"Yeah, Cap, the fire marshal is tied up on another job, so we need a backup fire marshal to investigate the fire on Fifty-Sixth Street." Backup fire marshal? Really!

"All right, I'm en route," I growled through my teeth.

Disappointed, I slammed the phone onto the cradle so hard that Flash actually did jump out of his chair that time.

I picked up a reserve fire marshal's car stored at 47's and was heading to Fifty-Sixth Street when a box alarm was dispatched for an explosion at Engine 34's firehouse in North Philly.

While 34's was at the extra alarm, Engine 27 was assigned to cover their station. They were backing inside when they noticed an accumulation of steam at the rear of the apparatus floor. Firefighter Eddie Friel, who had previously been stationed at 34's, was familiar with the station's problematic heater. As he led the way down the basement stairs to investigate, the boiler suddenly exploded. Friel, thirty-seven, a thirteen-year veteran, was killed instantly. Seriously injured were forty-year-old Firefighter Dennis Dougherty and fifty-one-year-old Captain John Harris. Firefighter Bruce Weber, thirty-three, was treated for minor injuries.

It was extremely difficult to focus on the fire investigation as word of another LODD spread around the fireground on Fifty-Sixth Street.

It was a bad month. Only nineteen days after the explosion at 34's, Firefighter Harry Henz of Engine 33 suffered a heart attack and died while responding to a call. We grieved like always, but things quickly returned to normal in the department, as they must.

With my increased responsibilities as captain, I asked to be removed from the qualified fire marshal's list after serving for nearly eight years. My request was granted just in time, because there was plenty to do at 49's. Fanning had scheduled a station inspection. For weeks, we stripped and waxed floors, cleaned walls and windows, pulled weeds from the cracks in the sidewalk, and waxed our apparatus to a brilliant shine. There was one final step—something I had learned from Charlie O'. Prepare a soup-to-nuts steak dinner on inspection night and invite Fanning to stay for supper. It was a bribe of sorts, but an accepted practice. The theory was that the chief's inspection would be less harsh if you fed him well. It worked!

Fanning's inspection was thorough, but he only found a few minor issues. Afterward we feasted on filet mignon, steaming baked potatoes, buttered veggies, and all the trimmings. Fanning hung around and chatted for a few hours. We even had a few laughs. His company was enjoyable.

July got really busy, but not because we were getting a lot of structure fires. City sanitation workers went on strike for about three weeks, and angry residents began burning their trash in the streets.

JULY 12, 1986—CAPTAIN, ENGINE 49

I had never seen Big Frank get so angry before. We were by the Seventh Street incinerator, extinguishing a huge pile of trash bags that most likely had been set ablaze by picketing sanitation workers, and they were breaking our balls.

"Just let it burn, firemen! As soon as you leave, it's going to burn again."

Big Frank suddenly snapped. "Fuck you, you motherfuckers! This is a public health hazard. You assholes shouldn't be allowed to strike. You and those pussy-ass schoolteachers, always holding the city hostage, both claiming how important your jobs are. If what you do is so damned important, you should have mandatory binding arbitration like us and the cops. No strikes allowed, period!"

Unbelievably, they got quiet. I don't know if it was because of Big Frank's words or the Halligan he was holding in his enormous hands. We didn't have any more fires there for the rest of the shift.

Chief DelRossi went on vacation that August, and I was ABC for four shifts. Battalion chiefs visited the firehouses in their battalion on their day shifts. We called it "making the rounds." At one of my stops, my comedic pal from 10's, Buddy Yeager, was the lieutenant. I should have known that he'd have something special planned for my first visit as ABC.

One of his firefighters had a reputation for being different, to say the least. As I walked in, the firefighter met me at the door and handed me a small folded piece of paper. My former coworker and his crew were at the kitchen table giggling as I unfolded the tattered note. It read, "I quit effective 0800 hours tomorrow." I slowly folded the paper back up, placed it back in his palm, and calmly walked him over to Buddy. "This is your lieutenant. Start out by going through channels!"

The giggles erupted into rolling laughter. Buddy snatched the paper out of the firefighter's hand. "You can't even quit right!" Then he looked at me. "All right, Cap, you had a golden opportunity to get rid of him and didn't pull the trigger."

I later found out that the firefighter was serious about resigning that morning but had a sudden change of heart. Every time he did something odd afterward, I got an anonymous prank call, and a deep throaty voice would say, "You missed your chance, Captain." *Click.*

I got my first fire as ABC on the following night shift.

AUGUST 15, 1986—CAPTAIN, ENGINE 49, ACTING BATTALION CHIEF 1

By the time we arrived, ugly black smoke was pouring from the second and third floors of the vacant row home on Fifth Street. I had made numerous fires similar to this one, but that night it was different; I was ABC.

Initially, I felt completely out of place, and very alone, standing outside the smoke-laden property, holding my radio and hand light. It seemed funny to be directing multiple companies instead of one tight-knit unit. DelRossi's advice from training was my only companion: "Use your experience and anticipate how the fire will spread, Bob. Think of each fire as a cube, and make sure you cover all six sides."

The first-in officer had placed both engines and ladders in service on the tactical box. When Ladder 11's officer got to the rear, he reported that heavy fire was extending laterally.

"Don't hesitate, Bob. If you need help, call for it early." More advice from DelRossi.

I told Joe Nolfi, Battalion 1's aide, to fill out the box and place the two additional engines in the left and right exposures. The fire was quickly surrounded. In short order, white smoke replaced the black ugly stuff. The fire was knocked down.

After checking with my officers and taking a peek inside for myself, I placed the fire under control. As DelRossi said, "Bob, if you're working with good companies and good officers, things usually run pretty smoothly." Luckily, that's exactly what happened on my first job as ABC. Amen.

At the time, Battalion 1 covered most of South Philly and was administratively responsible for eight companies and a fireboat. As ABC, I responded to more fires there than I did with 49's, so filling in for DelRossi was always a welcome change of pace. Though my opportunities were sporadic, almost every time I was there, we responded to either a working fire or an unusual incident. It was a great way to tiptoe into the waters of chiefdom.

Battalion chiefs investigate accidents involving the companies in their battalion. Most chiefs detest the task. The paperwork is extensive, and the chief is out of service during the investigation. We hadn't handled any accident investigations while I was training with DelRossi, though he reviewed the procedures. I wasn't looking forward to my first one.

NOVEMBER 28, 1986—CAPTAIN, ENGINE 49, ACTING BATTALION CHIEF 1

Nothing good ever comes from phone calls at 0400 hours. It was the FCC supervisor. "Cap, Rescue Fourteen's been involved in a major accident at Thirty-Eighth and Spruce. There's one injury, and the apparatus is not mobile." Shit!

As Nolfi zipped through the dark, desolate streets, a thousand things were going through my mind. "Who was injured? Suppose it was a firefighter? Do we need a tow truck? Where's the nearest reserve rescue? How bad does it need to be before I notify Fanning?" I glanced over my shoulder, wishing that DelRossi was sitting in the back seat as he had been during training. Ahead, it looked like a hundred police cars had responded to the accident. Red and blue flashing lights were everywhere.

Steam was still spewing from Rescue 14's badly crumpled grille, but its damage paled in comparison to the Chevy Malibu it had collided with. I got out of the car and casually scanned the scene, trying to act as though I had investigated a thousand accidents.

"Hey, Cap!" Nolfi yelled embarrassingly. "Aren't you going to need this?" It was the battalion's accident-investigation kit. So much for looking experienced.

I was wondering where to begin when someone behind me whispered, "Why don't you start by interviewing the firefighters from Rescue Fourteen?" The voice was welcoming, friendly, and familiar. I turned around, and Charlie O' was standing there puffing on his cigarette.

Recently promoted and assigned to Battalion 5, my former mentor had heard that I was ABC for the shift. "When Rescue Seven-M got dispatched here," he said, "I figured you might need a hand."

"Need a hand?" I blurted. "Jesus, Chief! If I had only one wish, it would be that you were here to walk me through this."

Charlie O' stuck around and guided me through the entire process. His advice, as always, was full of logic, wisdom, and, of course, a few judicious applications of Charlie O's principle. I gave him a huge bear hug when we were finished.

Battalion 1 responded to hazmat incidents with Engine 60 and Ladder 19. Whenever he had the chance, DelRossi would detail me there to get me familiar with the hazmat unit's equipment and procedures. I liked the technical aspect of hazmat response, the firefighters there were great, and I enjoyed the details. I didn't think anyone noticed.

Out of the blue one afternoon, I received a call from Commissioner Richmond's office. The commissioner wanted to know if I was interested in being transferred to Engine 60. Even though I liked the diversion of being detailed there occasionally, my goal was to get back to a busy company in

West Philly. Besides, I was annoyed that headquarters was constantly trying to recruit me for what I considered unappealing jobs. The year before, they almost had forced me to take a captain's position at the airport. Before that, they had called nearly every time a staff position opened up at headquarters. Irritated, I abruptly said, "No way!" With over a year under my belt at 49's, I was content to wait for my turn to be rotated. Besides, with the cold weather, we were catching our share of fires.

On some firegrounds Chief Fanning's Dr. Jekyll personality in the station would transform into his screaming Mr. Hyde. If your company wasn't the object of his wrath, it was funny to watch his tirades.

JANUARY 14, 1987—CAPTAIN, ENGINE 49

Damn, shit work again! Our trek through the rear alley was particularly trying. A huge German shepherd nearly sank his teeth into Flash's shoulder as we humped our hose line to the rear. The angry dog jumped to the top of the ramshackle fence and snapped his jaws, missing Flash by a fraction of an inch.

Danny barked back, "I'll fix that son of a bitch!" He took the nozzle and aimed it in a soldier's stance. When the snarling canine leaped again, Danny blasted him squarely between his barking jaws with the stream. The dog yelped, ran, and cowered in a corner long enough for us to pass. It's one of the tricks you learn when you're an experienced shit-work company.

After knocking down the fire on the first floor, 53's had advanced their line to attack the flames upstairs. We made our way inside and were mopping up on the first floor. Outside, we could hear Fanning screaming at somebody. We made our way to the window and could see him jumping up and down, yelling at 53's pump operator for some reason. It was always a comical sight when I wasn't the one being screamed at. We stepped back into the relative safety of the smoke, laughing our asses off until his outburst subsided.

Clad in his work jacket and soft chief's cap, Fanning was storming away from the dejected pump operator when suddenly a powerful hose stream from the second floor hit him square in the head and ran down the length of his body. His cap, scrambled eggs and all, twirled as it sailed through the nighttime air.

It was a funny sight, but was I horrified because I knew what was coming next. Dripping wet, Fanning retrieved his cap from a filthy puddle. His face was beet red, just as Brownie's used to get. Then Mount Vesuvius erupted. Screaming worse than I'd ever heard him before, Fanning steamed to the second floor, following 53's attack line.

"Get the hell outside and line up in roll-call formation. Now!" He was screaming so loudly that the fire-weakened structure was actually shuddering.

Outside, under a dimly lit streetlight, Fanning lined 53's crew up in roll-call formation. He paced back and forth, screaming in each man's face. "Are you assholes too stupid to look where you're aiming your stream? Please say yes! 'Cause if you aren't, that means you aimed at me." Fanning continued his diatribe for ten minutes, hoping that they'd crack under pressure and admit that they had hosed him down intentionally. But the well-disciplined crew stood fast. Soaking wet and chilled to the bone, Fanning abruptly ended his rant. "If you friggin' guys ever get a drop of water within ten feet of me again, I'll report the whole damned bunch of you!" He plopped his waterlogged cap on his head, and water splashed all over his forehead. "Shit!" he screamed, as he stormed his way back to his chief's car.

The entire battalion had a ball teasing 53's about Fanning's soaking. Rumor had it that they had been trying to splash a little water in his direction but misjudged.

That summer, we were called to assist the Philadelphia Police Bomb Squad at the old Publicker's Distillery. An environmental contractor was cleaning up the superfund site when they discovered a large bottle of organic peroxides. Crystals had formed around the bottle's lid, which meant it had become shock sensitive and could explode. The plan was to have the bomb squad place the bottle into their containment vessel and transport it to the police academy. A police sharpshooter was waiting at the firing range to shoot it and blow it up. Our job was to follow them along the route as a fire-suppression team, just in case it prematurely detonated.

As planned, we stood by with hose lines ready while bomb techs in their cumbersome garb cautiously loaded the bottle into their vessel. After the police stopped traffic in both directions of I-95, we joined two dozen emergency vehicles and followed the containment vessel for the ten-mile trek. It looked like a funeral procession, with the containment vessel serving as the hearse. A line of police cars at the rear held thousands of annoyed motorists at bay.

At the police academy, we stretched our hose lines again. Then the bomb techs gingerly walked the bottle to the business end of the firing range and placed it on a dirt mound. "Fire in the hole!" The sharpshooter fired and hit the bottle with pinpoint accuracy. But to everyone's dismay, it didn't explode. Instead, the peroxides splashed all over the range. The environmental contractor flung his arms in the air and then slapped them down to his sides. "Now we got to clean up this darn site too!" It wasn't the only hazmat incident we responded to that summer.

The Gulf refinery, where Ralph Campana, and seven other brother firefighters lost their lives, had become the Chevron refinery. Engine 49 was assigned on the first alarm.

AUGUST 9, 1987—CAPTAIN, ENGINE 49

Broad Street looked like a strobe-lighted discotheque as brilliant white lightning bolts danced around in the night sky. The accompanying powerful thunderclaps sounded like a continuous barrage of artillery, each one violently shaking the cab of our pumper as we pulled into Saint Agnes Hospital's driveway. As always, the electric storm had tripped their alarm system.

With all the storm-related activity, it was difficult to break through the radio traffic. I quickly depressed the microphone during a brief pause and reported nothing showing. Instead of an acknowledgment, a long beep came over the speaker. "Box five-nine-eight-eight, Penrose and Lanier Avenues. The fire's reported to be at the Chevron refinery." The hospital's security guard reported that the alarm had been caused by a power surge, and that was good enough for me. I told Big Frank to head to the refinery.

The FCC relayed that the fire was reported to be at the storage-tank farm across the Schuylkill. As we headed down the Platt Memorial Bridge, the view was surreal. To our right, flames were leaping from the top of a gigantic 130-foot-diameter storage tank in the center of the massive tank farm. The huge blaze and vivid bright lightning flashes eerily made it look as if we were descending onto an alien planet in the throes of a galactic laser war.

A drenched refinery worker wearing a white construction helmet anxiously waved us into the gate behind 53's. We followed them down a gravel road until they abruptly swerved to their left and pulled next to a yellow yard hydrant. Red flashing lights of refinery fire apparatuses were blocking the road ahead, so we had to back up several hundred feet to connect to a hydrant of our own. It was much farther from the fire than I had been hoping for.

Across a tank-containment dike, we could see another company slipping and sliding while struggling to drag their hose along the embankment. Time was of the essence. The tank adjacent to the fire was steaming, so I figured it best to pool our manpower and get their stream in service quickly and then work on ours. It was raining so hard that I couldn't tell that the other company was 24's until we were practically on top of them. Stanley, their lieutenant, welcomed the help.

It was hard to believe, but the storm got worse as we humped the heavy hose along the slippery dike. The thunder was deafening. Brilliant white flashes arced between low-hanging clouds and struck the ground all over the place. I was in the middle of the most horrific thunderstorm I had ever witnessed, and there we were dragging Dacron hose along an elevated embankment. Hmm! I couldn't help but recall the Greek scientist Thales of Miletus, who discovered static electricity by rubbing wool along an amber rod. Were we creating the same effect and, in a sense, inviting a deadly lightning bolt from the electrified clouds above? But there's no such thing as a rain delay in firefighting, so we pushed on. Regardless, I was terrified! All I could do was pray that we wouldn't lose someone to a lightning strike.

The blaze was at five alarms before we had 24's stream flowing. It took all of 24's large hose plus a few lengths of our own to get their stream to reach the tank. Charlie O' arrived on the second alarm and was assigned to manage our side of the fire. He told us to hold off stretching another hose line. He wanted to keep 49's in reserve in case the fire worsened. As always, Charlie O' was thinking two steps ahead. We rolled foam cans until our shift ended in the morning.

Fueled by a million gallons of gasoline, the fire raged throughout the day. Charlie O's decision to hold our pumper in reserve was a good one. Later in the day, 49's was repositioned to cover a more severely threatened tank. By the time we returned that night, the fire had grown to eight alarms, and huge fireballs were rolling into the sky. Despite our best efforts, and forty thousand gallons of foam, the fire eventually burned itself out. The nearby tanks survived the inferno.

Oftentimes, we found ourselves down the subway for various incidents. Unfortunately, it was usually to retrieve body parts of those unfortunate souls who jumped in front of trains. SEPTA and the fire department decided to evaluate our preparedness for a larger-scale subway incident. In order to simulate a mass-casualty train crash, they loaded three train cars with SEPTA employees and their families to act as victims. The simulated crash was set to take place between the Oregon and Pattison Avenue stations. Both stops were 49's first-in, and we were working day shift.

October 18, 1987—Captain, Engine 49

We reviewed our procedures and trained hard for the SEPTA drill, which was set to commence at 1000 hours. At 0950 I assembled the troops by the watch desk and waited for the Oregon Avenue subway box to be dispatched.

Just at that instant, Engine 10, Ladder 11, Battalion 1, and Rescue 14 were dispatched to the Tasker-Morris Subway Station for a person struck by a train. Gruber looked at me inquiringly. "Is that part of the exercise, Cap?"

I was just as surprised. Thinking that I might have missed something, I quickly flipped through the exercise plan. There wasn't a word in it about anyone being struck by a train. I was wondering if the drill planners were throwing us a curve ball. But ten minutes later an FCC dispatcher called and canceled the exercise. It turned out that as the train with its 125 mock casualties was approaching the drill site, a distraught woman jumped in front of the regularly scheduled train a mile or so behind them. SEPTA wisely canceled the drill.

A few weeks after the drill that wasn't, the 1988 officer's rotation list arrived in the department mail. After only two years and four months at 49's, my name was on it. I was surprised and tickled pink!

There were a few captain's spots open in West Philly, but I set my sights on Engine 65 at Fifty-Fourth Street and Haverford Avenue, which was busy and close to home. Chief DelRossi made a nice endorsement on my rotation memo, and on January 18 I received my first choice. I was going back to West Philly.

On my last shift at 49's, Chief DelRossi came over to say good-bye.

"Thanks for pulling for me, Chief," I said. "It was great working for you. Maybe someday down the road, if you're still here, I might even consider going to hazmat." I figured that he'd probably take my offer as innocent words of appreciation and soon forget about them. In hindsight, I guess I should have emphasized the words "down the road."

Ironically, my last run with 49's was a hazmat incident. A large styrene spill at a nearby chemical plant was a premonition of what was soon to be.

CHAPTER 24

Back to the West, Briefly

Less than a mile from 41's, at Fifty-Fourth Street and Haverford Avenue, the two-story red brick quarters of Engine 65 reminded me of a castle. Built in 1926, its impressive architecture suggested that structural splendor meant just as much as functionality back then. Two red, arch-style, manually operated apparatus-bay doors faced west on Fifty-Fourth. Originally it also had been the quarters of Ladder 24. When the ladder moved to 41's in 1959, 65's became a single-engine company and eventually home to West Philly's first mobile intensive-care unit (MICU), Rescue 9M.

Similar to 24's, 65's first-in Haddington neighborhood was small, but it had numerous fires. Geographically located in the center of West Philly's fire belt, 65's also responded to almost every working fire in the Eleventh Battalion and caught loads of work in the Seventh. When the department decided to strategically add another Squrt pumper, 65's was the logical choice. I was happy to be back in a busy company again.

JANUARY 20, 1988—CAPTAIN, ENGINE 65

I knew that Drew, Mike, and Wes were hard-hitting firefighters before we responded to a single fire together. We had made plenty of fires with 65's when I was at 41's, and they always had impressed me. Besides, the captain I'd replaced was my old buddy Johnny Fry. I knew he had trained them well and given them a strong sense of company pride.

In the kitchen on my first day at 65's, Drew said, "While Captain Fry was here, nobody ever stole our first-in jobs. Even with our two-story station and its antique manual doors, Cap, we hit the street in a flash." Our firehouse had a functional fire pole. "Hey, Cap," Wes asked curiously, "Are you going to slide the pole? We can't let Fifty-Seven's beat us in, you know."

Hesitant to reply that I'd never actually slid one before, I glanced up at its highly polished brass. "Yeah, I'll probably use it sometimes."

Drew sensed my hesitance and giggled. "You'll get used to it, Cap. We love it."

We made several runs on my day shifts, and I was lucky enough to be either near the stairs or on the first floor when the bells rang. But way past midnight, I was upstairs reviewing the station's policies. Fry had this place running perfectly, and I couldn't find a single thing that needed to be changed.

Suddenly the fire lights came on, and the bells rang loudly. From the watch desk downstairs, Mike screamed, "First-in! First-in!" The call was for a reported dwelling fire on Fifty-Fifth Street, only a few blocks from our station. Unfortunately, it was also only a few blocks from our adversary, Engine 57. As soon as I hit the hallway, Drew's head disappeared down the pole hole. Wes zipped down a second later.

Shit! I couldn't let 57's beat us in, so I had to slide the pole. As soon as Wes landed, I peered down the daunting twenty-foot drop. Gulp. I leaped onto the pole, and *whoosh!* Maybe it was because of my long-sleeved flannel officer's shirt or my inexperience with fire poles, but I couldn't apply the brakes. I dropped nearly as fast as I had when I fell through the roof years ago, except Hoss's head wasn't there to break my fall this time. *Wham!* I slammed onto the apparatus floor. I screamed in agony as my left ankle buckled. But despite my pain, I darted to our Squrt pumper and leaped into my boots. The engine was running, and everybody was on board by the time I yanked myself into the cab. My body slammed back into the seat as we darted out the doors.

As we dashed up Haverford Avenue, I silently prayed, "Please don't let Fifty-Seven's beat us in. Not on my first night here! Please!" But as soon as Drew swung the hard left onto Fifty-Fifth, we could see their flashing lights ahead; they were closing in fast. Drew gunned it hard, and luckily we beat them in, but only by a few car lengths. Flames were leaping from the front windows. "Thank you, God," I whispered to myself before I gave my report.

My throbbing ankle notwithstanding, I was delighted with my company's performance. Not only did we beat 57's, but by the time they dragged their line through the shit-filled alley, we had the fire completely knocked down.

When I got home, my ankle was badly swollen, but I hadn't broken any bones. I iced it all day and then returned for another night shift. Luckily, it was unusually quiet, and we only had one run. Needless to say, I didn't use the pole.

My ankle healed quickly, and by the time we were scheduled to work again, my limp was barely noticeable. When nobody was looking, I took a few practice slides down the pole, gingerly avoiding landing on my bad ankle. After I healed, I began using the pole during runs again. But whenever the opportunity presented itself, I preferred the relative safety of the stairs, lest I break a leg during a crash landing. The fireground was dangerous enough.

The fires were plentiful, but Rescue 9M's staffing issues were a major headache. Our paramedics were constantly being used as EMS training officers, resulting in Rescue 9M being downgraded to a limited MICU (a paramedic paired with a firefighter/EMT). In addition to paramedics' sickness, vacations, and injuries, the downgrades were taking a toll on my firefighters. Drew, Wes, and Mike were EMTs, and they needed to fill in on Rescue 9M nearly every shift. It was rare to have the three of them working together on 65's. I'd complained to EMS supervisors several times and even sent a memorandum to headquarters, but the downgrades kept coming.

But there were bigger problems brewing for 65's than the staffing of Rescue 9M. Once again, the city was suffering from financial woes, and rumors abounded about closing firehouses. With our small local area, the buzz was that 65's was at the top of the list. I found the gossip to be especially distressing. I had finally made it back to West Philly and was loving it. In less than two months, our platoon had responded to a dozen working fires, and we had been first-in at five of them. I was even sliding poles. If they closed our station, I'd wind up back in the pool again, and who knew where they'd send me from there.

Everybody in the station loved being at 65's and maintained their esprit de corps despite the rumors. The place stayed clean as ever, and the apparatus was bright and shiny as always. The guys still busted their tails to get out of the station quickly and were as aggressive as ever on the fireground. I was awfully proud to be their captain. But it wouldn't last much longer.

MARCH 25, 1988—CAPTAIN, ENGINE 65

Our house was empty when I came home from the station. Diane was at work, Alex was in school, and Maria was at prekindergarten. Bushed after two working fires, I climbed into bed hoping to catch a couple of hours before picking up Maria at noon.

As tired as I was, I couldn't doze off. An incident at our second fire the previous night had me giggling. We had been fourth in at a commercial building fire. I had battled a blaze in the same building when I was at the Nest.

After the fire was extinguished, we were restoring our equipment when a police officer from the Eighteenth District stomped over and angrily asked me why I had called his partner a jerk-off. I had no idea what he was talking about. Without looking at him, I continued to restore our hose line and replied, "You must be mistaken, pal. I didn't call anybody a jerk-off tonight."

The officer raised his voice. "Yes, you fuckin' did! We were here when you pulled up. You were mad as hell because our car was blocking the street."

There hadn't been any police cars blocking the street when we arrived. I slammed the heavy hose line down. "Let me ask you something, pal. Were any other fire engines here before we showed up?"

The invasion of his personal space must have irritated him, because he began screaming, "You know you were the first damned fire truck to get here! What difference does that make?"

I knew I had him. "Well, detective," I replied cockily, "we were still in our station—you know, the one way over on Haverford Avenue—when the first fire engines arrived. We weren't even dispatched until they asked for help. I guess we all look alike in these funny yellow helmets, don't we?"

The embarrassed officer turned around and screamed, "Fuck!" before storming away. His partner was down the block laughing his ass off. He had set him up. Cops liked to pull pranks on each other too.

By eleven o'clock I still couldn't sleep. That always happened when I was overtired. Then the phone rang.

"Bob?" It was a familiar voice on the other end.

"Yeah, this is Bob," I replied, trying to place a name to the voice.

"Bob, it's George DelRossi. How are you doing?"

"Eh, hi, Chief. I'm fine. How are you?" He'd never called me at home before. I immediately sensed that something was up.

"Bob, when you left Forty-Nine's, you mentioned that you might be interested in Hazmat."

Startled, all I could manage to say was, "Well, eh, um, er, yeah, down the road, Chief."

"Bob, I just got off the phone with the deputy commissioner. You're coming down to Sixty's on the C Platoon with me. Your buddy Lumpy is coming to Ladder Nineteen. It's a done deal!"

I was in a state of shock. "When's this happening, Chief?"

"The transfers will be down by the end of the day. You'll be in Sixty's on Monday night." DelRossi sensed my reluctance. "Listen, Bob, you're a perfect fit for the job. It's a great move for you career-wise. Besides, Ulshafer wants you there." (Roger Ulshafer had replaced Richmond as commissioner in early 1988.)

I was going back to South Philly.

I hated leaving 65's. It was busy, it was close to home, and it had an excellent group of firefighters. On the other hand, I wasn't sure it would be around much longer.

Regardless, I headed to 60's with a positive attitude. I had graduated from Temple, and Hazmat presented an opportunity to apply my technical education. It also offered more stability because Hazmat company officers weren't typically rotated. In my fifteen years on the department, 60's had been my thirteenth transfer.

It was the right move because Engine 65 was deactivated on June 18, 1988, less than three months after my transfer. Ironically, Rescue 9M was moved to 57's, but it still had its staffing issues. I guess 65's got the last laugh. Ha!

CHAPTER 25

Hazmat 101

W hen Mickey Mantle and Roger Maris hit back-to-back home runs, Yogi Berra exclaimed, "It's like déjà vu all over again." I repeated those exact words as I parked in the same parking space as I had on my very first day at Ladder 19. It had taken fifteen years to come full circle, but I was right back where I had started. I may have been the captain of 60's rather than a fresh-faced rookie in Ladder 19, but in a sense, I was a rookie all over again—a Hazmat rookie, that is.

Time and budgetary constraints had taken their toll on the sixty-seven-year-old firehouse that once had stood proudly. Its black slate-shingled roof was leaking so badly that its interior walls and ceilings were crumbling. Firefighters would sweep and mop the second-floor hallway every morning, but by the afternoon, a white glistening snow of plaster bits covered the floor. The walls were so bad that one night a partial section collapsed onto one of the bunks. Luckily, the firefighter was on watch duty and wasn't injured. The city was in a dither trying to decide whether to repair the costly roof or completely rebuild the entire block-long complex, which was also home to the First Police District. Either way, as the engine's captain, it was my responsibility to maintain the deteriorating firehouse until they came to a decision.

When it came to firefighting, Engine 60 was busier than 49's but not nearly as busy as my last stop, 65's. Since the fire station functioned as one of the department's two hazardous-materials response teams, there was always plenty to do. Engine 60 and Ladder 19 had the same duties as every other engine-and-ladder company in the city. But if a hazmat call was dispatched, they'd respond with Engine 60, Foam Pumper 160, and Chemical 1 as a single entity called Hazmat 1. Once on scene, they'd rendezvous with

Battalion 1 to form Hazmat Task Force 1 (HMTF-1). HMTF-1 covered the southern half of Philadelphia, while Engine 7, Ladder 10, and Battalion 10 operated as HMTF-2 and covered the northern half of the city.

There was a reason that Lumpy and I had been transferred there so quickly. The captain of 60's and lieutenant of Ladder 19 we were replacing had quarreled constantly. Their latest altercation intensified into a shoving match, and it was their last spat. Within a day they were transferred to opposite ends of the city.

On the other hand, Lumpy and I got along great. In addition to our stint as firefighters under Hoss's tutelage at 24's, we also had worked together there as lieutenants. Not only was Lumpy a fearless firefighter, but he'd developed into an extremely efficient and detail-oriented officer. With his great sense of humor, I knew right away that we were going to make a good team. But neither of us had much hazmat experience, and at the time, the department didn't have a formal hazmat training program. As the team's leaders, we had to learn quickly.

March 28, 1988—Captain, Engine 60

Engine 60's office had been a sacrosanct place when I was a rookie. My only task in there was to make Captain George's bed. As I sat in that very same office writing in my journal, it was hard to fathom that I was the company's commanding officer.

At the beginning of our shift, Lumpy asked apprehensively, "How the hell are we supposed to lead these guys without any hazmat experience ourselves? I don't know anything about chemical suits or the equipment they have here, do you?"

I feigned an encouraging smile. "Listen, Lump, Chief DelRossi had me fill in here often when I was at Forty-Nine's. These guys are great, and they really know their stuff. Starting tonight, we're going to make them train us. We'll train until we know every procedure and piece of equipment, inside and out. Don't worry; we'll be just fine." As I said it, I was hoping that I was right.

That's exactly what we did. We began training, drilling, and exercising each and every shift. We only allowed interruptions when either or both of our companies were dispatched to a call.

One of our first lessons was the proper selection and use of chemical protective clothing (CPC), more commonly referred to as hazmat suits. At the time, we had two types of suits: orange, made of butyl material, and green, made of Viton material. Both were Level A encapsulating suits, meaning that they were gas and vapor tight and completely cut the wearer off from his or her surroundings. There's no room for claustrophobia in the hazmat business.

Suit selection was determined by an extensive list of chemicals supplied by the manufacturer. If a chemical was highlighted green, Viton was used, and if a chemical was highlighted orange, butyl was the suit of choice. I was somewhat leery of the department's procedures, which stated that we must use Level A suits at every hazardous-materials incident. Suppose the material wasn't overly toxic? Suppose the only hazard was flammability? Some of the chemicals on the list weren't highlighted at all. What were we supposed to do then? Nobody seemed to know.

Donning a Level A suit was a tedious process that required the assistance of other firefighters. Since neither the butyl nor Viton materials offered fire protection, donning a heavy blue Nomex fire-resistant jumpsuit was our very first step. Then a specially fitted, thirty-pound firefighter's air pack was strapped onto our backs. It's difficult to speak and hear inside Level A, so headphones were placed atop our facemasks, and voice-operated microphones were strapped around our necks. A portable radio with its transmitter/receiver adapter was attached to the air pack's straps. The suits had heavy gloves attached to the fabric material, but we wore two pairs of latex undergloves for added protection. When we pulled on the suit, we were wearing well over sixty pounds of equipment.

If that wasn't restrictive enough, the suit's primary air supply came from an external air line via a bulkhead pass-through connection located at the suit's waist. We had to drag the air line everywhere we traveled. The only purpose of the tank on the wearer's back was to serve as an emergency escape reserve.

Switching from the external to the emergency air supply was difficult and scary. If we lost external air, we had to grab the tip of the left outer glove with our right gloved hand, tug the arm out of the glove, then disconnect the bulkhead connection using only the left hand. It was quite a challenging manipulation. After that, we had to reach around and open the internal air tank, again using only the left hand. We would be without air while we completed those steps. There was no easy way to get out of the Level A, so if we panicked and failed to follow the exact procedure, we could suffocate.

As a final exam of sorts during our training, the guys closed my external bottle without warning. I had just exhaled, and when I tried to take in another breath, my mask suddenly collapsed against my face. The feeling was absolutely terrifying! But since we had practiced the procedure so many times, I was able to stay calm and follow the steps. Afterward, I made sure everybody practiced the procedure routinely.

As Hazmat 1's captain, I didn't feel comfortable ordering my firefighters into a contaminated area (hot zone) wearing Level A suits until I had experienced it for myself. During my first two months, we responded to plenty of fires, which I liked, but nary a Hazmat call needing Level A suits. I knew it was only a matter of time.

May 29, 1988—Captain, Engine 60/Hazmat 1

There was no doubt that it was going to be an early summer as we pulled out of our station and lined up on Twenty-Fourth Street. At eighty-seven degrees with high humidity, we sweltered in the sun while waiting for all of our apparatuses to clear the doors. Five firefighters and I led the way in 60's. Two firefighters in Engine 160, our foam pumper, lined up behind us. And lastly, red-haired Rodger pulled Chemical 1 behind 160's, with Lumpy riding shotgun. (In

1982 the department had replaced the old soda-truck style chemical units with more modern vehicles.) As soon as the doors were closed, Lumpy waved. We were ready to go. I pressed hard on the siren, and our trio of apparatuses raced toward 68's district. Our Dalmatian, BLEVE (aptly short for Boiling Liquid Expanding Vapor Explosion), responded with us to all hazmat calls and rode in Chemical 1. I couldn't help but laugh when I glanced in the rearview mirror and saw the annoyed look on Lumpy's face when BLEVE climbed over his lap and poked her head out the passenger window.

Chief DelRossi was waiting for us when we arrived. Behind him, an abandoned fifty-five-gallon drum labeled "Toluene" was on the loading dock of a vacant warehouse. A pool of the clear, colorless liquid saturated the concrete around the drum.

DelRossi gave me a perplexed look when he saw me slipping on a Nomex jumpsuit. I knew what he was thinking; officers usually didn't make hot-zone entries.

"Chief, I've got to experience what it's like to do this myself," I remarked as Rodger and I suited up as the hot-zone entry team members.

DelRossi nodded with an endorsing smile. "Okay, I understand, Bob. Go ahead."

Firefighter Al Loughead rubbed his fingers over his thick graying mustache as he diligently flipped through the reference books. "Cap, toluene's a clear, colorless liquid with a petroleum-like odor. It's flammable and can be toxic by inhalation and skin absorption. It's highlighted orange, so we should use the butyl suits. I'll write its properties down, including the signs and symptoms of exposure." It hadn't taken me very long to realize that Al was my most knowledgeable hazmat technician.

The rest of the guys proficiently assembled all the tools and equipment that Rodger and I needed for our hot-zone entry. With the exception of our ridiculous-looking Care Bears kiddie pools, which we used to capture decontamination water runoff (commercial retaining pools were too expensive for the department's budget at the time), our setup looked somewhat professional. I don't think the guys from the Nest agreed. They were laughing their asses off at our setup. I'm sure a few especially hardy guffaws were aimed at Lumpy and me, both alumni of the Nest.

The heat and humidity were somewhat tolerable until I got into my long-sleeved Nomex jumpsuit. Suddenly I felt like I was in a sauna. After strapping on my air pack and donning my mask, I slid my feet into the suit's rubber boots. Al and Lumpy attached my communications equipment and connected my external air supply. Rodger and I screwed our masks into our regulators, and the guys zipped the suits over our heads.

Lumpy keyed the microphone. "Okay, guys, you're on air at thirteen seventeen."

The guys pulled us to our feet and spun us in the direction of the leaking drum. The mere act of walking was laborious. I plopped one foot in front of the other like the Frankenstein monster taking his very first steps. I couldn't hear a thing inside the suit except the rhythmic mechanical hiss of my regulator each time I inhaled. A freight train could have been heading toward me, and I wouldn't have had a clue. Even though Rodger was lumbering alongside me, I felt isolated and alone. Lugging our air lines in one hand, we rolled a hand truck loaded with a sixty-five-gallon recovery drum, bags of absorbents, and shovels with the other.

The rusted black drum had a faded red "Flammable" label on its side with the word "Toluene" scribbled across it. The product's liquid level had dropped below a small puncture hole that was slightly beneath its lid, so the leak had stopped. About two gallons of the liquid had pooled around the base of the drum.

Rodger and I carefully avoided becoming entangled in each other's air lines. Our suits were baking us in the hot sun. We tore the corners of two fifty-pound bags of absorbent and poured them over the spill. I was sweating profusely as I clumsily tried to spread the granules around evenly. A warning from Lumpy penetrated the silence of my headset: "Ten minutes left, guys." Because of the heat, we'd placed a fifteen-minute time limit on our operation. If we didn't speed up, we'd need to send in a second entry team to finish up. Neither of us wanted that, so we hastened our pace.

The next step was more difficult. We laid the recovery drum on its side and wrestled the bad drum into it while ensuring that the leak hole remained at the top. By the time we'd finished, my feet were swimming in pools of sweat that had accumulated in my boots. "Five minutes left, guys. Don't forget you need time for decon" (decontamination). Heeding Lumpy's advice, we quickly shoveled the soaked absorbent into the recovery drum and bolted its lid in place. We were done! It was just in time too, because my visor was completely fogged over. I could barely see a thing.

"Rodg, go through decon first. I'll follow you." I wasn't sending Rodger first because the officer should be first in and last out. The fact was, I couldn't see a thing except for the orange blur of his suit. I grabbed onto the back of his arm, and we awkwardly trudged toward our Care Bear pools like a pair of circus elephants.

Rodger stopped when he reached the first pool. I didn't. *Thunk!* I crashed into him, causing him to stumble and nearly fall. Lumpy urgently called over the radio, "Bobby! Hold up, kid! You almost knocked Rodger over." Later, Lumpy said that Rodger's arms were twirling when I bumped into him. It must have looked funny as hell. "Okay, Bobby. Just stay where you are. We'll guide you through as soon as Rodger's done."

It only took a minute for Rodger to pass through the shower, but it seemed as if I had to wait an hour as I continued to bake in the sun. I was concerned because my sweating had slowed and my heart was racing, two warning signs of heat stroke. Lumpy finally broke the silence again. "Okay, Bobby. Step into the first pool." That was easier said than done!

The sides of the pools were about a foot high. I lifted my right leg and stepped forward, but either the tip of my boot caught the lip of the pool or one of the Care Bears reached up and grabbed my foot, because I lost my balance and pitched forward. My foot slammed into the pool and splashed runoff water everywhere. Then I stumbled into the shower's piping and almost knocked the entire assembly over. By some miracle, I managed to regain my balance before falling flat on my face.

One of the decon guys, 141st classmate Billy Hopper, grabbed my arm and guided me through the rest of the process before I killed myself. Al was waiting at the end of the line, and he quickly unzipped my suit. I was drenched from head to toe in sweat. My socks were dripping as I lifted my feet from the half-inch pools of sweat in my boots. I was a little lightheaded, but I quickly recovered. It felt so refreshing to finally be out of that suit.

Well, it wasn't graceful, but I had my first Level A entry under my belt.

The experience was a real eye-opener, but I was glad I had done it. I had wanted to experience, firsthand, how bad it could get in those suits. I knew there was a safer and more efficient way to do things besides wearing Level A on all incidents. I just needed to figure out what it was, and convince the department's brass that their procedures were wrong.

June 7, 1988—Captain Engine 60

The morning started out when we responded to a horrific accident at Twenty-Sixth and Passyunk. A disabled woman, with hand-operated gas and brake controls, came flying over the bridge and slammed into a telephone pole. The pole won. The impact was so great that her car didn't come to a stop until the pole was sitting past the middle of her dashboard. It took us more than an hour to free her body from the tangled metal. We finished just in time to do some fire inspections.

Our first stop was a bar that was a well-known mob hangout. The bright morning sun was at our backs as we walked through the front door, wearing our soft uniform caps. A half-dozen men sitting at the far end of the bar suddenly began scuffling around and whispering. Thinking we were cops, they were scrambling to hide their number slips. A big burly guy with a thick glistening gold rope neck chain emerged from the darkness to head us off and stall for time.

"Can I help youse guys?" he said, squinting his eyes from the sun.

"Sure," I replied. "We're here for inspection."

"Inspection?" he asked, holding his hand up to shield the sun. "Sure, do whatever you got to do. Go ahead."

As my guys looked for fire violations, I seized the moment. "Would you like to buy some Hero Scholarship Fund tickets? They benefit the children of police and firefighters who've lost their lives in the line of duty."

A second man with a mustache and a thinner gold chain with a cross dangling from it came forward. I vaguely remembered him from one of Concetta's family gatherings. "How many you got?" he asked as he studied my face.

I pulled the tickets from my pocket. "Seven hundred sixty dollars' worth."

Without blinking, the first guy pulled out a wad of bills and peeled off seven hundreds and three twenties. "We'll take them all, okay?"

I tried to hide the shocked look on my face as we exchanged the tickets for the money.

The guy wearing the gold cross stared at my face. "Where do I know you from?"

"Uh," I stammered, "I was born and raised in South Philly, hung at Fifteenth and Moore and went to Southern High."

He shook his head. "Nah, I know you from someplace else."

Rodger yelled from the doorway, "Everything's good, Cap." I quickly thanked the men and darted for the door.

"Hey! Wait a minute," said the second guy.

I stopped dead in my tracks. "Oh shit," I thought. "They know we're not cops and want their money back."

With mistrust in his voice, he asked, "Which district are youse guys from?"

"We're from the firehouse on Twenty-Fourth Street," I answered honestly with a gulp.

He gave the first guy an angry look and growled, "I told you they weren't cops, you fuckin' moron." Then he turned to me and said, "Hey, Chief! Make sure the cops know we bought these tickets."

"Okay, sure will," I replied. We jumped on the apparatus and wisely headed to the other end of our district to continue our inspections.

Our second stop was a paint store. Sitting on a shelf were several five-gallon pails of toluene. Each one contained more toluene than had been spilled at our hazmat incident. I spun one of the pails around and read the precautions. "Caution—Use with adequate ventilation." There wasn't a word about Level A suits. If a painter could use the product without any protective gear, why should we take such precautions? Why should we risk heat strokes, slips, trips, falls, or suffocation if all we needed was adequate ventilation? Something was fundamentally wrong.

I hadn't realized it at the time, but the paint-store inspection was a major turning point for Philly's Hazmat program. After doing some research, I lobbied the department to change our procedures. We needed less cumbersome, safer, and simpler-to-wear Level B and Level C equipment. The cash-strapped department couldn't understand why they should spend more money to buy something that would protect us less. But Battalion Chief Gerry Janda, of the department's Hazardous Materials Administrative Unit, understood our plight. He cadged several cases of Level B and C supplies from a local chemical company.

I shifted our training sessions toward an analytical approach. In order to properly size up the dangers posed at hazardous-materials incidents, we needed to understand more about the properties of hazardous materials. If we understood hazardous materials better, we'd be able to do our jobs more efficiently and safely.

I felt that the essence of that foundation was a better understanding of chemistry. That fall, I headed back to college as a chemistry major. In the meantime, I read everything that I could find about hazardous materials and began to incorporate my learnings into our training exercises.

I was hooked on hazmat! It gave me a chance to apply the problem-solving skills I had learned in engineering school and went hand in hand with my childhood interest in chemistry. But most importantly, I was doing it while still responding to fires and other emergencies.

CHAPTER 26

The Return of EMS

JULY 8, 1988—CAPTAIN, ENGINE 60

We didn't accomplish any hazmat training during our day shift. The morning began with a call to the Sure-Kill Expressway after a motorcyclist who crossed paths with a truck was dragged a quarter mile and killed. So much blood and guts had been strewn along the highway that we needed our entire five-hundred-gallon tank of water to wash it all away. At one point, our stream accidently splashed into a large pool of blood and spewed a reddish mist into the morning's sun. I actually tasted the sweetish-salty mist suspended in the air. Yuck!

Next up was a massive first-in junkyard fire. We didn't return to our firehouse until change of shifts. There was a silver lining to the junkyard fire, though. I was able to finagle the junkyard owner into buying two hundred dollars' worth of Thrill Show tickets. But we needed to order more because the mob had cleaned out all the tickets we'd had on hand.

Tomorrow would be another day. I hoped we'd have some time for hazmat training.

Self-imposed pressure, fueled mainly by my OCD, made me feel negligent if we didn't do hazmat training during every shift. There was so much to learn.

There was no glory in battling junkyard fires, and 60's was first-in at several of them. To me, they were shit-work jobs with a capital *S*. On the other hand, fighting dwelling fires was well worth the interruption of our training, especially if we were first-in.

August 12, 1988—Captain, Engine 60

Billy Hopper comically recalled the B Platoon's last shift. Ladder 19's muscular tillerman George Owens had taken one bite of his Italian hoagie when they were dispatched to a reported dwelling fire. The tillerman had a bird's-eye view of the kitchen, and as they pulled out, Owens glanced over and saw BLEVE jump up and begin feasting on his hoagie. Hopper mimicked Owens's gruff words: "I screamed at that fuckin' mutt from the tiller cage, but she ignored me and kept chomping away. If we weren't first-in, I would have jumped off and killed that fleabag!"

I was still giggling at Owens's misfortune as we prepared for that night's hazmat exercise. Suddenly, the bells rang. "Everybody first-in!" As we dashed for the apparatus, BLEVE was looking wistfully at the oven, where a delicious-smelling tenderloin was safely roasting inside. No such luck tonight, BLEVE!

A column of black smoke greeted us as we swung the turn onto Snyder Avenue. "We've got a job!" I yelled excitedly to the guys in the crew cab. When we pulled up to the row home on Nineteenth Street, fire was showing from its first-floor front windows. We had it knocked down before the shit-work companies arrived.

An hour later, back in the kitchen, we cleared away our training materials and set the table for dinner. Unfortunately, the tenderloin wasn't very tender anymore. Lumpy took one bite and yelled at Hopper, "You chooch! I told you to turn *off* the heat when we got that run."

Hopper tossed a small piece of tenderloin into BLEVE's waiting jaws. "Come on, Lump! BLEVE isn't complaining. Besides, if we turned the heat off, Pepino would have gotten to it. I'd rather have my tenderloin a little tough than have mouse droppings in my gravy."

I was too hungry to complain. The meat was pretty tough, so I feasted mostly on potatoes and green beans. I was almost finished when the bells rang again. "Everybody first-in!"

I looked at BLEVE. "You're in luck this time, girl!" As I darted for the door, I tossed my last piece of tenderloin in her direction. It sailed way over her head, but she ran back and snared it like an all-star center fielder.

Minutes later, we crossed Eighteenth Street, and medium smoke was showing from the second floor of a two-story row home on Passyunk Avenue. Inside, we were met with six-foot piles of trash bags, rags, papers, and other junk. It was a hoarder's house! The smoke was banked down to the first floor as we inched our way along a very narrow path leading to the stairway. Scrap and debris snagged our hose on every turn. By the time we made the second floor, the fire had extended into the hallway and middle room. Fed by the junk, the blaze seemed to laugh at our stream. It was nearly two hours before we had it completely extinguished.

Exhausted, we made our way back to the fresh air outside. Normal etiquette didn't apply on the fireground. I stood by the curb, pressed my index finger against my left nostril, and blew hard. Curious bystanders gawked as black globules of mucus sprayed into the street. Neither embarrassed nor deterred, I did the same with my right nostril. A half-dozen other firefighters were doing the same thing.

"Move over, Engine Two!" I exclaimed as we restored our hose back at the firehouse. "Three fires in two tours for the big Six-O."

The bells rang again. "Hazmat One, cover Hazmat Two!" There was a chemical-plant fire in Northeast Philly, and we were being moved closer in case the second alarm was needed. We never got to our training, but I guess covering Hazmat 2 counted for something.

The dual role of working in a hazmat company was appealing to me. We might be called to handle a chemical spill at the beginning of a shift and then respond to a structure fire later in the day. But there was also a downside. One day we were dispatched to a dwelling fire. We were second-in, and Ladder 19 was first-in. As we headed up Twenty-Fourth, the dispatcher told us to disregard the call and sent us to a hazmat incident. As we turned around to retrieve Engine 160 and Chemical 1, we saw smoke in the distance. We had missed an all-hands working fire. I was pissed, and so was everybody else, but that was something we had to accept in hazmat.

The following shift we responded to a fatal high-rise fire in Center City. We were specially called because Chemical 1 had a three-hundred-foot air-line reel, which we hoisted to the upper floors to refill air bottles. A few firefighters staffed the refill station, while the rest of us got to do some firefighting. In a way, I felt vindicated because neither company would have responded to the high-rise otherwise.

I was so consumed with hazmat that I was caught completely off guard when the battalion chief's examination was posted. Somehow, it hadn't even been on my radar. A captain for only three years, I didn't feel ready to advance in rank, but Charlie O' had always told me to never pass up a promotional opportunity. I crammed a little, but hardly enough, and took the test anyway. I felt as if I had hit a weak grounder during the examination, and the results proved it. I finished a distant number 38 on the list, and there were only a dozen or so projected vacancies. It was easy to shrug it off because of my interest in hazmat, but I decided to study a little each day to prepare for the next one. Until then I was warm and cozy right where I was. Or was I?

December 27, 1988—Captain, Engine 60

"Jesus! It's friggin' freezing in here!" I shuddered, jolted awake by a blast of frigid air. At midnight the office bunkroom had been so stifling that I opened the window a few inches. But sometime during the night, the complex's huge antiquated boiler had gone out again. I jumped out of bed and slammed the window closed in anger. Shivering, I wrote a message for my relief on a yellow legal pad: "Damned heat's out again! Get portable heaters from 55's today." It was 0645 hours as I made my way down to the kitchen.

A few firefighters and BLEVE were huddled around the gas range's open oven door. "The heat is out again, Captain Bob!" Hopper quipped as he warmed his hands over the oven.

"Really Bill? I hadn't noticed," I replied cynically through my chattering teeth.

"Yeah, Captain Bob." He added, "Last year, when we lost heat, it was so cold that they relocated the First District's prisoners due to inhumane conditions. But we firemen and cops had to stay here and freeze our balls off. Those friggin' liberal assholes at city hall treat the prisoners with more respect than they do us. But least they're politically correct."

My frozen cheeks hurt as I giggled. Hopper's satire was interrupted by a box-alarm announcement. "Box three-two-seven, Thirteenth and Mifflin Streets, fire is located in the nineteen hundred block of Thirteenth, with a report of people trapped." Engine only! Fourth-in!

"Hey, Captain Bob, bring back some heat!" Hopper yelled as we darted out the door.

A wind-driven column of black smoke smudged the dawn's pretty pink hue as we raced down Passyunk Avenue. Adrenaline caused my teeth to stop chattering when 49's placed all hands in service. We were directed to cover the dwelling to the right of the fire. As fourth-in shit-work company, we were hunting for a rear alley entrance when I recalled an alley that Arthur and I had once used as a shortcut many years ago. It was a long hose stretch, but within five minutes we were all connected and ready to go. It's amazing how dragging eight hundred feet of hose can warm you up.

There was nothing but trapped smoke inside the exposure, so DelRossi redirected us into the fire building to extinguish a few small flare-ups. It wasn't much, but at least we got to squirt a little water after dragging all that hose line. When we were finished, I carefully stepped over the debris while looking for DelRossi to see if he had any further orders for us. Through the haze I saw him shining his light on the floor. That wasn't a good sign.

I knew the answer but asked anyway. "Did the people get out, Chief?"

"No, Bob," he replied in a sad tone. "We just found these two. They're fifty-two ninety-twos."

I casually shined my light at the grotesquely charred human remains and then nonchalantly looked back up. "We're done with the hot spots, Chief. Need anything else?" The sight of burned bodies didn't faze me anymore. I'm not sure how many I'd seen. I stopped counting after fifty.

"You're fourth-in, right?"

"Yeah, Chief."

"Okay. Give those hot spots another hit. Then you could take up."

Picking up sixteen lengths of hose was a lot more time consuming than stretching in. As we uncoupled them, the hose couplings drained and formed sixteen treacherous little skating rinks. Somehow we managed to roll our line up without falling on our asses, but by the time we finished, my teeth were chattering again. We headed back to the relative warmth of our ice-cold firehouse.

The complex's heater was repaired, but it broke repeatedly throughout that winter. I made sure that we hung on to the department's "temporary use only" portable heaters, refusing to return them to Engine 55's depot until that June.

Chief DelRossi, whom I affectionately called "my favorite chief," was unexpectedly rotated to the Tenth Battalion in early 1989. I was saddened to lose my mentor, but I had a very good working relationship with his replacement, Battalion Chief Fran Hanson. Fran had been a firefighter at 60's when I was a rookie at Ladder 19. The first day he made the rounds to our firehouse, he was appalled by how much the department had let it deteriorate since he left fifteen years ago.

But our crumbling firehouse wasn't the main issue for the administration. The department had recently been trashed by the media because of its overburdened and understaffed EMS system. The skyrocketing call volume caused severe delays in rescue-unit response times. There were even instances when no rescues were available for dispatch. The killing blow came when a rescue responding across the city took so long to arrive that the victim went into cardiac arrest and died in front of his shocked family. It was headline news for days, and it forced the fire department to completely retool its EMS system. Shortly thereafter, the First Responder Program we had piloted at 41's was implemented citywide.

In March of 1989, we were issued a resuscitator, backboard, and trauma kit. Suddenly it was nearly impossible to get through hazmat training without being dispatched to an EMS call.

April 7, 1989—Captain, Engine 60

I arrived at work intending to train on our new hazmat toy, a qualitative colorimetric tube kit. But every time we gathered around the kitchen table, we got an EMS call. I wouldn't have minded if they had been true emergencies, but our presence didn't make a lick of a difference at any of them.

0930: A woman passed out at the Acme Market. When we got there, she was sitting in a chair sipping water. We held her hand until Rescue 14 arrived. Then she refused to go to the hospital. Huh?

1007: We searched the area near Twenty-Eighth and Passyunk Avenue for a reported unconscious male. Unable to find anyone, we recalled the rescue unit.

1049: A man who slipped and fell in a junkyard was complaining of leg pain. There were no obvious breaks—just a few contusions. We waited until Rescue 19 took him to the hospital.

1158: We babysat a woman whose blood pressure was 180/90 until Rescue 7M arrived and took her to the hospital. She had run out of her blood-pressure medicine, but the prescription bottle had two valid refills pending. Say what?

1313: We entertained a five-year-old with a slight fever (one hundred degrees) until Rescue 13 arrived from North Philly. The mother didn't know that children's Tylenol might help reduce her child's fever. It didn't matter anyway because she didn't have any in the house.

1447: We headed to Southwest Philly for a reported seizure. Rescue 9M got there first and recalled us. Yes!

1553: We headed back to Southwest Philly for a man complaining of chest pains. When Rescue 19M arrived, they said that the man was a frequent flier. He had a habit of faking chest pains to get a free ride to his doctor's appointment at the hospital. Really?

1717: We responded a few blocks from the station for a seven-year-old who had swallowed his mother's wedding ring. Rescue 14 took him to the hospital.

1800: Our shift was over. I guessed we could play with our new toy the next day, or at least we'd try.

At the time, the main goal for dispatching FRCs was to get an EMT on scene quickly. Since we didn't have a rescue unit in our station, we were dispatched to nearly every medical call in our district. Our runs increased twofold. Three of my firefighters, Rodger, Dave, and Johnny B., were EMTs. Dave and Johnny B. were veterans of 24's, so they had plenty of experience from their days in the medicine wagon.

Although most of our EMS calls were nonsense, there were times when getting on scene quickly actually *did* make a difference.

May 10, 1989—Captain, Engine 60

The rules allow FRCs to make themselves available for "fire duty only" so they can wash up after a fire. That's exactly what I did after making us available from a two alarmer on Woodland Avenue. We reeked of smoke, had soot all over our faces, and were in no shape to make EMS runs. After everybody had a chance to clean up, I phoned the FCC supervisor and returned us to full duty.

The second I hung up, the bells rang. As we came running down the stairs, Hopper was standing outside the watch box grinning. "Engine only! Shoes!" Yes, the new term for EMS calls, "shoes," was becoming popular around the department. It meant we should wear our shoes instead of our boots and running gear.

"It's for a stabbing, Captain Bob," Billy said as he handed me the address. "We'll stay here to protect the district from fires." Ladder 19 didn't do shoe runs.

"Oh, that's just wonderful, Mr. Bill," I replied.

As we pulled out, Hopper mocked a hand salute. "Let's be careful out there, boys." I returned his offering with a gesture from my middle finger.

Not only did we beat Rescue 14 to the scene, but we also beat the cops. With the exception of a faint bluish light coming from the second-floor windows, the apartment on Point Breeze Avenue looked just like a vacant house. Its dilapidated front door was ajar, and when I slowly pushed it open, it creaked like Dracula's coffin. "Fire Department!" I yelled inside. "Did anybody call nine one one?" Nobody answered. Instead, I heard a familiar beeping and booping coming from the second floor. It was the same sound that Alex's Nintendo game made. His game only beeped and booped when he was at the controls, so somebody was playing Nintendo upstairs. Was it the stabber? The victim?

The police still hadn't arrived, and loss of blood from stab wounds could be fatal, so we slowly and carefully made our way up the steps. The opening lyrics of the Formations' 1968 hit single say, "At the top of the stairs there's darkness." In this case, at the top of the stairs there was darkness. There was also a man lying in a pool of blood with a butcher knife stuck in his chest. We could tell he was still alive because the knife quivered with each heart-beat. Dave and John quickly swung into action. They applied wads of gauze around the twelve-inch blade and administered oxygen.

Carefully sidestepping the blood, I headed into the bedroom where the Nintendo sound was coming from. I was hoping and wishing that the stabber wasn't in there playing *Super Mario Bros.* I was shocked by what I saw. A six-year-old boy, oblivious to all the commotion, was sitting in front of a television set, playing the video game.

I pulled the door closed behind me. "Who's the man in the hallway, sonny?"

Intently focused on the game, he replied without looking up, "I dunno. He don't live here."

"Who hurt the man?"

"I dunno," he mumbled.

"Is the man that hurt him still here?"

"I dunno."

"Where are your parents, sonny?"

"I dunno."

"Okay. Stay in here and play your game," I said, as I pulled the door closed. The police finally arrived, and I briefed them about the young boy while my guys struggled to carry the victim down to Rescue 14. I hoped the cops could figure that one out.

On another shoe run later that night, we found out that the previous stabbing victim was going to live. The knife had just missed his heart. ER doctors said that Dave and Johnny B.'s quick intervention probably saved his life.

We were constantly switching things around between fire, EMS, and hazmat calls. For fires we jumped in our gear and raced out the door. For EMS calls we wore shoes and latex gloves instead of fire gear, and for hazmats we changed vehicles before responding. Sometimes we got caught in between.

July 16, 1989—Captain, Engine 60

As a kid Paulie had been one of the biggest bullies in our South Philly neighborhood. Paulie had been strong, tough, and quick to use his fists. Nobody had dared cross him. Years later, I wasn't surprised to learn that he had become a leg breaker for loan sharks before garnering a low-level position in the mob.

But now in his forties, Paulie lay flat on the floor with his vacant eyes half-open. Johnny B. was vigorously pumping his chest, and Dave was filling his lungs with oxygen. "Clear!" Rescue 11M zapped him with their defibrillator. His wife and daughter screamed in horror as his huge frame jerked violently. But no matter how many times they zapped him or what drugs they pumped into his veins, the monitor remained flatlined. His once-mighty fists were totally limp, and an endotracheal tube was dangling from his mouth as we lifted him onto the hospital cot.

Johnny B. drove Rescue 11M, which freed the paramedics to work on Paulie. We followed them to the hospital, but when we arrived, Paulie was a goner. A miniscule coronary clot had brought down the man who had terrorized so many.

As we left the hospital, a tactical box was dispatched for a dwelling fire at Eighteenth and Moore. Normally second-in, we were only a few blocks away. We hastily squeezed ourselves into our running gear as Al sped to the fire. A minute later we stole the job from 24's. It was only a front-bedroom fire, but if it weren't for EMS, we surely would have been dragging our line up the alley.

Many people were confused when a fire engine, instead of a rescue unit, showed up for a medical call. On one call for an unresponsive man, I was wearing a recently issued stark black Nomex uniform shirt over my white T-shirt.

As I followed Dave and Johnny B. into the house, the man's daughter grabbed me by the arm and pulled me aside. "Oh, Father!" she said with tears in her eyes. "I'm so glad you're here. Can you please give him his last rights?" Hopper referred to me as Father Bob for the next few shifts.

Other times we were chastised by upset relatives who insisted that they didn't request or need a fire truck. Some people panic during emergencies and lash out at anyone who distresses them. In many cases, I tried to run interference as the guys tended to the patient.

August 7, 1989—Captain, Engine 60

Early in the morning, we were dispatched a few blocks from our firehouse for an unconscious man. His visibly shaken daughter began screaming at us the second she opened the door. "I didn't call for a fire truck. I called for a damned ambulance!" she yelled.

"Okay," I said, "take it easy, lady. The ambulance is on its way. My medics will make sure that your dad's okay until they get here."

"Unbelievable!" she shrieked. "I call for an ambulance, and they send me a fire truck!"

Upstairs, her mom was kneeling next to her dad, who was sprawled on the bathroom floor. His breathing was fine, and there were no obvious signs of injuries, so Johnny B. snapped an ammonia inhalant and wafted it under his nostrils. I was standing behind Johnny B., trying to keep the man's frenzied daughter at bay, when suddenly the man opened his eyes and stared directly at me. "Robert? What are you doing here?"

"Joe?" I replied in shock as I recognized him.

His wife looked up at me. "Robert?"

I looked down at her. "Madeline?" Then I turned to her daughter. "Claire?"

"Robert?" she answered.

Johnny B. looked back and parroted, "Robert?"

"Johnny B.?" I parroted back.

Still woozy, Joe began laughing, and everybody cracked up with him. Joe, Madeline, and Claire had been neighbors of ours when I was a little boy on Reed Street. I hadn't seen them for years and didn't recognize them until Joe said my name.

Regardless of whether it was tragic, sad, or humorous, EMS was part of my career again. Our shoe runs didn't decline until several months later when the department refined its dispatch criteria for FRCs.

CHAPTER 27

The Test

In 1990 Pennsylvania enacted new demanding hazmat-team regulations. The cost of complying with the new laws forced the department to cut back to one hazmat team. We never found out the real reason, but the department selected us to be that team. Engine 7, Ladder 10, and Battalion 10 were no longer in the hazmat business. They designed a new station patch calling themselves "Haz-Bins." Hazmat 1 was now covering the entire city.

Fire Commissioner Ulshafer was a progressive leader. Pennsylvania's new hazmat laws required hazmat teams to be state certified. Ulshafer ensured that we got the resources we needed to comply with the new regulations.

In the meantime, our fire station was falling apart. With another cold winter approaching, Ladder 19's captain, Jim McGarrigle, and I submitted a joint memorandum to Ulshafer describing the deteriorating condition of our firehouse.

Under pressure from the historical commission, the city was planning to remodel the block-long fire and police-station complex. The yearlong renovation included replacing the roof, windows, and doors; cleaning and repointing the brickwork; and installing separate heating and cooling systems to replace the antiquated central boiler plant. Our station's interior was going to be repartitioned, insulated, and remodeled. The commission was captivated by the complex's architectural splendor. They didn't flinch when we requested an elaborate training room, a laundry room, an exercise room, a modern stainless-steel kitchen, ample storage for Hazmat supplies, an intercom system, and a spacious recreation room wired for cable and surround sound.

But there was a major hitch in the plan. It called for temporarily relocating Ladder 19 and Chemical 1 to 47's Grays Ferry firehouse during the renovations. We were going to remain in our station with 60's pumper and the foam unit. McGarrigle and I weren't keen about splitting up the hazmat team, and we objected to that part of the plan. But the historical commission was intent on saving the building and wasn't about to let two disgruntled "hazmateers" discourage their efforts. We submitted another joint memorandum to Ulshafer emphasizing our opposition.

In mid-September 1990, Ulshafer sent Deputy Commissioner Harold Hairston and a contingent of officers and civilian employees to our station for a firsthand look. When they arrived that afternoon, glistening plaster chips were speckled all over the second-floor hallway. Hairston furrowed his brows and snapped at the D Platoon's lieutenant, Tommy Bitto, "When the heck was the last time your guys swept this darn floor?"

Tommy smiled back. "Nine o'clock this morning, boss." As Tommy was speaking, a plaster chip slowly floated down and landed squarely on the head of the department's facilities-maintenance coordinator. "See what I mean?" Hairston looked up at the deteriorated ceiling and shook his head. The group left without making any commitments.

SEPTEMBER 19, 1990—CAPTAIN, ENGINE 60

The weather was beautiful, so I wasn't surprised to see the D Platoon gathered outside when I turned onto Twenty-Fourth Street. Congregated in front of Ladder 19's open bay door, they were looking my way and giggling as I got out of my car. Tommy had a devilish smile on his face. Something was surely up!

"Eh, what's going on, guys?" I asked guardedly.

Among a flurry of snickers, they parted way to reveal a piece of brown cardboard covering Ladder 19's chrome numerals. The number 32 was written on it in black felt-tip. (Ladder 32, which had been housed with neighboring Engine 47, had been placed out of service several years prior.) "Oh shit!" I exclaimed. "Don't tell me that they're moving the ladder to Forty-Seven's? Didn't those assholes get our memo about not splitting us up?"

Everybody was rolling with laughter as Tommy placed his arm around my shoulder and walked me to the front of our pumper. "Yeah, Cap, they got the memo." There was another piece of cardboard, with the number 47 covering our chrome 60.

"Holy shit!" I exclaimed. "They're moving us all?" Tommy laughed so hard he could barely speak.

"Yep! It just came down about an hour ago. They're condemning the entire complex. We're moving to Forty-Seven's. This place is going to be demolished and completely rebuilt. To make room for us, they're placing Forty-Seven's out of service. We're moving on Monday."

On the outside, I was laughing with everyone else. But on the inside, my OCD was racing a mile a minute. Monday was only five days away! There was so much to be done to prepare for the move.

Certainly there were advantages of moving to 47's. Their firehouse was only fifteen years old and in good condition. Even its heater worked well. After spending several nights freezing like George Washington at Valley Forge, I considered that to be a huge plus. We'd also be covering 47's district along with the lion's share of our own. That meant more fires. And since our new quarters was a one-story building, we could get out of the station faster.

But there were also some disadvantages. A bigger response district meant that we'd also be making more shoe runs. We also were inheriting 47's plethora of alarm-system calls. The station's layout wasn't great either. Its kitchen, which also served as its television/training room, was termed the "fish bowl." Firefighters had given it that name because the offices had large windows that faced the kitchen, from which the officers could easily keep a watchful eye on their firefighters.

We felt bad for the members of 47's. Their notice was as short as ours, but even worse, they were all transferred to different companies. At least we were staying together. We'd never envisioned that they'd be disbanded for our sake. Rumors were that Chief Janda had been looking at a big vacant garage on Twenty-Fifth Street to serve as our temporary quarters, but it didn't work out.

Personally the move was one of the best things for my professional development. For the next six years, I'd be housed with one of the best fireground commanders I'd ever work with—Deputy Chief Richard Sottung. Under his tutelage I'd learn to refine my artistic side of firefighting and prepare for the next step in my career.

A few weeks after we moved to 47's, he waved me into his office for a friendly chat about firefighting. I was thoroughly impressed by his knowledge, experience, and wisdom. He had a great way of explaining things logically. It was the first of many gratifying learning sessions I'd have with him.

The following week, I was ABC in Battalion 1, and we caught an ass-kicking fire. When we arrived, there was so much smoke that we couldn't even tell which building was involved. When we finally narrowed it down to a large three-story L-shaped commercial property, we had an extremely difficult time locating the fire inside. If I hadn't had that first conversation with Chief Sottung, I'd most likely have pulled everyone out, requested the second alarm, and fought the fire defensively. Instead, I gave it a second thought and cautiously decided to hang in for a while longer. We took a brutal beating, but ten minutes later the fire darkened, and we saved most of the building.

After the fire, I was hunched over the curb blowing black snot globules into the street when Chief Sottung came up behind me. "Now that's the kind of interior attack I like! This was an ass-kicker, and your guys did an outstanding job holding it to a box." His compliment was extremely rewarding, and it gave me a tremendous feeling of pride.

In early 1991, the personnel department announced the battalion chief's examination. The test was a written-oral with two comprehensive problems—one a fire scenario and the other a management problem. Candidates were to take the test in two phases. In the first phase, we'd have one hour to write narratives for both problems. And at a later date, we'd be called before oral panels who'd challenge our narratives and change conditions to evaluate how we adapted.

To prepare, I scanned periodicals to learn the latest firefighting techniques, trends, and buzzwords. I also prepared general outlines for my narratives and committed them to memory. In my library, I had a book titled *Strategic Concepts in Firefighting* by Edward McAniff, a former FDNY chief of department. The book, which I bought in 1974, contained plenty of fire scenarios to practice writing my narratives. I had one distinct advantage over the other candidates: I was housed with Chief Sottung. He was a brilliant fireground strategist and an intellectually decisive manager. He knew that I was preparing for the exam and gave me several test-taking tips, things I never would have thought of otherwise. I felt that his coaching was more helpful than anything else I was doing to prepare myself.

In the meantime, we had settled into our temporary quarters, and things returned to normal.

January 8, 1991—Captain, Engine 60/Hazmat 1

We responded as Hazmat 1 to an illegal methamphetamine lab. A police chemist and I made the first entry wearing Level B suits to recon the area. The chemist was about as nervous about wearing a Hazmat suit as I was about triggering a booby trap. After our entry he pointed to one of the pictures we had taken with our Polaroid camera. "That's over a million dollars' worth of meth in those cooking tins."

"Let's go back in there with a recovery drum and split the profits!" I joked. He didn't crack a smile. I guess he didn't have much of a sense of humor.

During my Fire Science 101 course, Battalion Chief John Meskill often preached "The ultimate goal of a fire department is to put itself out of business through sound fire-prevention programs." We all laughed. But in the nineties, the Philadelphia Fire Department made a concerted effort to install smoke detectors in single-family dwellings, and it worked! We definitely saw the results in the firehouses. Residential fires were on the decline. Often referred to as "the war years" by our brethren in the FDNY, the busy firefighting days, which began in the late sixties and ran through the eighties, began to fade in the nineties. But there were still plenty of shoe runs to keep us busy.

January 29, 1991—Captain, Engine 60, MXT at Engine 57

The ashen seventy-three-year-old man was in ventricular fibrillation. On every fifth compression by one EMT, the other would fill his lungs with oxygen from the resuscitator. The defibrillator made a high-pitched whine as a paramedic charged the paddles. "Clear!" The two EMTs distanced themselves as the medic pressed the buttons. The man's body jerked in response to the jolt, and that was expected. But nobody expected the loud shrieky *reow!* that came from his cat. The feline had cuddled up under the sheet by the man's feet. The shocked cat rocketed into the air and spun around several times before landing and dashing away.

February 18, 1991—Captain, Engine 60

The D Platoon's shoe run sounded like a scene from a sitcom. At change of shifts, Tommy laughingly told me that during the run, a very soft-spoken young woman had been lying on her couch clutching her abdomen. Al Trav placed the stethoscope in his ears and took her blood pressure. "So what's bothering you today, honey?" he asked.

In a barely audible whisper, she replied, "I'm bleeding from my vagina."

Obviously, Al misheard her. He replied, "Yeah. There's a lot of that going around. I had the same thing myself, last week." The guys couldn't contain themselves as the girl stared wide eyed in utter disbelief.

I was off duty on the chilly evening of February 23, 1991, when linseed-oil-soaked rags ignited on the twenty-second floor of One Meridian Plaza, a thirty-eight-story high-rise office building in Center City. The resulting fire gutted eight floors and grew to twelve alarms. Unfortunately, it claimed the lives of Engine 11's Captain David Holcombe, fifty-two; firefighter Phyllis McAllister, forty-three; and Firefighter James Chappell, twenty-nine. They became lost and disoriented and ran out of air while trying to reach the roof to ventilate the heavy smoke conditions. Rescue teams were immediately sent upward after chiefs lost contact with them. One heroic team refused to quit searching and became trapped themselves one level below the roof. They were so low on air that they couldn't retreat back down.

Ladder 19's Jim McGarrigle was ABC in Battalion 1 that night. A helicopter airlifted him to the roof, and he pried open a roof hatch and rescued the rescuers. Engine 11's crew was found at 0215 hours after a search helicopter spotted a broken window on the twenty-eighth floor. Another team was sent up, but it was too late. The rescue effort became a body recovery.

The Meridian was the worst high-rise fire in the city's history. It was hampered by a number of issues. Improperly adjusted pressure-reducing valves (PRVs) installed on the standpipe system caused extremely low nozzle pressure on the attack lines. To make things worse, falling debris from the fire sliced through the hose lines feeding the standpipes, making it virtually impossible to get water onto the flames. Early in the fire, the building lost power, and its emergency generator failed to operate. Firefighters had to battle the blaze in complete darkness without the aid of elevators.

Holcombe, formerly from Engine 49, was a pleasant, soft-spoken gentleman. As fate would have it, he had transferred to 11's only months before his death. I knew him well. As I stood in formation saluting his casket at Rolling Green Memorial Park, I sadly recalled the fun we'd had when we trained him as a hazmat technician so he could fill in as ABC 1.

Shortly after the Meridian fire, Chief Sottung got detailed to the FAB to work on a special project. While Chief Hanson filled in for him, I filled in for Hanson as ABC 1. I was hopeful that the experience would help me prepare for the upcoming test.

April 4, 1991—Captain, Engine 60, Acting Battalion Chief 1

The PA speaker in 10's kitchen interrupted our lunch. "Box six-three-five-five, Philadelphia International Airport." Chief only! "It never fails!" I mumbled as I tossed my freshly made tuna hoagie back on the plate. The airport box was dispatched well over a hundred times each year. It was normally a milk run. After all, the only time I'd ever responded to an aircraft crash at PIA had been nearly fifteen years ago with Rescue 14.

This call was for a two-engine Piper Aerostar with an unsafe-landing-gear indicator. As usual, we headed to our standby position to wait for the aircraft to make a normal landing. I was so used to these unceasing calls (both 49's and 60's were also assigned to the PIA box) that I considered them nothing more than nuisance runs.

But this time, as we were coming down the Platt Bridge, Engine 78 shockingly reported, "The control tower reports that they lost contact with the emergency aircraft." My heart sank when I gazed north of the airport and saw a huge column of black smoke spiraling into the blue sky. Much to my horror, the aircraft had crashed.

The smoke looked to be coming from Southwest Philly, so with my eyes transfixed on the plume, I radioed that we were heading in that direction. When we reached Cobbs Creek Parkway, the smoke looked just as far away. The deceiving column was much farther than I had originally thought. But several dozen emergency vehicles, including Hanson in Deputy 1, were now following behind us. We tracked it completely across Southwest Philly and through West Philly before we eventually wound up on City Line Avenue, the city's border. Aware that the crash was out of our jurisdiction, I stuck my head out the window, looking back questioningly at the trailing vehicles. It looked like a hundred arms were frantically waving for us to continue forward. A Lower Merion Township police officer saw our procession and led us to the crash site. By the time we arrived, the Lower Merion Township Fire Department had extinguished the fire.

The crash involved two aircraft, the Piper and a helicopter. As the Piper was circling, the helicopter, which was trying to help, flew underneath it to see if the nose gear was down, but it ventured too close. The aircraft collided, and both plummeted straight down. They crashed in fireballs on the grounds of fully occupied Merion Elementary School.

The horrendous scene was surreal. The badly charred bodies of three people were clearly visible inside the blackened remains of the Piper. The helicopter, which ended up on the other side of the school, had once had two pilots, but all I could discern were gory body parts. The sights that disturbed me most were the blood-stained sheets covering the bodies of two first-grade girls. They had been playing in the school yard when the fiery debris rained down from above. Screaming mothers, with tears streaming down their faces, were arriving in droves.

That's when I realized that the devastating crash was only a few miles from Maria's elementary school! Unnerved, I told Nolfi to drive past her school on our way back. I had to reassure myself that she was okay.

US Senator John Heinz of Pennsylvania, who had been in the Piper, was among the seven fatalities. There were several injuries on the ground, including a seven-year-old boy who suffered severe burns over two-thirds of his body. Lower Merion firefighters and first responders did an outstanding job, and our assistance wasn't needed. I never considered box six-three-five-five to be a milk run ever again.

April 13, 1991—Captain, Engine 60, Acting Battalion Chief 1

In more than one way, it was test weekend. First was the relatively unimportant battalion chief's test. Yes, I said relatively unimportant, even though I'd been preparing for months.

Early Saturday morning we gathered at the MSB to take the written portion of the examination. With eighteen years on the job, thirteen of those as an officer, including six as captain, I felt ready to advance in rank.

With plenty of experience as an ABC and tutoring by chiefs like Charlie O', DelRossi, Hanson, and most recently Sottung, I was eager to run a battalion of my own. But, like all promotional exams, it was competitive. There were sixty-eight other qualified captains vying to get promoted too. As I scanned the room, I knew the competition was going to be fierce. Eddie Yaeger (CK-1), Johnny Fry, Bobby Skarbek, Eddie Schwartz, Joe McGraw, Billy Brightcliffe, John McGrath, Fran Gallagher, and Al Anderson, to name a few, were all sharp, knowledgeable, and proven test takers. I felt worried by their competition yet, at the same time, extremely proud to be part of such a well-respected and proficient peer group.

When the examination began, all the practicing I had done kicked in. I quickly read the fire problem and jotted down pertinent facts and issues. Then I reread it, making sure I hadn't missed anything. My narrative flowed easily. I had memorized my opening and conclusion, and I filled in the body by addressing the key points from my notes. I did the same thing with the administrative problem. I budgeted twenty-five minutes for each problem, which left five minutes to review and refine each one. The hour appeared to fly by in seconds.

When I returned home, I rewrote my responses from memory so I could practice defending them. I planned to ask Chief Sottung for his help. I wanted to be as prepared as possible for phase two.

Even though it was drizzling, damp, and dreary, I reported to First Battalion Headquarters Sunday night feeling enthused. I was optimistic about my chances of scoring well. Scheduled to testify in court for an arson fire in the morning, I lay down shortly after midnight. The bells rang before I could close my eyes. I trotted toward the chief's car, unaware that this call would be a much more important test than the one I had taken on Saturday.

Ladder 19's Billy Gaffney, Hanson's backup aide, started the engine. "Full box, Nine Seventeen East Passyunk Avenue, for an apartment fire. Engine Eleven's first-in, Cap." Billy was very thorough. With my aspirations riding high from the exam, I imagined that someday he might even be on my short list of possible chief's aides.

As we turned onto Passyunk Avenue, the midnight crowd at South Philly's landmark, Pat's King of Steaks, stared as we zipped past followed by

Ladder 11 and Engine 10. One potbellied guy was in the classic cheesesteak eating pose, leaning over the curb chomping away as globs of cheese wiz and grease oozed into the street. He flashed us the high sign as our sirens screamed past. Billy and I laughed at the comical sight.

Ahead, through a haze of smoke, we could vaguely make out Engine 11's red flashing lights. We had a job. Lieutenant Kenny Krauss, an excellent officer whom I'd crossed paths with in West Philly, reported medium smoke showing from the second floor of a three-story brick apartment building and placed two engines and two ladders in service. When we arrived, my first impression was that the fire involved one second-floor apartment unit. In the thirty seconds it took me to don my gear, conditions changed drastically. When I looked back up, heavy smoke was pushing from several large windows on the second and third floors. The fire was worse than I'd originally thought. I told Billy to place the last two engines in service and established a command post directly across the street.

The structure had a deceiving facade. Instead of one eighteen-foot by seventy-five-foot three-story row apartment, which was common in South Philly, it was actually three of them connected together. A "Shaftway" warning placard on the left side revealed that it once had been a fifty-four-foot by seventy-five-foot commercial building before being converted into apartments. I quickly realized that the redesigned floor plan was going to make it difficult for companies to find their way around. Sure enough, a few seconds later, Kenny reported that they were having trouble finding the stairs. I directed Engine 10 to advance their hose line through the front door to back them up.

Battalion 4 was the second-in battalion chief. Technically, he outranked me because I was only an ABC, but according to department protocols, I was officially the incident commander. Nonetheless, he was an outstanding fire chief, and I was glad that he was on that job, which unfortunately was getting dicier every second. Battalion 4 reported heavy fire showing from the rear, and I told him 53's and 1's were assigned to his position.

Angled Passyunk Avenue cuts diagonally through the square block bounded by Sixth, Seventh, Montrose, and Christian Streets. The only way to get to the rear was through a small gated courtyard off Sixth Street.

The narrow streets were choked with illegally parked cars, which blocked hydrants and made it difficult to maneuver fire apparatuses. I knew it was going to take a long time for the shit-work companies to stretch their hose lines back there.

Kenny radioed that they had located the interior stairs and were advancing up, with 10's right behind them. I then had Ladder 11 take out the huge windows to ease their advance. I also directed Ladder 5 to open up the roof. Fed by the supply of fresh air, flames began to lick from the windows. I was expecting to see the fire darken quickly as 11's advanced their attack stream forward. But instead, conditions got worse. To my horror, huge fireballs, reminiscent of those I'd only seen at refinery fires, began rolling twenty feet into the street. I had never seen a building burn so ferociously. The fire had quickly transitioned from dicey to ugly.

I asked Kenny for a progress report. He replied that they had water on the fire but weren't making much headway. I quickly reasoned that they didn't have the proper flow to deal with such fireballs. I was getting concerned that the extremely high temperatures might cause the third floor to collapse on top of them. Visions of the flag-draped caskets at the Meridian funerals flashed before my eyes. I radioed Battalion 4 and told him I was going to pull the companies out and fight the fire defensively.

"Bobby," he replied, "let's give them a chance to knock it down from the inside." Obviously he wasn't seeing what I was seeing.

Even though I was standing across the street, my face and hands were burning. I briefly turned my back to shield myself from the fire and asked Kenny for another progress report. The situation was the same. I glanced up and saw the cornices of several three-story properties behind me smoldering from the radiant heat.

I turned toward the fire building again, and the fireballs were even worse. Chief Sottung's words from one of our chats reverberated in my head: "Rely on your experience. If the situation gets bad enough, you'll know when it's time to get everybody out."

I took a deep breath. "Battalion One to Engine Eleven and Engine Ten, get the fuck out of that building now! I repeat! Battalion One to Engine Eleven and Engine Ten, get the fuck out of there now! Evacuate the building!" Then I radioed Billy. "Battalion One to aide, strike out the second alarm. Have all companies go in service with master streams. Have the ladders evacuate the entire west side of Passyunk Avenue."

I anxiously kept my eyes locked on the front door, waiting for 11's and 10's firefighters to emerge. It took less than a minute for them to exit, but it seemed like an eternity before I counted six yellow helmets. The last one was Krauss.

"Kenny, is everybody out?" I screeched.

He raised his right thumb. "We're all out, Cap." I felt like a thousand tons were lifted from my shoulders.

The intense radiant heat forced me to relocate my command post south of the fire. Billy had already backed the chief's car down the block because its plastic warning lenses were melting. When Chief Hanson arrived, he came to my new command post and exclaimed, "You've got a whale of a fire here, boy! I'm requesting the third and fourth alarms!" As he was talking, I heard two tremendously loud crashes. The third floor had collapsed onto the second, causing it to collapse onto the first.

Things were happening quickly, and it was a challenge to keep pace. I had to make many snap decisions, and at times I felt overwhelmed, even inept. But eventually the evacuations were completed; the fire was surrounded, and things began to stabilize.

That's when I began to develop self-doubts about my ambition to make battalion chief. There had been times when I felt helpless, especially when I was waiting for those six yellow helmets. I became paralyzed with fear when I thought about what might have happened if I had waited any longer before ordering them out. I also felt terrible about overruling Battalion 4, such an experienced and well-regarded chief. The enthusiasm I had felt when I arrived for work had rapidly drained away.

Later, when Chief Hanson placed the fire under control and said he was turning command back over to me, I dejectedly nodded my head. I guess he sensed that I was feeling low. "Let me tell you something, Bob. This is about as bad as it ever gets for a chief. You did a good job." His comments lifted my spirits, but I no longer felt the same zest for promotion.

At the following morning's court appearance, I couldn't imagine why I was getting odd looks. When I got home, I saw the reason. My face was as red as a bad sunburn. I had first-degree burns from the intense radiant heat. My hands were worse. They even had small blisters—second-degree burns.

When Diane came home from work, she was startled by my appearance. "Rob, what the heck happened to your face? It's all red!" I pooh-poohed my burns even though they were still stinging, but she dragged me upstairs and gently applied ointment to my burns and blisters.

Afterward, as we shared our usual cup of coffee before my night shift, she sensed that something else was bothering me. "What's the matter, Rob? You look really down." When I told her about my self-doubts, she pulled her chair close and gently began rubbing the back of my neck. "That's because you don't do the chief's job every day. If you get promoted, you'll adjust to it. I know you will." She had so much confidence in me. Her loving ways always made me feel better.

That night, back at the firehouse, the fire marshal called and said that the apartment building's hardwood floors had been heavily polyurethaned late that Sunday afternoon. The place was basically full of flammable vapors, which explained the fireballs.

My zest to become a battalion chief returned later that night. Firefighters from 10's and 11's told me they were thankful that they had been pulled out in time. Battalion 4 also called and acknowledged that I had made the right decisions. As I had suspected, Battalion 4 said that from his vantage point in the rear, things didn't appear as bad as they were. As I lay in my bunk late that night, I thought to myself, "Regardless of how I finish on the chiefs' list, the only test that really mattered this weekend was the one on Passyunk Avenue."

CHAPTER 28

The Luck of the Draw

On May 30, 1991, I received a letter from the city's personnel department, stating that information had been brought to their attention that necessitated them to invalidate the fire-problem narratives of the battalion chief's examination. The oral-defense portion for the management problem was still scheduled, but the fire problem was going to be readministered. I was crushed! I felt that the fire problem had been the stronger of my two narratives. Now I needed to study, practice, and take it all over again. When I heard gossip about why, my disappointment turned to anger.

The story was ludicrous. A few firefighters had complained to personnel that a candidate had inside information about the fire problem. Test makers had used an illustration from McAniff's book, *Strategic Concepts in Firefighting*, for the deputy chief's fire problem (the deputy and battalion chief's tests were given at the same time), and the anonymous people saw the candidate reading the book before the test. Really? I had read it too!

Many of us who were serious about professionalizing ourselves owned that book! With tons of illustrations, it was great for practicing and sharpening one's skills as a fireground commander. Even though the test makers did use one of its illustrations, they had changed the accompanying fire conditions drastically. If a building's occupancy, smoke conditions, exposures, location, and extent of fire are changed, the strategy and tactics used to fight the fire will change as well.

It was a stretch to infer, after merely observing a candidate reading a popular firefighting book, which had been around for seventeen years, that the candidate had inside information about the test. Besides, how had these anonymous people known about the source of the illustration, anyway? Did they themselves have a copy of the book? Why didn't personnel only opt to invalidate the deputy chief's test? Why did they annul the battalion chief's examination?

But the personnel department was satisfied that the complaint was valid. They in turn convinced the mayor's office that it was a form of cheating. So the mayor ordered the city's inspector general's office to conduct an investigation. The probe subsequently revealed that there was absolutely no basis to conclude that there had been any form of cheating. But the city refused to cede; the test was in limbo. Several candidates, who had studied hard for the examinations, complained to the Philadelphia Fire Officers' Union, who challenged the city to proceed with the oral tests for the fire problems, but it fell on deaf ears.

Despite the holdup, I practiced for and took the oral-defense portion of the management problem. The panel was difficult to gauge, but I felt that I had defended my narrative rather well. Nonetheless, I was annoyed that the fire problem was still looming. The officers' union was fighting hard for the city to proceed, but I knew it was going to take a while for them to resolve the issue. In the meantime, I was happy at 60's, and I directed all my energy into making us a better hazmat team.

In 1991, with a ton of support from the department's Hazardous Material's Administrative Unit (HMAU), we became the first hazmat team in the state to pass certification. Tommy Bitto and his D Platoon prepared a huge gourmet buffet for the state examiners. It was akin to the old feast trick we'd used to influence deputy chief's inspections, and we passed with flying colors! A contingent of brass from headquarters, including the fire commissioner, came to our station to present our certificate. We provided another gigantic lunch for that occasion too. Our certification was valid for four years—plenty of time for us to save enough money for the next banquet.

At the time, we were receiving much of our hazmat training from organizations outside the department, many of whom weren't emergency responders. Even though we were learning a lot, much of the training wasn't practical for the conditions we encountered in the field. I felt that in order to reach the next plateau, we should develop our own customized training program. Deputy Chief Gary Appleby, director of the Philadelphia Fire Academy, had founded an outreach training program that encouraged department members to develop and deliver training courses at the academy. It was just the opportunity we needed.

I had always felt that the 1975 Gulf-refinery tragedy might have been averted if on-scene commanders had had a better understanding of the properties of hazardous materials. I decided that our first course should give students the skills necessary to properly analyze and evaluate the threats posed by hazardous materials through the sound application of scientific principles. I presented the course outline to Chief Appleby, and he loved the idea. I began working on it immediately.

Tragically, 1991 ended with yet another firefighter fatality. On December 20, Lieutenant Stephen Yale, of Ladder 29, collapsed on the fireground at Third and Ashdale Streets. He died several days later. It had been a bad year for line-of-duty deaths, and I was glad that it was over.

January 2, 1992—Captain, Engine 60, Acting Battalion Chief 1

"Christ, Cap!" Ladder 11's Joe Krieble announced loudly in 10's kitchen. "Overtime *and* ABC tonight! Now I know why you have a Buick Riviera parked out back."

Joe's company mate, dark-haired and friendly Johnny Redmond, spun around, "It's almost eleven o'clock, and you just realized that he's ABC tonight? Where the hell have you been?"

Joe shrugged. "I don't know! I thought maybe he was working the engine."

Redmond shook his head. "You're unbelievable, Joe!"

I joined everyone in the kitchen laughing at the good-natured exchange between the A Platoon's comedy team.

Realizing that he had an audience, Joe continued. "Well, guys, look out! Because whenever Captain Bob's in the car, we work our asses off. Last August, I was working OT on the C Platoon, and Marchisello's ABC when a box comes in for the thirty-story Drake Hotel. We make the turn, and like a hundred people are waving towels and sheets from the windows. Thank God it was only one room. Then later that night—"

The bells interrupted Joe's forewarning, and we rushed out the door, headed to Pier 98 South, Delaware and Oregon. The pier, which juts over a hundred yards into the Delaware River, had ugly grayish-yellow smoke swirling from its midsection. As I was putting on my gear, Krieble pointed at me. "What was I just telling you guys? The captain's a jinx in the car!" The fire was extensive, but with the help of Marine Unit 1, we held it to a box alarm. Chief Sottung would have been proud of me.

Three hours later we returned to our station tired, wet, and shivering. As soon as we set foot in the warmth of our kitchen, the bells rang again. This time it was for a fully involved dwelling fire at Thirty-First and Tasker.

Lugging his power saw, Redmond was about to climb to the roof when he looked back. "Yo, Cap." He laughed. "The next time you're going to work on our platoon, let us know. We'll bring in extra cold-weather gear."

In early 1992, newly elected Mayor Ed Rendell (Philly's former district attorney) asked the district attorney's office to investigate the chief's examination. The result was the same. There wasn't any evidence of cheating. But the city still didn't concede. They continued to press for a retest of the fire problems. Unreal!

Later in the year, the city claimed that there was new evidence of cheating, and the case went to Common Pleas Court. There, Judge Sheppard ruled that there was no new evidence and that the claim was simply a rehash of old evidence. He ordered the city to proceed with the test. The city ignored the order, and the fire officers' union was furious. They continued to squabble with the city.

The whole thing was exasperating, but it didn't change life in the firehouse.

The Schuylkill River and a trash transfer station weren't far from our Grays Ferry firehouse. Needless to say, we saw more than our fair share of vermin. The city hired exterminators, but low bidders always won the contracts. We didn't stand a chance.

September 24, 1992—Captain, Engine 60

The shift was all about monkeys, bats, rats, and mice. Yes, that's what I said!

At change of shifts, the D Platoon's Joe Urick was telling us about when he had been at 24's and they had responded to an apartment where water was leaking from the ceiling. As they entered the apartment above, the television and radio were on full blast, the faucets were running, water was all over the floor, and there was a strong odor of natural gas.

"As we were walking around, turning things off, a screeching monkey suddenly charged at us from the back room. It scared the shit out of us! We collided with each other as we tried to flee. That little son of a bitch had gotten out of his cage and turned every friggin knob he could find in the apartment. We ran out and closed the door until they found his damned owner." Joe's tale set the tone for the night.

Shortly after shift change, I was in the hallway talking to Lumpy when, out of the corner of my eye, I spotted something odd hanging from the ceiling. "Shit, Bob!" I exclaimed. "Look, there's a friggin' bat hanging upside down!" Lumpy swiftly grabbed an iron poker, which for some reason was in Ladder 19's office, and after one mighty whack, the bat spiraled lifelessly to the floor. I suppose it had found its way in through the open apparatus doors.

We should have closed them, because just before dinner, a large black rat darted across the kitchen floor and ran directly into Ladder 19's office. Lumpy, who was sitting at his desk, was so startled by the rat, which scurried underneath him, he nearly jumped a foot in the air. Seizing the opportunity, Johnny B. ran over and slammed the office door closed. "Get him, Loo!"

"What the frig, John?" Lumpy screamed. "Thanks, you chooch!"

We laughed hysterically as curses, crashes, and bangs emanated from the ladder office. A minute later Lumpy emerged victoriously with the limp rat dangling from his trusty poker. It was his second kill of the night.

I figured that we had seen enough pests for the shift, but unfortunately, I figured wrong. Just as dawn was breaking, I heard a rustling noise coming from the trash can next to my bunk. I peeked over and spotted a little gray mouse spinning his wheels, trying to climb up the can's metal walls. Taking pity on God's tiny creature, I decided to spare his life. I carried the can out the back door and released him in the parking lot. The damn pesky mouse scampered from the can, ran several feet, then made an abrupt U-turn, and dashed back through a small crevice under my office window. "Next time, you're dead," I screamed, "you little shit!"

The lack of promotional lists was taking a toll on the department's operations. There were mounting chief's vacancies. Realizing that it could be a while before the dispute was resolved, Deputy Fire Commissioner Wauhop decided to fill the vacancies with ABCs for a year at a time. In December of 1992, Chief Sottung asked me to take one of the spots. I told him that I'd only accept it if the deputy commissioner guaranteed that I could return to 60's after my year was finished. Wauhop refused, and so did I. It would have been a great opportunity, but we had a lot going on at Hazmat, and I wanted to stay there unless I was officially promoted. Besides, I was getting plenty of time as an ABC anyway. To his credit, Ladder 19's Captain Jim McGarrigle declined a permanent ABC spot for the same reason.

On April 23, 1993, I celebrated my twentieth anniversary in the department. Engine 60, Ladder 19, Battalion 1, and Deputy 1 threw classmate Billy Hopper and me a filet mignon dinner complete with all the trimmings. They gave Bill an engraved ring, and I got a beautiful Italian wristwatch. Bats, rats, and mice aside, I couldn't imagine celebrating such a memorable occasion with any other group of firefighters.

July 30, 1993—Captain, Engine 60, Acting Battalion Chief 1

In my twenty years, I'd never seen it before. Sure, I'd heard about it several times, but I always had thought that it was simply an old fireman's tale. But here it was, right before my eyes. The guy who died after hanging himself was sporting a full erection. It was an impressive one, at that!

I don't know how I missed it at first, but I hadn't noticed it until a firefighter from 24's ribbed a pretty little paramedic: "Gee, Sherry, you're sexy enough to even arouse a dead man."

She casually glanced at the tent pole pushing up the guy's boxer shorts and nonchalantly replied, "They call it angel lust! It happens sometimes." Then she looked back at the firefighter who had kidded her. "I'll bet even in death, he's bigger than you'll ever be in life!" We had to restrain ourselves from laughing too loudly.

In the fall of 1993, Al Loughead and I delivered the pilot training course "Understanding the Properties of Hazardous Materials." Al concocted several experiments to liven up my lectures. His demonstrations were a smash, and the course was met with rave reviews. Chief Appleby loved it and asked us to deliver it to each platoon of Hazmat 1.

It was contagious. Captain McGarrigle and Lieutenants Bitto and Matt Black asked to get involved with the training. Appleby gave us permission to develop four more courses. Jimmy took the lead for a plugging and patching course; Tommy began working on a unit about personal protective equipment and Matt a decontamination course. Al and I began developing a module on analytical and monitoring equipment. I was hoping that down the road we'd put all the courses together and deliver them as a complete two-week hazmat-technician program. Appleby, enthralled by the idea, quickly coined our venture "The Five-Tier Hazmat Program." I had a ton of work to occupy my mind while the city and the officers' union slugged things out over the chief's test.

Specialized training courses by outside agencies still remained an essential part of our hazmat training. Later that fall we were at the Philadelphia Fire Academy receiving training on intermodal hazmat containers.

NOVEMBER 20, 1993—CAPTAIN, ENGINE 60/HAZMAT 1

The morning's training session was informative, even though it was all class-room stuff. After lunch we gathered around several intermodal containers that the trainer had brought to the academy. Earlier, he'd emphasized several times that our hands-on afternoon session might hold a surprise to challenge our minds.

As soon as we started the session, an academy staff lieutenant came jogging out of the building. "Hazmat One, you got a run!" I immediately became suspicious. Next to the address, the lieutenant had scrawled "Intermodal container leaking vinylpyridine."

I sneered at the course instructor. "Yeah, sure! How coincidental is this?" I was convinced that it was a setup, all part of the training.

As we raced down I-95, the trainer was hot on our tail. Certain that it was an exercise, part of our training, I had our vehicles turn off their lights and sirens. We crawled to the scene obeying traffic signals. When we arrived, the isolated intermodal container was spewing white smoke from its rear doors.

"Look, they even used a smoke generator to make it look realistic," I said to Johnny B. "Okay, let's play their game."

Vinylpyridine is a nasty chemical. It's flammable, toxic, and corrosive, and it can polymerize. The trainer slammed to a stop behind us and came running forward.

"Good choice of chemicals!" I yelled with a laugh.

He began waving his arms frantically. "Captain! I swear to my mother that this is not part of the training. It's real!" Just then a foul odor wafted by my nostrils. The incident was, in fact, real. We were there for the rest of the day. We learned much more about intermodal containers than we had expected.

In yet more budgetary cutbacks, the city deactivated Battalion 5 on July 1, 1993. In order to provide adequate coverage, Battalion 1 was relocated to

Engine 1's station on Broad, near Fitzwater. They were now covering both the First's and Fifth's old geographical areas.

JANUARY 1, 1994—CAPTAIN, ENGINE 60, ACTING BATTALION CHIEF 1

I was dog tired after fighting my way through the Mummers Parade crowd on Broad Street. It wasn't the walk as much as the lack of sleep. We had broken in New Year's Eve with two working fires the night before, one at 0220 and one at 0502.

After that night's shift, I left my car at 1's and walked to my parents' house, where I met Diane and the kids. A New Year's tradition, Mom prepared her usual feast of meatballs, roast beef, and potato salad. Like always, friends, family, and neighbors jammed into their tiny row home on Rosewood Street. Throughout the day, Diane and I took the kids to watch the parade. Whenever they got cold, we returned to Mom's to gorge ourselves and drink hot coffee. It was a great day, but by three o'clock it was time to kiss everybody good-bye and head back to 1's.

Smack-dab along the parade route, the quarters of Engine 1, Ladder 5, and Battalion 1 provided a warm friendly comfort station for firefighters near and far each New Year's Day. The station's enterprising members sold soup, hot dogs, hot chocolate, and coffee. The money earned helped offset their house dues.

The parade's main feature, the famous string bands, always stopped to perform in front of the firehouse. The Quaker City String Band was performing as I high-fived my way through the crowd of firefighters gathered on the sidewalk and entered the station. Even though I was bushed, I was glad to be part of the festive atmosphere.

Inside, several firefighters were laughing their asses off, some even rolling on the floor. The story was that Mayor Rendell had been all smiles as he led the string bands up Broad Street. Well, he had been all smiles until he approached the firehouse. Suddenly he was bombarded by a horrendous chorus of jeers and boos (under Rendell, firefighters had incurred two consecutive years of pay freezes). One off-duty firefighter's long-winded howling boo was more like something normally heard at an Eagles-Cowboys game. The mayor angrily spun his head and glared at the crowd of off-duty firefighters. Shortly afterward, a police cruiser showed up to videotape the entire crowd.

After shift change, Chief Sottung called. "Bobby, I think I know what your answer's going to be, but headquarters wants me to ask anyway. Do you know what happened in front of the station today?"

"No, Chief," I lied. "What happened?"

"They booed the mayor; that's what happened." He sniggered.

"Chief, there were hundreds of off-duty firemen out there today, even out-of-towners. I'm sure the culprits are long gone by now. What the heck could I possibly do about it?"

"Okay, if you hear anything, and I'm sure you won't, give me a call."

I never heard another word about the incident again. The year began with levity, but in the fire business, laughs can rapidly turn to tragedy. With shift work, it's simply the luck of the draw. On one shift the decisions are easy, the fires cooperate, and things run smooth as silk. Then the next shift, there's that monster job, the one where all hell breaks loose. If you happen to be off duty, you realize just how lucky you are that the luck of the draw has been on your side.

Chief Hanson was off, and I was ABC for the last chilly week of January. It was busy. We responded with Hazmat 1 to an oil-vat fire inside a manufacturing plant. We extinguished the fire using two fog streams, an operation more often studied in textbooks than performed in actuality. Then on the twenty-fifth, we responded to a horrendous residential gas explosion. Two firefighters from Ladder 11 made a daring rescue of a small child, and I put them both in for heroism awards. I was lucky to catch four shifts where things ran smooth as silk. My brethren, working the following four days, my days off, weren't as lucky. They had the misfortune to be working when all hell broke loose.

Church fires can be extremely difficult to fight, especially in those of older construction, replete with void spaces. Fires can spread quickly, with devastating results. Only two blocks from Battalion 1's headquarters, the Rising Sun Baptist Church proudly had served its faithful since 1846. Just after 1200 hours on January 28, the pyrolytic decomposition of wood beams near the structure's chimney caused a fire to break out in the basement. The A Platoon firefighters were just sitting down to enjoy their lunch when box four-four-nine was sounded for Twelfth and Fitzwater Streets.

The fire didn't appear too bad when firefighters first arrived. But somehow, as they searched for its source in the basement, the fire spread with lightning speed. Suddenly, several firefighters became surrounded by the flames, heat, and smoke. Tragically, two of them were killed and eight others were injured in the resulting five-alarm inferno. Dead were Ladder 11's good-natured Johnny Redmond, forty-one, father of four and a seventeen-year veteran, along with Rescue 1's Vincent Acey, forty-two, father of three and an eight-and-a-half-year veteran. Many firefighters sustained injuries, some critical, during the heroic attempts to rescue their comrades.

I was ABC again the four shifts after the church fire. It was busy again, but in a very different way. Twice a day, we went to the burn center to check on Firefighters Bob Crossfield and Walt Jackson. Both had suffered critical burns in the fire. There was also a lot to do for the funerals. Johnny's funeral was set for our first day off duty. Naturally, everyone wanted to attend the services, but we still needed to staff the firehouses. When word got out, firefighters from all over the city volunteered to work, pro bono, for those who wanted to attend the services. The demonstration of brotherhood made me feel proud as ever to be a Philadelphia firefighter.

Their funerals hit me harder than most LODD services. Most likely, it was because I understood that the shift that was on duty was simply the luck of the draw.

CHAPTER 29

Thermodynamics

Luckily, there was plenty going on with Hazmat to take my mind off Redmond's and Acey's tragic deaths. We were heavily involved with the design, layout, and specifications for a new hazmat response vehicle. Through the spring and summer, Al and I delivered our "Understanding the Properties" course to each platoon of Hazmat 1. In between, we worked our regular shifts in the firehouse.

February 23, 1994—Captain, Engine 60/Hazmat 1

What goes around comes around. We responded to a hazmat incident at Community College of Philadelphia. Dr. Gimm, the professor who taught my organic-chemistry courses, was racing down the fire tower as we were racing up. When I saw her, I jokingly said, "Hey, Dr. Gimm, your favorite student is here!"

Her eyes widened. "Robert, thank God you're here. A chlorine cylinder is leaking in the lab.

"Gee, do I need to know its reaction mechanism?" (Complex reaction mechanisms were something she had us memorize in class.)

"Forget that reaction-mechanism crap, Robert. Stop the darn leak!"

It was a simple repair—a loose packing nut that was easily tightened. As I was climbing into the cab of Engine 60, Dr. Gimm ran up and thanked us.

"You're welcome, Dr. Gimm," I replied. "You earned an A-plus for your evacuation procedures." She laughed.

March 22, 1994—Captain, Engine 60/Hazmat 1

Hydrogen sulfide is responsible for thousands of accidental deaths annually. The deadly gas has several industrial applications and is also a natural product of organic decomposition. Its toxicity is exacerbated by two main factors: It's heavier than air, so it hugs the ground. And after a few whiffs, its rotten-egg odor can destroy a person's olfactory nerve, rendering it virtually undetectable by smell. So it was only natural that I was on the edge of my seat as we responded through morning-rush-hour traffic to a reported hydrogen-sulfide leak.

The scene was chaotic when we arrived. Firefighters were banging on doors and ushering people blocks away from the incident. Police were blocking traffic in all directions, and SEPTA police had shut down the Market-Frankford Elevated Line.

"Chief, where's the leak?" I asked when we arrived. He pointed to a fiberboard drum behind a commercial building. I immediately knew something wasn't right. Gases are stored in cylinders, not fiberboard drums.

"How do we know its hydrogen sulfide, Chief?" I asked curiously.

"Bob, that guy over there works here. He speaks Spanish, but I clearly heard him say it's hydrogen sulfide."

My first impression was that rainwater might have reacted with a chemical in the drum, causing it to release the toxic gas. I walked over to the small-statured, dark-haired worker, pointed to the drums, and said, "Hydrogen sulfide?"

He nodded excitedly. "*Sí*, hydrogen sulfide!"

I squared his shoulders to face me. "*Dónde* MSDS?" (Where's the Material Safety Data Sheet?) He pulled a folded MSDS from his back pocket. The chemical's correct chemical name was clearly written across the top: sodium hydrogen sulfite. It was *not* hydrogen sulfide. I was extremely familiar with the less harmful chemical, also known as sodium bisulfite. It had been in every chemistry set I played with as a child.

Within ten minutes, the El was running again, the streets were open, the houses were reoccupied, and we were heading back to South Philly.

Thermodynamics (n.)—The branch of science concerned with heat and temperature and their relation to energy and work (Wikipedia).

Most people have no idea what the term means, but my engineering degree had required me to study two courses in thermodynamics.

June 18, 1994—Captain, Engine 60

The temperature was in the nineties, and the air conditioners were straining to remove the energy-sapping heat and humidity from our Grays Ferry firehouse.

I couldn't care less; it was pizza-pig-out night. Joe T. from 53's, a Haz-Back (we facetiously called our hazmat backups "Haz-Backs") was detailed to our company. As he'd done many times before, Joe T. had picked up a do-it-yourself pizza kit from a store near his home. The kit contained enough shells, cheese, and sauce to make ten delicious pies. The guys creatively enhanced each pie with onions, peppers, mushrooms, pepperoni, sausage, or even anchovies (yuck). There was always a wide enough variety to satisfy everyone's palate and fill our bellies. We all loved pizza-pig-out night, especially Chief Sottung, who turned down several dinner invitations at other firehouses to enjoy the night's feast.

I guess the only thing we didn't take into consideration was how much extra heat the oven added to our kitchen. Our air conditioners were completely overpowered, and we sweated up a storm, but the tasty pies were worth it. We devoured each pie as soon as it emerged steaming hot from the oven.

I always enjoyed when Joe T. was detailed to our station, and not just because of the pizzas he brought with him. He was a terrific firefighter and had been a trusty Haz-Back for years. But it was his hilarious wit that always made for an entertaining shift.

As we were stuffing ourselves, Joe had us in stitches as he ranted about his failed business venture with Lumpy. A few years ago, they had been partners in a pavement pole (bollard) business. They had thought they would make a fortune installing bollards in South Philly's tiny streets, where pavements often crack from cars and trucks that jump the curbs.

Joe T. was humorously berating Lumpy. "Yo, Lump! That was a friggin' brilliant idea you had. Yeah! Let's install pavement poles and make a fortune. Everybody in South Philly needs pavement poles, right?" Then he turned toward the rest of us. "So we each put up money for equipment and material, and after a year of advertising and spreading the word, do you know how many jobs we got? Two! Two friggin' pavement poles! And to top things off, they were Lumpy's paisans, so he gave them discounts!" I almost fell off my chair—I was laughing so hard.

By nine o'clock we were stuffed, but we stayed in the kitchen joking around and making small talk. Somehow our conversation shifted to ceiling fans. We were discussing the best way to install them so they wouldn't wobble, when the bells rang. "Engine, shoes!" Our conversation stopped as we dashed off to the Wilson Homes Housing Project.

The unmistakable odor of German roaches greeted us at the door as we entered the tiny masonry home. Dave and Johnny B. began tending to an elderly lady who had fallen in her living room. As they were taking her vital signs, Joe T. nudged me and pointed to the ceiling. "Yo, Cap, check out the wobble of that ceiling fan." I glanced up curiously and saw a huge brown roach buzzing its wings above our heads. I made a beeline for the front door and exploded with laughter once I got outside.

When temperatures rise, medical calls rise accordingly. At 1230 hours we were dispatched to the Tasker Homes Housing Project for a woman suffering from heat stress. Inside we found an obese woman reclined on her sofa. Two other very large women were fanning her with pizza boxes. Joe T. whispered in my ear, "Yo, Cap, it must have been pizza-pig-out night here too." Before busting a gut, I made an abrupt U-turn, slammed the clipboard into Joe's chest, and dashed outside. I sat laughing my ass off in the cab of our pumper until Medic 7 took the fat lady to the hospital.

At 0130 the bells rang again. This time it was a tactical box for a reported dwelling fire in the Tasker Homes. A gray-haired man in his seventies was waving to us as we pulled up. "Hey, Pop, what's on fire?" I asked as I jumped from the cab.

"Nothin', sonny! I just smell smoke," he replied in a gravelly voice.

An unfamiliar sour and pungent odor was in the air as we walked inside and methodically began checking each room. Masonry project homes retain the heat, and this one was scorching after baking in the sun all day.

In the middle of Pop's bedroom, we found a window air conditioner sitting on the floor. It was in a puddle of water and humming away. I wasn't sure if it was the source of the odor, but I knew darn well it was neither a safe nor an effective way to use an air conditioner. "Hey, Pop," I called out, "what the heck is this air conditioner doing on the floor? It's supposed to be in a window."

Pop furrowed his brow and snarled at me. "Put your hand over the vent, dummy. It's blowing cold air!"

I looked at him incredulously. "Put your hand on the other side, Pop. It's blowing hot air too!"

He shook his head and placed his hand over the cooling vent again. "Come here, dummy, and feel. It's blowing cold air."

"I know, Pop," I pleaded, "but it's blowing just as much hot air on the other side!"

"That don't matter none, dummy," he said. "As long as it blows cold air, it's working."

"Then why isn't it making the bedroom cool, Pop?" I asked incredulously.

"Cause it's hot outside, dummy!" he shouted back.

Frustrated and shaking my head with disbelief, at the behest of my engineering-trained mind, I exclaimed, "Pop, you can't use it this way. It violates the fundamental laws of thermodynamics!"

Puzzled, Pop scratched his head. "Thermo-who?"

Joe T. seized the moment. "Thermodynamics, Pop! You can't break those laws, or they'll throw you in jail." I turned my head, snickering.

Pop looked at Joe and then at me. "You're both crazy! I ain't breaking no damn laws!"

"Listen, Pop. We can't leave the air conditioner like this. It's not safe. You could get electrocuted. Besides, maybe it's causing the odor. We have to unplug it."

"Go ahead," he replied angrily, "but I know that ain't causing this smell. There's something else going on in this house."

We unplugged the air conditioner and checked the house again thoroughly. By the time we finished, the odor was gone. Satisfied, I cautioned Pop about not plugging the air conditioner in again before we left.

As we were backing into our firehouse, a car came speeding up Grays Ferry Avenue and screeched to a halt ten feet short of hitting our pumper. I was about to go scream at the driver when surprisingly Pop jumped out of the driver's side.

"I told you guys there was something else going on inside my house!" He handed me a stink bomb that somebody had slipped inside his mailbox. "My cat swiped this under the sofa! I told you dummies that it wasn't my air conditioner." Then he pointed at Joe T. "You and your damn thermo law. They should lock *you* up, boy!"

Firefighters witness people who do incredibly stupid things. Pop reminded me of a man whose house we had responded to when I was at 24's. The gas company had shut off his service for nonpayment, so he decided to place wood at the base of his forced-air heater, ignite it, and turn on the fan. Fortunately his neighbors smelled smoke and called the fire department before he killed himself from carbon-monoxide poisoning. Astonishingly, he had been just as adamant as Pop. I wasn't sure if it was an underlying reason, but a few years later, the gas company decided against shutting service to delinquent payers during the winter months.

In September of 1994, I received a letter from the officers' union stating that the city miraculously had shifted their position on the chief's test. The city admitted that no one had cheated in the examination. Instead, they claimed that the personnel department was at fault for poorly preparing the exam. They even brought in a subject-matter expert to testify how badly personnel had prepared the test. Unbelievably, the city was actually testifying against themselves! But their objective was still the same; they wanted a new fire problem. I simply shook my head.

At the end of 1994, as he'd done every year since the chief's test was put in abeyance, Chief Sottung asked me if I wanted one of the ABC spots.

My answer was the same. I didn't want to leave 60's unless I was officially promoted. It was the only way I'd leave my beloved hazmat.

July 8, 1995—Captain, Engine 60/Hazmat 1, OT, Ladder 19

Tommy Bitto was undoubtedly the best hazmat technician in the department. I never passed up the opportunity to work on the D Platoon with him. An outstanding firefighter, Tommy learned his skills working at 24's and in West Philly. He was also one of the best platoon supervisors I'd seen in my career. On his last performance rating, I had written, "Tommy, you run your platoon more like the father of a family rather than a platoon supervisor. It's no wonder that the D Platoon is outstanding both in the station and on the fireground."

Shortly after roll call, a box alarm came in for a building fire at Eighteenth and Christian. Engine 60 was fourth-in, and Ladder 19, which I was working, was second-in. When 24's arrived they reported nothing showing from the front, so Tommy and I took our positions in the rear. We spotted a man pointing down the alley, where a light haze was swirling in the humid morning air.

I reported our findings to the chief, and we went down to investigate. White fumes were coming from several wood shipping pallets lined against the building's rear wall. The wood was neither burning nor charred. The pallets were completely wet, yet they were spewing white fumes. The chief popped his head out the back door and looked at us questioningly. Tommy and I looked at each other, nodded, and simultaneously said, "They're soaked with hydrochloric acid, Chief!"

Sure enough, they were. The pallets were off-gassing hydrogen-chloride vapors, which looked exactly like smoke. A firefighter who was watching us remarked, "What are you guys, the Hazmat Bobbsey Twins?" We returned to get our hazmat vehicles and cleaned up fifty gallons of the spilled acid.

Meanwhile, the city and the officers' union were still bickering about the chief's test. Finally, in the fall of 1996, nearly five and a half years after it all began, the city got its way. I received a letter from the personnel department stating that I was scheduled to retake the narrative portion of the fire problem. I was extremely annoyed but had no choice other than to study and practice all over again.

It came as no surprise that the second fire problem was easier than the first. Two months later I finally completed phase two of the battalion-chief's test. Our fire-problem scores were to be averaged with our scores from the management problem we had taken back in 1991.

The fiasco made firefighters of all ranks frustrated with the promotional process. Because of an unfounded complaint, several careers had been placed on hold. There was a logjam of captains who had not been eligible to take the 1991 test, and many of them were justifiably angry. Many others felt that using subjective oral boards as the sole basis for promotion was ridiculous. I agreed! In actuality, removing the multiple-choice portion actually hurt the department. Those who studied the department's equipment, procedures, directives, rules, and regulations usually became better at their jobs! Objective knowledge of those subjects wasn't evaluated in the subjective oral tests.

For those of us who completed the 1991–96 exam, there were expected to be between twenty to twenty-five vacancies, nearly three times those of a normal list. In addition, nineteen of the original sixty-eight candidates who applied for the examination had either retired or lost interest. With the competition reduced to forty-nine eligible captains, it was a golden opportunity to make battalion chief.

Our new response vehicle, Hazmat 1, arrived in early December. Tommy and I were tasked with training each platoon to drive and operate the huge truck. It was an exhausting eight-day schedule, but the overtime pay kept us happy.

On Friday, December 13, 1996, I was excited because we officially placed our new vehicle in service. We spent nearly all day methodically organizing our equipment neatly and efficiently. My OCD didn't help matters; I wanted everything to be perfect.

Around noontime, I heard a rumor that the chief's lists were going to be announced by the end of the day. I had been so busy with the new vehicle that I had completely forgotten about the test. At 1730 hours, Chief Sottung was still sitting in his office doing routine paperwork. If the lists had been announced, division headquarters surely would have been among the first to know. I figured that the rumors were false and left for home thinking more about what I wanted to accomplish with our new truck in the morning rather than about the chief's list.

When I arrived home, Diane was at the back door excitedly jumping up and down. "Call Chief Rosini! The chief's list came out!" I instantly knew that I had done well, because if all she knew was that the list was out, she'd have been nervous, not excited.

"Did Rosini say how I scored?" I asked, smiling.

She threw her arms around me. "You finished number two!" As we stood there embracing, the telephone rang. It was the fire commissioner calling to congratulate me. I was only a physical examination and an interview away from becoming a battalion chief!

CHAPTER 30

HMAU

As I sat outside of the office of the deputy commissioner of operations waiting for my battalion chief's interview, I was instead waved into the office of the deputy commissioner of technical support. I knew what that meant; I was going to staff.

Truthfully, it didn't come as much of a surprise. Chief Whalen had faithfully served his term as chief of the HMAU (141st classmate Jim Whalen had replaced Janda a few years ago). "I hope you do well on the chief's test," Whalen often had teased, "because you're going to be my ticket out of here." I would have much rather been assigned to the field, but I felt it was my duty and obligation to fulfill a staff position as a chief officer. At least I'd be doing it in hazmat.

"Well, you probably know why *I'm* interviewing you," Deputy Commissioner Matt McCrory said as I sat across from him.

I replied that I had a hunch that I'd be going to the HMAU and was okay with it. He looked relieved that I wasn't whining or complaining about it.

"Bob, you're the most qualified guy for the job. It has its perks: a secretary, staff, cell phone, pager, and a take-home SUV. You'll report directly to me. I'll give you plenty of leeway to run your unit as you see fit."

Having worked closely with Whalen, I was fairly familiar with the nature of the job. My main question for McCrory was "How long will I be in staff?"

He shuffled a few papers and then looked up. "Listen, Chief, it will take you a year to learn the job. Give me a year after that." We shook hands, and my new boss wished me luck.

My last few shifts at 60's were busy. Though I knew I'd be leaving, I wanted to make sure that Hazmat 1 was set up perfectly. Maybe it was

322

my OCD, or perhaps it was because I was still going to be involved with hazmat, but I didn't want to leave any loose ends.

Christmas Eve was my last shift as a captain. The guys held a huge celebratory farewell dinner at the firehouse. We feasted, kidded, and joked all night. At 0500 hours on Christmas morning, I made my last run with 60's. It wasn't a fire call or a hazmat run. No, poetically, my last call as captain was another detested shoe run. As we pulled onto Grays Ferry Avenue, I exclaimed with glee, "Merry Christmas to all. This is my last freaking shoe call!"

On December 27, 1996, Diane, Alex, Maria, and our parents proudly looked on as I was officially sworn in as a battalion chief in the Philadelphia Fire Department. The ceremony was held in the Mayor's Reception Room at city hall. Unlike Mayors Rizzo and Goode, Rendell only posed with groups of promotees. I was quickly ushered to stand with the mayor and four other newly promoted battalion chiefs for a group photograph. Maybe he was too busy for individual shots. Then again, maybe he was still harboring ill will from the New Year's Day, 1994, booing incident.

December 30, 1996—Battalion Chief, HMAU

There was no easy way to make the twenty-mile trek from our Overbrook home to my new office at the Philadelphia Fire Academy. On a good day, it took forty-five minutes each way. But at least I was using a city-fueled Ford Explorer. My new "apparatus" was white over red, with "HU-1" stenciled in large white letters on the rear side windows. I was on call 24-7 to serve as the hazmat liaison at hazardous-materials incidents.

Jim Whalen and I would be working together for a week-long transition. That morning we were methodically working our way through the files when they pulled the second alarm for a fire involving hazardous materials.

Within minutes we were responding southbound on I-95 toward Whitaker Avenue. As liaison, my job was to interact with facility personnel and outside agencies and provide technical support to the incident commander. Stevie, the unit's tall blond-haired compliance officer, had looked up the facility's

Tier II forms, which list the hazardous materials stored on its premises, so we had a good idea what we'd be dealing with before we even got there.

Companies were fighting the well-involved two- and three-story structure fire with exterior master streams when we arrived. Several loud explosions ripped through the plant during the firefighting effort. As I scanned the Tier II forms, the chemical likely responsible for the blasts jumped off the page: sodium, a metal that reacts violently with water.

Pow! We nearly jumped out of our skins as another blast ripped through the east end of the building. The plant manager was standing nearby, so I asked where they stored the sodium. Sure enough, it was the east end. We relayed our findings to a chief, who repositioned the streams away from the area. The explosions subsided shortly thereafter; then they stopped altogether. "Wow," I thought. "If every day is like today, my two-year hitch will fly by!"

The rest of the transition wasn't nearly as eventful. Within a week, Jimmy was happily transferred to Battalion 13, and I was running the show.

My job actually got easier as soon as it began. Ineligible for the chief's exam, Charlie Crowther was one of those unfortunate captains whose career had been placed on hold because of the 1991–96 test standoff. Pleased with the job he had done as an ABC at fire prevention, Fire Commissioner Hairston offered him his choice of assignments. Charlie, who had previously been a lieutenant in the HMAU, wanted back in. The unit's captain's position had been left unfulfilled for several years because of budgetary cutbacks, but the commissioner granted Charlie his request. Not only was it great for him, but it was terrific for me! Charlie quickly became my right-hand man.

February 10, 1997—Battalion Chief, HMAU

It didn't take very long for Charlie to show how beneficial he was to the unit. During a meeting with my staff, I mentioned that the department was upset over the high cost an environmental contractor planned to charge to dispose of a pallet of old firefighting foam. The foam was slightly toxic to the environment, but only if spilled in large quantities.

Charlie, who had a great knowledge of hazardous materials' laws, rules, and regulations, asked for a copy of the MSDS and disappeared into his office. A few minutes later, he returned with a big smile on his face. "I got a great price, Chief. We could get rid of that stuff for free!" His contact at the city's wastewater treatment plant had said that they could properly treat and dispose of one five-gallon can per day. In fact, they said that it was actually good for the digestive enzymes that broke down organic wastes in their effluent.

I did the math, and the entire pallet would be gone by spring. Headquarters couldn't approve fast enough. We assigned the one-can-a-day project to a light-duty firefighter assigned to our unit.

Aside from the travel, it was much nicer working at the academy than at the Fire Administration Building. Bustling with in-service training, the outreach program, and cadet classes, the atmosphere there made me feel closer to the field. To make our unit feel even more like the firehouse, I held our daily meetings informally, in the academy's kitchen.

The Nunn-Lugar-Domenici Weapons of Mass Destruction Act of 1996 stipulated that first responders in the nation's 120 largest cities be trained to respond to nuclear, biological, and chemical (NBC) terrorism incidents. Philadelphia was the first city to receive the Domestic Preparedness Program, which involved a week of train-the-trainer courses, a tabletop exercise, and a full field exercise. I scheduled my staff and our tier-program instructors to take the Awareness, Operations, and Hazmat Technician courses. The instructors subsequently incorporated the lessons they learned into their respective courses.

The program was delivered in August. Some of the instructors were chemical-weapons experts from the United States Army's Aberdeen Proving

Ground in Maryland. Their depth of knowledge and experience was awesome. They stole the show.

The last day, Friday, was the tabletop exercise, and lunch was provided. Shortly before noon, Charlie and I were taking a break from the tedious exercise. As we gazed out the academy's windows, two sheriff's vans pulled up. We watched curiously as guards unshackled a group of prisoners and had them tote several packages into the cafeteria. It was our lunch! Inmates from the prison's job-training program had prepared lunch exclusively for our exercise group, which was mostly made up of police and firefighters. Charlie and I looked at each other. "Prisoners serving lunch to cops? Nah!" We ordered our lunch from a nearby deli.

After the exercise, the Domestic Preparedness Program director asked if I was interested in a part-time position on their training team. I had accrued plenty of compensatory time from my after-hours duties as hazmat liaison, so I jumped at the opportunity. So did Chief Rosini and two other members of the department. We were quickly validated as instructors at the Aberdeen Proving Ground. Over the next four years, ironically ending in 2001, we taught terrorism response around the country. Unfortunately, terrorism remained a hot topic for the rest of my career.

One of the duties of the HMAU chief was to serve as the department's representative on Philadelphia's Local Emergency Planning Committee (LEPC). LEPCs are mandated by federal law to plan and prepare for hazardous materials' releases and accidents. One of the committee members constantly referred to industrial hygienists as penultimate hazmat gurus. It wasn't the first time I had heard that said. Industrial hygienists use a scientific approach to provide safe working environments.

I had stopped taking chemistry courses when I felt they no longer had practical applications to hazmat. But Temple University offered a master's of science degree in environmental health (MSEH) with an industrial-hygiene concentration. The program was open to those with undergraduate degrees in the hard sciences or engineering. It was right up my alley. Mystified by what industrial hygienists knew, I began classes in September 1997.

October 10, 1997—Battalion Chief, HMAU

In the morning we received a call from a small family-owned pharmacy in Germantown. The pharmacist said that he was trying to hire an environmental contractor to properly dispose of some old chemicals. But every time he reached one of the chemicals on his list, the contractors hung up on him. The chemical was picric acid, a yellow crystalline solid that had been used to prepare pharmaceuticals. Picric acid is relatively safe when stored in a container full of water. But if it dries out, as it often does during long-term storage, it becomes a dangerous shock-sensitive explosive. We told him not to disturb the container until we got there.

Courteous and friendly, Mom and Pop had quietly operated the family-oriented pharmacy for more than thirty years. Mom led us down to the basement, where several containers of old chemicals were neatly spread on a small table. Smack in the center was a clearly labeled amber glass jar that was half-full of picric acid. It was bone dry! When we told her that we had to call the police bomb squad to remove the jar, Mom fell backward onto a chair. "Oh my God. I don't want any commotion. This is such a quiet neighborhood."

We ushered Mom and Pop down the block while making a few phone calls. Minutes later Engine 9, Ladder 21, Battalion 9, Medic 10, and half the local police district came screaming to the scene. Police closed Germantown Avenue in both directions as firefighters evacuated the block. The bomb squad arrived towing their huge blast-containment vessel. Bomb technicians donned their heavy protective blast suits and entered the basement. Minutes later, they emerged walking gingerly with the jar and placed it inside the containment vessel.

Mom was down the block sitting on a beach chair and being consoled by several neighbors. I tried to comfort her. "Okay, Mom, it's almost over. Pretty soon you—"

"Fire in the hole! Fire in the hole!" the bomb technicians suddenly screamed. *Boom!* A tremendous explosion lifted the containment vessel a half foot in the air. Mom let out a ghastly screech, her eyes got wide as saucers, and she passed out. The technicians had decided to render the jar safe in the vessel.

As the medics were tending to Mom, she slowly opened her eyes and looked at me. "I thought I said I didn't want any commotion, young fella. What are you going to do next? A fireworks display?"

The Philadelphia Fire Academy had the grim task of planning and coordinating LODD funerals. It was one aspect of their operation that I was hoping not to witness while stationed there. Sadly, things didn't work out that way.

On October 27, 1997, Engine 63 was dispatched to Sydenham Street near Sixty-Eighth Avenue for downed power lines. After they cordoned off the area and called for the utility company, a nearby resident ran outside and told them that his basement was on fire. Lieutenant Terry McElveen, forty-three, and rookie Firefighter Jimmy Hynes, twenty-seven, stretched a hose line inside to battle the blaze. They never came out. Both perished when they became disoriented in the trash-strewn basement and ran out of air.

Unfortunately, the Fire Academy had plenty of experience preparing funerals. Nonetheless, I was amazed by the organization and efficiency of Chief Appleby and his staff. The amount of work was staggering, yet they meticulously covered each minute detail and planned for every possible contingency.

Sorrowfully, three months later they had to do it all over again. On January 27, 1998, Lieutenant Stephen Murphy, forty-seven, of Ladder 1, collapsed from a heart attack while operating on the fireground at Garnet and Jefferson Streets. He died on February 3.

The recent LODDs unnerved Diane more than any had since we met. The day after Murphy's services, I asked her if she'd take my dress uniform to the dry cleaner. She cuddled up and began gently rubbing the back of my neck.

"Rob, you're going to turn fifty this year. Maybe you'd be happy at the HMAU for the rest of your career?"

I shot her my best "are you out of your freaking mind?" look.

"Okay, okay, it was just a thought," she replied apologetically. "I was just thinking that it'd be less strenuous and safer as you grow older."

I tried my best to reassure her. "Di, if and when I get back to the field, I promise to be super careful. Right now, I'm safe and sound in staff."

She smiled sympathetically. "I know. It's just as important to me that you're happy. I just want you to come home safe every day." I kissed her softly, knowing full well that I couldn't have married a more understanding woman.

JULY 13, 1998—BATTALION CHIEF, HMAU

It seemed like the last time I was first-in at a fire had been eons ago. But that changed drastically when Charlie and I went to pick up a few items at the uniform store. Just as we tossed our packages into the back seat, a hazmat box was struck for an explosion at Delmar Drive and Southampton Road.

"Whoa," Charlie exclaimed excitedly, "that's only a few blocks away!"

I didn't have a clue how to get there, but I didn't need one. A column of smoke guided us to the nearby waste-oil-reclamation facility. As we pulled into the main gate, smoke was pouring from a garage where waste-oil trucks routinely drained their contents into storage tanks. Workers were hurriedly dragging a severely burned man from its open bay doors. He was screaming in pain. We slammed to a halt, and Charlie jumped out to tend to the man while I reported nature and conditions. Engine 58 arrived moments later and quickly knocked the fire down, but we still had a major hazmat situation. An ugly brown river of waste oil was running out of the building and into nearby storm drains.

I jumped into my gear and went inside to investigate. Hundreds of gallons of oil were pouring from a baseball-sized hole near the bottom of a reclamation truck's charred hulk. Firefighters worked frantically and constructed earthen dams to protect the sewers. It took Hazmat 1 forty-five minutes to fight their way through the lingering morning-rush-hour traffic, but the torrential leak hadn't slowed by the time they arrived. They used decontamination pools to temporarily capture the oil and transferred it into recovery drums using hand pumps.

Our investigation subsequently revealed that the burned man had been the truck driver. He had climbed to the top of the tank truck to check the waste-oil level. When his flashlight didn't work, he used a butane cigarette lighter instead. It was a very bad move! Vapors from the waste, which most likely contained gasoline and other volatile hydrocarbons, ignited with explosive violence. The blast flung the driver from the truck, burning him severely. Paramedics transported him to the burn center with third-degree burns.

Working at the HMAU could be a springboard to environmental and public-safety employment opportunities. During my tenure as chief, four of my staff landed jobs and retired from the department. I was glad for them, but each one left a tremendous gap in our ranks. One of those vacancies was filled by hilariously funny Bill Emery.

For me, humor was essential to staff. It brought a firehouse feel to the office. I was as much of a practical joker as anybody, and Emery, with his great sense of humor, was one of my favorite targets. But if you dish it out, you've got to be able to take it, even if you're the chief.

While I was in Denver with Domestic Preparedness, the guys borrowed HU-1. When I came home, it was parked in front of my house as promised, but it was facing the wrong way down our one-way street. When I started it up to turn it around, I almost jumped out of my seat. The AM/FM radio blasted Spanish music, the front and rear wipers flopped at high speed, and the heater fan was roaring on high. To top things off, my neatly stored gear was completely disheveled. It took me a half hour to straighten things out and check for other booby traps, but I giggled the entire time. Emery had gotten me!

That wasn't all. I often drew happy faces on correspondence with my staff and our secretary. The following morning I opened the door to my office, and large yellow happy-face posters were plastered all over the walls.

My computer's screen saver was scrolling a happy face, and happy-face stickers were strewn about the room. The kicker was a large happy-face blow-up doll sitting at my desk wearing a yellow construction helmet. He had gotten me again!

I leisurely strolled into the kitchen, where the guys were quietly sitting with guilty smirks on their faces. I said good morning, poured my coffee, and sat down across from Emery. He shuffled in his chair conspicuously and asked, "So, how was Denver, Chief?"

"Well, Bill, let's see," I said, glaring at him. "My rental car was perfectly quiet when I started it up. There weren't any happy faces plastered on the walls of my hotel room, and I didn't find a happy-face blow-up doll lying in my bed." Resounding laughter filled the second-floor hallway. I turned to Charlie. "The next time, I'm giving *you* the keys to HU-One *and* my office." Then I pointed at Emery. "Don't dare give them to *him!*" We laughed all day.

The end of my second year in staff came quickly. My hitch was supposed to be over, but McCrory asked me to stay another year. Since I was earning tons of compensatory time to use for my Domestic Preparedness travels and was off duty to attend night classes at Temple, I agreed.

It was a productive year. That spring, for the first time, we offered the five-tier program as a complete three-week Hazmat Technician Course. We also completely revised the department's hazmat operational procedure, adding addendums for terrorism and mass decontamination. In addition, we spent a lot of time working on Hazmat 1's state recertification. The busier we were, the faster time passed.

That fall, the city announced the deputy chief's examination. "How could I possibly be a deputy chief if I don't have any field experience as a battalion chief?" I reasoned. I didn't feel comfortable about advancing in rank, so I took the test without studying. My rank on the list was thirteen, not high enough for the few anticipated openings. I wasn't disappointed at all.

On Monday, May 3, the Fire Academy sadly prepared for yet another LODD funeral. Firefighter Eric Cassiano, forty-one, of Engine 2, fell through the floor while battling a dwelling fire in the 2200 block of North Orianna Street. He laughed it off and continued to battle the blaze. After

2's returned to the station, Cassiano went to lie down. He didn't make their next run. He was dead from an apparent spinal injury and internal bleeding from the fall.

June 21, 1999—Battalion Chief, HMAU

Startled awake, I sat on the edge of the bed in a stupor, trying to process the simultaneous ringing, beeping, and buzzing in my ears. When I finally realized that the annoying sounds were coming from both our house phone *and* my pager, I darted toward our desk, as did Diane. We collided head on in the darkness. She handed me the phone as she rubbed her head.

"Chief, we just struck out the second alarm at the Sun refinery."

The fire, which involved a heat-exchanger unit, escalated to four alarms. By the time I arrived, master streams had the unit surrounded, and plant workers were operating valves trying to isolate and divert the flow of product into another exchanger. Because of high start-up costs, refineries typically try to keep their process running, even during major fires. My job was to act as the interface between the plant's manager and our incident commander. Our chief was getting annoyed because of the amount of time it was taking for the rerouting operation.

Shortly after I explained the refinery's position, plant personnel stopped the flow of product, and the fire went out. I returned home just in time to take a shower and go to the office. Drat!

June 25, 1999—Battalion Chief, HMAU

During rush hour we raced to the subway concourse at Fifteenth and Market for an odor that was making people ill. As we rushed through the Friday-morning traffic, foremost on my mind was Aum Shinrikyo's 1995 deadly sarin attack in Tokyo's subways.

When we got there, the first-arriving units had shut down rail traffic, evacuated the concourse, and cordoned the area off. Hazmat 1 members were donning their suits and setting up their decontamination equipment. As I was questioning a concourse employee, I noticed a faint rotten-egg odor and immediately suspected what it was.

Hazmat 1's recon teams confirmed my suspicion. They entered the concourse and found several leaking commercial batteries. The spilled sulfuric acid was reacting with organic material and producing trace amounts of hydrogen sulfide.

According to department procedures, the HMAU chief's job was to serve as hazmat liaison, but many incident commanders didn't mind if I got involved with the operational aspect of handling the incident.

July 23, 1999—Battalion Chief, HMAU

We responded to a two-alarm blaze involving a large open vat of Stoddard solvent inside a manufacturing plant. Chief Mack was waiting for a sufficient supply of foam before sending an attack team inside to extinguish the fire.

I scanned the MSDS. The flammable liquid's flash point was one hundred degrees Fahrenheit. "We could knock this thing out with a couple of fog streams," I informed the chief.

He looked at me with doubt in his eyes. "Fog streams?"

"Yep," I replied, recalling the vat fire on Lancaster Avenue. "We actually did it before. If it's okay with you, I'll go inside and coordinate the operation."

He smiled and gave me a hearty thumbs-up. "You've got it!"

We cautiously advanced the two fog streams, angled 120 degrees apart, and quickly smothered the fire. As I was putting my gear in the hatch of HU-1, Mack walked up and said, "You know, you should stay at HMAU until you retire."

"You sound just like my wife, Chief," I replied. "Nag, nag, nag!" He laughed.

On July 29, 1999, the Fire Academy prepared for the fifth LODD during my reign as HMAU chief. Firefighter Richard Devine of Engine 28 collapsed and died while operating on box eight-three-eight, Amber and Westmoreland Streets.

September 14, 1999—Battalion Chief, HMAU

I never made it to the office. As I was leaving for work, a Hazmat box was struck for Allegheny and Tioga. I flipped on HU-1's lights, turned on the siren, and raced down Haverford Avenue.

Sixty-two cars of a Norfolk-Southern freight train uneventfully crossed the railroad overpass on Allegheny Avenue. Cars number sixty-three and sixty-four weren't so lucky; they derailed. One of them, a DOT 111 tank car loaded with twenty thousand gallons of molten phenol, plummeted onto the busy roadway below. Actually, it could have been worse. If the derailment had happened only thirty seconds earlier, it would have crushed a fully occupied school bus.

The tank car landed upside down, and its top valves were crushed. A river of phenol poured into nearby sewer inlets before Hazmat 1 could construct retention dikes. The water-treatment plant said that the phenol was actually good for their digesters. Again? What *don't* those darn digesters like?

Our entire HMAU staff spent the next thirteen hours working with Hazmat 1, railroad-emergency responders, and cleanup contractors. With only four months left in staff, I was so ready to get back to firefighting.

A month later we were at another derailment, this time at Frankford Junction. One of the chiefs asked me if I was putting in for Battalion 1. I hadn't known that the rotation list was out. There were two spots in the First. I submitted my transfer request listing Battalions 1, 11, and 7 as my choices.

At two o'clock in the morning on December 29, 1999, I was startled out of a deep REM sleep by the phone again. "These damned hazmat calls are killing me!" I mumbled under my breath before answering.

"Robert?" It wasn't the FCC; it was my mother. Her voice was trembling. "I just called nine one one. Dad's having a congestive-heart-failure attack again."

It wasn't my first late-night run to South Philly. Since 1980, my dad had had his share of heart problems. In addition to heart failure, he'd had a triple bypass, angioplasty, stents, and even a pacemaker. But this time things turned out differently; Dad died later that morning. Instead of festively welcoming in the millennium, we quietly planned a funeral. For the first time since I was six years old, Mom didn't host an open house for the Mummers Parade.

After Dad's funeral, I took a week off to help Mom adapt to her new life as a widow. The adjustment was extremely difficult for her. Having suffered from bouts of depression since she was a young woman, Mom quickly spiraled downward. Her depression became so bad that we had to admit her to the hospital. I knew that when she got discharged, she'd need a lot of care.

Battalion 1 was only a mile from Mom's house, and being stationed there would certainly help out. Deputy Commissioner McCrory took care of me and made sure I got the First.

My replacement at the HMAU was veteran Battalion Chief Bill Doty. Our transition week was mutually beneficial. As a matter of fact, I probably learned more from his experiences as a field battalion chief than he did from me about the HMAU. I left knowing that the unit was in very capable hands.

On April 14, 2000, after three years, three months, and nineteen days of staff, I finally made it back to the field—not that I had been counting.

CHAPTER 31

Decomp

B attalion 1's lineage dates back to March 15, 1871, when it was organized as one of six assistant engineers in Philadelphia's newly paid fire
department. At that time, Assistant Engineer 1 (Battalion 1) covered the
southeastern portion of the rapidly developing city.

When I was hired in 1973, Battalion 1 was quartered at 49's, and it
covered deep South Philly. Battalion 5, which was housed with Engine 1
and Ladder 5, covered the remaining portion of South Philly and the lion's
share of Center City.

To provide better coverage for the sharp rise in structural fires during the
war years, Battalion 5 moved to Engine 43's station in 1975, and Battalion
1 shifted north to the quarters of Engine 10 and Ladder 11. Battalion 1's
district had expanded to cover most of South Philly.

In 1993, when structural fires began to wane, Battalion 5 was disbanded
for financial reasons. Battalion 1 moved to Battalion 5's old quarters at Engine
1 and Ladder 5. In effect, they were now responsible for the former geographical
areas of both Battalions 1 and 5. Their new district covered the bulk of Center
City and nearly all of South Philly, and they ran citywide for hazmat calls.

In addition to its ten companies housed in six fire stations, Battalion 1
was also first-in with some companies in the Fourth and Seventh Battalions.
Their district was large and heavily populated, and it included a wide diversity of fires and other emergencies. Personally, there wasn't a better place to
hone my skills as a fire chief.

APRIL 14, 2000—BATTALION CHIEF, BATTALION 1

It was fabulous to be in the firehouse kitchen again. I was taking small
sips of my coffee while off-going Battalion Chief Joe McGraw provided the

entertainment. Promoted at the same time as I was, Joe was quick witted and could find humor in just about anything. He was one of the funniest storytellers I ever met. Smart, well-educated, and hazmat-qualified, Joe was perfect for the battalion's other rotation opening.

Joe's first assignment as chief had been the Ninth Battalion. The kitchen was in an uproar as he recalled one of the runs he'd had while there. The call was to assist the police. Joe was scanning the dispatch printout for more information when he saw the word "thon" printed on the bottom line. "Thon?" he said to his aide. "What the heck is thon?" Station printers sometimes wrapped words to the line below, so Joe checked the line above. The last word on that line was "py." They were responding to an incident involving a deadly constricting snake, a *python*.

The large snake had somehow escaped its cage and was tightly coiled around its owner when Joe arrived. The police, unsure what to do, asked, "Any ideas, Chief?"

"There's nothing in the training manual about handling pythons coiled around people," Joe said. "I could only think of one thing to say. 'Yeah! Shoot it!'"

The lady's eyes were popping out of her head, and she could barely breathe, but somehow she managed to eke out, "No! No! Please don't kill my snake!"

The cops looked at Joe, who looked back at them. "It's either her or the damn snake. Shoot it in the head!" he screamed. "Shoot it!" Suddenly, as though it sensed its pending doom, the huge python had uncoiled itself, slithered away, and slunk back into its cage.

As I listened to Joe, my side was hurting from laughing. But deep down inside, I felt like I had missed so much while I was in staff. My promotional peers had over three years of field experience, while I'd only dealt with hazmats. I was behind the eight ball. But alas, the bells rang. "Chief only! Thirtieth and Market for a jumper." My aide Jimmy steered our Chevy Suburban onto Broad Street.

Perched on the bridge over the dirty brown Schuylkill, the shaggy-haired young man's cleanly pressed fraternity sweatshirt clashed with his tattered jeans. He looked more frightened than anything else. Hanging on with a white-knuckled grip, he didn't look sincere about jumping. Regardless, I positioned Ladder 9 and Rescue 1 on opposite banks of the river and had Marine Unit 2 launch their speedy two-manned whaler. If he jumped, we were ready for him.

A young plainclothes police officer began talking to the man, approaching closer and closer as he spoke. Before long, the officer had climbed over the guardrail and was within range to snare him. But just before he could make his move, the shaggy-haired man, who was wound up as tight as a snake, relented. He slowly unraveled his arms, slithered over the guardrail, and slunk into the back of Medic 7. Just like Joe's python, he survived to live another day.

The First Battalion's companies on my D Platoon had excellent firefighting reputations. Doty couldn't stop raving about how fortunate he had been to be their chief. I quickly found out how right he was. After only a few working fires, I found out that they were well trained, motivated, and aggressive. To make things even better, I had an impressive group of officers leading them.

The First and Fourth Battalions responded to many incidents together. Pat Campanaro, of the Fourth, was a superb veteran chief who had been one of my fire-science instructors. I was delighted to be working with the man I affectionately called "Uncle Pat." Even though we were equal in rank, I considered him a mentor. At the fires we'd already worked together, he had given me tips and pointers about the finer aspects of chiefdom. My cup was never too full. I always left room in it to learn from others, especially knowledgeable veterans like Uncle Pat.

May 18, 2000—Battalion Chief, Battalion 1

The beautiful spring weather reflected my good mood while I was driving to work. One of my favorite songs, "My Back Pages" by the Byrds, was playing on the oldies station. I cranked up the volume, still trying to make sense of Dylan's 1964 lyrics as I parked on Kenilworth Street, next to the firehouse.

After three grueling years, I finally had earned my master's degree. As a reward, if only in my mind, we headed to 10's for chicken parmesan shortly after shift change. A long beep on the radio diverted us to 1100 South Cleveland on tactical box six-eight-nine. Medium smoke was pouring from a two-story row dwelling. Its two well-involved rooms were quickly knocked down by 24's, and a half hour later, we arrived at 10's.

As we were waiting for Ladder 11 to return from Cleveland Street, 10's tall, friendly Lieutenant Joe Ingram and I were chatting outside his office. Delicious wafts of fried chicken were making my stomach growl. Chicken parm is one of my favorites. But a few feet away at the watch desk, a box alarm sounded for Pier 34, South Wharves. We were second-in. An occupied pier had collapsed into the river.

Built in 1909, Pier 34 had been a commercial pier for cargo freighters, coal ships, and passenger liners during Philly's industrial boom. In the seventies, when most of the city's manufacturing plants had either moved or closed, many similar piers either were torn down or became the scenes of spectacular multialarm blazes. Even though 180 feet of it had collapsed into the Delaware in 1994, Pier 34 survived by transitioning to the entertainment business. Club Heat, a newly opened restaurant and nightclub, sat on the end of the structure. Approximately forty people had been enjoying the beautiful spring weather when it suddenly collapsed at an angle and dumped them into the murky sixty-five-degree water.

The aroma of fried chicken was still in my olfactory bulb as Jimmy turned onto Washington Avenue. All of a sudden, Uncle Pat's voice boomed over the radio. "Battalion Four, we have a major pier collapse. Several victims are trapped under the debris, and others are being swept downstream." In addition to the second alarm, Uncle Pat initiated the department's mass-casualty and river-emergency operational procedures. He also requested the department's marine units, along with rescue craft from the Coast Guard; police; and communities on the New Jersey side of the river to respond.

Piercing screams were coming from the twisted remains as I approached Uncle Pat's command post. Behind him I saw first-arriving firefighters heroically attempting rescues. Two firefighters were floating chest deep and holding a pinned woman's head above water while performing CPR on her. Other firefighters were swimming and dragging victims behind them or were precariously perched on the shifting debris as they pulled those within reach from the river.

"Pat, where do you need me?" I shouted over the din.

Unfazed by all the chaos, Uncle Pat calmly turned around and said, "Bob, here's how we're going to work this: I'll handle the rescue end up here. I need you back at the street end of the pier. Send me the second-alarm companies and medic units as I need them. As we pull the people out, I'll send them back to you for triage and transportation. Okay? Oh! And be careful. I can still feel the pier shifting under my feet." He gave me an encouraging slap on the back and got back to work.

Back at the base of the pier, I placed a second-alarm chief in charge of staging and EMS officers in charge of triage and transportation. Maybe it was because of my OCD, but to avoid confusion, I instructed units going into the pier to stay to my right, while returning litter bearers came back on my left. It gave me a better picture of what was happening. The pace was hectic, and at times I felt more like a traffic cop than a fire chief. By the end of the night, we had transported thirty-seven people to area hospitals. Eight of them were firefighters.

We ate our chicken parmesan at 2300 hours, and I had reflux all night.

Three young women, aged twenty-one, twenty-five, and twenty-seven, coworkers from the New Jersey State Aquarium, were killed in the collapse. Unfortunately, they chose Club Heat that night to celebrate the twenty-five-year-old's birthday. Criminal charges were filed against the owners of Pier 34 and Club Heat, alleging they had been aware of the danger. Several firefighters and fire department units were later awarded commendations for their heroic actions.

Despite the tragedy, Uncle Pat's system had worked perfectly. A resident of South Philly, he brought more than experience to the fireground.

He was also very familiar with the neighborhood. A few weeks later, we were first-in at a fully involved dwelling fire not far from Uncle Pat's home. As the companies were stretching their hose lines, he tapped me on the shoulder.

"Bob, I'm familiar with this place. It was just rebuilt using lightweight truss construction, so don't send anybody inside." Moments later, the building came down with a thunderous crash. Uncle Pat smiled and winked. The fire-science course he'd taught me several years before had been Building Construction.

Although I had handled a few as an ABC, I didn't have much experience with elevator-rescue incidents. But with the large number of high-rise buildings in the First, I was forced to learn quickly. I had an old elevator training manual, which was helpful, but the practical experiences proved to be much more enlightening.

JUNE 28, 2000—BATTALION CHIEF, BATTALION 1

"You know, they shouldn't send us to stuck elevators," I complained to Jimmy as we responded up Broad Street. "Elevators should be a ladder-company operation, not ladder and chief. Who am I supervising? One supervisor? I bet they send a chief because several years ago some ladder company wrecked an expensive elevator door. Hold the company officer responsible for his actions, just like any other single-unit operation, right?"

Jimmy laughed. "Aw, come on, boss, you're upset because this run came at dinnertime."

"Yeah, that meatloaf smelled pretty darned good." I laughed.

This stuck elevator was in a parking garage. It was a brand-new glass-walled beauty designed to traverse the exterior wall. I guess they figured that its scenic view might offset its exorbitant Center City parking rates.

Stuck only a few feet above ground, the elevator was crammed with riders. Apparently going to the nearby Forrest Theatre, they looked like well-dressed sardines tightly packed in a glass jar. "We'd better get them out quickly," I thought. It wouldn't be long before the heat and humidity caused their body odor to overwhelm the sweet scent of their perfume and aftershave.

Elevator keys were normally stored in little boxes next to the door opening. All we needed to do was unlock the mechanism, slide the doors open, and help the sweaty people down. It should have been a piece of cake. It wasn't!

The key was missing from the little box. Strike one! The parking attendant didn't have a clue where it was. Strike two! And Ladder 23 hadn't been issued a key for the new elevator. Strike three!

Okay, it was time for plan B. I asked the goof in the booth if he had an ETA for the elevator company. He looked at me like I was asking for a bologna sandwich. "ET who? What company?"

"The elevator company!" I said, raising my tone. "You did call them, right?" He didn't. As a matter of fact, he had to make three calls just to get their phone number. Time was ticking; the sardines had already been in their jar for nearly fifteen minutes.

During weekdays elevator mechanics roam Center City doing repairs and routine maintenance, and response is usually quick. But this was nearly eight o'clock on a Friday night, and the elevator company gave the dullard in the booth an ETA of thirty to forty-five minutes. Great!

To calm the sweltering crowd and keep them informed, I tapped on the glass and said that an elevator mechanic would arrive shortly. As I told my fib to them, an elderly white-haired woman rolled her eyes and collapsed in a heap. Did she pass out from heat stress? Was it a heart attack?

Okay, it was time for plan C. "Battalion One to Ladder Twenty-Three. We have a person down in the car. Pop the darn doors with the Jaws of Life, now!" Within a minute, Ladder 23's powerful Jaws completely destroyed the decorative doors, and we carried the unconscious woman to fresh air.

As the paramedics began to assess her condition, she miraculously regained consciousness, quickly jumped to her feet, and brushed herself off. Then she turned to her husband. "Come on, honey, the show's about to begin." As they were walking away, she looked back, gave me a snide wink, and giggled.

I stood there scratching my head, wondering if I had just been duped.

After only a few months in the First, I began to feel as though I had earned a degree of sorts in elevator rescues. By the time fall arrived, we had responded to top rescues, bottom rescues, hatch rescues, and lateral transfers between cars in blind elevator shafts. We'd even rescued a worker who severed his arm on a piece of machinery before falling down an elevator shaft. He was at the bottom of the pit, but his arm was on the third floor.

Engine 60 and Ladder 19, who had moved into their new four-bay firehouse while I was at the HMAU, were assigned to the First Battalion. I was blessed to have Tommy Bitto on my platoon. After so many years working together as captain and lieutenant, we really clicked as battalion chief and lieutenant. Every time I was about to ask him to handle something, he already had it done. It became a running joke between us. Sometimes I'd intentionally pause halfway through my sentence. "Tom, did you take care of…?"

"Decon?" he'd reply. "Yeah, boss, they're setting it up now."

"And how about…?" I'd pause again.

"The overpack drums? They're ready to go too, boss."

One of the tasks we routinely handled when I was at the HMAU was coordinating household-hazardous-waste events throughout the city. It gave city residents the opportunity to dispose of old oils, paints, pesticides, and other hazardous materials in a safe and proper manner. They were held for years without incident. Then the city decided to host a similar event for its operating departments to properly dispose of their hazardous wastes. Things didn't go exactly as planned.

November 8, 2000—Battalion Chief, Battalion 1

At 0930, we were making our daily rounds when we got dispatched with 53's and Hazmat 1 to Delaware Avenue. With all the truck traffic in that area, I was thinking that it was most likely a ruptured diesel saddle tank. Instead, as we turned the corner, we saw a yellow city-owned stake-body truck parked on the side of the road. In the truck's rear bed were two open fifty-five-gallon drums that had toppled on their sides. Ugly brown waste oil was dripping from the rear gate, and about eighty gallons had pooled along the curb. The oil-stained driver waved us down as we neared.

It didn't take a rocket scientist to figure out what had happened, but I asked anyway. The driver replied as he scratched his thinning hair, "My boss told me to take these barrels to that hazard-waste thing. But when I made that last turn, they fell over, and all this crap came pouring out."

I peered into the back of the truck. "Where are the lids?"

"We didn't have any that fit," he replied while shrugging his shoulders. He didn't have shipping papers either. I began scratching *my* head. At least somebody had had enough sense to place yellow "Waste Oil—Non PCB" stickers on the drums.

When Hazmat 1 arrived, Tommy ran a few field tests to confirm that it was, in fact, simply waste oil. Then his crew pumped most of the oil back into the drums, placed lids on them, and lashed them to the side of the truck, as they should have been in the first place. While Hazmat cleaned up the residual spill, Jimmy and I followed the truck to the hazardous-waste collection site to ensure it got there without further incident.

Once the truck was safely inside the perimeter, we turned around and headed back for the gate. Ahead of us, another city stake-body truck, this time a white one, was heading our way. I couldn't believe my eyes. The driver and passenger were hanging their heads out the side windows just like Ace Ventura did in *Pet Detective*. Astonishingly, their heads were enveloped in a white cloud, and they were gasping for air. With tears streaming from their eyes, they waved for us to stop. It turned out that a thirty-gallon pail of muriatic (hydrochloric) acid, which had been carelessly loaded with other waste containers, had tipped over and popped its lid. The acid then poured over the truck's hot exhaust pipe and created a vapor cloud. I had FCC dispatch a medic unit along with Hazmat 1 as soon as they finished cleaning up on Delaware Avenue.

Medic 11 was evaluating the driver and his passenger when Hazmat 1 arrived. Tommy bent over with laughter. "Don't tell me we got another one, boss."

"Yeah, Tom." I snickered. "What a clusterfuck! This time we got about thirty gallons of hydrochloric acid spilled under all that crap in the truck's bed."

"Okay, boss, we got it," Tommy replied. As he turned to head back to his crew, a van from the medical examiner's office rumbled its way over several potholes behind him.

A few minutes later, as the paramedics were preparing to take the acid victims to the hospital, several loud blasts of an air horn echoed through the air. I swung my head around and saw the environmental contractors scrambling for safety, screaming, "Picric acid! Picric acid!" Unbelievably, somebody at the medical examiner's office had placed a container of dry picric-acid crystals in their van. By some miracle, it hadn't exploded when they hit the potholes.

The event was delayed until the bomb squad arrived. Once again, shouts of "Fire in the hole! Fire in the hole!" filled the air. Blowing up picric acid in their containment vessel was getting to be a routine thing.

After we returned to the station, I forwarded a memorandum advising that in the future, environmental contractors should travel directly to the city departments to properly collect and dispose of hazardous wastes. I wanted to make the subject of the memorandum "How to avoid hazardous-waste clusterfucks," but I chickened out.

All or parts of the First, Third, Fourth, Sixth, Ninth, and Seventeenth Police Districts were within the First Battalion's boundary. The calls to assist the police were as common as those for stuck elevators. Most of them involved raising ladders to rooftops or windows so the cops could search for suspects, weapons, or signs of forced entry. Some involved opening car doors where parents had accidentally locked their keys *and* their children inside the car.

Others were to help police gain access to houses in order to check on the welfare of elderly residents who hadn't been seen or heard from for a while. But every once in a while, the call was way outside the realm of what would be considered ordinary.

November 10, 2000—Battalion Chief, Battalion 1

Our red flashing lights reflected off parked cars, windows, and street signs as we responded silently down Broad Street. There was hardly any traffic, so why wake anyone with our siren?

I studied the printout closely for further information or worrisome words like "thon," but it simply read, "Assist Police—No further information." As I wiped the sleep from my eyes, I yawned and said to Jim, "It's probably just another asshole burglar on the roof. I hope they catch this one too."

Only two weeks before, just as early in the morning, we had responded to another assist-the-police call with Ladder 27. A pair of not-so-bright burglars had cut a hole in the roof of an old theater that had been converted into a variety store. They tied a rope to the chimney, and the dumber one shinnied his way down and stepped onto what he thought was the floor. It wasn't. The imbecile stepped onto a suspended fiberglass ceiling panel, which immediately gave way and plunged him twenty feet to the real floor below. Adding insult to injury, his bone-crunching crash set off the burglar alarm. When we arrived, he was sitting there writhing in pain from a broken leg. A few cops had their weapons drawn and were looking up at the hole. As the paramedics treated him, a police sergeant looked at the hapless suspect and growled, "You asshole. Did you really think that a suspended ceiling tile would support your fat ass?" I didn't have much pity for burglars and couldn't help but chuckle. Ladder 27 raised their main ladder to the roof, but the other suspect was long gone. He hadn't given a damn about his partner in crime.

As we approached this morning's scene, Ladder 27's shiny huge tiller ladder was sitting on Sixth Street, just short of the intersection. Several police cars and two private ambulances were parked farther down the block. Police had stretched yellow tape to keep the curious crowd of onlookers away from one of the row homes. A tall police lieutenant was standing on the corner with Tommy, Ladder 27's acting lieutenant. Out of the corner of my eye, I saw two ambulance attendants, wearing snug surgical masks and Tyvek chemical jumpsuits, hastily retreat down the steps of the taped-off house.

"Uh-oh, that's not a good sign," I muttered under my breath. I had a pretty good idea why we had been called. Hoping my suspicions were wrong, I asked Tommy what was up.

But the tall chisel-jawed police officer cut in before he had a chance to answer. "We have a decomp, Chief—a bad one too! She's got to be at least five hundred pounds, boss, and she's wedged inside the bathroom."

Trying to grasp the enormity of the situation, I nodded my head toward the two parked ambulances. "What, pray tell, are they doing here, Loo?"

"Oh, them. They got the medical examiner's contract to pick up bodies. But I don't think they imagined in their wildest nightmares that they'd ever encounter anything as gruesome as this. The first-arriving ambulance called the second for help, but even the four of them can't dislodge her. These guys don't have a clue, Chief. I told them that you'd talk to them when you got here."

The officer's words jogged my memory. I had read in the paper that some employees from the medical examiner's office had been accused of stealing money and valuables from the dead. The article went on to say that until the investigation was finished, the task of picking up bodies was going to be privatized. At the time, I didn't figure that it would have an impact on fire-department operations. I figured wrong.

"Okay, Loo, we'll figure something out," I replied to the officer. "Come on, Tommy. Let's go talk to them."

One of the attendants was sitting on the back bumper of his ambulance, looking pale as a ghost and gagging. The young man, who appeared to be in his late twenties, had a surgical mask pushed over the top of his forehead.

"Hey, buddy, who's the head honcho?" I asked. He pointed toward the front of the ambulance and then lowered his head and began gagging again. Fearing that his vomit would bother me more than the decomp, I darted toward the front cab.

His cherub-faced boss wasn't much older and was talking to a higher supervisor on his cell phone. "Okay, boss, the fire chief is here. I'll tell him what you said." At least he wasn't gagging. "Hi, Chief, thanks for coming. My boss wants you guys to get her out so we can take her to the morgue." Obviously he was trying to pawn the worst part of the job, getting her out, onto us.

"Is she *too heavy* for you guys?" I retorted, implying that four ambulance attendants should be able to lift a lot of weight.

"Well, yeah, she's heavy, chief. Maybe five hundred pounds. But somehow she got stuck between the toilet and sink. We can't budge her."

Apparently this was going to be more of a challenge than I'd thought. We had a huge smelly decomposing body wedged tightly in a confined area. How nice! Just like Thon, this one wasn't in the training manual either! There was only one way to develop a game plan. "Okay," I told the ambulance supervisor, "let's go inside and take a look."

"Okay, Chief," he replied as he handed me a surgical mask, "but I think you're going to need one of these too."

I'd had the misfortune of smelling death before, so taking his advice, I pulled the elastic band over my head and snapped the mask into place. It didn't help at all. As soon as we walked inside, the unique horrible stench cut right through my flimsy filter. Many have tried to describe the odor of death before. To me, it smells like a mix of ethyl mercaptan (the odorant added to natural gas), human feces, and body odor with just a dash of sharp provolone cheese.

I apprehensively peeked into the first-floor powder room. The ill-fated woman's decomposing body was sitting on the toilet. The gruesome sight was worse than I had imagined. Clad only in a bra and panties, with a hypodermic needle dangling from her left arm, she had slumped with her purplish head on the sink. Brown fluid, with tinges of pink on the edges, had oozed from her mouth and pooled in the basin. Her bloated body was reddish purple, but her extremities and eyelids were blackened by decay. She was stuck because her right arm had fallen between the toilet tank and the sink before swelling with bloat. In my opinion, the estimates were conservative. She had to be nearly six hundred pounds. In spite of my overwhelming urge to dash outside, I took a few minutes to study the situation.

"Okay," I said, turning to the ambulance supervisor. "Let's go outside, and I'll explain what *we're* going to do." We darted for the door.

Fresh air never had tasted so sweet, but unfortunately I knew it wasn't going to last very long. In a meeting with Tommy, the police lieutenant, and the ambulance supervisor, I explained the plan. The police were to move the crowds to the end of the block. It was going to get very smelly outside. Tommy would send two firefighters to the basement to shut the main water valve, while the rest of his crew would lash two wraparound stretchers together. They'd place the stretchers outside the powder room along with hand tools, in case we needed to break the porcelain sink apart. Once everything was ready to go, the four ambulance crew members, along with two firefighters from Ladder 27, would remove the body and place her on the stretchers. I would go in with them to personally supervise the operation.

The ambulance supervisor raised his eyebrows when he heard that his crew was going to play such an integral role in removing the body. This was their job, and we were assisting them. I wanted to make sure they were part of this wonderful experience. I didn't give him a chance to object before I quickly turned to Tommy.

"Tom, pick two guys for the lifting part. Tell them to wear their bunker gear and latex gloves. If they want, they can pack up." Like a quarterback coming out of the huddle, I clapped my hands. "Okay. Everybody be ready to go in five minutes."

Selecting two men was a no-brainer for Tommy. The task fell to the two newest members of the company, John and Eddie. It's fire-department tradition. If something distasteful needs to be done, it goes to the new guys. Neither of them opted to wear SCBAs, so I gave them surgeon's masks. I knew what they were thinking: if the ambulance crew could hack it, so could they. They made me proud.

After everything was ready, our seven-person entry team assembled by the front steps. In many respects, it was like a hazmat hot-zone entry, except it was much more grotesque. I'd prefer methyl-ethyl bad stuff any day. After snapping my mask in place, I gave a hearty thumbs-up and led the way inside. The stench was just as bad the second time around. John and Eddie positioned themselves in such a way that they could reach behind the victim's body and push. John pulled the needle out of her arm and tossed it in the bathtub. I positioned the ambulance crew to grab her arms and legs. We had two pushers and four pullers.

"Everybody, on the count of three," I announced through my mask. "One...two...three!"

Flatulent noises and sickening ripping sounds mixed with the grunts of the six men as they lifted her body. The toilet seat was stuck to her rear end, and it lifted with her. Halfway up, it detached and slammed down. To my amazement, her arm popped free much easier than I had thought it would. Decayed chunks of human flesh were stuck to the sink and toilet seat behind her. The water in the toilet bowl was a gross mix of blackish-brown goo. Unbelievably, the stench got even worse. The ambulance attendant who had been sitting on the back bumper earlier began gagging again. If he heaved, I'd surely heave with him, so I shoved him toward the door. He jumped at the chance and was gone in a flash. I joined the remaining five lifters, and we hoisted the ghastly remains to a standing position before sheer weight caused her to buckle and collapse to her knees.

We tried to gently lower her onto the stretchers, but momentum took over, and she slammed down. Unfortunately, she landed only partially on the stretchers. It took another five minutes of rolling and shimmying until the stretchers were completely underneath her.

After the body was secured and covered with sheets, I gave everyone a few seconds to catch their breath, as foul as the air might have been. I glanced back to see if our path was clear, and I caught the blur of someone darting past the powder room.

"Who the hell is that?" I shouted to the ambulance supervisor. He was just as surprised as I was. I chased the blur into the living room, only to find an extremely thin, haggard-looking woman with tattoos all over her arms rummaging through the furniture. "Who the hell are you?" I yelled. "Are you a relative? You shouldn't be in here, lady!"

"No, she's got my stuff. I need my stuff!"

I didn't argue with her. Instead, I went to the front door and called out to police, "A druggie came in the back door and is in here looking for drugs."

A powerfully built officer with arms bulging under his short sleeves ran up the steps. But the stench of death stopped the weightlifter dead in his tracks. From the doorway, he screamed, "What the fuck's the matter with you, lady? Get out of there." Undeterred and clutching a small plastic baggie in one hand, she ignored him and continued her drug quest. The officer shouted, "What the fuck!" He stuck his head outside and drew a deep breath before rushing in. He grabbed her scrawny arm and dragged her outside kicking and screaming.

As soon as they disappeared into the fresh air, I cleared a few pieces of furniture to ensure a wide path. "Is everybody ready?"

"We're ready, Chief," Eddie exclaimed. "We want to get the hell out of here!" He was right. We had been inside for twenty minutes. With grunts galore, we dragged the lifeless woman to the door. Then we lifted her, struggled our way through the narrow foyer, and carried her down the front steps. The rear of the ambulance appeared to sag a foot when we slid her body inside.

Several curious neighbors were looking from their open second-floor windows. Suddenly I heard one woman scream, "Oh my God, what is that awful smell?" All the open windows slammed shut in rapid succession.

I thanked the ambulance crews and Ladder 27 for a job well done. It was four thirty when the sagging ambulance lumbered away.

Back at the station, I took a quick shower to wash the stink from my reeking hair and changed into a fresh uniform. I splashed aftershave all over myself before heading to the kitchen for coffee, but the stubborn stench refused to leave my nostrils. Unsure whether anyone else could detect my stink, I sat in a corner chair instead of my usual spot on the long wooden bench.

Before long, the oncoming shift began arriving. An overtime firefighter brought in soft pretzels. "Have a pretzel, Chief," he said cheerfully, but I politely declined. For some reason, I didn't have much of an appetite.

That evening I was preparing for another night shift. Ever thoughtful, Diane always made sure we shared a light snack before I left for work. As I sat at the table, she was slicing something on the cutting board behind me. It sounded like an apple. Having finally regained somewhat of an appetite, I eagerly awaited the cool, refreshing taste of fall. She reached over my shoulder and slid a small dish directly under my nose. The smell hit me like a ton of bricks. My nostrils flared in flashback as several slices of ultrasharp provolone cheese sat before me. I quickly slid the plate way across the table.

Shocked by my reaction, Diane widened her eyes. "You love provolone, hon. What's wrong?"

"Eh, I'm just not in the mood for cheese today," I lied. "Do you have any apples?"

Before the medical examiner's office was allowed to resume normal operations, we assisted other ambulance crews with several more heavy corpses and decomps. The worst one, even worse than the six-hundred-pound woman, came on a warm spring afternoon. The putrid odor had drifted throughout the block, and neighbors were slamming their doors and windows closed as we approached the scene. Flies were buzzing all around the tiny row home, and maggots were swarming all over the body. The man was so huge that we had to widen an interior doorway with a circular saw in order to get him out. All of a sudden, stuck elevators didn't seem to bother me anymore.

CHAPTER 32

BPH

At many an ass-kicking fire over the years, I had heard exhausted older firefighters grumble: "This is a young man's job." Nowadays, I guess it's more politically correct to refer to firefighting as a young *person's* job. Regardless, I never gave it much thought until I returned to the field. During my first year at Battalion 1, I turned fifty-two.

Physically, I felt fine. I'd always believed that physical fitness was part of my job. The Philadelphia Fire Department didn't have a mandatory physical-fitness program like some others, so throughout my career I followed a daily exercise regimen. Stretches, push-ups, sit-ups, jumping jacks, and jogging helped preserve my stamina and kept the beer belly away.

Earlier in my career, we were required to take physical examinations every two years. In order to do that, firefighters had to be pulled from the staffing quotas, and more often than not, they were covered by overtime members. Once again, the almighty dollar prevailed, and the physicals were eliminated. Personally, I believe that mandatory physicals and a sound physical-fitness program could have prevented many serious firefighter injuries and maybe even some fatalities caused by the rigorous physical demands of the job.

My exercise routine was helpful, but it didn't prevent my body from aging. Like many people in my age group, I had developed high blood pressure, which was easily controlled with medication. I was also diagnosed with gastroesophageal reflux disease (GERD). That little purple pill helped tremendously, as long as I avoided those late-night firehouse meals.

Then I developed benign prostate hyperplasia (BPH). BPH is a non-malignant prostate condition that causes frequent urination. It wasn't well suited for a man who loved coffee and had an occupation that kept him away from the bathroom for extended periods. During our rounds every day, I marked my territory, so to speak, at my six firehouses. Many times that wasn't enough. On quite a few firegrounds, I found myself dancing around like I was at a discotheque. I finally decided to seek medical attention, and the doctor prescribed Flomax. The medication sounded more like the brand name of a high-pressure fire-hose nozzle.

NOVEMBER 25, 2000—BATTALION CHIEF, BATTALION 1

Diane was off on Saturdays, but that never stopped my loving wife from waking up at 0500 hours with me. As always, when I stepped out of the shower, a piping-hot cup of coffee was waiting on the vanity.

My first brew was in my belly before I was in my uniform. I headed down to the kitchen and poured myself another. "Rob!" Diane exclaimed. "That's two cups already! Shouldn't you cut back until you're sure the Flomax is working?"

"Nah!" I assured her like a know-it-all. "I took a pill before bedtime just like the doctor told me and didn't wake up once to pee all night. I'm sure it's working."

After I finished my second cup, Diane walked me to the garage and tenderly kissed my lips. "Please don't drink too much coffee in the firehouse until you're sure that the medicine works."

"Oh, I'll be just fine." I shrugged. Famous last words.

The two cups of coffee were dripping into my bladder when I entered the back door of the firehouse. Bob Noble, the C Platoon's chief, was washing in the office bathroom, and my bladder wasn't overly uncomfortable, so I headed directly into the kitchen. Yes! I poured myself another cup of coffee.

The kitchen was full of giggles as two military veterans, one a Coast Guardsman and the other navy, were trashing each other's branches of service. A former marine jumped in and destroyed both of them with a well-placed artillery round. Everybody was roaring. The hilarious banter somehow shifted to army versus navy and then transitioned into engine versus ladder. The entertainment was a distraction for my rapidly expanding bladder.

After I downed two more cups of coffee, the bells rang. "Engine fourth-in and chief first-in, Nineteenth and Arch, a building fire."

That's when the first warning signals from my bladder alerted my brain. I had to pee! Instead of heading to the bathroom, I dutifully dashed for the apparatus floor, hoping that I'd be able to quickly place the fire under control. No such luck.

"Engine Forty-Three, we're investigating smoke in the area but can't find its source." Great! Even a mild breeze could make smoke drift unpredictably around Center City's high-rises.

After nearly twenty minutes of searching, Ladder 9 finally found a large burning Dumpster over a block away. I gleefully picked up the microphone, placed the fire under control, and directed my backup aide, John Narkin, to head back to our station at warp speed.

Our firehouse was in sight when a long beep sounded over the radio. "Please, no!" I sighed. Luckily, the box was for a building fire in West Philly. Yes! But my bliss was brief. A second tone followed immediately. It was for a dwelling fire in the Seventh Battalion. Since Battalion 7 had been dispatched on the previous box, guess who was dispatched in their place? Oy!

My bladder twinged as we bounced our way over the Grays Ferry Bridge. Just as we were coming down the west side, 68's placed the fire under control. Yes! I was never so proud to be an alumnus of the Nest.

"Johnny," I exclaimed, "head directly to Forty-Sevens, pal. I got to pee!" John giggled as he steered us toward the porcelain bowls I once commanded on Grays Ferry Avenue.

In the meantime, the other fire in West Philly had gone all-hands. As we rode down the bridge, I waved to Deputy 1 responding up the other side in his Crown Victoria. In two minutes, I'd be able to relieve my bladder in his toilet and pee in style. But my hopes were dashed when another tactical box was dispatched. Yep! It was in the Seventh Battalion again. Laughing uncontrollably, John swung a U-turn at the base of the bridge, and we bopped our way back over heading to Sixty-Third and Kingsessing. My eyes crossed in pain as we rumbled over the trolley tracks on Woodland Avenue. As I was pondering which firehouse toilet would be closest after this run, the FCC upgraded our assignment to a box alarm. They were receiving reports of people trapped. I was sitting on my hands with my legs crossed when 40's reported heavy fire conditions. I had no choice but to suck it up as we sped toward the smoke in the southwest sky.

When we arrived on the fireground and I was able to stand, the pressure in my bladder eased. Don't get me wrong; I still had to pee badly. But with plenty of decisions to make and things to do, my brain no longer considered bodily functions to be of utmost priority. Directing companies to attack the fire and search for a missing person consumed all my cognitive abilities. For nearly twenty minutes, I all but forgot how badly I had to go. After the fire was knocked, we discovered a man's charred remains in the front bedroom. We had to wait another twenty minutes for a fire marshal and department's photographer to arrive. That's when the need to drain my bladder returned...and with a vengeance.

The only bathroom in the house had been completely destroyed by the fire, and its soot-stained toilet was sagging precariously on weakened floorboards. I briefly entertained the thought of using it anyway. But how would it have looked if the chief crashed to the first floor with his bunker pants pulled down to his ankles? I'd surely be on the front page of the *Daily News*. With no other option than to hold it in, I thought about Jerry Seinfeld's fear of "uromysitisis" in the hilarious parking-garage episode.

Trying not to look like a lunatic, I pranced around the fireground for the half hour or so it took for the fire marshal to complete his investigation. As soon as the body was loaded into the back of a police van for its trip to the morgue, I made a mad dash for our Suburban. "John, go to Fortys, on the double! I'm going to pee my friggin' pants!" As incredible as it might sound, another beep sounded as soon as I jumped in. Yep. We were dispatched to Sixtieth and Chestnut for another dwelling fire. I screamed in agony, "You gotta be friggin' kidding me! Where the heck are Battalions Seven and Eleven?" John was laughing so hard, I thought that *he* might pee his pants.

Engine 35 was covering for 41s, and they placed the fire under control just as we turned onto Chestnut. Their pump operator looked at us oddly as we flew past them with our lights still flashing. My bladder was throbbing, and John was racing to 57's, the next nearest toilet. As soon as we crossed

Fifty-Ninth Street, the implausible happened. Another long beep. "What are the odds?" I thought. I couldn't believe my ears when the dispatcher's first words were "Hazmat box." Once again, my yearning for white porcelain was spoiled. John, who was absolutely hysterical by then, redirected our Suburban toward Twenty-Fifth and Christian for a sodium-hydroxide spill.

As we sped down Fifty-Second Street, I recalled my shame when I had peed my pants in first grade. Deathly afraid to ask Mrs. Panzer for permission to use the boys' room, I was unable to contain myself. I piddled all over my chair and tried to blame it on a mystery man who appeared out of nowhere. After Panzer embarrassingly yanked me out of the classroom by my ear, I had vowed that it would never happen again. Yet, here I was, some forty-six years later, contemplating the humiliating consequences of doing it all over again. Surely I couldn't blame this one on some mystery man. I pressed my legs tightly together and tried to think about anything other than my urgent need to pee as we bounced our way over the bridge once again.

I jumped out of the car as soon as we arrived, hoping my bladder pressure would ease upon standing again. It didn't! Not in the least. I tried to focus my attention on the leaking drum of corrosive sodium-hydroxide solution that had splashed onto the truck driver when he lifted the rear gate. As 24's decontaminated the man with their booster line, the sound of the splashing water almost made me lose control. I had to walk away. The walking helped. So after the patient was safely in the hands of paramedics, I continued to size up the incident by prancing in circles around the hot zone. I'd be lying if I said that my sizing up didn't include looking for a nearby toilet. Unfortunately, there weren't any. To make things worse, the sirens had drawn a large crowd of curious onlookers. A discreet alley pee was out of the question.

Curious as to what I was up to, Tommy Bitto began following my orbital path. By the end of our third lap together, we had developed a game plan. Tommy spun off tangentially and headed to brief his crew as I continued to rotate around the truck. It was the first time I ever had used the orbiting-command-post method of incident management. It seemed to work just fine. Forty-five minutes later, the spill was cleaned up and the leaking drum was overpacked. I veered out of my trajectory and darted toward the chief's car.

I hopped into the front seat and shrieked, "John, *do not*, I repeat, *do not* make us available. Go straight to our station, *now!*" John was laughing so hard that he could hardly drive. We raced down Christian and onto Broad before finally pulling onto our apron. As we came to a stop, I jumped out of the car and made a mad dash for the bathroom. The firefighters gathered in the kitchen gaped curiously as I dashed past, wondering if something was wrong. Fumbling with my zipper, I slid to a halt in front of the welcoming white throne in the chief's quarters. Finally! Relief! I rolled my eyes as if I were experiencing my first orgasm. As my stream splashed into the bowl, I could swear that I actually felt a nozzle reaction like those produced by fire hoses. The length of my pee rivaled Tom Hanks's famously long urination scene in the movie *A League of Their Own*.

It was past noon by the time I zipped up. I felt like a new man. Without distress signals coming from my bladder, my brain could now process the luscious aroma coming from the kitchen. Ladder 5's Keith Woods was frying up his signature cheesesteaks. With hunger pangs, I strolled into the kitchen to a chorus of laughing firefighters. John had filled them in.

"Did you have a nice pee, Chief?" giggled Ladder 5's veteran John Norvilas.

"Johnny," I replied, laughing, "I had more liquid in my bladder than Ones has in its booster tank!"

Determined not to go through that hell again, I made a conscious decision to consume no more than two cups of coffee in future mornings and to empty my bladder as soon as I felt the slightest urge. Unfortunately, I also should have thought about the afternoons.

Like most Philly firehouses, our firehouse treated firefighters detailed from other stations to free meals. As a show of thanks, most of them brought doughnuts or soft pretzels for us to nosh on at the beginning of the shift. Of course, that day's detail man had bought something different: twenty-four-ounce bottles of Coca-Cola. I'm not sure if it was the cheesesteak, the mound of potato chips I had with it, or all the peeing I had done, but I was extremely thirsty. Before I realized it, I had downed the entire bottle.

I finished just in time for the alert tone to sound again. "Attention, Engine Twenty-Four, Ladder Eleven, Battalion One, and Medic Fourteen, Twenty-Three Hundred Fernon, assist the police for a barricaded man."

Even a monkey learns from his mistakes. There was usually no urgency for assist-the-police calls, so I dashed to the bathroom instead of the apparatus floor. Unfortunately, the twenty-four ounces hadn't hit bottom yet. I couldn't produce a single drop! Frustrated, I zipped up and darted outside, where John was patiently waiting on the apron.

The best way for police to resolve barricaded-person incidents is to coax the individual into surrendering peacefully. Unfortunately, that can take quite a while. For an hour we provided fire protection, medical support, and raised ladders for SWAT before the man finally walked outside with his hands over his head. It was just in time because SOS signals were coming from my bladder again.

While we were on Fernon Street, there was an all-hands building fire at Emerald and Boston Streets. It was far from our district, so I didn't give it a second thought. But as we headed back to our station, two long beeps sounded over the radio. You guessed it! We were dispatched on the second alarm. I crossed my legs again and cursed myself for stupidly downing the entire soda. By the time we arrived, the fire was up to four alarms, and so was my bladder. Deputy 2 assigned me to an exposed six-story vacant factory. Its upper floors had caught fire from radiant heat. Once again my urinary distress temporarily faded as I busily positioned companies to protect the faded memory of Philadelphia's former industrial might. When things finally calmed down, my urge to pee returned. I wasn't at the same critical stage as I had been in the morning, but I had to go!

Under the guise of checking the factory's interior, I headed inside hoping to find a working toilet. Evan a nonworking toilet would have sufficed at that point. But as soon as I stepped in the door, Deputy 2 called me back to the command post. I suppressed my growing need and obediently hastened around to the front of the fire building. The good news was that he was releasing us from the fireground. The bad news was the reason. We were needed to respond to a hazmat incident. John pulled up, I crossed my legs, and we raced toward a leaking propane tank in West Philly.

I'm not sure how much liquid an adult male's bladder can hold, but I believe mine was reaching its capacity as we zigzagged our way to Fortieth and Walnut. As soon as we arrived, I went into orbit again, this time around a hundred-pound hissing propane tank. Tommy Bitto was scratching his head as I circled the hot zone once more. I'm sure he thought I'd completely lost my mind. He waited until I came full circle before joining my orbital path. As we circumnavigated the perimeter, we could see the frost line on the tank. It was half-full. At the rate it was leaking, it would be hours before it was empty. My bladder surely would have exploded by then!

On our third roundabout, we sent two hazmat firefighters to try to stop the leak, but they were unsuccessful. It was time for plan B. As we arced around the tank again, I said, "Tom, if we can't stop the leak, let's expedite it." He knew exactly what I meant. We had used the technique a few times before. His crew stretched their booster line and directed a stream of water below the tank's frost line. The relatively warm water increased the tank's pressure and sped up the leak. It worked so well that the tank was empty in less than fifteen minutes. By then, the pressure in my own tank had gotten critical. As soon as the hissing propane stopped, I raced back to the car, and John zoomed toward Engine 5's station. Relief was only a few blocks away.

The bodily-function gods must have a sense of humor, because the radio squawked, "Attention, Engine Forty-Nine, Ladder Twenty-Seven, Battalion One, Rescue One, and Medic Eleven, Twentieth and Pattison, an accident."

I rolled my eyes in pain. "Do you friggin' believe this?" John was laughing as hard as he had in the morning. When we arrived on Pattison Avenue, the driver of a crumpled SUV was still trapped inside. I boogied to the puttering rhythm of the Jaws of Life's engine as I directed the fifteen-minute rescue operation.

As soon as the man was loaded into the back of Medic 11, I sprinted back to the car, jumped inside, and snatched the microphone from its cradle. "Johnny Boy, do not make us available until I'm standing before the toilet in Forty-Nine's station. Let's fly!"

As we sped toward 49's, a box sounded over the radio for a reported apartment fire at Broad and Tasker. It was our first-in. No matter how much pain I was feeling, I wasn't about to let anyone steal my fire. I grabbed the microphone and moaned, "Battalion One is available and responding." There was a chance that things might have worked out better that way, anyhow. The reported fire was less than ten blocks from our firehouse. If 10's placed the fire under control quickly, we'd zip right past them, and I'd be standing in front of my own porcelain bowl even sooner.

The odds were good for a betting man. But they weren't good for a non-gambler like me. As soon as we turned onto Broad Street, 10's reported that fire was showing. "Screw it!" I screamed. "If I pee myself, so be it!" Luckily, the fire attack went well, but we were in service for nearly twenty minutes. There were no rhythmic Jaws of Life to boogie to this time, so I hummed Marcia Griffiths's "Electric Slide" as I danced around the command post.

The pain signals from my distended bladder must have made me delirious. When I got into our Suburban, I absentmindedly, and astonishingly, radioed that we were available. Furious with myself, I screamed, "What the heck did I just—" Before I could finish, we got dispatched again.

Since the end of World War II, a hand grenade had sat undisturbed in the basement of a tiny row home. That day, of all days, when I had to pee worse than ever, the homeowner had decided to call 911. It took nearly an hour for the bomb squad to fight their way through traffic. My back teeth weren't actually floating, but I could swear that I was tasting my own urine. Somehow, I managed to hold it in. As soon as the bomb technicians rendered the grenade safe, I hopped back in the car, and John sped off. After lasting so long, I felt that it was now a challenge. I was determined to use my own toilet. I told John to head directly to our station. I tried everything to prevent my bladder from bursting during the five-minute ride: tapping my foot, counting cars, and even humming. The last few blocks were the worst. My brain sensed that relief was near and began sending premature "prepare to empty" signals to my bladder.

People walking by our firehouse scrambled for safety as we jumped the curb. I sprang out of the car like a jack-in-the-box and dashed inside. As I tore through the kitchen, Norvilas laughed loudly. "Uh-oh, the chief's got to pee again."

The kitchen was roaring with laughter, but I couldn't care less. I had finally made it. I sighed as I urinated for nearly five full minutes, a new personal record.

Needless to say, the events of that day called for major adjustments to my fluid intake. From that point on, I had one cup of coffee with Diane before leaving for work. When I arrived at the firehouse, I urinated as soon as I walked inside. I only allowed myself one more cup at the kitchen table. I also made a trip to the bathroom before we made our daily rounds and, as usual, at each firehouse. For lunch and dinner, my limit was only twelve ounces of soda. For the most part, it helped. But there were still firegrounds to come where I'd dance the jitterbug, the hustle, and even the boogaloo.

CHAPTER 33

The Age of Terrorism

During the first week of 2001, it was my turn to be qualified as an acting deputy chief (ADC). Just as in ABC training, I ran the division under Deputy 1's watchful guidance. For me, the difference from commanding a battalion to managing a division was hardly as drastic as the transition from company captain to ABC. There were more meetings to attend, the paperwork was a bit heavier, and five battalions' worth of information flowed through division headquarters. An infamous former chief once summed up the deputy chief's position by saying, "You're one step further from the excitement of firefighting and one step closer to the lunacy of headquarters." After one day of shuffling papers, faxes, e-mails, and phone calls, I understood exactly what he had meant.

Deputy chiefs don't respond to nearly as many calls as battalion chiefs. They aren't dispatched unless all hands of a box alarm are placed in service, the second alarm has been requested, or the incident involves something unusual. They manage the fireground more strategically by dividing it into smaller segments called sectors or divisions, each commanded by a battalion chief or company officer.

During my training, I picked up plenty of advice and tips. Much of it was pragmatic and not found in textbooks. "In most cases give your chiefs a chance to work the fire. You don't need to bust out of the door like you do at the battalion. Take a piss first, if you need to."

"If I need to?" I thought. "That's one aspect of the dep's job I'll definitely take advantage of."

We only responded to two working fires during my training. It wasn't nearly enough practice, but it gave me a feel for the job. Final anointment of my qualification as ADC rested with the deputy commissioner of operations. His memorandum of approval was faxed to division headquarters on my last night of training.

After four long shifts at division, it felt good to get back to the hustle and bustle of Battalion 1. I didn't realize how much I'd miss the fires, accidents, assist-police calls, hazmats, and even those dreaded stuck elevators. Most of all, I missed the rush of busting out the door on the initial dispatch, even if my bladder was half-full.

January 14, 2001—Battalion Chief, Battalion 1

Snow flurries were falling as we raced through the streets of Center City. Motorists and pedestrians alike snapped double takes as we zipped past them. Their looks of awe weren't because of our siren and flashing lights. No, they were because I had my head stuck out the window like a German shepherd panting in the breeze. I'm sure they thought that I was insane, but it was something I had to do. We were responding directly from another decomp, and I was hoping that the wind whirling through my hair would blow the stench away. I was chilled to the bone, but so be it. I didn't want the residents of the apartment to which we were responding to catch a whiff and think that the fire chief had the worst case of BO they'd ever smelled. Luckily, we pulled up behind 43's before my frozen ears snapped off in the bitter wind.

I got strange looks as I walked into the lobby, but it wasn't because of my stench. I kept too far away from the residents for that. No, they were staring at me because of my bright-red face and wind-blown, just-seen-a-ghost hairstyle. As I made my way down the sub-subbasement for a reported electrocution victim, I tried to comb my hair back into place. It was no use! The snow flurries had frozen it in place. It felt like an entire bottle of maximum hold had been sprayed on my head.

At the bottom of the steps, a new odor replaced the scent of decaying flesh in my nose. It was burned flesh! The smell was coming from a critically burned maintenance man who had been zapped while working near the building's main power feed. Firefighters had removed him from the electrical room, and he was being treated by paramedics.

I explained to the building manager that no one should enter the room until it was declared safe by a licensed electrician. As I told him that he'd be getting a visit from the Department of Licenses and Inspections, I couldn't help but notice that his eyes were transfixed on my hair. His nose was twitching too. God only knows why he thought I'd styled my hair like Don King and was wearing eau de provolone aftershave.

Fighting fires in the tiny streets of South Philly is a unique challenge. Once fire apparatuses are positioned, it's very difficult to make adjustments.

MARCH 2, 2001—BATTALION CHIEF, BATTALION 1

At 0530 this morning we were in the 1900 block of Moore Street looking for a reported house fire. The distinctive odor of burning wood was in the air, but where was it coming from? It certainly wasn't where the 911 caller had said it was. I was becoming more and more concerned as we unsuccessfully fanned out looking for its source. The narrow streets of South Philly were bad enough, but at that hour, parked cars jutted out into the intersections. It was going to be difficult to relocate our apparatus if the fire was found somewhere else.

Sure enough, my dread became reality. Jimmy relayed that police were reporting a dwelling fire three blocks away. To make things worse, they said people were trapped inside. Companies scrambled backward and forward as everybody tried to relocate to the 2100 block of Mifflin. We followed Ladder 19 as they backed a full block down Twentieth. We scooted past them before they tried to negotiate the tight turn onto Mifflin.

There wasn't any traffic as we bucked two blocks up Mifflin to a middle-of-the-row porch-front dwelling. Heavy black smoke was pushing from its second-floor windows. Unfortunately, we arrived before everyone else in our hoseless, ladderless Chevy Suburban. Luckily, 60's swung a sharp turn from Twenty-Second Street just a few seconds later. Whew!

One of Tommy's men dashed upstairs to conduct a search while the rest of his company stretched an attack line through the front door. Ladder

19 finished their turn and screamed toward us just as Ladder 11 turned off Twenty-Second. Things were shaping up.

I was sizing up the fire conditions when all of a sudden the second-floor window exploded with a loud crash. A large object suddenly emerged from the smoke and hurtled directly toward me. I ducked as it sailed over my head and slammed into the parked car behind me. *Boom!* It was a thirteen-inch portable television. A second later, Tommy's search-and-rescue firefighter flew out the same window and rolled to a landing on the porch roof.

Thankfully, the firefighter wasn't injured. He had been searching the front room when flames erupted behind him. He tossed the television through the window and jumped out only seconds before the room flashed over. After an extensive secondary search, we learned that everybody had gotten out before we arrived. Tommy instantly gave the firefighter a new nickname—"the Boom-Tube Man."

Just like my thermodynamics buddy who placed his air conditioner in the middle of his room, people sometimes do amazingly crazy things. I began calling those types of calls "crazy calls."

May 20, 2001—Battalion Chief, Battalion 1

At first, I wasn't sure whether to classify the run to West Philly as a hazmat call or a crazy call. While trying to exterminate a severe German-cockroach infestation, an elderly man poured several gallons of concentrated household ammonia around the baseboards in every room of his tiny row home. While it didn't seem to bother the roaches much, the irritating ammonia vapors drove him, his wife, and their adjoining neighbors out into the street. It took us nearly an hour to clean up and air out the house. His wife was screaming and yelling at him the entire time. "What the hell's the matter with you? If you hired an exterminator like I wanted, you wouldn't have to make such a *crazy call* to nine one one!" I thought so!

Since 49's was in the First Battalion's geographical district, so was South Philly's sports complex.

SEPTEMBER 2, 2001—BATTALION CHIEF, BATTALION 1

A win would have kept the Phillies tied for first place in the National League East. But the ugly 5–2 defeat by the last-place Expos had me down during my drive to work. When I pulled up to the firehouse, my gloom quickly faded, and I began laughing uncontrollably. Six grunting and straining B Platoon pranksters emerged from the rear parking lot lugging a tiny sports car. They carried their unsuspecting comrade's car around front and dropped it into a parking spot on Broad Street. The little roadster's owner had made the mistake of dozing off in the TV room, and his opportunistic platoon-mates quickly devised the hoax to make him think his prize possession had gotten stolen.

Everybody was at the kitchen table waiting to see the firefighter's reaction when he walked outside to the parking lot. But no sooner had I sat down than the dispatch printer began to clatter. "Chief only! Veteran's Stadium with Ladder 27 for a stuck elevator!" I had to miss the best part of the practical joke because of another friggin' stuck elevator. Damn!

Aging Veterans Stadium recently had made headlines after a preseason game between the Eagles and Ravens was postponed because of uneven patches in the artificial turf. Referees and coaches unanimously agreed to cancel the game, fearing that ripples in the playing surface might cause injuries to the players. To add to the embarrassment, that same night eighteen reporters sweltered for nearly forty-five minutes when their press elevator got stuck between floors. As we raced down Broad, I was hoping that we weren't going to be caught in the middle of another media frenzy.

Luckily, this time only three people were in the stalled elevator. The car was ten feet above the first level and twenty feet below the second in a blind shaft. Usually the safest course of action was to await a certified mechanic to override the controls and reposition the car to a floor opening. But that day, a man inside was screaming that his baby daughter was about to pass out from the heat. We quickly killed the power, lowered a ladder to the top of the car, opened the roof hatch, and lowered another ladder inside. The entire operation only took fifteen minutes, but by then, the man with the baby girl in his arms was irate.

"This is the worst stadium in all of baseball!" he ranted as he passed his daughter to Ladder 27's firefighters. "This place is an embarrassment to the Phillies. I'd rather be playing anywhere else!" That's when I recognized him as one of the Phillies' utility players. Once he climbed out of the shaft, he rudely snatched his daughter from the arms of the firefighter and stormed away without an ounce of gratitude. Maybe he was miffed, like I was, because they had lost the game.

The player got his wish to play elsewhere. The following year he spent most of his time in the minor leagues. Less than three years later, the Phillies moved into their new stadium a few blocks away, Citizens Bank Park.

The Domestic Preparedness Program had attained its goal of preparing the country's 120 largest cities for an NBC terroristic attack. While delivering the courses, we had discussed many different types of attack scenarios. But in our wildest nightmares, none of us imagined the events that would occur on September 11, 2001. The tragic loss of 2,996 lives that day was shocking enough, but for those of us in the fire service, the unimaginable had happened. The collapse of the World Trade Center Towers killed 343 of our brethren in the FDNY. The sense of loss was overwhelming to firefighters everywhere.

I was between night shifts that Tuesday and had just finished mowing the lawn when Diane called from work and told me about the first plane crash. I turned on the TV just in time to see the fireball of the second plane as it crashed into the South Tower. I watched horrified as the nation's worst terrorist attack unfolded before my eyes. When the towers collapsed, I knew that scores of heroic firefighters had to be among the casualties.

By noon, Diane and the kids were home, and I was dressed in my uniform in case of a recall. Instead of my usual shift at Battalion 1 that night, I was detailed to Emergency Management's mobile command post, CP-1, in front of the Police Administration Building. Thankfully, things were uneventful in Philly.

Never was the bond shared by firefighters more apparent than after those attacks. For the next few weeks, Philly firefighters hit the streets and collected thousands upon thousands of dollars for the families of our murdered FDNY brothers. The outpouring of generosity from the public was unbelievable. At the end of each shift, we transported several heavy cash bags, collected by our companies, to Local 22's headquarters. Our assistance didn't end there. Most firefighters donated at least twenty dollars apiece to the same cause. Off-duty Philly firefighters also packed buses daily and traveled to New York to help dig at the collapse site. I was proud of how our firefighters rallied in support of the tragedy that had befallen our brothers ninety-six miles northward.

The tragic events of that day caused us to approach incidents with a warier eye. A few weeks later, during a horrendous rainstorm, Uncle Pat was dispatched to the Delaware River for a large barge drifting aimlessly. Fearing that it might be loaded with explosives and headed toward the Benjamin Franklin Bridge, the Coast Guard was dispatched to chase it down. We boarded Marine Unit 1 with an LBC and followed them up the river. Everyone let out a huge sigh of relief after it harmlessly passed under the bridge. About a mile farther, the barge uneventfully crashed into an abandoned pier. It had simply broken away from its moorings in the storm.

As fall approached we had our usual increase in fires. Though we'd never forget 9/11, there was something comforting about fighting Philly's more typical fires. But the normality was short lived. On October 5, an anthrax-laced letter killed American Media photo editor Bob Stevens. Fears of another terrorist attack abounded as more anthrax letters were discovered over the next several days. Terrified people began calling 911 whenever *they* deemed a piece of mail suspicious. For the next few weeks, it wasn't uncommon for us to respond to a dozen hazmat calls each shift. As the city's only hazmat team, we were running around like crazy. Something had to be done.

Under Deputy Chief Rosini's leadership, we put together seven rapid-assessment teams. Each one was staffed with a hazmat officer, a hazmat technician, a police officer, and a representative from the city's health department. Strategically located in firehouses around the city, each rapid-assessment team (their amusing nickname was RAT) responded in SUVs equipped with basic hazmat gear, supplies, and equipment. Dispatched with the first-in engine and battalion chief, the RAT's mission was to assess the credibility of each call. If warranted, the call would be upgraded to a full hazmat response.

Tommy Bitto and I developed a *target, threat,* and *substance triangle* procedure for the RATs to follow as guidelines. The concept was simple. Since most calls weren't about high-risk *targets* like elected officials or didn't contain *threats,* most of them were quickly dismissed. Some didn't even contain a *substance!* The more legs of the triangle present, the more carefully the incident was scrutinized. The RAT concept worked well, and Hazmat 1's calls dropped drastically.

Since Battalion 1 covered such a large chunk of Center City, we also responded to many calls with the first-in engine and RAT. Weekdays, when the office buildings were occupied, were very busy. It was amazing how nervous the general public had become about anything remotely suspicious. Some of the calls were humorous; some were ridiculous.

10/12: The bomb squad x-rayed an unattended suitcase on the sidewalk. The x-rays were inconclusive, so they fired their disrupter (explosive charge) at the expensive piece of luggage. The mysterious owner's underwear and a few sex toys flew in all directions. No other hazards were found.

10/12: Responded to a report of white powder in the street. It was paint splatter from a lane-marking crew earlier in the day.

10/13: A SEPTA bus was evacuated when a rider spotted white powder on a seat. It turned out to be talcum powder. Somebody had overpowdered his or her crotch that morning.

10/19: A panicked lawyer sat frozen at his desk when he spotted white powder on his pants. While interviewing him, I saw the same white powder around his lips. More implicating was the opened box of white-powdered doughnuts on the table behind him. A quick sugar test confirmed our suspicions. He had eaten a doughnut before opening the mail. Guilty *and* sloppy!

10/20: A woman thought she saw powder disperse in the air when she pulled the zip tab of a Fed-Ex envelope. We had her sit in the exact same position, gave her a similar envelope, and had her pull the tab again. "Oh my God! I'm so embarrassed," she cried as a small amount of cardboard dust danced in the morning's sun rays.

11/19: A woman became hysterical when she saw white powder on a toy she had ordered through the mail. We called the company; it was plastic mold release agent.

11/19: Workers scrambled from the Tioga Marine Terminal after unloading Chilean grapes that they thought were covered with white powder. By the time we got to the grapes, the powder was gone. It was frost! It had melted in the sunlight.

11/22: People evacuated a company cafeteria when they saw something unusual on the table. It was smeared banana.

12/05: An office building was evacuated because someone saw a suspicious powder in the coffee-room trash can. It was aspartame sugar substitute. The small blue package was also in the trash can.

The 2001 anthrax attack killed five people and infected seventeen others. The chief suspect, Bruce Ivins, a government scientist at Fort Detrick, Maryland, died on July 29, 2008, from an overdose of acetaminophen. The FBI linked the anthrax's DNA strain directly to him and was about to file criminal charges just before he died.

By the end of the year, the suspicious-incident responses dropped off, and the RATs were disbanded one by one.

Occasional suspicious-incident calls remained part of Battalion 1's repertoire. On January 17 we responded to a major university dormitory for an unknown substance in a stairwell. It turned out to be phosphoric acid. One of the students had "borrowed" it from a chemistry lab. Then on January 30, Engine 2 found a box affixed with radioactive warning labels in the back of a burning panel truck fire. Police were concerned that the stolen truck contained a dirty bomb. It didn't. It was an industrial radiography machine used for nondestructive tests. I explained that it was unlikely that terrorists would place the proper DOT shipping labels on a secret bomb.

My aide Jimmy got promoted to lieutenant, and I replaced him with Bill Gaffney. Bill had been my aide during the 1991 polyurethane-fueled three-alarm inferno on Passyunk Avenue. Detail-oriented, conscientious, and experienced, Bill was a perfect fit for my OCD. He had been a backup aide for years and had a great sense of humor.

A chief's aide is much more than just a driver. Together, the chief and his or her aide function as a team. Aides act as a second set of eyes and ears on the fireground. I was extremely comfortable with Bill serving as my executive officer.

February 8, 2002—Battalion Chief, Battalion 1

A dirty gray column of smoke was rising in the chilly eastern sky as we zipped past 53's empty firehouse on Snyder Avenue. They were already on scene at Pier 80, one of the few piers in South Philly in which I hadn't already fought a blaze. Billy, who was once with Ladder 27, briefed me about the pier's construction, size, and occupancy during our two-mile run. When we pulled up behind 53's, I felt like I had designed the thousand-foot wharf myself.

"Chief, Marine Unit One's underway. I'll have FCC dispatch a LBC to Marine Unit Two, just in case." It was an excellent suggestion.

The fire, which involved approximately five hundred square yards of baled cardboard, was located on the land end of the pier. Luckily, we cut it off before it extended to the rest of the structure. We didn't need the services of either fireboat, but it was reassuring to know that they were there. Just like my trusty aide Bill, they had my back.

February 15, 2002—Battalion Chief, Battalion 1

For five years, the huge diesel-fueled emergency generator sat idly on the grounds of vacant Mount Sinai Hospital. Nearby residents probably thought it was no longer functional. But the area was hit by a power failure, and the enormous beast sputtered, groaned, rumbled, and reluctantly roared back to life louder than ever before. Its lack of upkeep had taken a toll. Clouds of dense black smoke belched from its exhaust and quickly spread throughout the neighborhood. Alarmed residents quickly flooded 911 with calls, and shortly afterward, we arrived on the box alarm.

Unable to determine the building's current owner, I had Billy request a representative from Licenses and Inspections, but their ETA was over two hours. I wanted to put the colossal air-polluting hunk of machinery out of its misery sooner than that. A few feet away from the generator was an exterior basement stairway, and maybe there was a shut-off switch inside. As Ladder 11 was hammering away at the door, Billy called on the radio. "Chief, Deputy One is on the cell and wants a progress report. I told him that I'd call him back." Billy had cleverly stalled for time.

"Good move, Bill," I replied. "Downplay it! Tell him that we're in the process of shutting the generator down." Like most battalion chiefs, I didn't like relinquishing command to my boss unless absolutely necessary.

Billy called Deputy 1 back and was speaking to him when the generator suddenly exploded. Pieces of machinery whizzed over our heads.

"What the hell was that?" the dep exclaimed.

"What was what?" Billy replied innocently.

"That noise! It sounded like an explosion!"

"Oh, that? A truck backfired, Chief. And by the way, the generator is shut down."

Now that's an aide who can think on his feet!

Billy and I had a lot in common. Both of us grew up in South Philly, were the same age, and had been stationed together when I was at 60's. As the fire service entered the uncertain era of terrorism, it was comforting to know that I had a stalwart aide to rely upon.

CHAPTER 34

The Diverse First

Other battalions in the city might have had more fires, but none of them were as diverse as the First.

On April 29, 2002, we responded to a major ammonia leak in a large cold-storage facility. A damaged pipe was spewing a steady stream of the deadly gas in a remote section of the building. In addition to being toxic, ammonia can also be flammable under certain conditions, and the interior concentration was so high that I was concerned about the possibility of an explosion.

Tommy and his team made six separate entries into the extremely hazardous atmosphere. They thawed frozen valves, isolated piping networks, and eventually stopped the stubborn leak. I was so impressed by their teamwork and innovative ideas that I put them in for, and they received, a well-deserved unit citation.

Anything involving unknown chemicals had the potential to cause terrorism hysteria. One day we were dispatched to a major trauma center where a patient claimed to have downed a dose of poisoned cold medicine. When he whipped the half-full bottle out of his pocket, the medical staff panicked. By the time we arrived, they had the ER evacuated and shut down.

The victim's only complaint was mild nausea. Other than that, he was conscious, oriented, and alert. After Tommy took the bottle outside to test it, I told the head nurse that it was safe to reopen the ER. She gawked at me with disbelief. "Really? How could you possibly think that it's safe to do that?"

"Ma'am," I replied, "first, the bottle was capped. Second, it's now safely outdoors." Then I pointed to the victim on the gurney. "And third, look at the man who *drank* the stuff. He's fine!" The man waved to us and smiled.

She still wasn't convinced. "Listen, ma'am," I added. "Even if the medicine *is* tainted, do you really think that one ounce in his stomach can cause harm to others? On the other hand, what's happening to those seriously ill and injured patients being diverted to the next closest trauma center? Isolate him in a treatment room and open up!"

"Oh," she replied, as the logic finally sank in. She quickly signaled her staff to reopen the ER. Tommy's tests revealed that the bottle of medicine was contaminated with a small amount of paint thinner.

Regardless of how farfetched many of the calls were, the department knew that it had to be better prepared for the age of terrorism. In addition to Hazmat 1, the only other special-operations unit in the department was Rescue 1. Rescue 1 was an elite specialized company that handled technical-rescue situations (building collapses, swift-water rescues, high-angle rescues, etc.).

Chief Rosini asked me to represent hazmat at a meeting regarding the issue. As a result of our meeting, we decided to double our capabilities by converting two engine companies into squad companies. In addition to their regular engine duties, squad companies would be trained and equipped to handle both hazmat and technical-rescue incidents. It was a proven concept the FDNY had been doing successfully for years. We estimated that it would take two years to purchase specialized apparatuses, select the best personnel, and then train and equip them.

As soon as the program was approved, hundreds of firefighters filed applications to transfer into the squads. It was only a matter of time before we'd be training them to be hazmat technicians. In the meantime, I was enjoying my time at Battalion 1.

JUNE 26, 2002—BATTALION CHIEF, BATTALION 1

The kitchen topic at change of shifts was the illegal hooch-still explosion we responded to the other day. Personally, I was amazed that there was such a demand for illegal moonshine. The sophisticated distillery must have cost a fortune to construct. But despite the still's intricate design, the budding entrepreneurs didn't foresee that their attempts to conceal the alcohol's odor could cause its vapors to reach an explosive concentration. Ethanol vapors accumulated inside the tightly sealed building and eventually found an ignition source. The powerful explosion rocked the neighborhood. When we arrived, rivers of moonshine were flowing down the streets.

"Surprisingly, there wasn't much fire," I explained, "but we had a major hazmat mitigation on our hands. If it weren't for some helpful local residents, many more gallons of ethanol would have gotten into the sewers."

One of Ladder 5's firefighters stared at me curiously. "Did they help block the sewers, Chief?"

"Well, not exactly," I explained with a smile. "They used glasses, pitchers, and bottles to scoop up gallon after gallon of the hazardous liquid. I guess they really did care about their environment." The kitchen was roaring as the printer clattered in the background. "Chief only!"

The words on the printout were vague, as usual: "Assist police—No further information." It was humid and ninety-two degrees as we zipped down Broad Street. I turned to Bill. "I hope this isn't another friggin' decomp, Mr. Bill. I don't think I could handle the stench in this heat!"

Billy laughed. "Yeah, me either! You stunk up the whole car last time."

Fortunately for both of us, it wasn't. But the beaten young man dangling upside down and bleeding profusely on a nine-foot alley fence wasn't as lucky. The ill-fated burglar had been breaking into the rear of a home when its residents entered the front door. He fled down the alley and tried to scramble over a security fence. But when he reached the top, his pants snagged on sharp spikes, and he lost his balance. The crook flipped upside down and was wriggling frantically when angry neighbors, seething from a recent rash of burglaries, caught up to him. In a dose of vigilante justice, they beat him senseless with baseball bats and broom handles. I'm not sure how many bones they broke, but he was completely limp when Ladder 11 got him down and placed him on a backboard.

Minutes later we were back in the comfort of our air-conditioned firehouse. It was so hot and muggy outside that I couldn't have cared any less if we got any more calls during the shift. Engine 1's flurry of alarm systems and shoe runs had delayed our dinner. It was 2130 hours when I finally began stuffing myself with meat and potatoes. The detail man brought chocolate and butter-pecan ice cream for dessert, and I couldn't resist. It was late, but was I willing to risk another GERD attack for my favorite flavor combination.

I knew that I'd sinned and there'd be hell to pay if I lay down within the next few hours, so I hung around the kitchen. We were talking about how the other day the C Platoon had needed to rip open the walls of an apartment so police could remove a body. A man had allegedly killed his wife and tried to conceal her behind a false drywall partition.

I was so engrossed by our morbid conversation that I wasn't paying attention to the fire-radio chatter in the background. Shortly after 0100 hours, we got dispatched on the second alarm to a vacant-factory fire in North Philly. I was familiar with the place; it was the streetlamp company where I had been a draftsman many years ago.

The fourth alarm was in by the time we arrived. Closed for years, my former place of employment was a three-story irregularly shaped structure that was 400 feet long by 150 feet wide. Flames were through the roof; it was a goner for sure.

My job was to protect the exposures on the east side—a row of three-story apartment buildings. Baseball-sized flaming embers were sailing over their roofs, and their cornices were smoldering from intense radiant heat. It took several trips up and down the block, venturing into rear alleys and climbing ladders, to assess the most effective placement for the four engines I was assigned. The hose lays were long, and it took a while before we finally had water flowing.

As I paced along the block checking our progress, I suddenly began to feel light-headed. The heat, the humidity, and my heavy bunker gear had taken their toll. Having gorged on a late meal certainly didn't help. I staggered backward against one of the exposed apartments and slowly slid into a sitting position. The fire across the street was getting dim, but it wasn't because of our hose streams; it was because I was losing consciousness from heat stress.

"Hey, Chief! Are you okay?"

I looked up groggily, and the blurry image of a helmeted man slowly came into focus. He was a member of Philadelphia's Second Alarmers Association.

"Let's get that heavy gear off you, Chief." My cumbersome running coat was soaked with perspiration as he slid my arms out of the sleeves. He caringly brought a paper cup to my lips. "Here, Chief, take a few sips." It was the Second Alarmers staple: ice-cold lime drink. The haze in my mind slowly disappeared, and within minutes I was back on my feet.

"Chief, let's have the medics check you out," he urged.

At my age that would certainly have meant a trip to the hospital. "Nah, I'm good!" I replied. "You guys are the best! You're a lifesaver, brother." I gave him a huge brotherly hug.

He was reluctant to leave my side until I shooed him away. As he made his way toward a group of exhausted firefighters manning a master stream, he kept glancing back to see if I was okay. Each time I faked a smile and gave him a thumbs-up.

Truthfully, I was drained. I stood there watching my old office burn to the ground. The machine shop, the assembly line, and the little cafeteria where Concetta and I had shared so many lunches together were gone forever.

I felt old, tired, and weary as I wrote in my journal. For the first time ever, I was having thoughts about retirement. But the thoughts hurt like hell because I still love this damned job so much.

Never before had I come so close to passing out from the heat. It was an awful night for firefighting, but I had done it so many times before and had never had a problem. I was hoping that it was only a fluke, but deep down inside I knew that age was catching up with me.

Thank God the Second Alarmers came to my rescue that night, or I'd surely have wound up in the hospital. Organized in 1921, the all-volunteer canteen service has been providing beverages and sustenance to Philly firefighters, paramedics, and police ever since, offering ice-cold drinks during hot weather, piping-hot drinks during cold weather, water, snacks, ice packs, hand warmers, and comfort stations. It wasn't the first time they had soothed and nourished my sapped body. They are truly Philly's unsung heroes.

My zeal for firefighting was also changing. Unlike during my days as Captain Blood the Rookie, an occasional quiet shift didn't bother me at all. If we were busy, that was great. But if the bells didn't ring, I really didn't mind. Besides, a quiet shift meant no firefighter injuries. No one under my command had yet suffered a major injury—or worse, a LODD. I often prayed for God's guidance to help me make the right calls.

July 2, 2002—Battalion Chief, Battalion 1

Dripping hot tar was the culprit on this humid afternoon. It burned five of my firefighters as they valiantly tried to reach people reportedly trapped on the third floor. But conditions weren't improving at the Catherine Street apartment fire. My artistic side knew it was time to pull everybody out, give up our search, and fight the fire defensively. Only moments after the last firefighter was safely outside, the stubborn flames broke through the roof. Minutes after that, the roof collapsed onto the third floor.

The reports of people trapped were erroneous. Dear Lord, thank you for watching over my firefighters.

Though my tactics were common to Philly's aggressive style of firefighting, the close call on Catherine Street spooked me. There's a fine line that separates aggressiveness from recklessness on the fireground. Years of experience factored into my decision to evacuate that building. But risks had to be taken when lives were at stake. Suppose I wasn't so perceptive next time?

July 26, 2002—Battalion Chief, Battalion 1

People on the sidewalk were screaming hysterically. A man was trapped inside. Engine 10's old firehouse on Morris Street had been converted into apartments years ago, but heavy smoke was pushing from every one of its windows that morning. An aggressive interior attack was our only chance to save him.

Only one set of stairs led to the second-floor apartment. Engine 10 had made the turn on the second floor, and they were advancing their line toward the fire in the front room. Other firefighters were beginning to conduct a search when suddenly the rear room flashed over. Many of them got caught in the huge fireball and came tumbling down the steps. Fortunately, I had 53's backing up 10's. Poised on the stairway, they quickly opened their hose nozzle and battled the flames back.

After the fire was knocked down, we found the man's remains in the back apartment. Everyone was glum because we didn't make the save. But the fire marshal's investigation revealed that he had been dead before we even got the call. The poor guy had a bullet hole in the back of his head. The fire had been set in an attempt to cover up the homicide.

At the time, we'd had no idea that the man was already dead. Amazingly, the firefighters who got caught in the fireball weren't injured. They quickly dusted themselves off, ran back upstairs, and resumed their search. Their valiant effort to make the rescue was perilous, but in that case, I had to take the risk.

Most times when we were called to make river rescues, the people either had drowned or had gotten out on their own accord. Sometimes they obviously needed to be rescued, but sometimes we weren't sure whether they were dead or alive.

November 7, 2002—Battalion Chief, Battalion 1

The man floating face down in the frigid Schuylkill was most likely DOA. The passerby who called 911 said she had watched the object float for nearly twenty minutes before she'd realized it was a body. Regardless, there was still a chance that the chilly river had slowed his metabolism. I knew it was a long shot, but revival might have been possible.

I instructed Marine Unit 2's small whaler to retrieve the body and transfer him to paramedics at the bulkhead. As the whaler approached him, he abruptly plunged below the murky green surface. I was shocked! What had made him sink so suddenly? Did water find its way inside his body and cause him to lose buoyancy? Was an air pocket under his jacket disturbed by the wake of the whaler? He went down so quickly! For a fleeting second, I even wondered whether Jaws or some other sea creature had sunk its teeth into him and pulled him under. We probed the river using long hooks until the police dive team arrived. Our combined efforts failed to recover the victim.

I never found out why the body sank. A week later, my friend Battalion Chief Mike Iraci, who worked at Battalion 7, recovered the man about a mile downstream. I asked Mike if he had noticed any huge bite marks on the corpse. He looked at me like I was crazy, but thank God he said no.

NOVEMBER 24, 2002—BATTALION CHIEF, BATTALION 1

If at first you don't succeed, try, try again. I thought so, anyway. We responded to the Walnut-Locust stop of the Broad Street subway for a man on the tracks. Nobody seemed to know whether the gray-haired man had been pushed, had jumped, or simply had lost his footing. We stopped rail traffic, shut off the third rail, and lifted the slightly injured man onto a stretcher before sending him off to the hospital.

Much later that night, we were returning from a dwelling fire when we got dispatched to the Snyder Avenue stop for a man underneath a train. Snyder is only four stops from Walnut-Locust. This victim wasn't so fortunate; he was DOA. As we removed him from the tracks, I noticed that he had gray hair too. His sneakers also matched those of the earlier victim. I couldn't tell if it was the same guy for sure because his face was mangled too badly by the impact.

December 26, 2002—Battalion Chief, Battalion 1

It was 05:44 a.m. and time to assist the police again. This time it was the 2600 block of Earp Street. I was familiar with that block because we'd had so many fires there before. About half of the homes were vacant, and many of those were dilapidated or burned out. I glanced at the printout. "Ladder 19, Battalion 1, assist police—no further information."

"Why isn't there ever any further information?" I said to Bill. "Doesn't anybody ever ask questions?"

As we turned onto Twenty-Sixth, Ladder 19's lieutenant, Arty, was chatting with a police sergeant. Arty was sporting a huge grin and shaking his head as I approached. "Uh-oh, what do we have, Arty?" I asked, rolling my eyes. "It isn't a big snake, is it?"

"No, Chief, but this one does involve the animal kingdom. It's *rats!*" Arty pointed to a man poking his head from the second-floor window of a row home. "That guy told us that giant rats are crawling around on his first floor. He's afraid to come downstairs with his wife and kids. He wants us to get them down with a ladder."

The man's home looked to be in decent condition, but the adjoining vacants were in bad shape. Both had been boarded up, but crackheads had pried off the boards, and rubbish and debris had accumulated in both of them.

"Yo! Buddy!" I yelled up. "Can't you and your family just run down the steps and out the door? The rats are more afraid of you than you are of them. I promise they'll run away."

"Ain't no friggin' way, man!" he shouted. "Those rats are as big as cats. My kids are two and four. I ain't taking them nowhere near those rats, man."

I turned to Arty. "Check the front door. Maybe we can shimmy it open."

Arty smiled. "Already tried that, Chief. It's double locked with deadbolts."

I looked back up. "Yo, man, toss down the keys. We'll make sure the rats don't bother you."

"I can't do that, boss. The keys are downstairs with the rats, and I ain't going the hell down there to get them. And don't be busting my door down either. They'll rob me blind around here."

A rusted mideighties Buick was directly in front of the man's house. To complicate matters, it was half parked on the pavement. If we placed a ladder there, the climbing angle would be extremely steep, especially for untrained climbers. I'd much prefer to bring the family down the interior stairs. "Whose car is this, buddy?"

"It's mine, man."

"Let me guess," I replied. "Your car keys are downstairs too, right?"

"You got it, man! All my keys are in my jacket. It's hanging at the bottom of the stairs."

It was time for another plan. I had Ladder 19 place a ladder between the car and house. The angle was even steeper than I had originally thought. "Okay, Arty, send one of your guys up and have him retrieve the keys."

Without hesitation, Calvin volunteered. "I'll go up, Chief." I'd known Calvin Graham for a long time. He was the senior member of the company, yet he still volunteered for almost everything.

Not long ago, we had been called to check on the welfare of a senior citizen. While we checked the first and second floors, I asked someone to check the basement. Calvin volunteered and trudged down the steps. All of a sudden, I heard two loud thumps as Calvin flew back up in two leaping bounds, his eyes wide as saucers. When he had gotten to the basement, he'd tripped over the dead lady and fallen right on top of her.

Now here he was again, volunteering for rat duty. I was really surprised because he was muttering about how much he hated rats. Nonetheless, he easily scaled the steep ladder and quickly disappeared inside the window. Seconds later, he climbed back out and zipped back down.

"Cal?" I asked snidely. "Didn't you forget to get the family out?"

He smiled, reached into his pocket, and pulled out the man's keys. "I went halfway down the steps and snagged his jacket. I did my job. Now somebody else can deal with the damn rats. I'll be in the truck." Everybody, even the guy at the window, cracked up.

We didn't see any rats when we entered the front door. Surely they had scurried away by then. We guided the guy and his family down the stairs and into the back of a police car. Our job was done. As I made my way back to our SUV, Calvin was sitting in the cab of Ladder 19, safely away from the rats. I waved, calling, "You're the best, Cal!"

DECEMBER 27, 2002—BATTALION CHIEF, BATTALION 1

Shortly after midnight, we were dispatched with Ladder 23 for a man trapped in a stuck elevator. The poor guy had been ringing the emergency bell to no avail, so in desperation, he called 911 on his cell. Problem solved? Not really. The man had no idea what building he was in. All he knew was that he was in a parking garage near city hall. It took us forty-five minutes just to locate the correct garage.

JANUARY 18, 2003—BATTALION CHIEF, BATTALION 1

We were going from 60's to 49's while making our rounds when we saw heavy black smoke coming from the refinery. "Zip around, Bill. Let's see if they need our help." Seconds later we pulled up to the main gate. The security guard had his back to us and was talking on the phone when Bill gave him an attention-getting yelp from our siren. He spun around, still clutching the phone.

"I just called nine one one," he exclaimed. "How the hell did you get here so fast?"

"What can I tell you, buddy?" I said, smiling. "We get out of the station fast."

We handled the fire in Furness Unit 868 with one alarm and plant personnel.

FEBRUARY 18, 2003—BATTALION CHIEF, BATTALION 1

I certainly never read anything in the training manual about that day's type of call. We were called to the Philadelphia Naval Shipyard because a decommissioned destroyer escort was taking on water and listing badly. It was docked in the middle of a row of other decommissioned ships, and Navy Yard firefighters were concerned that if it toppled over, it could take out the entire row of ships in a domino effect. We were there nearly all day in subfreezing temperatures, pumping water from its hull. Navy divers arrived late in the afternoon and patched the leak.

MAY 19, 2003—BATTALION CHIEF, BATTALION 1

The aroma of fried onions filled 1's kitchen, and lunch was almost ready. Keith's signature cheesesteaks were the main course. We gathered in the kitchen, anxiously waiting for our sandwiches to emerge from the grill. There was a pecking order for cheesesteak day in our firehouse: detailed firefighters ate first, then paramedics (if they were in the station), the chief and his aide, the company officers, and finally the firefighters. Keith always ate last.

A few hungry firefighters were joking about the recent B Platoon fire in a funeral home on South Broad Street. They had rescued dead bodies. Yes, dead bodies! While firefighters battled the stubborn blaze, others carried caskets containing human remains outside.

"Hey! Maybe they'll get a citation!" mocked one firefighter.

"Yeah!" sniped another. "As long as they leave out the part about the people they rescued already being dead."

The detail man and paramedics were chomping their sandwiches, and we were next. Yes! Then the bells rang. No! "Everybody first-in, Nineteenth and Lombard, a hazmat box!" Shit!

The subway grates clanked as we emptied onto Broad Street with our sirens wailing. "Attention all companies responding on hazmat box four-six-one, Eighteenth and South Streets, the incident's reported to be a leaking tank truck at Nineteenth and Lombard. All companies use caution while responding." I thought I heard laughter in the background as the suspiciously giddy dispatcher was speaking.

As we headed up Lombard, I mused on the possible scenarios. Could it be a leaking heating-oil truck? A gasoline tanker? Maybe there was an issue with a liquid-oxygen delivery vehicle at Graduate Hospital.

Bill slowed down after we crossed Eighteenth, careful not to drive into the middle of a hot zone. Halfway up the block, I got out and continued on foot. When I reached Nineteenth, I could see the tanker sitting two hundred feet south of Lombard. Was it an MC306? MC307? MC312? Its DOT classification might provide a clue about what it contained. Oddly, it didn't appear to be any of the above.

I ventured a bit closer for a better look. As the tanker came into focus, so did an awful stench. Yep, it was hazardous, all right, but not in the classic sense. The tanker was a septic-system cleaning truck, for God's sake! Feces, urine, toilet paper, and God knows what else had erupted from the vacuum tank's broken sight glass. Brownish goo was dripping off walls and parked cars. Pools of waste had turned Nineteenth Street into an open cesspool. A man holding his nose dashed by as he fled the area. Seconds later an impeccably dressed woman's high heels clickity-clacked as she ran gagging her way across the street.

"Battalion One to aide. Place the incident under control. Have Engine One and Ladder Five evacuate and isolate Nineteenth between Lombard and South. Have Hazmat One proceed in and stage behind our command post."

Tommy Bitto called me on the fireground frequency. "What do we have, boss?" he asked eagerly.

I just had to have a little fun with him. "Tommy," I replied, "this is pretty nasty crap. We have an active leak and a major cleanup. It's going to be a real shitty job."

"What type of crap, Chief? Is it flammable? Corrosive? Toxic?"

"Tom, I guess you could say it's toxic, and the gas it gives off can be flammable. When you get here, proceed to my location, and we'll develop a strategy."

"Okay, boss. We're arriving now." I could tell by his voice that he was all geared up. Yes!

As he approached, I stopped him short of Nineteenth. "Tom, I've given you some shitty assignments before, but this one tops them all. Are you up for the challenge?"

"Yo, boss, you know we are," Tommy snapped back, offended. "We train for this all the time."

I placed my arm over his shoulder and walked him to the corner. "Good, Tom, now carefully take a gander down Nineteenth."

Unsure what to expect, he hugged the wall and cautiously took a peek. He paused for a second before erupting with laughter. "You son of a bitch! You got me good! I'm thinking chlorine, pesticides, even Zyklon B, but never a friggin' shit truck!" Got him!

After laughing wildly for five minutes, we got to work. The first thing to do was stop the crap from oozing out of the tank. Who else but my main man, Calvin Graham, climbed up and hammered a conical wedge into the leaky sight glass. I'll never forget the sight of him wearing a hazmat suit and capping the leaking feces.

This class of hazardous materials actually *belonged* in the sewer, so we washed the fecal matter and urine away with booster lines before disinfecting the area with bleach solution.

After decontaminating everything and everybody, we headed back to our firehouse. It was a shitty day, yes. But that couldn't keep me away from Keith's delicious cheesesteaks. Mmm! I moaned with delight as I took my first bite.

For some reason, we had a resurgence of suspicious calls during the summer of 2003. The first one was a balloon filled with an unknown yellow fluid in city hall's courtyard. It turned out that the "balloon" was actually a condom. We tested the fluid and found that it was urine. It was a weird way to pee for sure. I briefly entertained the thought of carrying an emergency condom in my running gear for my BPH, but my better judgment prevailed.

The following week someone called because an abandoned toilet contained a mysterious blue liquid. Yep, it was blue toilet disinfectant.

August 5, 2003—Battalion Chief, Battalion 1

While two SEPTA police officers were eating breakfast in Old City, their radiation detectors simultaneously sounded alarms. Concerned about a possible terroristic attack, they evacuated the diner and cordoned the area off before we arrived.

We didn't detect any radiation in the restaurant, but when we scanned the evacuated patrons, our readings went through the roof. Eventually we pinpointed the source to an elderly man. He had been injected with radioactive technetium-99m that morning for a diagnostic medical procedure.

The cops were embarrassed, but I assured them that they had done the right thing.

August 13, 2003—Battalion Chief, Battalion 1

Blaring sirens added to the hustle and bustle of Center City as we converged on city hall. The problem? As one of Mayor John Street's mail screeners was opening envelopes, an ounce of white powder had poured onto her desk. She didn't panic until she read the ominous letter inside: "Death to Mayor Street! Death to America! Allah is great!" It was a concerning situation because all three legs of the terrorism triangle were present: a substantial amount of *substance*, a *threatening* letter, and high-profile *target*—Mayor Street.

The security staff had closed the mail-room door and told the woman and her coworker to remain at their desks. I guess they never heard Paracelsus's quote: "*Sola dosis facit venenum*" (The dose makes the poison). As I gazed through the glass door, I could see that they were sitting right next to the powder. I angrily barked at the security staff, "Why didn't you tell them to move away? The more those women inhale, the higher their dose!" Shaking my head, I tapped on the glass and told the women to walk to the other side of the room.

"Yo, boss, what's up?" It was Tommy Bitto.

"Tom, let's get these ladies deconned and follow our evidentiary procedures with the powder."

We had handled this type of incident several times. Tommy decontaminated the ladies, bagged their clothing, and had them dress in Tyvek suits for modesty. Another team went into the hot zone, retrieved a sample, double bagged the threatening letter, cleaned up the spill, and disinfected the area with bleach. After the sample jar, evidence, and team members were decontaminated, Tommy's crew tested the powder.

Tommy's guys had placed the letter and its envelope into clear plastic evidence bags in such a manner that police could easily examine them. Everybody breathed a sigh of relief when officers immediately recognized the postmark. It was from a state penitentiary. What were the odds that an inmate would have access to a harmful powder? The threat was most likely a hoax.

Our field tests indicated that the suspicious powder was nondairy coffee creamer, something a prisoner could easily obtain. As a final check, we had the testing team dissolve some of it in black coffee. It certainly looked like coffee creamer. To improve the odds that our assumption was correct, we ran two more tests, a concept we call "confirmation theory." Both tests suggested coffee creamer. As an added precaution, I asked police to send the sample to the crime lab for definitive results.

The incident had stirred up a media circus outside, so a few officials, including me, were summoned to the mayor's office for a prepress briefing. A mayor's aide led us to Street's decorative office and signaled us to wait in the hall. Honestly, I was nervous. Had I overstepped my bounds by yelling at the security staff? Twenty minutes later, the door finally swung open. The mayor was sitting at an ornate throne at the head of the table.

"Okay," he said, "I understand that some of my employees were exposed to coffee creamer or something that was sent here from a prison. What are my options?" The ball was in my court.

"Mr. Mayor, I'm Bob Marchisello, the fire department's hazmat chief. We're ninety-nine percent sure that the substance is nonhazardous. We can't be a hundred percent sure without results from the crime lab. As I see it, you have three options. The first option, which I *don't* recommend, is that we play this to the extreme. This means shutting down city hall and performing mass decontamination of all civilians and employees. The second option, which I *also don't* recommend, is to act as though this never happened. Just tell the media it was a hoax and go about your business as usual. However, the third option, which I *do* recommend, is to take a common-sense middle-road approach. Shut down the mail room. Discreetly send the two employees for medical evaluations and then send them home. When the lab results come back negative, as I'm sure they will, you may resume all normal operations."

"Okay," he said decisively, "it will be the third option." Imagine that—Charlie O's principle actually made it to the mayor's office.

CHAPTER 35

The Roulette Wheel

Hazmat training for the squad companies began on October 6, 2003. By then, our course had grown to a twenty-day ProBoard-certified hazmat-technician program. In order to reduce overtime costs, the squads only attended training during their day shifts, which meant we had to teach each platoon in two-day bursts. Hazmat training for the squad companies and their backups took nearly six months to complete. It was a job unto itself just to keep track of each platoon's progress. Like the other instructors, I worked at the firehouse whenever I wasn't teaching.

Our second day of class got off to a bad start when the department suffered another LODD. On October 7, 2003, Firefighter James Allen, forty-three, of Ladder 16, collapsed while operating on the roof of a burning building. Despite firefighters' desperate efforts to revive him, he was pronounced dead at the hospital. It was an eerie foreboding of what was to come next.

Special Operations Command (SOC) had done an outstanding job of selecting personnel for the squads. All the firefighters and officers were energetic and highly motivated. While some had technical backgrounds or were skilled tradesmen, others had either attended or graduated college. They all had one thing in common: a strong desire to learn.

One of Squad 72's officers in particular impressed us all. Lieutenant Derrick Harvey, forty-five, was a former chemistry major in college. The fifteen-year veteran spent extra time during his breaks trying to master every concept we taught. He was especially interested in ways to sustain his platoon's hazmat skills after they completed their training.

On January 9, 2004, at 0626 hours, Harvey's platoon of Squad 72 responded first-in to a basement fire. While battling the blaze, Derrick fell through weakened floorboards and was quickly enveloped by flames. He was rushed to the hospital, suffering severe burns. Training for the squad companies continued while Derrick clung to life in Temple University's burn unit.

January 15, 2004—Battalion Chief, Battalion 1, Detailed as Hazmat Instructor

Lieutenant Harvey's condition deteriorated during the night. His platoon heard the news but stoically arrived bright and early for training that morning. After promising to keep them informed, I called the deputy commissioner's office first thing. I wanted to be notified if there was any change in Derrick's status, as soon as headquarters knew.

I tried to be as upbeat as possible during class, but inside I sensed the worst. Understandably, the usually spirited class was subdued all morning. Thankfully the phone remained silent, and no news was good news. Derrick was a strong person, and I was hoping he'd make a comeback.

But it was not to be. That afternoon the class was quietly taking an examination when the phone's piercing ring shattered the silence. Derrick had succumbed to his injuries. With a lump in my throat, I slowly paced to the front of the class. They knew what was coming. Their eyes were transfixed on my every step. Sobs broke out when I tearfully made it official. We dismissed the class indefinitely, pending Derrick's funeral arrangements.

As I saluted Derrick's casket, the right side of my brain caused tears to flow down my cheeks. But my left brain was busy calculating the odds that the next LODD might possibly happen under my command. With eleven battalions and four platoons, the odds were one in forty-four. That was only six more numbers than a roulette wheel. Where would the spinning silver ball land next? It made me feel uneasy. Suppose the next LODD was because I had made a bad decision? I'd never be able to live with myself! The thought had me horrified.

Tier 1 of the Hazmat program was finished by the end of January, and I was back in the firehouse until Tier 5 began in April. Despite the dangers,

I didn't want to miss any more of the harsh winter's fires. At least that was the plan.

January 31, 2004—Battalion Chief, Battalion 1

A major water-main break had flooded several South Philly row-home basements. Chief Noble sent his aide to pick up Billy and me at shift change. In turn, I took over the scene while Billy drove Noble back to our firehouse. It's normally how battalion chiefs exchange relief so there's no disruption of command. As soon as Billy and Noble left, I sent Ladder 27 back to their station to exchange shifts and requested that Engine 49 be relieved on scene.

It was windy, eighteen degrees, and I was shivering as I carefully made my way along the ice-encrusted street, monitoring conditions. Portable pumps were sputtering in the background. Water-department crews were frantically working to close valves, and utility crews were scrambling around cutting gas and electric to the affected homes. Our job was rather dull. We were merely pumping water out of flooded basements and providing standby support. My greatest concern was to avoid making a spectacle of myself by slipping and falling flat on my ass.

Five minutes after Billy drove off, the water department stopped the gushing leak. That was great! As soon as he returned, I'd slide my way down the street and make us available. Less than a minute later, a box was dispatched for a store fire at Fifth and Wolf. It was only nine blocks away, but I didn't have a vehicle. Instead, I listened helplessly to the sirens in the distance. I felt like the little buff of years ago, yearning to be part of the action.

Engine 53's message squawked over the portable. "We have heavy fire showing with a report of people trapped."

"Shit!" I screamed, my breath lingering in the frosty air. If there was a fire in my district, I wanted to be there! Hoping for Billy's quick return, I skated my way toward the corner and was gliding along fairly well until Engine 60 and Ladder 19's passing sirens broke my concentration. As I looked up, I suddenly spun out of control, my arms flailing. My superb double axel had a lousy ending. I flopped down on my rump and skidded ten feet before slamming to an ungracious halt against the curb. I had slipped and fallen on many firegrounds, but this was by far my greatest spectacle. It even rivaled Brownie's gold-medal performance back in 1977. "Shit!" I screamed again with frustration.

As I struggled back to my feet, the fading sirens were replaced by an approaching electronic siren. Billy was racing back to get me. I made it to the end of the block as Billy came screeching around the corner. Finally away from the ice, I dashed up the street and jumped in before he skidded to a stop.

I quickly snatched the microphone. "Battalion One is available and responding to Fifth and Wolf."

It was too late. "That's negative, Battalion One. Battalions Four and Seven are on the fireground. We'll make you available." After replacing the microphone in its cradle, I couldn't help but scream a third and final "Shit!"

As it ought to be, fire dispatchers need to maintain adequate coverage. I couldn't, and wouldn't, have overridden their authority. Ladder 27, however, was only a block from the fire when 53's gave their report. Although they were technically still in service at the water-main break, they made themselves available and responded to the fire. It was a good call, and I was fine with it. Despite their speedy response and valiant efforts, three people perished in the blaze.

After the 2000 anthrax attacks, new technology came on the market to detect several types of biological-agents. In early 2004 we received a brand-new immunoassay testing device. The following week we used it at a hazmat call and it momentarily scared the pants off us.

February 5, 2004—Battalion Chief, Battalion 1

Workers at a plush Center City hotel were cleaning a room when they discovered a suspicious white powder. The staff immediately suspected anthrax and called 911. Even though only one leg of the terrorism triangle was present, *substance*, it was a good time to try our new biological-agent testing device. During our training on the state-of-the-art immunoassay machine, the instructor stressed that it would never yield a false positive. Wrong!

Judging by the unidentified substance's color and consistency, I was expecting it to be cocaine. But after we ran a sample on our machine, we were shocked at the results: Positive—Anthrax. Alarm bells reverberated in my astonished brain. I had them run the test again, and the result was the same: Positive—Anthrax. To say I was concerned is an understatement. Panicked, I called the machine's manufacturer.

"We just received back-to-back readings for anthrax on your machine. We were told that it doesn't false positive. Is that correct?"

Instead of being horrified, the voice on the other end was cool and calm. "Well, it shouldn't false positive. Well…that is, unless you place too much sample in the device. Cut down on your sample and test again."

We did, and the third test was negative. I angrily told the man to talk to his trainers. The scary lesson reinforced my adage: "In Hazmat, never say never, and never say always, except to say there are always exceptions." We ran a test for cocaine, and the result was positive.

My stalwart aide Billy retired in 2004. Selecting Ladder 11's Chuckie Cassidy as his replacement was a no-brainer. The ex-marine was an outstanding firefighter who had been a dedicated backup aide for years. I certainly missed Billy but was every bit as comfortable with Chuckie as my wingman.

During Billy's last shift in the firehouse, I briefly thought about my own retirement. Several of my 141st classmates had already retired or enrolled in the Deferred Retirement Option Plan (DROP). Firefighters who opted to DROP froze their pensions but could remain employed for up to four years with full salary and benefits. During that time, they'd also collect their pensions in a city-controlled escrow account that was payable upon separation.

I was fifty-six years old but still felt physically capable of performing my duties. As I downed a piece of Billy's retirement cake, I decided that I wasn't mentally prepared to leave yet. But two more LODDs that summer made me reconsider.

On August 20, 2004, Engine 28 arrived first-in to a basement fire in a row home. What they didn't know was that it was an illegal marijuana-growing operation. The basement contained a maze of wires, fans, lights, and heaters. As they were advancing their hose line through the cluttered basement, conditions deteriorated rapidly. Captain John Taylor, fifty-three, a highly decorated veteran, sensed an imminent flashover and ordered his company to retreat. As they tried to exit, forty-two-year-old Firefighter Rey Rubio's air pack got tangled in wires. Taylor heroically refused to leave his side. As he frantically tried to free the firefighter, they both ran out of air and were overcome.

Theirs marked the fortieth and forty-first LODDs in my thirty-one-year career. The roulette wheel had spun again, and this time the silver ball had landed in the Tenth Battalion. Just as with Harvey's death ten months earlier, I was unnerved. Where would the next ball land? After the funerals, I discussed my retirement plans with Diane for the very first time. It was a difficult decision for me. On one hand, the prospect of leaving the job I loved so much was terrifying. On the other, the thought of losing a firefighter under my command was petrifying. I decided to enter the DROP in two years. Having a plan in place made me feel somewhat better.

A few weeks later, we responded to a working basement fire on Twenty-Eighth Street. I nearly flipped out when I detected a hint of marijuana in the air. Squad 47 must have thought I was nuts because I kept asking for progress reports every thirty seconds. It turned out that a young man was blissfully smoking a joint in the crowd behind me. I think I got higher than he did when I realized that he, not the fire, was the source of the unique smell.

Over the years, there were many times I fought more than one fire in the same building. Oftentimes conditions dictated that I use similar strategy and tactics. I never imagined that one day my fireground decisions would be influenced by what Arthur and I had seen fire chiefs do during our fire-chasing days many years before.

February 7, 2005—Battalion Chief, Battalion 1

I recognized the old storage building as soon as we turned the corner. Its upper three floors had been destroyed by a six-alarm blaze that Arthur and I had buffed as young boys. The lower floors were now occupied as a day-care center (front cover photo). At 0911 hours on that chilly Monday morning, heavy black smoke was pouring from its windows. My heart dropped. I knew there could be dozens of children in there.

Thankfully, the staff had safely evacuated all the kids. They were safe and sound in a store down the block. Their fire drills had paid off!

I guess buffing all those fires with Arthur had its dividends. Using the same tactical approach that I had seen chiefs use back then, I placed many companies in the same exact positions. The flames quickly darkened. Even though I had pulled two alarms, I didn't use any second-alarm companies.

Afterward, I submitted civilian commendations for the entire staff. They were the real heroes that day.

In the fire business, things often happen in bunches. For a spell in 2005, it seemed that more was happening below ground than above. A crash of two underground trolleys was followed a week later by a Market-Frankford Line subway derailment. Both mass-casualty incidents were labor intensive. The injured had to be immobilized, placed on backboards, and carried to street level. As in many transportation accidents, some "victims" seemed to feign their injuries. Surely they were hoping for huge pain-and-suffering settlements from SEPTA. Suspicions aside, we treated everyone according to protocol.

We also responded to two underground power-line fires. One of them flipped manhole covers in the air like tossed coins. The other made the ground rumble as though a huge dragon were under our feet. Though not uncommon incidents, their timing was coincidental. Our subterranean streak lasted three shifts.

It was relatively easy to keep my firefighters safe during our underground jaunts, but a fire later that summer posed more of a challenge.

July 9, 2005—Battalion Chief, Battalion 1

This morning's fire at the twenty-four-hour porn cinema was scary. The occupied four-story brick building was a hundred feet wide by seventy-five feet deep. The scary part was the nasty dense grayish-yellow smoke pushing from every door and window. The red devil was in there lurking. But where? More importantly, was anybody trapped inside? We had to mount an interior attack.

Inside, pack men searched for victims while four attack teams snaked their hoses through a labyrinth of viewing booths, private rooms, and sex-novelty shops. As I suspected, they were having trouble finding the fire. Outside, shards of glass rained down as ladder companies took out the upper-floor windows. The defiant smoke only seemed to worsen.

My heart was pounding. "Another minute and I'm pulling the plug… forty-five seconds…thirty seconds…"

"Engine One to Command. We have water on the fire!" Whew!

Diane and I planned to move outside the city after I retired. In the fall of 2005, I said that we should begin looking for a house.

"Rob, what about the residency requirement?" she exclaimed.

"Listen, Di, many other firefighters have vacation houses down the shore or up the mountains," I replied. "We'll live here in Overbrook, but *our* vacation home can be in the suburbs. There's absolutely no difference!" We bought a house in Springfield Township, Delaware County, that November. It was a small step toward retirement. In five years, making life-and-death decisions would be part of my past, and the roulette wheel wouldn't matter.

January 28, 2006—Battalion Chief, Battalion 1

It was nearly four thirty in the morning, and unlike in my younger days, I couldn't fall back asleep. Only two hours ago, we'd had a dwelling fire on Twentieth Street and then responded to a hazmat call. Eyes wide open, there was nothing better to do than listen to a working fire in the Eleventh Battalion. The fire was soon placed under control, and my eyes were finally getting heavy. As I made my way to my bunk, a panicked radio call jolted my eyes open again. "Firefighter down! Dispatch a medic unit!" There was nothing I could do to help on the fireground five miles away. All I could do was listen, and it didn't sound good. The firefighter was transported to the hospital with CPR in progress.

The roulette ball landed again. Firefighter Tracy Champion, forty-nine, of Engine 54, was a twenty-one-year veteran. He collapsed while overhauling and was pronounced dead at Lankenau Hospital from an apparent heart attack. Another LODD. The following month I pulled the trigger and signed up for the DROP. I'd be done in July of 2010.

CHAPTER 36

An Unexpected Rung

On July 17, 2006, I formally entered the DROP, and my sails were cast on a four-year journey toward the shores of retirement. It was a tough decision, and I had mixed emotions about it. I was relieved that when my time was up, I'd no longer be responsible for the lives of others. But I'd also be leaving the job I loved thoroughly.

More insidious than LODDs, but just as frightening, was the fact that many firefighters die from cancers and other diseases due to smoke exposure. The high incidence rate of cancer in firefighters has prompted many states, including Pennsylvania, to enact cancer presumptive bills for firefighters. Such bills often consider the disease to be service connected.

Tommy Bitto got promoted to captain, and after a short stint at Engine 1, he returned to hazmat. It was a hazmat no-brainer because Ladder 19's Jimmy McGarrigle had retired. Even though I'd no longer be working with Tommy (he was on another platoon), I was glad that he was once again a major player in hazmat. The transfer was great for both Tommy and the department. Sadly, it was short lived.

In July of 2006, Tommy collapsed on a fireground and was rushed to the hospital, and on August 28, cancer claimed his life. My good friend and coworker was only fifty-five years old. Like everybody else who knew him, I was crushed.

Tommy joined a long list of firefighters I'd known who died young from cancer and other job-related illnesses. Statistics don't lie. The smoky beatings we took over the years were surely responsible for many of them. In the toxicology course I studied for my master's, I learned that smoke doesn't only cause lung cancer. Its toxic byproducts could cause cancer to develop in many other organs. It was scary! The department didn't formally recognize Tommy's passing as a LODD, but I knew it probably was. So did other firefighters. His funeral procession was nearly a mile long.

A month later we kicked off another Hazmat Technician Training Program with a moment of silence for Tommy. Driven by his memory, we set our glum feelings aside and delivered the program as best we could. Tommy had been one of our best instructors. As usual, I alternated between the Fire Academy and the firehouse during the program.

OCTOBER 3, 2006—BATTALION CHIEF, BATTALION 1

The unidentified yellow powder on the grounds of police SWAT headquarters looked exactly like the agent we used in our fire extinguishers. As I peered at the spill through binoculars, I sneezed. Then I sneezed again and again. Could I be wrong? Was it riot-control agent instead? The probability fit the scenario.

Two suited hazmat technicians retrieved a sample, but as we got deep into our testing protocol, the powder remained unidentified. The next step called for us to heat a small amount of the powder in a test tube and observe the results. Even though I was five feet away as Calvin held the test tube over a flame, I sneezed again and then again. At that point, I was fairly certain it was riot-control agent.

I summoned a member of SWAT to the scene so he could observe the powder and confirm my suspicions. As I held the jar against the light, the burly chisel-jawed officer studied it with squinted eyes. "It just might be, Chief. There's only one way to know for sure." Before I could react, he snatched the sample from my hand, removed the cap, and took a deep whiff. He immediately began running around the yard choking, coughing, sneezing, and gagging. After he composed himself, he calmly walked back up to me with tears pouring from his eyes. "You're a hundred percent right, Chief," he said, sniffling. "That's the riot-control agent we use."

I had never missed a promotional opportunity. But since I was enrolled in the DROP, I had no intentions of taking the upcoming deputy chief's test.

With nearly ten years of experience as a battalion chief, I felt qualified but preferred to spend the rest of my time in the First Battalion. Besides, the deputy's job was boring, and the possibility of another staff position might accompany an advancement in rank. When the test was announced that fall, I figured I'd pass it up.

OCTOBER 8, 2006—BATTALION CHIEF, BATTALION 1

Franny Dougherty, Ladder 5's captain, was one of the finest firefighters I'd ever worked with. Courageous, knowledgeable, professional, and personable, Doc loved the job as much as anyone I'd ever met. Under his leadership, Ladder 5 was, no doubt, one of the best-run companies in the city. I deeply respected Doc's thoughts, ideas, and opinions.

After our traditional Sunday firehouse grand-slam breakfast, I was catching up with routine paperwork when Doc walked into the office. "Hey, boss, can you do me a favor tomorrow? When you deliver your application for the deputy chief's test to Personnel, would you mind dropping off my battalion chief's application?"

I had completely forgotten that the examination had been announced. With my recent entry into the DROP, I had no intention of taking the test. I told Doc that I wasn't applying but would gladly drop his application off. His reaction caught me by surprise.

"Yo, boss! How could you not take the test? Don't you remember what you said last time?"

His words jogged my memory. After the last deputy chief's list was published, I had been at a divisional meeting where a battalion chief enrolled in the DROP was complaining about a candidate who had finished near the top of the list. "DROP or no DROP," I chided him, "you have no right to complain, because you didn't take the test. Maybe if you did, you might have scored higher and blocked his promotion."

Before I could reply to Doc's words, the bells rang. "Everybody, first-in!" Doc tapped the application on my desk with his index finger. "Fill it out, boss!"

As thick black smoke billowed above their heads, I counted ten faces perched at the second-floor windows. Gasping for air, they were oozing tears and snotters. Before I got out of the car, one jumped and plopped on the ground. He sprang to his feet and quickly scurried away. Encouraged, others soon followed suit. A raggedy woman grabbed my arm as I was putting on my gear. She was screaming hysterically. "There's thirty-five of them in there! Please save my cats!" Yes, they were all cats.

Known in her neighborhood as "the Cat Lady," the woman had turned her unkempt, run-down house into a cat's nest. It was a sight to behold as Doc's crew raised ladders and made several cat rescues. Some cats scampered over firefighters' helmets and down their backs. Others needed to be carried down. One frightened feline bit through a rescuer's glove as he grabbed her off the window ledge. "Ouch! You little shit!" he screamed while cradling the adorable tan Maine coon.

All the cats survived. We summoned the SPCA, and 1's submitted a referral to Licenses and Inspections for unsanitary conditions. As we pulled away, police were trying to maintain order. The Cat Lady was being lambasted by angry neighbors as she ran around collecting her pets.

When I returned to the station, I reluctantly completed the application that Doc had left on the desk. "Okay, Doc, I'll take the damn test," I mumbled.

I delivered our completed application forms to the MSB during our rounds the next day. Unfortunately, it was my last shift in the firehouse for the next five months.

We spent the rest of the week at the Fire Academy teaching the hazmat program. Sadly, it was the last time I'd be teaching with my faithful sidekick, Al, who was retiring in December. For one final time, Al's dazzling demonstrations and comical wit brought my drab lectures to life. It was his best performance ever. Though we had capable replacements learning his routine, I was going to miss him terribly.

That Saturday, October 15, Diane and I were working on a few projects at our Springfield home. While climbing down a small ladder, I made a misstep, fell, and fractured my right humerus. As I lay there in terrible pain waiting for the ambulance to arrive, a comforting thought came to mind: "I have an excuse for not taking the deputy chief's test!"

The fracture required doctors to surgically insert a metal rod in my arm. The surgeon said that it might take up to nine months of physical therapy before I could return to work. I wasn't happy with that. I was responsible for my battalion and wanted to get back to work as soon as possible. I was religious with my physical therapy, and things progressed faster than expected. I ambitiously set my goal to return to work in mid-March.

Consumed with rehab, I had completely forgotten about the deputy chief's test. But in January a letter arrived from Central Personnel. I was scheduled to take the examination in a few weeks. I threw the letter in my desk drawer. Out of sight, out of mind!

Since I had gotten injured, firefighters often called to see how I was feeling. In addition to offering their warm thoughts and encouraging pep talks, they kept me abreast about what was happening in the department. Many of them also expressed concerns about a few candidates who were planning to take the deputy chief's test. "So-and-so has been in trouble during his entire career; so-and-so screws up every fireground he's on; and so-and-so hasn't worked one day in the field as a chief. He's always been in staff! Chief, please don't let them run unimpeded to the end zone. Take the test!"

My heart wasn't in it, but on the morning of the test, I found myself on the Market-Frankford El headed toward the MSB. I had decided to take the exam. I wouldn't have even gotten that far if Diane hadn't shaken me out of bed. "Wake up, Rob!" she yelled. "You said you're taking the deputy's test today!"

I groggily replied that I had changed my mind. "I don't feel like paying twenty bucks to park in Center City. It's a waste of time and money!"

She put her hands on her hips and, with her head bobbing up and down, chided, "You've never missed a promotional exam before! Maria will drop you off at the terminal on her way to work. Come on, get up!" I reluctantly dragged myself into the shower.

It didn't dawn on me until the El reached Fifty-Sixth Street that I was completely unprepared for the exam. I thought briefly about my plan of attack and decided that I'd simply handle whatever they threw at me as though it were happening in real time. I had done several shifts as ADC, so I had some experience. Besides, what did I have to lose? I still had Battalion 1 to look forward to if I didn't place well on the list. For the first time in my life, I walked into the civil-service examination room completely calm and relaxed.

As I sat waiting my turn, I thought about how much the testing process sucked! The candidates had thirty minutes to convince three boards of fire chiefs, all strangers from other cities, that they were worthy to be promoted. Knowledge, experience, background, reputation, formal education, training, and performance weren't factored into the final grades.

Deputy chief's examinations once had contained a multiple-choice portion, but it had been discontinued. That was ridiculous! Deputy chiefs need to make decisions based on their knowledge of the department's organization, directives, procedures, equipment, techniques, firefighting, supervision, and management. Everyone in the department had an equal opportunity to master the concepts. A multiple-choice examination, unlike an oral test, was totally objective. Either you knew the answer or you didn't. Eliminating the multiple-choice test left the very subjective oral examination as the sole basis for promotion.

As I continued to wait, I decided to try something a successful candidate told me he had done a few years prior: sneak in the phrase "cultural diversity." When I went before the boards, I did just that, over and over again. Somehow, I even managed to insert it into the fire problem. Satisfied that I had done my duty to act as a blocker, I returned home and quickly forgot about the test. My bigger goal was to finish physical therapy and get back to the First Battalion.

On March 17, 2007, five months and two days after my injury, I finally returned to the firehouse. It was great to be back. I didn't realize how much I had missed the kitchen banter. Captain Doc had been ABC most of the time I was gone, so the battalion was in great shape. I gently eased my way back into the swing of things.

I was off duty on Friday, March 23, when a friend from fire headquarters called me at home. "Bob, the fire commissioner's about to call you."

My immediate response was defensive. "Why? What the hell did I do?" I couldn't imagine why he'd be calling me at home.

"You finished high on the dep's list, you dummy!" He laughed. I was astonished!

Just then, the other line clicked. It was the fire commissioner. He congratulated me for placing number five on the deputy chief's list. I hadn't given much thought to my placement, let alone the anticipated vacancies. But as we spoke, I counted on my fingers. There'd be at least five openings by July. I hung up and stood there with a bewildered look on my face. I wasn't sure whether to be happy or sad.

Diane came running in from the kitchen. "Did I hear you talking to the fire commissioner? Is something wrong?"

"Do you remember those diversity comments I used in the dep's test?" I replied.

"Yes, why?" she asked warily. "Are you in trouble for *that*?"

"No!" I half smiled. "I guess they liked them, because I'm going to be promoted."

I felt compelled to accept the promotion in order to fulfill my duty as a blocker. It was a totally unexpected rung up the promotional ladder.

CHAPTER 37

The Reluctant Deputy

On July 1, 2007, I was transferred to Division 1, B Platoon, as the assigned ADC. A formal promotion ceremony wasn't scheduled until that fall. Having spent more than six years at the Grays Ferry firehouse, it was a familiar haunt for me. After 60's and Ladder 19 moved back to their newly constructed fire station, 47's had returned to service and was now one of the city's two-squad companies. I knew 47's firefighters very well from their hazmat training.

But no matter how acquainted I was with my surroundings, it felt odd to return there as division commander.

July 1, 2007—Acting Deputy Chief, Division 1

I hoped nobody had noticed that I'd mistakenly pulled into the wrong parking spot that morning. I had parked in the same spot I had used more than ten years ago as captain of 60's. Red-faced, I quickly backed across the lot and into the spot clearly marked DC 1.

At 0630 hours I walked into Deputy 1's office as divisional commander for the first time. It was humbling to think that I was now holding the same title that Chiefs Sottung, Appleby, Fanning, McCrory, and even my old nemesis, Les Misérables, once held. I felt so out of place, like I didn't belong.

Geographically the city was split into two divisions. Deputy 1 was responsible for Center City, South, Southwest, West, and a portion of North Philly. Battalions 1, 3, 4, 7, and 11 made up the First Division. I was blessed to have an outstanding group of battalion chiefs. Bernie Cowden, Pete Curtis, John

Hawthorne, John Grillone, and my old company-mate from 24's Al (call me "John") Fry were seasoned veterans.

With loads of paperwork and staffing issues to handle, a division chief needs a knowledgeable and reliable aide. I inherited one of the best in Ed Hutt. A thirty-year veteran, my new blue-eyed aide had worked both divisions and knew the city like the back of his hand. He was an expert at balancing the division's complex staffing quotas and had a great sense of humor. We immediately hit it off.

Squad 47 on my platoon was led by Lieutenant Kenny Pagurek. Impressive as a student during hazmat training, Kenny was even better as a firefighter. A true leader in every sense, he kept his platoon well trained, highly motivated, and prepared to handle any emergency. Kenny's firefighters were a nice blend of veterans. The tight-knit bunch loved having fun as much as they loved the challenges of the fireground.

Despite the positives of working with such good people, I wasn't enthused with my new position. I missed the thrill of busting out the door when the bells rang. Deputy 1's dispatch printer didn't budge unless all hands were working on a box alarm, the second alarm had been requested, the incident involved something unusual, or there were fire fatalities.

All-hands fires often fell into two categories. One was where things were going well. In those cases, the battalion chief usually placed the fire under control as soon as he or she heard that the deputy was responding. (I knew; I had done it myself!) The others were TARFU incidents (things are really *fouled* up). The deputy's job in those cases was to try to gain control before it became a FUBAR incident (*fouled* up beyond all repair).

Unlike in the busy seventies and eighties, it wasn't unusual for a deputy chief to go through an entire shift without a run, let alone a fire. Some shifts felt like *The Day the Earth Stood Still*. Some deputies couldn't stand the boredom, so they dispatched themselves even though all hands weren't in service. I'd never liked when that happened to me as a battalion chief, so as division commander, I didn't respond unless we were officially dispatched. It was a page out of Chief Sottung's book. Even though I craved the action, I wasn't about to be a hypocrite. Besides, I felt that if I showed up *uninvited*, it might make my chiefs feel that I didn't have confidence in them. Nothing was further from the truth.

I felt disconnected from headquarters. The administration kept the field deputies at arm's length. They rarely sought input regarding policies, plans, or even personnel matters. Each deputy's main focus was limited to those issues that affected his or her platoon and division. The consequence over time was that each platoon was run a little differently. As a battalion chief, I had often referred to field deputies as the heads of the "eight families." Suddenly, as if one of them had been whacked by a retirement bullet, I had become *Don Roberto*, boss of Division 1's B Platoon.

In a way, I didn't feel connected to firefighters in the field either. Unlike battalion chiefs who made daily rounds, deputy chiefs didn't get to see their personnel nearly as often. Sure, there were dinner invitations, station inspections, and firegrounds, but with forty-two companies in the division, it was a challenge to get to know everyone well.

Managerially, I allowed my battalion commanders plenty of space to resolve their own issues. I'd always believed that problems should be resolved at the lowest level. If I heard rumors or rumblings about something going on in the division, I waited until the battalion chief came to me before taking action. I had never micromanaged before and didn't want to begin at my new rank. It was a page right out of Charlie O's book.

July 10, 2007—Acting Deputy Chief, Division 1

Headquarters notified me that one of my firefighters was being temporarily transferred. Since I had reviewed the division log for the past year (I'd actually had time to do that!), I knew that the department had issued the female firefighter her own refrigerator to store the breast milk she pumped for her baby.

"That's fine, Chief," I replied, "but we also need to transfer her refrigerator!" There was a pause on the other end.

"Oh shit! I forgot about that."

Both transfers were approved pending the arrival of a warehouse truck to move the fridge. I'm not sure, but I think I was the first division commander in the history of the department to have a refrigerator transferred.

Squad 47's firefighters were an innovative bunch. They knew how to blend new technology with techniques of the past. Sometimes it worked; sometimes it didn't.

August 29, 2007—Acting Deputy Chief, Division 1

It was way past midnight when Ed backed our Crown Vic into the station. We'd just returned from an enjoyable dinner at 16s. But something odd was happening on Grays Ferry Avenue. It was way too early for the kitchen to be completely dark.

"Something's up, Ed," I cautioned as I grabbed the handle of the full-view kitchen door. An eerie glow was coming from the center of the room. Five silhouettes were huddled around the glow.

"Shh, we're about to get that little son of a bitch," one of the silhouettes whispered.

I tiptoed quietly toward the group of 47's firefighters who were staring into the lens of their thermal-imaging camera. There he was, directly in the center of their screen. It was our elusive firehouse mouse. I watched as the little fellow took a few steps, paused, and sniffed. He knew something was up. The chunk of cheese ahead of him was too big to be true. He was right. The cheese was underneath a cardboard box propped up by a stick. The stick was tied to a string, and Terry was holding its other end.

The mouse inched forward and sniffed again. A few more steps—another sniff. Suddenly, the crafty little rodent darted into the trap and snagged the cheese. Terry quickly yanked on the string, but it was too late!

Before the box thudded on the floor, the pest scampered victoriously under the stove. "Fuck!" seven voices shouted in unison. We were laughing so loud that I think they heard us in Division 2.

As for the mouse, even with the hunk of cheese clamped in his jaws, his face looked familiar. I believe he was a relative of the mouse I had set free in the parking lot several years ago.

On November 16, 2007, I officially became the third member of Class 141 to reach the rank of deputy chief. John Devlin and CK-2 had gotten promoted a few years earlier.

Diane, Alex, Maria, and Mom watched proudly as I repeated my oath of office. It was my first promotion in which I wasn't silently humming Stallone's victorious *Rocky* theme song. I tried my best to look excited for my family, but the zeal and enthusiasm just weren't there. Though I felt some pride at having achieved the department's highest civil-service rank, I didn't have any passion for my new job. Nonetheless, I vowed to try my best.

One of the duties of field deputies was to respond to fire fatalities within their division.

DECEMBER 19, 2007—DEPUTY CHIEF, DIVISION 1

"Do I really need to see my umpteenth Bubba?" I muttered under my breath as I begrudgingly trudged up the stairs. Moments before, I had decided to spare my mind from yet another ghastly charred body. Battalion 7 had confirmed the fatality, so I felt no need to view it, nod, and say, "Yep, it's a fifty-two ninety-two, all right."

At least that was my plan until our shift fire marshal, Tommy, popped his head out of the second-floor window. "Hey, boss, I think you might want to take a look at this victim."

"Oh well, one more won't scar me," I thought.

The rear bedroom was hazy and steamy. The grisly remains were lying face up on the floor, its arms and legs burned away by unusually high temperatures. "I guess they used gasoline, huh, Tommy?" I said from the doorway.

Kneeling beside the victim, Tommy looked over the top of his glasses. "Not only that, boss. Come and take a look at this."

Drat, I had to get within smelling range to see what he was pointing at. Tommy's high-powered light was focused directly on the center of the victim's chest. "See the bullet hole?" A nine-millimeter hole was clearly visible in the victim's charred sternum. This person had been set ablaze to conceal a homicide. I decided I'd skip having bacon with my eggs in the morning.

Two months after the promotion, I commanded my first big fire as a deputy chief. Thankfully it wasn't a TARFU job. My battalion chiefs were too good for that.

JANUARY 20, 2008—DEPUTY CHIEF, DIVISION 1

It was one of those nights that I actually *didn't* want to go to a fire. It was a frigid nineteen degrees, and the winds were howling at thirty-five miles per hour. I'd have been content to spend another boring but cozy night at division headquarters. Of course it didn't work out that way.

CK-2 was on a roll (CK-2 was assigned to Division 1's A Platoon). I tried to avoid spilling my coffee from laughing so hard as he recalled and mimicked our 141st instructors and classmates. He remembered every little quirk they'd had. Shift change with CK-2 was as enjoyable as when he'd held court at the coffee urn in Fire School.

I was still giggling when the bells rang. "Squad and chief. All hands working on the box at Front and Thompson." Battalion 4 had placed all hands in service at a warehouse fire.

The multistory structure in North Philly was loaded with display cases, cabinets, and furniture. It was about three hundred feet wide by a hundred feet deep. As we raced down I-476, Chief Hawthorne wisely sounded the evacuation signal and requested the second alarm.

When we arrived, wind-whipped dense yellow-gray smoke was pouring from the century-old brick building. Naturally, my first concern was for my firefighters. Had everyone made it out of the building? The transition from an offensive to a defensive strategy could be dangerous. There was always a chance that the firefighters wouldn't hear the evacuation signal or would get disoriented during their retreat. I waited nervously as each company reported that they were safely outside. The fire was spreading rapidly, but my mind was at ease. Everybody was accounted for!

Before positioning the second-alarm companies, I requested the third alarm. Moments later, the fire was through the roof, and I requested the fourth. Bernie Cowden needed the entire fourth alarm to cover the Bravo (south) side, so I requested the fifth. When windswept embers blew over the Market-Frankford El and headed toward nearby homes and businesses, I asked for the sixth. Two hours later, the fire was under control.

I was frozen solid, but my first big one was under my belt.

Other than occasional fires, life at division headquarters was humdrum. The paperwork was monotonous, and dealing with headquarters over personnel matters was insanely frustrating at times. But I was happy to be in the field.

Devlin, who had been appointed as the deputy commissioner of technical support, asked if I'd be interested in a staff position. I asked whether I had a choice in the matter. Surprisingly, he said yes. Maybe he considered my past staff experience, or maybe it was a classmate thing. Regardless, I respectfully declined. With less than three years until retirement, I didn't want to spend the rest of my time bouncing off the walls at headquarters. Boredom and an occasional bone-chilling fireground notwithstanding,

I wanted to finish my career right where I had started, in the firehouse. Besides, I really enjoyed being housed with Squad 47. The guys treated me like a king, the meals were great, and we had a lot fun.

JUNE 19, 2008—DEPUTY CHIEF, DIVISION 1

The scrumptious aroma of roasting tenderloin had my stomach growling. The table was set, dinner was ready, and as usual, the dispatch printer began clattering. Squad 47's crew dashed for the door, third-in to a reported laundromat fire. "You'll be back in a flash!" I yelled confidently. "Laundromats are usually nothing more than small duct fires. I'll keep the food warm."

The tenderloin was back at the firehouse when I placed the fire under control a half hour later. As the burned-out laundromat smoldered before us, 47's crew took turns walking past my command post, loudly yelling to each other, "Yep, these laundromats are nothing but duct fires. Look! There's a piece of duct sitting in the fire debris." I shook my head and snickered each time. I loved those guys!

From that night on, whenever a laundromat fire was dispatched anywhere in the city, there'd be snickers and chatter from the kitchen. "Relax, guys, it's only another duct fire!"

As usual, when those fires were quickly placed under control, I'd let out a boisterous "Hah! Told you so!" The snickers would turn to laughter.

NOVEMBER 16, 2008—DEPUTY CHIEF, DIVISION 1

Well, it was official. I'd responded to an aircraft incident at every rank. A multiengine commuter aircraft's nose gear failed to deploy. Sparks flew as it came to a sliding halt on the runway at PIA. I had the second alarm standing by, but 78's did an outstanding job foaming the aircraft and removing the passengers.

One of the most tedious duties of field deputies was processing daily overtime forms. Often there were up to fifty overtimes per shift. For some reason, the department didn't hire enough personnel to keep pace with the retirements. It was incredible! One of the city's benefits from the DROP was that Human Resources should have been able to anticipate vacancies. Some speculated that city officials felt that it was more cost efficient to use overtime than to hire more firefighters. I disagreed. Entry-level firefighters' wages were much lower, and their benefits were about a third of their salaries. Overtime firefighters, on the other hand, earned time and a half. The math didn't make sense. Whatever the reason, in order to reduce overtime, the city disbanded Engines 1, 6, 8, 14, and 39, along with Ladders 1 and 11.

To avoid the political ramifications of completely closing firehouses, disbanding the above listed engine companies created five single-ladder companies. The administration obviously didn't study their department's history. By the midsixties all single-ladder fire stations had been eliminated. There had been far too many fires where single ladders arrived first on scene, without pumps and water tanks and with limited hose line, and in some of those cases, people had died.

I was heartbroken. Not only did they close Engine 8, which had roots dating back to Benjamin Franklin's original fire company, but they also closed my childhood favorite, Ladder 11. The move left only three ladders to cover all of densely populated South Philly. Working fires called for three ladder companies, the last of which was a rapid intervention team (RIT). With Ladder 11 gone, every South Philly fire stripped the area of ladder coverage.

There were better options for closures. Thirty years ago at Research and Planning, we had developed a long-term strategy to close, relocate, and combine fire stations. At the time, single-ladder stations were strictly taboo. The plans we had developed were sound and cost effective, and they wisely anticipated population shifts. Our proposals had one flaw: they didn't consider politics. Not one of the January 2009 closings had even been on our radar back then.

Shortly after the closures, one of South Philly's remaining ladder companies was sent for four consecutive day shifts of training. Unsurprisingly, their absence left a huge gap in coverage. For the first three shifts, I painstakingly shifted ladders from other areas of the division to cover their station. The moves created gaps in those areas. I felt as if I were playing Russian roulette. How could I predict where the next fire would occur? On the fourth shift, I refused to cover the South Philly ladder.

An hour into the shift, I received a call from a friend who worked at the FCC. He had just received a call from "the West Wing" (a term we used to describe the department's administrative offices) inquiring why South Philly didn't have cover-up ladder. As he was speaking, the phone clicked. It was wrath from the West Wing.

"Why didn't you move a cover-up downtown?"

I don't like to answer questions with questions, but I felt I had no choice but to answer with three.

"Why was Ladder Eleven closed?" I replied. "Didn't the plan consider the consequences? Do we really need to move covers down there every time training is scheduled?"

"Just cover them up, *Chief*!" *Click.*

On May 19, 2009, Ladder 8's Lieutenant Stephen Cospelich collapsed shortly after fighting a fire. The fifty-six-year-old veteran never regained consciousness, and he died on May 20. I tried not to dwell on it, but my LODD odds as a deputy chief were now down to one in eight.

As my retirement date neared, I spent much of my off-duty time remodeling our family room. Most days I was joined by Squad 47's Tommy Richey, a skilled carpenter. The layout of the room made the remodeling task difficult. Tight clearances, odd angles, and complex miter cuts called for lots of ingenuity. Oftentimes we used a Dremel rotary tool to sand, grind, or make cuts in areas that were too small for larger power tools. Our running joke, when faced with such a task, was to chant melodiously, "It's Dremel time!"

August 23, 2009—Deputy Chief, Division 1

Tommy and I were discussing the best way to install a banister, when the phone rang. It was the FCC supervisor. "Chief, what resources do we have to cut a case-hardened steel ring off someone?"

I knew that we had ring cutters, but they were designed for soft metals like gold and silver. I pressed the Hold button and asked Tommy if they carried something better on Squad 47. "Yeah! We have tools that could cut hard metals."

"Okay, go get Kenny," I said, referring to Lieutenant Pagurek. "I got a run for you."

The supervisor said that the ring victim was at a local hospital. When I asked him to dispatch Squad 47 and Battalion 1, he replied, "Okay, Chief, but there's just one more thing."

"What's that?" I questioned as I jotted the address on a notepad.

"Eh, the ring, Chief; it's not on the guy's finger."

"No?"

"No, Chief. It's on his penis."

"Oh my!"

"Also, when they get there, they're to ask for Dr. Dickson."

"Dr. *Dick*son?" I giggled. If I didn't recognize the supervisor's voice, I would have certainly thought that I was being set up.

Excited to make a special-operations run, Kenny sprinted into the office. "Chief, Tommy said that you need us to cut a case-hardened steel ring off somebody's finger. Where do we need to go?" I smiled as I handed him the address.

As he turned for the door, I chimed, "Oh, Kenny, it's not on a finger… it's on a man's penis. It's a cock ring!"

Kenny stopped dead in his tracks.

"Now, when you get there, ask for Dr. *Dick*son." I added.

"You're screwing with us, right, Chief?"

I couldn't help but giggle. "No, Kenny, this is for real. I'm sending Battalion One with you."

"Oh well. I guess that's why they call us *special* ops." He laughed as he headed toward their pumper. "Squad Forty-Seven, do or die, boss!"

About two hours later, when Squad 47 returned from the run, I greeted them as they strolled into the kitchen. "Well, did you cut it off?"

"No, Chief," Kenny replied, smiling, "we didn't cut his penis off."

"Not his penis, the ring!"

"Oh, the ring?" He cackled. "Yeah, we cut the ring off."

"What tool did you use?" I asked curiously.

Tommy proudly pushed his way forward. "Chief, I took one look at that ring and said, 'It's Dremel time!'" We laughed all night long.

Now, I don't know much about cock rings, but this one wasn't on the penile shaft where I would have imagined. Somehow it had slid over the man's scrotum. Dr. Dickson had tried everything possible to remove the ring before calling the fire department.

Squad 47's operation was executed with precision and sensitivity. They carefully folded towels, placed them under the man's buttocks, and covered his legs with sheets. To avoid accidentally cutting his scrotum, they slid tongue depressors between the ring and his skin. Then, to prevent the ring from overheating, they ran a stream of IV fluid over the area while cutting. After two careful cuts, they safely removed the ring in two pieces.

November 9, 2009—Deputy Chief, Division 1

Here's another first! I got to see an incident on television before actually responding to it. A SEPTA commuter train loaded with passengers caught fire in West Philly that morning. Squad 47 busted out of the door as soon as Battalion 11 placed all hands in service. As I was making my way to our Crown Vic, the fire was on TV, and news helicopters were providing a great overall view of the entire incident. I paused a few moments to study the scene before responding. It was very helpful for my incident management plan. Thank you, *Action News!*

The days rolled by, and my retirement approached quickly. I didn't know it at the time, but the last major fire of my career came at the end of June. It was a huge vacant-building blaze in the Spring Garden section of the city. I donned my gear and took command for the last time. Two weeks later I arrived at the firehouse for my last shift.

July 12, 2010—Deputy Chief, Division 1

I just can't believe it. I'm spending my last night in the firehouse writing my last journal entry. My career of thirty-seven years, two months, and twenty-four days is over. We didn't turn a wheel, not even a "recall the deputy chief" run. But Squad 47's sendoff for me was spectacular. Those guys are a class act! I couldn't have spent my last few years with a better bunch of firefighters.

Only hours ago, a delectable blend of aromas had filled the kitchen. Spread over the counters were roast beef, meatballs, potato salad, macaroni salad, cheeses, chips, dips, and pretzels. The centerpiece was a delicious porchetta, complete with an apple in its mouth. A giant cake bore the words "Congratulations Deputy Chief, 'Haz-Mat Bob' Marchisello, Philadelphia Fire Department, 37 Years of Service." It was surrounded by a plethora of tasty deserts and cookies.

Diane, Alex, Maria, and Maria's boyfriend (and future husband) Matt were here to join the celebration. Companies from around the division stopped throughout the night to bid me a fond farewell. Hundred and Forty-First classmates John Devlin and CK-2 joined the dozens of off-duty and retired firefighters who packed the firehouse. They gathered at tables in the kitchen and on the apparatus floor. Even my very first mentor, Uncle Frank, was here. I got choked up when he gave me a big bear hug and said, "Bobby, I knew from your very first day in the firehouse that you'd rise to the top." Then he whispered in my ear, "But don't forget, you were the *second*-best pump operator in the city. *I was the best!*" We laughed like crazy.

Around ten o'clock I was presented with gifts and plaques. Squad 47 gave me a beautifully engraved wooden bench, which Diane quickly earmarked for our front porch. I made a small speech to pay tribute to my many mentors and fellow firefighters. The party lasted until way past midnight.

The crowd was long gone by morning, and I didn't get a wink of sleep. I just lay in my bunk with my eyes open, reflecting on my career. When the first shimmers of daylight broke through the windows, it was time to write these final lines in my journal.

Tears are dripping on the page. In a few minutes, my relief will be here, and my career as a Philadelphia firefighter will be over. I feel blessed. Ever since I was a little boy, this had been my dream job, my fantasy. With hard work, prayers, and a little luck, I enjoyed a wonderful career. I may no longer be employed by the department, but in my heart, I'll proudly be a Philadelphia firefighter until the day I die.

In stark contrast to that first gorgeous spring day at Fire School, no birds were chirping on the morning of July 13, 2010; it was raining instead. The gray, dreary sky reflected my mood as I loaded cardboard boxes into my car. Many of the mementos they contained had followed me from firehouse to firehouse throughout the years. Fittingly, the last cardboard box contained my journal.

I made my way through the kitchen for a last round of bear hugs and good-byes and then stepped out the back door for the last time as an active firefighter. I dodged the raindrops as I ran to my car and started the engine. I wasn't ready for what came next. A formation of Squad 47's firefighters lined both sides of the parking lot's exit. Rain was dripping from their helmets as they stood at attention. As I pulled between them, Kenny yelled, "Hand—salute!" I rolled the windows down, stopped, and returned their salute. "Ready—two." Tears poured down my cheeks as I pulled onto Grays

Ferry Avenue and headed toward home. Madonna's "This Used to Be My Playground" was playing on the radio. My tears turned to sobs.

The house was silent and still when I got home. Everybody was at work. Depressed and blue, I trudged upstairs as though I were headed for the gallows. I sat on the edge of the bed and took off my uniform shirt for the last time. I stared at my badge, "Deputy Chief, Fire Department, Phila." My eyes swelled, and I had a lump in my throat. I pulled a small notebook from my shirt pocket and slid out the tattered and stained piece of paper neatly folded inside. It had accompanied me throughout my career. It was a quote from Edward Croker (1863–1951), a former chief of the FDNY:

I have no ambition in this world but one, and that is to be a fireman. The position may, in the eyes of some, appear to be a lowly one; but we who know the work which the fireman has to do, believe that his is a noble calling. Our proudest moment is to save lives. Under the impulse of such thoughts, the nobility of the occupation thrills us and stimulates us to deeds of daring, even of supreme sacrifice.

Suddenly I began crying hysterically. Was it survivor's guilt because forty-three of my brother Philly firefighters had lost their lives during my career and I hadn't? Was it relief because none of them had been under my command? Or was it sheer, utter sadness because my career was over? Maybe it was all three, but for a half hour, I lay on the bed crying uncontrollably. Then, as fast as they began, my tears stopped. I haven't cried about it since.

EPILOGUE

After spending nearly four decades as a Philadelphia firefighter, I've happily settled into partial retirement. Hazmat was very good to me. My little niche in the fire service landed me part-time jobs with Delaware County Emergency Services, Philadelphia Community College, Bucks County Community College, and other consulting jobs. In between, I enjoy spending time with my family, traveling, pursuing hobbies, reading... and of course, I enjoyed writing this book. Now I can safely tuck my journals into a plastic tub and hoist them into a dark attic, where they'll sit next to other dust-covered boxes filled with seldom-viewed family relics and old pictures.

I thoroughly miss being a firefighter. It will always be in my blood. Anytime I hear a siren or see a fire truck racing down the street, I still get goose bumps, and once again I'm that little boy in the third-floor flat, pressing my face against the screen, watching the fire trucks go by...

ACKNOWLEDGMENTS

First and foremost, I'd like to thank my lovely wife, Diane, for her devotion, encouragement, and support during my career and during the writing of this book. In many ways it was more difficult for her to be the wife of a firefighter than for me to put the wet stuff on the red stuff. Thank you to my wonderful children, Alex and Maria. I'm so proud of you. I'm very sorry for missing so many Christmas mornings, birthdays, and other holidays. Thanks to my late parents, Rose and John. I was lucky enough to have you present at every milestone during my career. Unfortunately, Dad passed before my last promotion, but I felt his spirit smiling down proudly.

Thank you to my best childhood friend, the late Lance Corporal Arthur Anthony Johnson, USMC. We had so much fun chasing fire engines together as little buffs. I'm so sorry that you never got the opportunity to join the PFD. You certainly would have been one of the great ones. I dedicated my career to you.

I'm especially grateful for my very first mentor, Lieutenant Frank "Uncle Frank" Castellucci, whose guidance laid a splendid groundwork upon which to build my career. Also, to the many mentors I've mentioned in this book. My career was a composite of the things you taught me, directly and indirectly. To those of you who didn't make the pages, it was not out of neglect; it was for the sake of space. I'll never forget you.

A special thanks to Battalion Chief George DelRossi. Hazmat was the perfect niche for me. Without *my favorite chief's* direction, I'd never have realized my hazmat potential. To firefighter Albert Loughead, my company-mate, my coinstructor, and fellow *hazmateer*, your enthusiastic experiments gave life to my rather drab lectures. I miss teaching with you so much. My sincere appreciation to my friend Deputy Chief Gary Appleby, whose outreach program opened the doors to make our hazmat training program one of the best in the country.

A big, big thank-you to my friend Battalion Chief Michael Iraci for making sure my retirement party was so special. Your zest for the job kept my head in the game during the waning days of my career. And to Squad 47, B Platoon, Medic 37, and ES 8. Thanks for the tremendous last night-work send-off, the engraved bench, and the flag, as well as for making my last few years on the job so enjoyable. Also to Deputy Chief Joseph McGraw for letting me use his "thon" story in this book.

I'm deeply indebted to PFD historians Jack Wright and John-Jack W. Oswald. Thanks for helping me make sense of the chicken scratch in my journal and brushing the cobwebs off many dusty memories. To Jack Wright, Gary Appleby, and Sergeant Greg Masi, Philadelphia Police Department, and chief of the Second Alarmers Association—thank you for allowing me to share your photos in this book.

Thanks to Sandra M. Bennett and Doreen McGettigan for the many tips I picked up in your Creative Writing and Getting Published courses at Delaware County Community College. And to my good friend, author, and journalist, Bill Tonelli, for his literary advice.

I will always be very proud to be affiliated with the Philadelphia Fire Department; the Philadelphia Firefighters' and Paramedics' Union, Local 22; the Philadelphia Fire Officers' Union; and the Philadelphia Retired Firefighters Association. A special thank-you to the Springfield Fire Company (Delaware County, Pennsylvania) for selecting me as an honorary member.

Two other organizations hold a special place in my heart: the Philadelphia Second Alarmers Association—I don't know if I'd have made it through my career without your sustenance and support; and Local 22's Widows Fund—their generosity provides financial support to so many spouses of firefighters who died far too soon. Partial proceeds of this book will benefit both organizations.

Finally, to firefighters everywhere, active and retired, career and volunteer. Whether you respond to ten thousand calls a year or only one, you are my brothers and sisters. Please be careful out there and stay safe.

ABOUT THE AUTHOR

Robert Marchisello retired as a deputy chief from the Philadelphia Fire Department after over thirty-seven years of service. He holds an associate's degree in fire science from Community College of Philadelphia, as well as a bachelor's degree in mechanical engineering and a master's degree in environmental health, with a concentration in industrial hygiene, both from Temple University. He currently serves as a Hazardous Materials Specialist for Delaware County, Pennsylvania.

Made in the USA
Coppell, TX
01 March 2020